Conflict Termination in Europe

CONFLICT
TERMINATION
IN
EUROPE

Games Against War

Stephen J. Cimbala

PRAEGER

New York
Westport, Connecticut
London

Library of Congress Cataloging-in-Publication Data

Cimbala, Stephen J.
    Conflict termination in Europe : games against war / Stephen J.
Cimbala.
        p.   cm.
    Includes bibliographical references.
    ISBN 0-275-93592-2 (alk. paper)
    1. Soviet Union—Military policy. 2. Europe—Defenses.
I. Title.
UA770.C56   1990
355'.033547—dc20   89-77107

Library of Congress Catalog Card Number: 89-77107
ISBN: 0-275-93592-2

First published in 1990

Praeger Publishers, One Madison Avenue, New York, NY 10010
An imprint of Greenwood Publishing Group, Inc.

Printed in the United States of America

The paper used in this book complies with the
Permanent Paper Standard issued by the National
Information Standards Organization (Z39.48-1984).

10 9 8 7 6 5 4 3 2 1

To Betsy

Contents

CIMBALA, STEPHEN J.   ORDER NO: 21638
                        ORDER DATE: 02/14/91

CONFLICT TERMINATION IN EUROPE : GAMES AGAINST N
WAR.   T
                                               A
                                               S

GREENWOOD PUBLISHING G 1990   1 VOLS
                           45.00 CLOTH
0-275-93592-2 89-77107
NO-602735

                    QTY ORDERED: 001
                    QTY SHIPPED: 001
                               540903/1009

BLACKWELL NORTH AMERICA

FLORIDA STATE UNIV-BACKRUN | 1129800023| JUTA-B

Preface

On December 18, 1940, Adolf Hitler issued his directive for the invasion of the Soviet Union, "Case Barbarossa." The German dictator and his war machine were riding high at that moment. The German armed forces had swept to victory over their opponents in continental Western Europe. Great Britain remained in the war but unable by its own resources to launch a counteroffensive that could drive the Führer back into his lair. The United States was not yet committed to war, remaining in its prewar isolationist cocoon insofar as much popular and media opinion was concerned. Franklin Roosevelt and Winston Churchill both knew that the New World would have to come to the rescue of the Old before Hitler and his minions could be defeated, but Roosevelt recognized only too well that the timing of such a move was everything in mobilizing U.S. public opinion behind the war effort.

Hitler's reason for attacking the Soviet Union as soon as he did was complex. He had long sought "living space" in the East, and this could only be obtained at the expense of the Soviet Union. He could not subdue the British without a cross-channel invasion, for which his forces were inadequate. He convinced himself that defeating the Soviet Union would force his other opponents to make peace on terms favorable to Germany. Despite the skepticism of some members of the German army's high command, he proceeded with plans for an invasion of the Soviet Union in the spring of 1941. This action was postponed on account of diversionary operations underway to put the lid on contrapuntal developments in Yugoslavia and Greece. The German offensive into the western USSR was finally programmed for June 22, 1941. It was not without irony that

Napoleon had begun his fateful offensive into Russia on the same date in 1812.

British historian H. R. Trevor-Roper has collected Hitler's wartime directives in a very useful compendium.[1] Directive No. 21 for Case Barbarossa was limited to nine copies for reasons of security: "It is of decisive importance that our intention to attack should not be known."[2] Incredibly, it was not, and Stalin was deceived with regard to the exact timing and operational cast of Hitler's attack until the very moment.[3] The Germans were to achieve a series of stunning tactical and operational victories with their experienced ground forces, led by armored spearheads and preceded by preemptive attacks against Soviet air forces. However, the nagging question was, What then? The effort to answer that question resulted in an ambiguous compromise, built into the very planning process of Barbarossa. Directive No. 21 had laid down that "the German armed forces must be prepared, even before the conclusion of the war against England, *to crush Soviet Russia in a rapid campaign* (Case Barbarossa)."[4]

This was all very well said. The question was whether a campaign could be mapped that would achieve the political aim of Soviet withdrawal from the war in addition to the military aim of rapid and successful destruction of the Soviet Union's most important armed forces. The issue of how to connect the military-operational objective with the political one was all-important. As early as July 21, 1940, von Brauchitsch, the commander-in-chief of the army, had been discussing with Hitler the issue of war aims in the East. The results of the discussion were listed in the meticulous diary kept by General Franz Halder, head of OKW (the armed forces high command, which was directly subordinate to the Führer and gradually came to take over from the military services the direct operational planning for the war).[5] The discussion, according to historian Albert Seaton, produced nothing meaningful. The establishment of new political states in the Ukraine, Belorussia, and the Baltic, plus enlargement of Finland, followed from the campaign plan and fell short of stating the political aims on which termination of a war against the Soviet Union could be based.[6]

Planning for Case Barbarossa was also campaign oriented rather than war oriented. The problem that confronted Germany's planners in 1940 and 1941 was the same as that which had confronted Russia's adversaries for centuries: how to accomplish decisive war aims in the vast space of the Russian heartland. Napoleon had succeeded in reaching and occupying Moscow, only to learn—contrary to his suppositions—that the collapse of the Russian government and the surrender of its armed forces did not follow.[7] The German army and armed forces high commands therefore planned for a campaign in two stages. The main body of Soviet armed forces was to be trapped near the western frontier of the Soviet Union; everyone agreed on this as the logical first stage. The second stage was more controversial. Halder and von Brauchitsch favored concentration of subsequent efforts on the axis of advance toward Moscow. The capture of Moscow would drive the Soviet government off its pedestal and cut off the Soviet Union's communications and transportation hub from the rest of the country. The importance of Moscow as an administrative and industrial center would force the Soviets to muster the bulk of their remaining forces to defend it; having destroyed those forces defending Moscow, the Germans would simultaneously have defeated the Red Army.[8] Hitler demurred, favoring a three-pronged advance in the general directions of Leningrad, Moscow, and Kiev (Army Groups North, Center, and South), which was the path eventually taken. In the first few weeks of war it made little difference. But by the late summer and autumn of 1941, when more important decisions had to be considered, it made a substantial difference whether concentrated or dispersed axes of advance were to be emphasized. Members of the German armed forces high commands then, and later, would argue that had the Wehrmacht concentrated its efforts on al all-out offensive to capture Moscow, the Soviet Union would have been effectively defeated.[9]

But would it have? The capture of Moscow would not in itself have destroyed the Soviet war effort or the Soviet unity of command. The Germans would have been holding onto the first thousand or so miles of Soviet territory, but the remainder of the eleven time zones to the east would remain in hostile hands. On June 11, 1941, Hitler drafted Directive No. 32, "Preparations for the period after Barbarossa." This directive was sent to the commanders-in-chief of the three services (army, navy, and air force) on June 19 to provide a context for their postcampaign planning. After the Soviet armed forces had been destroyed, according to this directive, Germany and Italy would "be military masters of the European Continent" with the temporary exception of the Iberian Peninsula, a situation Hitler proposed to remedy in due time.[10] The defense of the areas already conquered *and* foreseeable future offensive actions would "require considerably smaller military forces than [had] been needed hitherto."[11] With smaller military forces and with the armaments industry tasked primarily for the production requirements of the navy and the air force, the Germans could consolidate their existing holdings and undertake new ventures in several directions. These would include attacks on British possessions in the Mediterranean and western Asia, involving convergent axes from Libya through Egypt, from Bulgaria through Turkey, and perhaps from Transcaucasia through Iran. Also foreseeable, "if the collapse of the Soviet Union has created the necessary conditions," were preparations for a motorized expeditionary force from Transcaucasia against Iraq. Operation Felix to capture Gibraltar in order to close the Mediterranean to British use, with or without the cooperation of Franco, would also be embarked upon at the first opportunity (and had in fact been included in previous planning studies). Finally, the "Siege of England" must be resumed "with the utmost intensity" by the German navy and air force "after the conclusion of the campaign in the East," with the ultimate objective of "bringing about a final English collapse through a landing in England."[12]

Historians might debate whether it is the Führer or Napoleon who deserves the all-time honors for ambition overreaching grasp. There are always revisionists waiting in the wings to support heterodoxy, and some have contended that Hitler "could have won" under the properly support-ive conditions: a timely Japanese entry into the war against the Soviet Union; a refusal on Hitler's part to declare or wage war against the United States, playing off America's isolationism against its desire to aid Britain; or postponing the war against the Soviet Union until the war in the West was buttoned down. These theories make for interesting fireside reading, but speculations about what "might have been" are insensitive to the central problem that brought Hitler down: the coupling of force and policy. Policy must demand of the armed forces no more than what is feasible for them to accomplish; preferably, policy makes the road to that which they can accomplish smoother. Success in war is preceded by success in diplomacy, as Bismarck's experience showed. Just as policy must be sensitive to the limits of force, so must the armed forces be used not as an end in itself but in support of coherent policy objectives. From the standpoint of war termination, the postwar world should be preferable to the prewar or else the war is ill begun.

Hitler's grand strategy failed both tests: of policy sufficiently apprecia-tive of war and of force properly subordinated to policy. The first charge has been documented, but the second is not usually pressed against the Führer. He seemed the embodiment of personal, political triumph over the armed forces, and he eventually directed operations down to the tactical level on the Eastern Front. The operative phrase, however, was "force properly subordinated to policy" and the word *properly* is where the Führer's policy fails the test. For Hitler committed the same mistake as Ludendorff: He assumed that the aims of war and the aims of policy are the same, until the one is swallowed up by the other. Evidence for this lay in the kind of war Hitler planned to wage in the East. It was to be a total war of annihilation, sparing neither the economic resources nor the noncombatant inhabitants of the conquered territories. It was a massive explosion of hatred loosed against the Führer's imaginary and real enemies alike:

The liquidation of the commissars, communist intelligentsia, gypsies, Jews and civilian hostages in the early stages of the war was to be followed by Führerbefehle, forbidding the acceptance of the surrender of Leningrad and Moscow, and ordering the encircled cities to be razed to the ground by shell fire and bombing. The female population of Stalingrad was to be transported and the males destroyed. The Soviet High Command and the Red Army troops were of course equally guilty of similar barbarities. Never in modern times was a war to be waged so pitilessly.[13]

One might say that we are being too hard on the German war plan, allowing Hitler to be held accountable for his fantasies instead of viewing the German war plan on its own terms. So let us suppose the connection between force and policy that is *assumed* in German planning—that the collapse of the Soviet Union would follow the successful completion of the three-pronged offensive to form a defensible glacis from Archangelsk to the Volga. Within this framework of assumptions there is additional room for a mismatch between strategy and force application.

These shortcomings of the German campaign planning have been recounted by many historians, so a résumé of the more salient difficulties should suffice. The first category of difficulties lay in the area of logistics and supply. The second was the unusually harsh winter, even by Russian standards. The third was the unexpectedly stiff resistance from Soviet forces, whose size and competence the Germans had underestimated. We will assume that there was little the Germans could have done to change the weather, which affected the Soviets as well. Therefore, the difficulties of the first and third categories—of logistics and faulty intelligence appreciation—merit further remark.

German logistical capabilities simply were inadequate to sustain a conflict much beyond the duration of the campaign against France in 1940. This was not unknown to German military and economic planners. Only a small proportion of the divisions available for war in 1939 were fully motorized; most of the supplies for standard infantry divisions were carried on some 1,200 horse-drawn wagons.[14] Motor vehicles were concentrated in a relatively few units, especially in those formations designated as armored and motorized and tasked for rapid movement, while the rest of the army moved at the traditional pace of shoe leather. As a result, fast-moving panzer units in particular frequently outran the slower infantry, which would then obstruct the supply columns of the armored spearheads unless carefully controlled in movement.[15] In any event, motorized transport could not supply the forward-moving German armies beyond an approximate range of 300 miles (500 kilometers); beyond that, transportation depended on railways that were never adequate to the task. The transfer points from German to Soviet trains bottlenecked the entire system of logistics.[16] The summary verdict by historian Martin Van Creveld, with regard to the probable outcome of a best-case scenario for Army Group Center, is of interest:

There is no doubt that the logistic situation would not have allowed an advance by Army Group Centre on Moscow at the end of August. At the very best, a force of between 14 and 17 armoured, motorized and infantry divisions might have been so employed, and whether this would have been enough, even in September, 1941, to break through the city's defences is very much open to question.[17]

If the German operational strategy was insufficiently cognizant of logistical realities that should have been foreseen, it was also based upon some wishful intelligence estimates. German knowledge of the Soviet armed forces and their state of preparedness had lagged significantly since Hitler assumed the chancellorship. The collaboration of German and Soviet armed forces that had developed in the pre-Nazi years gradually disappeared in the atmosphere of ideological distrust between the two governments during the 1930s. The Soviet Union was not an easy target for intelligence penetration, and the German military intelligence staff tasked with Soviet and other "Foreign Armies East" assessments was not inclined to give the Soviet Union a higher priority than the armies of the Scandinavian countries, China, Japan, and some Balkan countries.[18] The German army had no reliable way of estimating the numbers of peacetime Soviet army divisions, tanks, and aircraft or of other order-of-battle indicators that are customary components of net assessments. The German handbook on the Soviet armed forces of January 1941, an official and secret document, concluded that Soviet forces were not fit for modern war.[19] This expectation was based in part on knowledge of Stalin's purge of his military high command in the late 1930s, which had indeed crippled the Soviet military leadership at a critical time.[20]

Most astonishingly, the Germans failed to anticipate that Soviet resources for an extended war would be superior to their own, despite the acknowledgment that Germany had not, as late as 1941, fully mobilized its national resources for the war effort. Hitler attempted to follow a "guns and butter" policy until the reversals of German field forces in 1942 and 1943; in addition, the eventual entry of the United States into the war forced other decisions upon him.[21] The Germans simply dismissed the problem of relative resource bases for a long war with the operational assumption that their field armies would settle the issue in eight to ten weeks.[22] The assumption of a rapid defeat of the Soviet armed forces leading automatically to a political capitulation of the Soviet state was then fed back into the "analysis" of relative economic potential.

Equally astonishing was Hitler's declaration, on December 11, 1941, of war against the United States following the December 7 Japanese attack on Pearl Harbor. Perhaps Hitler assumed that he would have to fight America anyway; Roosevelt and Churchill certainly shared that assumption. Nevertheless, the declaration of war so soon against the United States was both gratuitous and revealing of Hitler's hidden assumption that the war against the Soviet Union would be short. In an extended war, the U.S. and Soviet industrial capacities would soon overwhelm the German, and therefore the allies would outproduce Berlin even if they could not outfight Germany. This is in large measure what happened. At the tactical level, the casualty-exchange ratios of Germans to opponents, on the Eastern and Western Fronts, favored the Germans by large margins. Man for man and unit for unit, German ground forces fought more effectively than their opponents.[23] Yet they lost, on account of a mismatch between political objectives and military means. In so doing they followed the path of Napoleon, who wasted the best army in Europe in an extended retreat from Moscow to the Berezina.

We have looked closely at German decision making with regard to the campaign against the Soviet Union because it introduces the subject matter to follow with exceptional clarity. Other examples of the gap between policy aims and military means might have been chosen, from the Peloponnesian Wars to Vietnam. But the Nazi-Soviet conflict is of special interest because it occurred in Europe, because it involved modern armed forces by present-day standards, and because one of the two combatants is still standing as a nuclear-armed superpower facing the Western alliance. Moreover, the Soviet armed forces of today study, in exhaustive detail, the campaigns of the Great Patriotic War, as they refer to it (Great Fatherland War in some translations).

This war is the defining event of modern Soviet history for an entire generation of leaders just now passing from power with the advent of Gorbachev and his new thinking. The past is prologue to the present and the future, and the West—no more than the East—can escape it. Nowadays the West relies on nuclear deterrence to prevent war and a conventional force to delay an attack until there is time to make the nuclear decision. As we shall see, there is no clear policy for what happens then, especially at the end of the road. The planners of NATO deterrence and defense strategy are in the same position as were Hitler's economic and military planners in 1939 and 1940: They can foresee the first moves but not the later actions, so optimism about the latter is built into the earlier decisions. Thus it is presumed that NATO's initial uses of nuclear weapons in Europe will somehow cause any attack to desist short of accomplishing its objectives, but also short of the escalation that escapes control by both sides. The Soviet recognition of the difficulties inherent in nuclear dependency has led to Gorbachev's very forward arms-control diplomacy, but withdrawal of nuclear weapons from Europe could leave NATO at a substantial disadvantage in conventional defenses. Few NATO Europeans want to raise the nuclear threshold at the price of lowering the threshold for conventional war; they also are reluctant to pay for the additional conventional forces that would allow them to attain a more credible conventional deterrence. The implications are that, from either the Soviet or the Western standpoint, it is difficult to see acceptable paths to war termination in Europe, as the chapters that follow will attempt to demonstrate. Therefore, all the marbles are placed on the prevention of war, as if this were strictly a technical or procedural matter. But war is fundamentally a human enterprise. The failure to think through how war might be ended is tantamount to assuming that governments and organizations that have failed in the past cannot fail again.

SYNOPSIS

Chapter 1 provides an overview of the problems and choices attendant to ending war in Europe under contemporary conditions or in the near future. These choices are bounded by the constants of European politics, U.S. commitments, and Soviet security interests. Therefore, there is not a great deal of room for maneuvering once war has begun, and even less once nuclear weapons have been detonated. This spells trouble for NATO, which relies on the credibility of its threat to set off nuclear charges in order to deter conventional aggression. What is touted as a virtue for deterrence—the disproportionate destruction caused by nuclear weapons—becomes a liability once the improbable nuclear threat has actually been fulfilled.

Chapter 2 considers the philosophical and practical issues related to the problem of preemption. Preemption is the more likely path to nuclear war between superpowers than is preventive war. Preventive war is an altogether unexpected and unprovoked attack on an unsuspecting victim. Preemption is the act of striking first, in the expectation that the other party has already decided to do so but has not yet succeeded in carrying out its decision. This means that preemption can be mistaken, based on faulty indicators. The different kinds of preemption are contrasted in terms of their implications for the philosophical state of nature on which deterrence theory is based. Americans and Soviets share a limited community of interest in creating a nuclear-deterrence "sovereign" in the fashion of Hobbes' *Leviathan.* For this they must surrender some of their liberties, as did Hobbes' citizens; the right of first strike or preemptive attack no longer pays dividends because a system of mutual deterrence leaves both sides vulnerable to unacceptable retaliation. However, this philosophical satisfaction is mitigated by the practical difficulty of manipulating the threat that nuclear sovereignty makes inefficient to execute and, if deterrence fails, by the difficulty of reestablishing a state of nature in the postattack environment.

Chapter 3 considers the problem of military stability in general and in terms of its specific applications to modern Europe. The transformation of politics in the Eastern bloc, so dramatically evident in the disestablishment of Communist governments in Eastern and Central Europe in 1989, could lead either toward military stability or away from it. Military stability is that condition in which neither NATO nor the Warsaw Pact expects to be attacked or sees reasons for its opponent to do so. The future of military stability in Europe is dependent upon controlled political evolution toward domestic pluralism within the non-Soviet member states of the Warsaw Pact. At the same time, the function performed by the Pact, as a security glacis for the Soviet Union's declaredly defensive military doctrine, must be preserved. The risk of military destabilization in Europe is one of inadvertent war or escalation growing out of a crisis in which political leaders are beset by uncertainties and military plans are dependent upon rapid mobilization and deployment. The risk is significant whether either side contemplates using nuclear weapons or withholding them as a threat by which to coerce an acceptable war termination by the opponent.

Chapter 4 is the first of two chapters that visit the problem of Soviet strategy for war in Europe. Soviet military planning for most of the 1980s was thought to prefer a rapid and decisive conventional offensive, which would throw NATO off its bearings and destroy the cohesion of its defenses. The Soviet plan for conventional war would also have attempted to destroy as many of NATO's nuclear systems as possible before NATO could authorize nuclear release. The difficulty with this Western understanding of Soviet planning, even before 1989, was twofold. First, there was some reason to doubt whether the expected Soviet model for war in Europe, as opposed to the preferred one, was based exclusively on the use of conventional weapons. If it was, then the Soviets were counting on "force multipliers" such as the destruction of NATO C^3 (command, control, and communications) sites; the use of chemical weapons, at least selectively; and the possible political collapse of the Western alliance at an early stage. Also, even if the Soviet short-war campaign succeeded in paralyzing NATO without triggering nuclear escalation, a long war might ensue that would not be to Soviet advantage. The current Soviet leadership seems to appreciate that a restructuring of their economy is required before they can field even competitive short-war strategies for the 1990s, let alone strategies and forces for an extended war.

A second view of the Soviet strategy for war in Europe, presented in Chapter 5, revisits some of the issues raised in the preceding chapter, but from a different perspective—that of command and control. The Soviet war plan as envisioned by Western analysts would place a great deal of stress on NATO C^3. Necessarily, it would also stress the Soviet command system, which is highly dependent on a centralized, although not rigid, system of control. The Soviet system does not subdivide "command" and "control" functions to the extent that Western theory and practice do. The Soviet tradition is of one-man command, which has extended in their experience from Frunze to Gareyev; the commander is solely responsible for the execution of command and control missions. The difference can be seen quite clearly in the U.S. response to the truck bombing of the Marine barracks in Lebanon in October 1983, compared to the Soviet response to the landing of an intrepid West German aviator in Red Square. In the U.S. case President Reagan accepted responsibility that should have extended much further down the chain of command. In the Soviet case, the defense minister was fired and other heads rolled in the military hierarchy. The Soviet system of command and control will somehow have to reconcile this system of top-down accountability with the desire for flexibility and initiative on the part of lower-level commanders.

Chapter 6 explores the Soviet view of war termination. The Soviets write almost nothing about the subject. Their analytical framework is derived from Marx, Lenin, and Clausewitz, notwithstanding the recent antinuclear declamations of Gorbachev, which have implied that Clausewitz's view of the proper relationship between war and politics does not include the use of nuclear weapons. The Soviet view is that the danger of imperialist wars against Communist states is never absent, although *glasnost* has led to diminished expression of an imminent fear of Western attack. Their opinion of how war might be ended is related to the expectations held by Soviet leaders about how war might start and what the objectives of the USSR and its opponents will be. The idea of fighting a solely conventional or limited nuclear war in Europe is not excluded in Soviet planning studies and doctrinal writings. Indeed, in the last decade, the possibility of either or both less-than-total conflicts has received more serious scrutiny than formerly. This involves some contradiction of previous views that are no longer incontrovertible, but the military leadership has adjusted to the cues provided by the party hierarchy. There is some prospect of a growing divergence between the socio-political level of Soviet military doctrine and the military-technical one. The socio-political level has in recent years emphasized a strategic defensivism and a "reasonable sufficiency" as adequate yardsticks of Soviet military preparedness. At the military-technical level, the professional officer corps is apparently more skeptical of bilateral superpower arms control as a long-term guarantor of security, and the military hierarchy is positively hostile to unilateral reductions. Further, the Soviet view of escalation, influenced by the military-technical level of doctrine as well as the socio-political, is not as sanguine about escalation control as is the Western view. The Soviets are able to exercise restraint over their own forces if need be, but their reading of NATO doctrine does not make them optimistic about Western capabilities for limiting expansion of a conflict once it begins.

Chapter 7 contrasts the orthodox view of mutual assured destruction with the strategic revisionism of defense dominance or mutual assured survival. The latter supposes that a deterrent system based on offensive retaliation can be supplanted by one that relies on deterrence by denial. Near-perfect defenses will be deployed by both superpowers, in this vision, and offenses will be reduced to ineffectual levels. There will be no incentive to attack since offenses will be too weak to accomplish any logical missions. But there are several problems with both the orthodox and the revisionist schools in terms of their implications for conflict termination. The orthodox position, of deterrence by threat of retaliation, has only in theory provided for limited nuclear options that might fall short of triggering expansion to uninhibited counter-city exchanges. In fact, many of these limited options could not be distinguished from the onset of a massive counterforce attack aimed at disarming the opponent. The problem is less the lack of sufficient numbers of launchers and warheads than it is the limitations of the C^3 systems of both superpowers and their respective alliances. The revisionist or defense-dominant view of deterrence provides little more in the way of consolation, with regard to the control of escalation and the termination of war, than the orthodox position. The early defense technologies will be difficult to distinguish from offensive ones as they will have credible ASAT (antisatellite) capabilities, thus useful for preemption against the opponent's warning and communications satellites. The defense-dominant view also does not fully explain how we get from where we are to a condition in which defenses are truly preeminent. Finally, the perspective of mutual assured survival is uninformative with regard to control of escalation and war termination because advocates of this position have thus far concentrated on proving its value for transcending deterrence. As the SDI research and development process shifts toward partial systems, including those that might be transmuted into ATBMs (theater ballistic missile defenses) for Europe, the problems of escalation control and war termination could receive more serious attention.

The problem of nuclear surprise is that it would be alarming if nuclear weapons were used at all, especially in a "bolt from the blue" first strike. Nevertheless, forces are sized on the assumption that this worst-case scenario must be dealt with. If the worst conceivable case can be handled by U.S. strategic retaliatory forces, then they can handle lesser cases as well. The assumption of greater-to-lesser does not follow because the worst-case scenario has a logical simplicity that is absent from other, more realistic cases. War is unlikely to start with a premeditated attack by one superpower against another. Nuclear war between superpowers is much more likely to result from a miscalculated escalation or a loss of control that follows the outbreak of conventional war, or that follows from the breakdown of a superpower crisis. For analysts, the problem of surprise attack is that the two processes—of uncontrolled escalation after conventional war and of crisis deterioration—are very different. Thus different treatments would be required to effect cures. The onset of conventional war would immediately raise troubling issues of protecting those assets related to nuclear deterrence that are threatened with destruction in conventional war fighting. In Europe this is especially the case with NATO C^3 systems. Competing tendencies will exist between the need for the most competent conventional-defense measures, which may require elaborated destruction of the opponent's forces and command systems, and the avoidance of a panic over conventional losses, which would set in motion the chain of nuclear escalation. In order to fight a conventional war in Europe the NATO and Warsaw Pact coalitions must agree to limits that stop short of a traditional notion of victory or defeat. While combat is taking place, both superpowers are going to be in a state of highest readiness should either side be tempted to preemption. It might be thought that the problem of strategic nuclear surprise is assumed away once conventional war has broken out. That is, once fighting has begun, its escalation would not be totally surprising, and forces and command systems are placed at higher levels of alert. This last observation is true but insufficient; it does not take into account the complexities of alert management and escalation control. It might seem that intra-war deterrence remained intact above some thresholds, such as that between conventional and nuclear war, only to have one side decide that the opponent was vulnerable to surprise in midstream. Once forces had been alerted and then stood down, they might be more vulnerable to attack than if they had never been alerted in the first place.

The concluding chapter recapitulates themes from preceding chapters and offers some analytical perspectives on the problem of war termination in Europe. Among the central themes is the recognition that one cannot get away from nuclear weapons if the context is the deterrence of war in Europe or the fighting of war if it comes to that. If deterrence has failed, it is of course preferable to terminate any war before nuclear weapons are used. If that objective cannot be accomplished, then the fewer nuclear weapons used, the better. This seems agreeable and obvious from the academic perspective. But military operations are not so easily managed and military commanders have competing priorities. Once war begins they are more concerned with the prompt execution of strike orders than they are with the diplomacy of violence. Political leaders who want to use military force in a calibrated fashion, in order to limit the collateral damage of war and make the use of force correspond closely to policy, may find that their reach into bureaucratic procedure in wartime is limited. Few leaders understand the intricacies of military planning to begin with, and in peacetime they largely avoid the subject of war plans, especially nuclear war plans. The problem of civil-military disconnection is exacerbated by the problem of reciprocal effects created by the superpowers' and their allies' command systems. Once war has begun, each side's warning, intelligence, and response systems will be integrated with the other's, producing a positive feedback loop that reinforces escalation instead of dampening it. None of this precludes the possibility of war termination. To the contrary, most of what is said in the pages that follow demands that the issue be thought through more carefully. However wise this is, the result should not be optimism about controlling war in Europe, but rather the sober realism that planning for war termination before the event begins may prevent a bad situation from getting worse.

NOTES

1. H. R. Trevor-Roper, ed., *Blitzkrieg to Defeat: Hitler's War Directives, 1939–1945* (New York: Holt, Rinehart and Winston, 1964).

2. Ibid., p. 49.

3. Barton Whaley, *Codeword Barbarossa* (Cambridge, Mass.: MIT Press, 1973).

4. Trevor-Roper, *Blitzkrieg to Defeat*, p. 49.

5. Albert Seaton, *The Russo-German War, 1941–45* (New York: Praeger Publishers, 1971), p. 52. Hitler is reported to have decided by July 31, 1940, that "Russia is the factor by which England sets the greatest store. . . . If Russia is beaten, England's last hope is gone." See Walter Warlimont, *Inside Hitler's Headquarters 1939–45* (New York: Praeger, 1965), pp. 113–14 (first published in Germany under the title *Im Hauptquartier der deutschen Wehrmacht 1939–1945*, translated by R. H. Barry). This is an example of the Führer's geopolitical logic at its self-defeating best. The defeat of the Soviet Union as a prerequisite to the defeat of Great Britain was a necessary connection only if the global political objectives of the regime were unlimited. But if they were unlimited, then Great Britain could not be expected to sue for peace, for there would be no incentive to do so. Sooner or later it would have to grapple with the absolutism of Germany's ambitions.

6. Seaton, *Russo-German War*, p. 52.

7. Nigel Nicolson, *Napoleon 1812* (New York: Harper and Row, 1985), esp. Ch. 9.

8. Earl F. Ziemke, *Stalingrad to Berlin: The German Defeat in the East* (Washington, D.C.: Office of the Chief of Military History, U.S. Army, 1968), p. 7.

9. See, for example, Heinz Guderian, *Panzer Leader* (New York: Ballantine Books, 1957).

10. Trevor-Roper, *Blitzkreig to Defeat*, p. 78.

11. Ibid.

12. Ibid., pp. 79–81.

13. Seaton, *Russo-German War*, p. 55.

14. Martin Van Creveld, *Supplying War: Logistics from Wallenstein to Patton* (Cambridge: Cambridge University Press, 1977), p. 144.

15. Ibid., p. 145.

16. Ibid., p. 160.

17. Ibid., p. 176.

18. Seaton, *Russo-German War*, p. 43.

19. Ibid., p. 46.

20. On Stalin's purges of the Soviet military leadership, see Malcolm Mackintosh, *Juggernaut: A History of the Soviet Armed Forces* (New York: Macmillan Co., 1967), Ch. 5, pp. 84–97.

21. Albert Speer, *Inside the Third Reich* (New York: Avon Books, 1970), esp. pp. 287–88.

22. Ziemke, *Stalingrad to Berlin*, p. 7.

23. According to Max Hastings, U.S. Army assignment of a low priority to infantry recruitment and the filtration of better-educated and more physically fit men to the specialized technical branches of all the services had, by 1944, resulted in rifle companies of very low-quality enlisted personnel and shortages of competent NCOs and officers. Moreover, "Few American infantry units arrived in Normandy with a grasp of basic tactics—a failure for which many men paid with their lives. The American airborne units showed what was possible on the battlefield, what the American soldier at his best could achieve. But only a handful of other formations proved capable of emulating the 82nd and 101st. The belief that fire-power could ultimately save the infantry from the task of hard fighting underlay many difficulties and failures on the ground." See Hastings, *Overlord: D-Day and the Battle for Normandy* (New York: Simon and Schuster, 1984), pp. 167, 316.

Acknowledgments

I am grateful to Jacob Kipp, David Glantz, Graham Turbiville, Harry Orenstein, and their colleagues at the Soviet Army Studies Office, Fort Leavenworth, Kansas, for suggestions with regard to reference materials. A similar acknowledgment for valuable references is made to Christopher Donnelly, Peter Vigor, and Peter Podbielski of the Royal Military Academy, Sandhurst, Great Britain, and to Phillip Petersen and Joshua Spero of the Policy Support group in the Office of the Secretary of Defense. I am also indebted to Edward (Ted) Warner and John Hines of RAND Corporation for sharing copies of works in print and in progress, and to their RAND colleagues William Martel and Paul Davis for their contributions to my understanding of U.S. strategy and strategic planning methodology. Desmond Ball, Keith Dunn, and George Quester deserve credit for stimulating my interest in the topic of war termination, and Gregory Treverton for help in clarifying issues pertinent to Europe and NATO. I am especially grateful to Raymond Garthoff and Leon Goure for reading portions of the manuscript and providing helpful comments, and to Vernon Aspaturian, Mary Fitzgerald, and Trond Gilberg for guidance to useful and important sources. Paul Bracken, Bruce Blair, and Ned Lebow have contributed very much to my knowledge of crisis management and war termination. I am particularly grateful to Diane Wolf, Madlyn Hanes, and Edward Tomezsko for administrative and departmental support, and to Mary Glenn of Praeger Publishers for her interest in and encouragement of my work. Lauren Pera of Praeger supervised the production process, and Talvi Laev served as project editor. Most important, my wife Betsy has endured still another production with patience and tact.

None of the above persons or institutions bears any responsibility for the arguments or errors contained in the manuscript, nor for mistakes in translation.

Conflict
Termination
in
Europe

1

Conflict Termination and Risks in Europe: An Introduction to Problems and Choices

The subject matter of conflict termination is quite complicated, and it can be approached from a number of perspectives. The decision maker is interested in accomplishing as many of his or her objectives as possible. The policy analyst wants to understand why some situations can be managed to a successful connection between the use of force and the attainment of policy goals, while others cannot. The scholar wants to fit theories of international relations and foreign-policy decision making into the crucible of political experience at three levels: the international system and the balance of power, the national character and decision-making processes of states, and the particular attributes of individual decision makers and their group dynamics.

This study considers the problem of conflict termination in Europe. This choice is made on account of Europe's importance for both superpowers; conflict termination must be pertinent to the most significant cases if it is to have any continuing interest for policy planners. The case of Europe also allows us to apply knowledge of U.S. and Soviet concepts of escalation and force planning to the issue at hand. We will see that our knowledge of East and West is not identical, nor does it lead to parallel conclusions. A third reason for focusing on Europe is that it highlights the difficulty of terminating coalition wars, since the political complexity of those conflicts is apt to be less manageable than it is for two-party conflicts.

Discussion of war termination in the context of Europe requires a perspective on forces and command systems. The approach here is to emphasize the importance of command systems and decision making as keys to the control of crisis and wartime escalation. Ending wars after they have started has some definite relationship to a state's or an alliance's approach to peacetime readiness and crisis management. Forces and decision-making repertoires not instituted under normal conditions cannot be improvised in emergencies without running a high risk of failure. This is especially so with U.S., Soviet, and other nuclear weapons tightly coupled to warning and intelligence systems. In addition, the superpowers have dispersed nuclear weapons with their general-purpose forces deployed outside their borders. Vertical integration of warning and intelligence with nuclear responses is combined with synoptic war plans that integrate strike planning for theater and strategic nuclear forces.

This perspective differs from the more common one of comparing force attributes such as survivability, lethality, and mobility. It would be equally legitimate to study how the superpowers' nuclear and conventional forces are conducive to crisis management and war termination. Some elements of this force-attribute perspective are significant for the discussion of conflict termination, and will be so noted. Sometimes these force elements are the doctrines for using forces, as well as the forces themselves and their basing modes. The U.S. and Soviet expectations about how rapidly their strategic and other nuclear forces might have to be used—and against what—condition each's approach to command and control of those forces. In turn, this influences the prospects for crisis management, control of escalation, and war termination. The discussion that follows considers the interactions of forces and command systems from three vantage points, relative to conflict termination in Europe: First, the relationship between war and politics as perceived by Soviet and "Western" planners will be noted; second, the superpowers and their coalitions' likely views on the process of escalation in Europe will be compared; third, the command, control, and communications (C^3) perspectives implicit in U.S. and Soviet writings and deployments will be assessed for their implications with regard to war termination. A final section reviews force-related issues as they pertain to strategic and theater nuclear command and control problems, with reference to the problem of ending wars within some policy-relevant framework.

WAR AND POLITICS

The views of Lenin and Clausewitz have had a well-understood influence on the development of Soviet military thought.[1] As distilled through Lenin, Clausewitz is understood by Soviet military strategists to have explained the connection between war and politics. Politics is the intelligent faculty, and military forces are the instruments, for the advancement of state interests.[2] In the Soviet version of this, politics is determined by the historical unfolding of the international class struggle, and the aspirations of the international working class are embodied in the Soviet Union and its leadership, especially the party hierarchy. This sense of historical mission implies that the long-run objectives of the Soviet Union can be constant although the methods of approaching them can change in the short run. Thus crisis, arms control, détente, arms races, and subversion are among the carrots and sticks with which Soviet leaders challenge their opponents, who have no one to blame but themselves for a misappreciation of Soviet objectives. In the most recent version of Soviet declaratory policy with reference to international affairs, Gorbachev's emphasis on *perestroika* is judged to have brought about a reformulation of Soviet global objectives as well.[3]

As devotees once removed of Clausewitz, the Soviets have, since the nuclear age, come to appreciate another of his maxims: that war, left to itself, takes an absolute form. During the 1950s and much of the 1960s, the Soviet leadership expected that any major coalition war against the West would involve the immediate and massive use of nuclear weapons.[4] This one variant model was not too dissimilar from the U.S. "massive retaliation" declaratory policy, which was abandoned by the Kennedy administration in favor of "flexible response." The Kennedy and Johnson administrations had some difficulty convincing U.S. allies in Europe of the rationale for the shift from massive retaliation to flexible response, which was finally adopted as official NATO policy in 1967 (MC 14/3).[5] The Soviets, meanwhile, were also rethinking their military doctrine, and in 1966 an important shift in emphasis was first indicated, with important overtones for later doctrinal debates.[6] This was the subject of numerous discussions among the Soviet leadership until the latter 1970s, but the direction of the trend was clear much earlier. The Soviet Union was going to have to be prepared for more than one variant of war, since NATO strategy might require a response calling for an extended conventional phase of war or an extended conventional war.[7]

The Soviet expectation that they had to prepare for more kinds of wars, either in Europe or globally, did not adjust the priority of Soviet political interests in determining military policy. During the Brezhnev era the Soviet Union used a combination of détente and arms control and a sustained military buildup to accomplish two very important politico-military objectives. The first was to nullify the perception of U.S. strategic nuclear superiority and to substitute a perception of parity, or essential equivalence in the overall U.S.–Soviet strategic nuclear balance. The second objective was to strengthen Soviet forces for conventional war in

Europe and for global power projection. This was done in part to redress the downsizing and deemphasis on ground forces during the Khrushchev era. It was also a response to the establishment by NATO of flexible response, and the apparent Western Assumption that a war in Europe would have a meaningful conventional phase.

Western military strategists have also been influenced by the expectation that war and politics are related as instrument is to intelligent faculty. However, in the United States especially and in parts of NATO Europe, the coupling of war and politics to conclude a conflict on acceptable and realistic terms poses a special challenge on account of alliance relations and domestic politics. Americans tend to view peace and war as antithetical states—one exclusive of the other. Europeans want little or nothing of any war in Europe that does not include the prompt involvement of U.S. nuclear forces, in order that this expectation dissuade Soviet aggression, including conventional. Americans also view war in Europe as one possible component of a global war that might be protracted, while Europeans understandably see war on their territory as the main, if not sole, event. Finally, Europeans, including NATO members, do not see the Soviets as presenting an imminent military threat to the extent that Americans do, although the differences in views attributed to mass publics on either side of the Atlantic are greater than those held by leaders within the Atlantic alliance.[8]

ESCALATION AND THE CONDUCT OF WAR IN EUROPE

Western concepts of the Soviet view of escalation are frequently dated. The tendency to base U.S. views on the one variant model of war that the Soviets have long since rejected is characteristic of both liberal and conservative U.S. strategic policy analysis. Conservatives argue that the Soviets will not recognize limitations or thresholds in coalition war, so as to impress upon the public mind the size and diversity of the Soviet nuclear and conventional force structure. Liberals object to any suggestion of Soviet interest in graduated escalation, on the grounds that East and West might "collaborate" to make war in Europe thinkable, and therefore fightable.

The irony is that, despite a large outpouring of Western literature on the subject of escalation since Herman Kahn first made this terminology fashionable, the United States and NATO today are no better prepared to initiate escalation, and to control it, than are the Soviets.[9] NATO's approach to escalation is essentially mechanistic if its declaratory policy, which it might not follow under actual wartime conditions, is to be believed. If conventional defense fails, deliberate but selective nuclear escalation follows. The last measure is the initiation of strategic nuclear war. Had NATO completed its INF Pershing II and cruise missile (GLCM) deployments in Europe in lieu of an INF agreement, one might have added another "rung" of escalation—a Eurostrategic step on the ladder—somewhere between battlefield nuclear war and strategic nuclear war.

When the United States had a perceived strategic nuclear superiority compared to the Soviet Union, this strategy was feasible. Equivalent Soviet strategic nuclear forces deter U.S. escalation to the top of the ladder unless the United States and its allies are willing to run greater risks than the Soviets. However, there is no reason to assume that the West is more risk-inducing than the East, especially if the evolution of a crisis or conventional war has allowed time for public opinion to make itself felt. The common assumption that the West is always going to be more strongly motivated to "play chicken" than the Soviets, on the basis of a jointly understood Western "defensive" motivation and a Soviet "offensive" one, is not justified by the evidence of previous crises during which U.S. policymakers have contemplated the use of nuclear weapons.[10]

If Soviet capabilities to control escalation in Europe are at least equivalent to Western ones, it does not follow that their doctrine is similar. The Soviet view is apt to be derived from both politico-military and military-technical aspects of their military doctrine.[11] The politico-military aspects suggest to them that a war against the Western coalition is not about a piece of territory in West Germany. What such a war would be "about" would be the postwar distribution of power in Eurasia. From this would follow, according to the military-technical aspects of Soviet doctrine, a reluctance to get into any war for which their forces were unprepared.[12] And it is difficult to see how, absent national territorial ballistic missile defenses, the Soviets can expect to have their forces adequately prepared for general nuclear war. Therefore, their military planning must hope to avoid the nuclear devastation of their forces as they attempt to accomplish their war aims in Europe. Even more fundamental is their requirement to avoid nuclear devastation of the Soviet Union itself.[13]

The Soviets would recognize thresholds in war that conform to these politico-military and military-technical expectations. Thus they would prefer to conduct front and TVD (theater of strategic military action) operations in a decisive manner to minimize unnecessary diversion of efforts against low-priority or superfluous targets. Soviet diplomacy should have prepared the way for Soviet arms by dividing the Western coalition in the period preceding the actual outbreak of war.[14] NATO nuclear weapons and weapons storage sites, air defenses and air bases, and command and control centers would be prompt targets in a theater-strategic conventional offensive designed to remove the opportunity, and incentive, for NATO nuclear escalation. Soviet strategic and theater nuclear forces would remain as counterdeterrents to NATO escalation. In the event that these theater or strategic nuclear forces have to be used, according to the judgment of the highest Soviet leadership, they would be used selectively instead of indiscriminately. The Soviets may have accepted mutual deterrence as the basis of East-West arms agreements, but they have not accepted mutual assured destruction as a basis for targeting their nuclear forces.[15]

NATO AND SOVIET C³, ESCALATION AND CONFLICT TERMINATION

The possibility that the Soviet Union and the Warsaw Pact, instead of the United States and NATO, would be able to employ selective nuclear options more effectively in support of European war aims creates great sensitivity on both sides of the Atlantic. For example, the report of the U.S. Commission on Long Term Integrated Strategy, *Discriminate Deterrence*, noted that strategic nuclear retaliation was an option of last resort. For attacks regarded as more plausible, including selective nuclear ones, the United States and NATO would have to rely on other options.[16] This was hardly news. Since the "Schlesinger doctrine" of 1974 (National Security Decision Memorandum 242), the United States had indicated that limited strategic options would be preferable to larger retaliatory strikes in some instances. Of equal importance was the insistence of Schlesinger and his successors upon building truly limited options into the United States' Single Integrated Operational Plan (SIOP), as opposed to larger numbers of massive retaliatory strikes.[17] These limited options were not designed to launch prevailing strikes or to improve firepower ratios. They were designed to attack discrete targets with the objective of sending a specific political message.

Although the United States' declaratory policy of enhanced LNO (Limited Nuclear Options) was widely controversial, the operational war plans went in the direction of multiplying discrete options for many reasons. One was presidential desires not to be trapped into a choice between all-out war and capitulation to the demands of the opponent. Actually, no president after Kennedy really faced a choice so stark.[18] A second reason was the multiplication of U.S. warheads available for targeting the various categories of wartime objectives, should deterrence fail. The categories of targets, according to Desmond Ball, have remained remarkably constant over the decades as the available warheads and their allocation schemes in the U.S. SIOP have been adjusted to fit changes in doctrine and technology.[19] For example, SIOP 5, which was approved in December 1975 and took effect in January 1976, allocated weapons among four general target categories: Soviet nuclear forces, conventional (general-purpose) military forces, military and political leadership, and economic and industrial targets. Attack options were grouped into Major Attack Options, Selected Attack Options, and Limited Nuclear Options, with the last designed to "permit the selective destruction of fixed enemy military or industrial targets."[20]

The two reasons stated for increased reliance on LNOs in U.S. war plans involved presidential assumptions about making deterrence more credible and about improving crisis stability. They also involved a reasoned effort to apply the "abundance" of U.S. MIRV technology to the objective of attack discrimination. But a third—and, for our purposes, the most important—objective of increased reliance upon LNOs was the goal of war termination. Schlesinger made this clear in his report to the U.S. Congress on the fiscal year 1975 defense budget: "To the extent that we have selective response options . . . we may be able to bring all but the largest nuclear conflicts to a *rapid* conclusion before cities are struck."[21] This was arguably an attempt to define a limited strategic war with an opponent who could not be assumed to be interested in playing the game by the same rules. The Soviet view of "limited" nuclear options was less one of bargaining during war in order to terminate it on some mutually agreeable terms and more the question of the most economical assignment of weapons to targets while preserving intact any societal assets they might need for postwar recovery. Two versions of "limited" nuclear war seemed improbable in the Soviet reckoning: limited strategic war involving attacks on the Soviet homeland, and war limited to Europe geographically, which was less than strategic in its political import. Here Americans and Soviets, by virtue of their divergent heritages, were far apart in their perceptions of Europe and its relationship to the defense of their respective homelands.[22]

The United States, in its effort to develop selective strategic or theater nuclear options, also walked into a mine field of command and control issues. The first was whether the U.S. and NATO command systems could handle the physical stress of regional conventional or conventional-nuclear war in Europe and then respond with larger, but still selective, components of the NATO nuclear operations plan or the U.S. SIOP. The second was whether even physically intact—or mostly so—command systems could be counted on to follow through procedurally in real crisis and wartime scenarios, compared to peacetime simulations. The third was the synergy of the two sides' nuclear command systems and the possibility that during a crisis or war they might interact in unpredictable ways.[23]

On these three issues the United States and NATO did not necessarily stand up better than their prospective opponents. The second issue—of comparative NATO and Warsaw Pact command follow-through—has paradoxical aspects. Proponents of U.S. and NATO theater command systems argued in favor of Western flexibility compared to Soviet rigidity. But some U.S. analysts disagreed. John G. Hines and Phillip A. Petersen have noted that Soviet high commands of forces on a TVD (theater of strategic military action) scale have been established for the continental and maritime sectors of northern, western, and southern Europe.[24] These high commands are intermediate between STAVKA/VGK (Headquarters, Supreme High Command) and the front operational commands in various theaters. The precedent for a high command in a strategic theater of military action was the Soviet Manchurian campaign in 1945, for which a special Far East Command was established.[25] These strategic theater of operations commands in the western, northwestern, and southwestern TVDs would provide the Soviet leadership with a regionally based level of peacetime planning and wartime coordination that allows for a smoother progression from normal peacetime conditions to war readiness. NATO might be comparatively underprepared for the peacetime transition to war readiness, and for wartime force management, at the "echelons above corps" level.

The first issue—of physical destruction or disruption of command systems and communications—is also not necessarily one that encourages optimism about conflict termination favorable to NATO. A conventional war in Europe would involve destruction of NATO C^3 assets that would also be useful, and in some cases necessary, for the execution of theater or strategic NATO and U.S. war plans.[26] NATO Follow-on Forces Attack (FOFA) operations would be intended to destroy Soviet rearward echelons and to disrupt or destroy the rear-to-front communications on which the movement of Warsaw Pact forces depends. This conventional deep strike is thus expected to throw off the timing of Soviet force movements along the various axes of their advance. The Pact offensive is thought to be highly stylized in terms of its expectations about the accomplishment of objectives within formatted guidelines or norms.[27] Disruption of echelonment patterns and movement norms would demolish the Soviet game plan, and so grind the offensive to a halt.

One problem with this reasoning is that the Soviets may not echelon in a formatted way, in order to confound deep-strike planners and to conceal their real intentions with regard to likely axes of advance. More reliance may be placed upon the use of forward detachments and Operational Maneuver Groups (OMGs) as spearheads of the army and front offensives. These formations would be tasked to establish selective penetrations of NATO forward defenses and to exploit or conduct breakthroughs into NATO's strategic (i.e., operational-strategic) depth.[28] Built-to-order raiding forces of this type will create the proverbial "fog of war" in NATO's defenses as they attempt to regroup and resist the first probes of Soviet forklike punctures along the defense line. If the Soviets succeed in forcing NATO into an early state of confusion, the NATO deep attacks against reinforcing echelons may be superfluous, in that NATO will have lost its effective cohesion and C^3 much further forward. This point bears reemphasis. The threat from the Pact's first echelons and raiding or disruption forces is not so much that they will eliminate NATO's capacity to defend by a process of attrition; instead, the more subtle problem is that of eroding NATO's cohesion through the proliferation of Soviet and Pact "oil slicks" onto key communications nodes, command posts, and other targets the loss of which would cause Western coordination to suffer appreciably.[29] Another issue in conventional deep strike is that the Soviet Union can certainly develop its own "reconnaissance strike" systems and invert the dilemma that FOFA poses to the Soviets, against an opponent with diversified command and control systems, military doctrines, and political priorities once war has begun.

The third issue is the potential for effects of interaction between the U.S. and Soviet, or NATO and Pact, command systems. This is an unavoidable problem if there is to be any hope of terminating a theater conventional or nuclear war before it erupts into strategic exchanges between superpower homelands. Even earlier, the problem is apparent during the process of managing nuclear alerts, at least from evidence available from Western sources.[30] The U.S. and Soviet nuclear forces have apparently never been alerted simultaneously. Thus there is great uncertainty about what would happen if simultaneous NATO and Pact or U.S. and Soviet alerts took place. One problem is that the alert of U.S. and European NATO forces might not be synchronized, especially if some of the European members of NATO felt that the causes of the crisis were ambiguous.[31] Another problem is that NATO has little evidence of the Soviet process of nuclear alert management; estimates must be extrapolated from past Soviet practices in response to U.S. alerts, in some cases under force balances much more favorable to the West than now. A third problem is that the U.S. and NATO alerting processes would involve measures that seem defensive and protective to Western planners but provocative to Soviets who fear NATO preparations for preemptive attack.[32]

The alerting process might not seem directly related to the issue of war termination, but it is. During the alerting process NATO and Pact forces would be going through a transition from peacetime to war readiness. The safety catches that prevent the outbreak of accidental or inadvertent war, while remaining nominally in place, would in reality be dissolving gracefully, as commanders anticipated having to react quickly to unexpected, and potentially devastating, surprises.[33] Political leaders in the U.S., NATO European, or Soviet hierarchies are unlikely to give blanket or permissive delegations of contingent release authority to battlefield commanders. Nothing so explicit would be permitted or encouraged, but something less explicit and controllable might take place instead. Organizations depend upon standard operating procedures and rehearsed drills in order to provide a rapid and appropriate response to threats or policymakers' demands. They can do only what they have been programmed to do; what is not in their repertoire will not be done or, if done, will be executed poorly.[34]

If, during the alerting process for U.S. or Soviet forces, either side's policymakers appear to be losing control of military operations in the field, the opponent will be motivated to move into war—or, if in war, to escalate rapidly and decisively. Something of this sort was at issue during the Cuban missile crisis. U.S. Navy standard operating procedures called for aggressively trailing and forcing to the surface any Soviet submarines capable of delivering a nuclear strike against U.S. shore targets. The implications for crisis management or for escalation control if deterrence failed were unrecognized by U.S. leaders until the operations had been underway for some time and had forced a number of Soviet submarines to surface.[35] Had altercations involved even limited use of nuclear weapons deployed at sea, the Soviets might have concluded that the United States had set in motion the first stage of a comprehensive war plan. Collisions at sea between Soviet and U.S. vessels have occurred with regularity in peacetime; under conditions of crisis or limited war, they would be more ominous, especially if they involved ships armed with nuclear weapons.

For war termination to occur after either side has used nuclear weapons, there are several requirements in addition to limiting the scale of destruction and the number of strikes against key targets, especially cities. Commanders and command posts, communications, and authoritative political succession must be preserved during any regional or global war. In addition, there must be some incentive structure such that U.S. and Soviet leaders *want* to stop the war. The capability to stop is insufficient. Devices such as the U.S.–Soviet Direct Communications Link ("Hotline") or the nuclear risk reduction centers provide the capacity for crisis-time communications to correct misunderstandings that might contribute to accidental or inadvertent war.[36] But they are not expected to survive beyond the early phases of any superpower nuclear conflict, and the problem of postattack communications between adversaries would have to be solved in some other way if doing so were deemed desirable. There is some doubt whether U.S. or Soviet nuclear command organizations and policy-making systems would, under the stress of strategic nuclear war, be able to recreate protocols that would identify unambiguously the surviving national leaders and their rank for giving authoritative commands.[37] Even if nuclear attacks against the superpowers' homelands were spared, nuclear strikes into Eastern and Western Europe could lead to intra-alliance defections, antigovernment revolts, and postattack bloc disintegration with which command systems organized for peacetime would be unable to cope. The problem of extended deterrence has bedeviled U.S. nuclear war planners for several decades in peacetime. Under wartime conditions, the more acute problem of extended command over nuclear weapons systems dispersed among general-purpose armies, navies, and air forces would be among the largest barriers to war termination on any acceptable conditions.

PERSPECTIVES ON FORCES AND COMMAND

The preceding discussion has emphasized issues of control and doctrine. But the problem of force characteristics cannot be isolated from the issue of war termination. Forces that have been designed for one kind of mission are not easily adapted, if at all, to another. The U.S. and Soviet nuclear arsenals, and their conventional force structures, may contribute to the outbreak of kinds of wars that neither side has expected or planned for. This could make war difficult to end under severe conditions or when political issues are in dispute.

NATO and Warsaw Pact forces are not like general-purpose military forces of the past. They are general-purpose forces equipped to fight with nuclear and conventional weapons. However, their military doctrines are based in part on the military histories of the member states. Those histories include, in the Soviet case, the World War II and its impact upon Soviet doctrine and strategy. For Western analysts, this has meant that the Soviet

Union, if it decides to go to war at all, would come at NATO with a conventional *blitzkrieg* designed to achieve rapid and decisive war aims and to preclude NATO nuclear escalation.[38]

If one looks at actual NATO and Pact force structures, several things weigh against the likelihood of this. One is that NATO is not so weak, relative to the Pact, in numbers of active-duty and potentially mobilized reserves, force-to-space ratios, armored division equivalents on the Central Front, and other static indicators of the success or failure of any short-warning attack.[39] The second is that the level of destruction attendant to even a short conventional war would be unprecedented. Both sides would suffer from shortages of logistics and effective operational reserves if the war continued beyond several weeks. Neither would be able to establish a predominant position before its ready forces and rapidly mobilizable capacity were used up. Therefore, and contrary to common wisdom about conventional war in Europe, an extended war of attrition may follow a short war of material exhaustion and command disruption. If so, the extended war offers the challenge of negotiating for war termination.[40]

A third concern for the Pact is whether its command, control, and communications will be adequate to fight a widely dispersed war across several fronts simultaneously. On one hand, the establishment of high commands of forces in the various western TVDs will, as noted, allow for smoother transition from peacetime to war readiness. On the other hand, this improvement in higher levels of command must be matched by flexibility and innovation down below, or the Soviet command system will find itself having been "decapitated" by organizational inflexibility, on account of the incompetence of its tactical leadership for fluid and confused battlefields.

A fourth concern for the Soviets must be that, even if all goes well for their side of any plan for conventional victory in Europe, NATO's force structure may not allow the West to "cooperate" by avoiding escalation to nuclear weapons. If you were a conservative Soviet war planner, you would assume that any war in Europe might go nuclear at any time. Thus your forces would only be concentrated at the very moment of an attempted breakthrough of important defense positions; afterward they would be dispersed and concealed. The electronic battlefield will be a competition between detection and deception, of nullifying the grids of the opponent while attempting to improve the verifying of your own. Creating, in the electronic indicators that are sucked up by the opponent's vacuum cleaners, the right kind of misinformation may be the key to victory or defeat. Thus the Soviets practice "radio-electronic combat" as part of their peacetime war planning, which includes jamming and spoofing enemy emitters and protecting their own transmissions (electronic countermeasures, ECM and counter-countermeasures, or ECCM).[41] But they can be less than fully confident in the performance of their computer decision aids and electronics compared to those of the West, which has maintained a significant lead in this area for decades.

If conventional war might turn out otherwise than expected, as a result of forces or force multipliers that do not yield preferred solutions, so might nuclear war. The issues of deterrence stability are widely understood in the academic and military communities as they pertain to prewar and crisis behavior. The basic objective of U.S. and Soviet nuclear forces is to preclude surprise attack by posing to the opponent the plausible risk of societal devastation. But forces are expected to do other things, too, and this is where outcomes might deviate from planned objectives.

Among the other things that nuclear forces are expected to do is to contribute to escalation control and war termination. U.S. and Soviet forces as now deployed are partially maladaptive to either of these missions. Both sides have important force components in basing modes that are vulnerable to preemptive attack. In the U.S. case, its silo-based ICBMs and all bombers not on ground alert could be destroyed in a preemptive attack. The Soviet Union has a higher proportion of its warheads and megatonnage on land-based missiles than does the United States. Both sides thus deploy forces of which substantial components invite attack on themselves and provide little in the way of poststrike negotiating leverage.

On the other hand, the United States maintains programs for modernizing its bomber-cruise missile forces and its sea-based ballistic missiles (SLBMs) and cruise missiles (SLCMs). The sea-based forces could be used for prompt or delayed attacks, and the bomber-cruise missile force is being modernized by planned deployment of the Advanced Cruise Missile, the B-1 bomber, and the B-2 (Stealth) bomber now in research and development.[42] The Soviet Union has begun to upgrade its strategic bomber force by deploying long-range cruise missiles (ALCMs) on some of its Bear-H bombers and by the planned deployment of Blackjack intercontinental bombers.[43]

The Soviet Union is also diversifying its land-based missile force. The SS-24 rail-mobile missile will have an estimated ten warheads, while the SS-25 single-warhead missile is already widely deployed on road-mobile vehicles.[44] The United States, following the lead of the Scowcroft Commission, has proceeded through advanced development for the Midgetman small, single-warhead, mobile ICBM. However, the Reagan administration was less than enthusiastic about Midgetman, and offered it as a potential bargaining chip to the Soviet Union in arms control negotiations. Then secretary of defense Frank Carlucci indicated in his annual report for 1989 that the administration would not fight continued congressional funding for Midgetman, but would prefer to invest in mobile-basing schemes for MX/Peacekeeper, including a rail-garrison deployment that appeared promising to Air Force planners.[45]

It seems conceivable that the U.S. and Soviet deterrents of the 1990s would look very different from those of earlier decades if new deployment modes and technologies were combined with arms control breakthroughs. The superpowers at Reykjavík moved very far toward a commitment to reduce by half the number of their warheads on land- and sea-based strategic ballistic missiles. These and subsequent discussions led to proposed reductions in the range of 6,000 strategic force loadings for each side, with some 4,900 to 5,100 based on ICBMs and SLBMs. With reduced numbers of warheads and launchers, the survivability of the remaining forces would become more important (statistically, not substantively), and the incentive for mobile and deceptive basing schemes would be stronger. Mobile land-based missiles would be more valuable in a restrictive arms control regime in which the survivability of each component was presumably more critical, compared to a situation of great force-size redundancy. On the other hand, the Soviet ICBM force would also be mobile, and thus harder to target. For a variety of reasons, the Soviet Union was unlikely to shift its emphasis from land- to sea-based systems as drastically as did the United States, although the SSBN-SLBM force was improved considerably in the 1970s and 1980s.

Superpower force structures that are less heavily dependent on prompt response are less capable of preemption. They also contribute to whatever potential there is for intra-war deterrence and war termination.[46] Mobile land-based, airborne, and sea-based forces would resist prompt and comprehensive destruction. Even if deterrence failed, neither side would have a realistic hope of destroying the forces of the opponent without a sustained and debilitating campaign. The inability to destroy the opponent's forces rapidly would change the time factor, from one of compelling urgency to that of launching the most comprehensive attack possible. It might make more sense to launch selective attacks and then negotiate. As the technical possibility for preemption seemed more remote, the willingness to use nuclear weapons in a selective way might increase. However, the uses to which nuclear weapons can be put, other than as instruments of deterrence, are very few. They are not going to be used casually. And in a slow-paced nuclear war, leaders of both sides are going to have more to say about how the war is conducted than they would in a war of 30 to 60 minutes.

Forces that offer this diversified survivability would also contribute to a less panic-stricken assessment of command vulnerability. Assessments sometimes confuse the issue of scale in attempting to discern the survivability of U.S. or Soviet C^3 systems. The nuclear command system of the United States, for example, is not expected by planners to survive an attack designed to destroy it. By targeting enough warheads, if they so chose, the Soviets could destroy the physical apparatus of U.S. postattack command. The price, however, would not be cheap; strikes of this magnitude would encourage comprehensive U.S. retaliation against any available Soviet targets, and the Soviet warheads gratuitously expended against U.S. C^3 targets would not be available for strikes against surviving U.S. weapons. In other words, there is a trade-off between the tasking of forces for a massive surprise in an expected short war and the assignment of targeting priorities on the basis of a protracted but limited war.[47] Even in less than massive attacks, strikes against the command system of the opponent may be self-defeating. Attacks against the U.S. or Soviet command system that would leave forces undestroyed and a command system cut into pieces would not benefit the first striker. The second striker would unleash destructive forces controlled by a divided brain, a recipe for unlimited and uncontrolled devastation. In the case of attacks against an alliance command system, the problem is compounded. Soviet planners could, for example, never be certain what the French or British would do with their national strategic deterrents, even if those forces and command systems were temporarily spared during superpower exchanges.

The point that nuclear wars between superpowers may be protracted and therefore limited, or short and massive, deserves repetition in another context. There were some early misunderstandings of Reagan declaratory strategy, in which readers assumed that the United States was planning its forces and command systems with the expectation of fighting an extended and comprehensive nuclear war. The Carter administration, when it attempted to explain publicly countervailing strategy, also found itself discussing "protracted" nuclear war, which some audiences took to mean extended and massive exchanges.[48] Further grist for this mill were the perennial academic or Pentagon threat assessments in which the Soviet Union is depicted as dug in with bunkers and command redundancy for an extended global war.[49] Reagan modernization plans for elements of the U.S. strategic nuclear "Triad" of ICBMs (MX/Peacekeeper), SLBMs

(Trident II), and bombers with air-launched cruise missiles (B-1 and B-2) suggested to skeptics an across-the-board attempt to confront the Soviet Union with a counter-counterforce strategy that could win or equalize prompt exchanges and sustain combat into the extended phases of any conflict.

Soviet threat assessors and Reagan critics share a misapprehension here. The United States, at least since the days of Secretary of Defense James R. Schlesinger, is not planning for a protracted nuclear war in the sense of a total war. The Schlesinger doctrine was for the selective use of forces in order to get away from the fixity of large, and therefore potentially immobilized, SIOP options. Carter Secretary of Defense Harold Brown sought to continue the Schlesinger doctrine in a new planning context— one that emphasized C^3 modernization and the targeting of Soviet C^3 assets other than national leadership. These latter were to be spared initially from strikes aimed directly against them, in order to induce them to negotiate.[50] Academic strategists are appalled by this and argue that it is part of the slippery slope toward Armageddon; we will not get into that argument here.[51] Planners did not see it that way. There was no point in planning for an uncontrolled, apolitical exchange of weapons. A fruitful planning assumption was that exchanges would be less than total, communication would be preserved between leaderships, and surviving forces would be withheld for postattack coercion.

It was also argued, by a different set of critics, that the planning assumptions about bargaining during nuclear war were signs of weakness instead of U.S., or NATO, strength. The willingness to engage in less-than-total SIOP counterforce attacks into Europe or the European Soviet Union would signal lack of resolve and would encourage the Soviets to raise the ante by several orders of magnitude. This criticism also missed the mark as a critique of planners' assumptions. The intent of the Schlesinger-Brown doctrines was not to win a counterforce war but to induce the Soviet Union to enter a process of coercive bargaining. Withheld strategic forces, and perhaps surviving general-purpose forces widely dispersed, would provide postattack bargaining leverage. These withheld forces would be the most survivable, such as U.S. and Soviet SSBNs (ballistic missile submarines), and their major value would be that they would *not* be used unless all hope for restraint was abandoned. As U.S. and Soviet SSBN forces evolve toward the inclusion of greater counterforce potential, the preceding statement will be modified, but not drastically. The point was that neither U.S. nor Soviet planners could remove their cities from the assured retaliation of the other, even after substantial numbers of counterforce exchanges had taken place and some destruction of C^3 on both sides had occurred. Evidence for this argument, in the U.S. case, is the absence of electronic Permissive Action Links (PALs) aboard ballistic missile submarines. They are designed to provide a capability for retaliation even if, and after, the command systems that normally support them are destroyed.

The only way out of this condition—vulnerability in the later stages of war to counter-societal destruction regardless of the results of early counterforce exchanges—was for either side or both to deploy nationwide BMD (ballistic missile defenses) systems. A major unknown is whether the United States will continue the SDI program through research and development and into deployment of any missile defense system. Any system deployed within the next several decades would be a partial one designed to reinforce deterrence instead of supplanting it, contrary to the president's initially stated (and probably unattainable) objective. The limited U.S. system might defend land-based missiles that are silo based or mobile, and it might also protect command centers and other C^3 assets.[52] However, it could be argued that arms control is a less expensive way of accomplishing this. Passive measures to increase the survivability of forces and command systems might also be cost-effective compared to even limited BMD systems. For example, a point defense system might work interactively with mobile ICBMs to increase the leverage of the defense. On the other hand, a sufficiently mobile land-based missile might not require BMD at all. A pertinent issue is how many warheads are required to survive on each leg of the U.S. force structure and what their targeting assignments are. To revisit an earlier point, if U.S. planners assume a need to strike comprehensively and promptly against the Soviet nuclear force structure, then a large armada of survivable ICBM warheads will be needed (whether on single-warhead or MIRVed launchers is another question). If the assumption of planners is, instead, that more selective retaliatory strikes are more probable, then survivable warheads can be distributed among land-based, sea-based, and airborne platforms, with emphasis on the latter two.

It was suggested by the Reagan administration that the basis of super-power deterrence might be moved from its current reliance upon offensive retaliation to a new condition in which offenses have been nearly disarmed and non-nuclear strategic defenses are preeminent.[53] The transition from offensive retaliation to defensive damage denial as the basis of deterrence would require superpower cooperation in limiting BMD deployments in each phase. The superpowers would also have to cooperate in restricting innovation in offensive countermeasures that might defeat either side's BMD system, and to jointly limit the deployment of antisatellite (ASAT) weapons or other defense suppression capabilities. This would require a climate of superpower political relations that admittedly is far from the present one.

Moreover, the transition to "defense dominance" also risks confusion about matters of scale, with regard to command and control of defenses, in the same way that confused terms of reference inhibited understanding of C^3 vulnerability and its relationship to offenses. An omnivorous attack against the missile defenses and supporting command systems of either superpower, once those defenses were deployed, would signal a lack of interest in maintaining political limitations on war. For one thing, the command system that supported terrestrial or space-based components of any BMD system would have to be commingled with the command system that supported offensive retaliation. The president is the president, and the Politburo is the Politburo, whatever the dominant technology. The idea that war in space could be limited to that "theater of operations," as if space were a U.S. CINC or a Soviet TVD, rests on assumptions about U.S. and Soviet command systems that are not politically astute.

At the same time, it is a fallacy to suppose that any attack against a U.S. or Soviet BMD component, however ambiguous in origin or light in destructive consequences, will result in war on earth. The leaderships of the two sides are not going to go to war, especially total war, without more provocation than that. Much depends upon whether anticomponent attacks occur under normal peacetime conditions, during crises, or after limited war has begun. The Soviet view of command and control in this regard is that wars are to be avoided if possible, especially nuclear wars that involve attacks on the Soviet homeland. If war cannot be avoided, the Soviet objective is not to lose.[54] Soviet BMD provides insurance against losing if war proves to be unavoidable. This is not taken by the Soviet military leadership to mean that BMD—or antinuclear strategic defenses overall, including missile and air defenses—can provide a sufficient basis for prevailing in a war. Defenses must be complemented by the capability for preemption, if war is deemed unavoidable and evidence of enemy intent to attack is considered probative. If preemption cannot be justified, then a capability for launch under attack or launch on warning must be maintained as the next-least-destructive option.[55]

Again, confusion of scale must be guarded against. The tendency in U.S. strategy is to set technologically driven missions for forces and to measure system performance against theoretically optimal performance criteria. Invincible countermeasures by the opponent are also assumed. One can defeat almost any U.S. (or Soviet) BMD system by this method and, for that matter, any U.S. or Soviet offensive system (consider how the rush to MIRVing was justified by the Western assumption of highly competent Soviet BMD capabilities). So, too, with measures and counter-measures for what is now termed the BM/C³ (battle management/command-control) components of SDI or Soviet BMD systems. If they are required to survive omnicompetent threats against them without any fault tolerance, then U.S. or Soviet BM/C³ systems are by definition defective. If they are that easily defeated by offensive countermeasures, however, who designed the countermeasures? And cannot designers from the same disciplines design counter-countermeasures?

This issue cannot be resolved by technology alone, but only by relating preferred strategies to technological possibilities. Briefly, it is not inconceivable that NATO will need to rely on limited nuclear options more than will the Soviets. This requires more subtlety in command systems but not resistance to worst-case attacks. European theater ballistic missile defense systems (ATBMs) deployed by both NATO and the Warsaw Pact would arguably benefit the Pact more by denying LNOs to NATO, which it would otherwise have. However, it would also allow NATO to improve damage denial on behalf of important force and command targets that might be subjected to early, devastating attacks. If so, conventional deterrence could be improved. NATO has no command system that has been tested under anything approaching wartime conditions. Perhaps the Soviet assumption—of a truncated escalation ladder after more than several demonstrative nuclear weapons have exploded in Europe—is more logical than the NATO one—an elongated ladder with numerous stopping points.[56] If so, the targets that defenses protect may mean less than the assumptions made by policymakers about the meaning of attacks against those defenses. Attacking the defenses that protect command systems could be interpreted as another signal that restraints are no longer considered to be important or, even if important, feasible.

It has been suggested that the entire basis of deterrence could be changed if both superpowers deployed perfect or near-perfect defenses of their homelands. This would also solve, in theory, the problem of command preemption. However, near-perfect defenses, even if they could be built, are mixed blessings for the Western alliance. They would provide protection for the U.S. homeland but leave Western Europe comparatively exposed to conventional or nuclear aggression, against which U.S. responses would not be guaranteed. One might argue that a defended U.S. homeland would improve extended deterrence of Soviet coercion against NATO Europe, but this argument presupposes that Western strategic or theater defenses are vastly superior to Soviet or Pact ones. If defenses of the two sides are essentially equivalent, then each will worry that the other has a slight advantage, and so be deterred from nuclear coercion. In a crisis this will leave matters to the side with superior conventional forces. NATO has the wherewithal not to fall so far behind the Pact that its position is one of crisis-driven vulnerability. NATO should, in the near term, maintain parity with the Pact in modernization of important technologies and weapon systems. The West should also be prepared to use arms control to negotiate a more favorable military balance on the Central Front, or at least to diminish the prospects for the successful surprise attack (one object of the conventional stability talks).

CONFLICT TERMINATION AND WAR OUTSIDE EUROPE

It would be wrong to assume that a war fought in Europe necessarily must begin there. The more probable situation is that the superpowers' allies or clients will clash initially outside Europe and will subsequently drag in the Americans and Soviets. Local or regional conventional wars in the Middle East, the Persian Gulf and Southwest Asia, or Northeast Asia could expand into a coalition war in Europe. Both strategic and political complexity would be multiplied with escalation from extra-regional perturbations, compared to a situation with an intra-European source of conflict.[57]

The complication is that not all conflicts outside Europe are equally important for the security of Europe, the United States, or the Atlantic alliance. The U.S. problem of conflict assessment is sufficiently complicated in itself. Two dimensions of this problem—of defining security priorities for defense commitments—are perennial trouble spots in executive-congressional relations. First is the issue of how many conventional wars the United States is prepared to fight simultaneously. Second is whether U.S. general-purpose forces can be used outside Europe with the same assurance of host-nation receptivity and infrastructure. Host-nation infrastructure includes ports, airfields, and other support for U.S. forces deployed far from the continental United States.

The first problem—how many wars the United States can expect to fight simultaneously—has both strategic and structural faces. It is not good strategy to use combat forces in all cases in which U.S. or allied interests might be jeopardized. If they are used, combat forces might best be employed in noncombatant roles. However, the assignment of combat forces to noncombatant roles—say, peacekeeping—is a tricky business, as Americans learned in Lebanon in 1983. Not only did the U.S. combat forces in Beirut suffer devastating losses, but U.S. (and European) policy suffered a severe setback when "peacekeeping" forces were perceived as siding with one faction in Lebanon's civil war.[58] It probably is wise to keep superpower forces out of peacekeeping missions, especially those in contentious zones involving U.S. and Soviet allies.

As to the ubiquity of U.S. or European combat forces in combat roles outside Europe, there is the problem of agreement on policy objectives, which must precede the commitment. In 1956 the British and French collaborated with Israel in order to prepare a military attack on Egypt, only to have the Americans disestablish the plan by siding against U.S. allies. This U.S. decision, and the U.S.–Soviet agreement on preventing Nasser's downfall, alerted British and French planners to two things: the need for self-reliance on issues of vital interest, and their dependence on the United States for sustained, out-of-the-area commitments.

Academic commentaries have supposed that, during the Kennedy and Johnson administrations, the United States was prepared to maintain general-purpose forces that would make possible the fighting of two and one-half wars: a major war in Europe, a second major war in Asia, and a minor war elsewhere. Vietnam showed, however, that the American public was not tolerant of protracted wars and military stalemates, especially in regions far from North America. In this regard, the Vietnam pattern to some extent replicated the U.S. experience in Korea. However, Vietnam occurred in a different U.S. domestic political context. In the eyes of many U.S. elites and European observers, the entire U.S. geopolitical framework of "containment" was suspect, as a result of the Vietnam experience or of popular understandings of it. Europeans sought to distance themselves from the U.S. commitment, and this in turn created reciprocal reaction from Washington. The Nixon administration attempted to change declaratory policy to a one and one-half war strategy, which seemed consistent with the president's objective of improved relations with the People's Republic of China. This, too, was something of a misnomer since, as in the Kennedy-Johnson case, the commitment was more rhetoric than reality. The truth was that the United States and NATO were not prepared to fight the "one" conventional war in Europe for very long without nuclear escalation. Therefore the issue of fighting simultaneous conventional wars was a theoretical more than a practical one. Practically speaking, the United States would have had to throw everything into the pot in Europe and hope nothing else erupted at the same time.

The Reagan administration perhaps wisely declared that it had no specific formula for how many conventional wars the United States should fight simultaneously. However, the Reagan declaratory strategy implied that the United States might have to be prepared to fight in Europe, Asia, the Middle East, and Latin America with U.S. combat forces.[59] It was not clear whether this meant simultaneous or sequential fighting; either way, it led to a substantial "strategy-force mismatch" between commitments and resources. Another issue in the Reagan case was "horizontal" or geographical escalation, in which the United States might respond to an attack on one vital interest by striking at a different but equally valuable target outside the initial theater of operations.[60] Although his administration gave fewer public indications of interest in multitheater war-fighting capabilities, Carter's State of the Union Address in 1980, declaring the Persian Gulf to be a vital U.S. interest, prefigured the evolution of the Rapid Deployment Force into the Central Command and a major U.S. planning contingency.

The United States has boxed itself in. Assuming commitments for several decades that implied at least prompt conventional defense of Europe, South Korea, and Israel if the last were threatened with catastrophic losses, U.S. leaders and planners have now added the Persian Gulf and the Iranian oil fields to their commitments.

There have been several complications with this most recent add-on to the list of global U.S. military commitments. First, it was not entirely clear what scenario the U.S. planners envisioned. If there were a major Soviet invasion of Iran to occupy the oil fields of Khuzistan, the Soviets would have the problem of insurrection behind their advancing forces. Even after they expelled the U.S. expeditionary force defending the Khuzistan region, they would have to contend with the pacification of Iranians, for which the Soviet experience in Afghanistan does not augur well. In addition, the logistics of mounting such an invasion through northern Iran might be more formidable than stopping it, given the few attractive routes from the Soviet Union into northern Iran and the ease with which air interdiction might create impassible choke points.

Second, any U.S. president would be loath to send U.S. combat forces to defend Iranian oil fields without European support, politically and militarily. A multinational force would involve all the problems of crossnational collaboration, but a unilateral U.S. intervention could invoke the War Powers Act and other démarches against continuation of a costly commitment. The U.S. Congress would clearly be interested in sharing any successful commitment and divesting itself of responsibility for failure.

Third, a Soviet invasion of Iran was less likely than the collapse of that or other Gulf regimes from internal causes. The United States would then face the problem of defining the prevention of internal political decay in another country as in America's security interest, on account of that country's geopolitical value. This situation was faced by U.S. experts on

China in 1949, and has presented itself on other occasions since, including in the Philippines in recent years. What U.S. combat forces, perhaps supplemented by outside diplomatic or military support, could do to prop up a tottering Saudi or other Gulf regime threatened by internal pressures is difficult to specify. CIA operations of the kind mounted in Guatemala or Iran during the Eisenhower administration would be inconceivable now, on account of the differing political climate for clandestine operations.[61]

Fourth, a war in Iran against Soviet forces would not be a "limited" war, in the sense that limited wars are conceived by planners who suppose that the United States can fight one or several of them in addition to a war in Europe. The outcome of any direct combat between uniformed U.S. and Soviet forces would be unpredictable. The odor of escalation would be in the air from the moment the first U.S. bullet struck a Soviet soldier, or the reverse. Also, such a war would not be limited geopolitically. It would be "about" preserving Western access to vital oil supplies, hence about the survival of NATO in its present form and about the vulnerability of Western Europe to further Soviet coercion. Lastly, the Soviet attack, if successful in creating a temporary setback in NATO cohesion and durability, might have a permanent opposite effect. A greater sense of European dependence on U.S. economic as well as military protection could result. A NATO alliance thus headed for polycentrism could revert to a situation of U.S. hegemony, to the ultimate detriment of Soviet ambitions.[62] Witness, for example, the effects of the Soviet invasion of Afghanistan in 1979.

The second major issue regarding U.S. and/or allied military intervention outside Europe is the receptivity of those being rescued to the rescuers. Iran presents an interesting and paradoxical case. If the Iranian regime or its mirror-image successor were suddenly threatened with internal collapse, and there followed an heir apparent who resembled Mengistu or Tarraki, would the Soviets send in military forces to provide "fraternal" assistance? If so, how would the United States or its allies respond? Apparent threats to deprive the West of its oil supplies might not be made explicit until long after a revolutionary regime had consolidated its power. Even then, regimes of anti-Western ideological character have nonetheless supplied vital resources if the price is right, as in the case of Libya. Soviet intervention in such a situation of domestic instability would in all likelihood be indirect rather than direct, and would include foreign and military intelligence, counterintelligence and security services, and, if necessary, *spetsnaz* (special designation) forces.

Indirect Soviet intervention would not necessarily make Iranians, Saudis, or other Gulf regimes sympathetic to U.S. or Western counterintervention. Governments might lean one way and popular support lean another way. The Carter administration apparently was confident that the Shah was secure as long as the armed forces and the security services supported him. This was a correct reading of the balance of power in the establishment but not in the bazaars or in public opinion. Nor did it foresee the Shah's irresolution to mobilize his own "repressive base" on account of his illness, confused signals from his U.S. allies, and abundant indications by 1978 that repression was part of his problem instead of the solution. The point is not to pillory Carter with the wisdom of hindsight, but to illustrate how little is known reliably about the internal politics of Gulf and Middle Eastern countries and about the political psychology of their leaders. Yet U.S. or allied intervention would be betting military forces and campaign strategy on the accuracy of assumptions about internal politics in authoritarian societies, about which U.S. (if not European) cultural understanding is demonstrably fallible. Consider, for example, the U.S. and Israeli misreading of Anwar Sadat's intentions for war on October 6, 1973.[63]

The Arab-Israeli war of 1973 illustrates the potential for connecting mis-estimates of the internal politics of regional combatants with a chain of events leading to direct superpower confrontation. The superpower confrontation of 1973 was not as simple as the Cuban missile crisis of 1962, although it appeared to be less risky of actual U.S.–Soviet nuclear war. In the Cuban case there was U.S. surprise and anger after obtaining photographic evidence of the Soviet missiles in Cuba, and the embarrassment of having been duped diplomatically. The situation from then on was exclusively two-sided. Allies and observers, including the Cubans, played but a negligible role in resolving the crisis.

But in 1973 the United States was entangled with Israel and the Soviets with Egypt. Moreover, the United States was attempting to lure Egypt out of its connections with the Soviets as a basis for establishing an Israeli-Egyptian peace settlement of issues left over from the war of 1967. Egyptian feints of having severed umbilical ties to the Soviet Union turned out in fact to be part of the Egyptian deception campaign prior to the attack.[64] The United States was not unequivocal in its support of Israel, as it would presumably be in the case of Soviet coercion against Western Europe. U.S. officials cautioned Israeli leaders repeatedly against the risk of preemption, which had worked so successfully for Israel in 1967. Israeli leaders were warned that their preemption might be followed by withdrawal of U.S. political and military support. At the same time, U.S. intelligence estimates contributed to Israel's self-assurance that Sadat would not dare attack unless he could improve his capabilities for air-to-ground and air-to-air combat (whereas in fact the plan for Operation Badr was more dependent upon improvements in Egyptian air defenses, canal-bridging capabilities, and portable antitank weapons).[65]

Even after war began, with an unequivocal aggression by the Egyptians and Syrians (plus advanced planning, including the Saudis and Jordanians with regard to an oil embargo), the U.S. policy-making establishment was a divided house. The Nixon administration could not agree on the issue of war termination: How rapidly did it want the war to end, and on what terms? One might contrast a State Department and a Defense Department perspective very generally, allowing for injustices to individuals. The State Department notional view would favor even-handedness with respect to Arab and Israeli postwar interests. The objective of the war would be to get an acceptable stalemate, followed by enhanced willingness from the Egyptians, who had rescued their pride from 1967, to negotiate outstanding issues. This eventually became the rationale or rationalization offered by Kissinger for the U.S. position, although it may be a tendentious explanation for what happened in "real time."[66] A notional Defense Department view might have been more decisively supportive of Israel early in the war.

The U.S. policy-making community was more united on what it did not want the Soviets to do, which was to intervene militarily before a cease-fire could be worked out. Thus Brezhnev's offer of a joint superpower intervention to stabilize the fighting, and his suggestion that the Soviets were prepared for unilateral intervention if necessary, galvanized the U.S. bureaucracy into action. A worldwide military alert was declared, and the Soviets were clearly given to understand that deployment of Soviet combat forces in Egypt would create a serious risk of war, including nuclear war.[67] U.S. intelligence indicators suggested serious Soviet preparations for intervention if the Politburo so decided, including the movement of airborne divisions to points of debarkation and the trailing of U.S. vessels in the Mediterranean by combat-ready Soviet trackers. According to Bruce G. Blair, Brookings Institution expert on command and control:

Within about twenty-four hours after the U.S. forces moved into DEFCON 3, Soviet surface action groups had formed and prepared for attack. For the next eight days they maintained continuous high readiness to engage U.S. forces in battle.[68]

Thus, partly as a result of mis-estimates of Egyptian intentions and domestic politics, Americans and Israelis almost blundered into a wider war over which their control was far from certain.

Nor is the Soviet record of estimates relative to the attainment of political objectives through intervention, followed by successful war termination, arguably better than the U.S. record. The war in Afghanistan has proved not only a diplomatic setback for the Soviet Union in the Third World but a military stalemate as well. The Soviet agreement in 1988 to withdraw their combat forces from Afghanistan and to confine their role to military and other assistance provided a face-saving escape from an acute politico-military embarrassment and an intelligence failure. The ability of the Afghan government to mobilize its strength against the *Mujaheddin* without an overbearing Soviet military presence was clearly insufficient.[69] The continuing Soviet commitment of their own combat forces created a drain on resources, loss of lives, and a bonanza for the U.S. intelligence community, which supported the guerrillas with clandestine arms shipments. Gorbachev's decision that enough was enough was parallel to the decision by Johnson administration advisors not to provide General Westmoreland with additional combat forces in 1968. In each case, termination of the conflict was unilaterally decided upon and imposed on the host government by the responsible superpower.

For the Soviets in Afghanistan and the Americans in Vietnam, more was at stake than the desire to cut losses, however strong that was. There was also the declaratory or de facto revision of war aims. In the Soviet case, the decision was to live with a politically acceptable regime of limited effectiveness, instead of demanding one that could button down all political opposition. In the U.S. case, the decision was to accept a time interval during which South Vietnamese independence and survival could be guaranteed, instead of an open-ended commitment of U.S. forces to meet those objectives. Withdrawal of U.S. combat forces was followed by a North Vietnamese military victory, certainly inconsistent with the initial U.S. war aims but not with the revised ones. The South Vietnamese were put on notice shortly after Nixon's election that the United States would gradually withdraw its combat forces and shift the burden of fighting onto the Army of the Republic of Vietnam. This also alerted the North Vietnamese that a temporarily expedient diplomatic agreement would eventually pay larger dividends. The South Vietnamese defeat was also a U.S. "defeat" provided the original U.S. war aims had not been altered—but they had been.

Not all allies and clients are as susceptible to domination by their U.S. and Soviet advisors. Sadat accepted Soviet help to wage the war of 1973, after which he effectively dissolved the Soviet influence on his government and its policies. The Shah of Iran led all others in OPEC in gouging higher prices from U.S. and allied European oil consumers in 1973. During the Reagan administration the United States sought to support the Duarte government in El Salvador and to disestablish the regime in Nicaragua (which the United States had initially supported following the overthrow of Somoza in 1979). But support for Duarte required the United States to collaborate in suppressing right-wing forces, including death squads, which impeded the creation of a democratic political process. However, this process itself was also jeopardized by antidemocratic forces of the left, in the form of revolutionaries that the United States charged were supported by Nicaragua and Cuba. Thus U.S. policy called for supporting a middle-of-the-road alternative in El Salvador, despite a State Department assertion that the enemy was a multinational front. A fledgling middle-of-the-road Salvadoran regime would be overmatched by a multinational front, so either the United States was exaggerating the size of the opposition or it was underwriting a precarious position. And if the U.S. analysis of Nicaraguan objectives was correct—that the Sandinistas were the key in spreading Marxist revolution from Cuba through Central America—then displacement of the Sandinista regime was required before Duarte could be saved. Moreover, the U.S. Congress was skeptical of Reagan rationales for aid to El Salvador and opposition to the Sandinistas, and polls repeatedly showed that large majorities of U.S. citizens could not distinguish which side the Reagan administration favored in either nation.

The United States acquiesced in Reagan's second term to negotiations between the Sandinistas and the U.S.–supported *contra* opposition. However, the *contras* proved to be of divided leadership, and each segment had its own umbilical ties to U.S. intelligence or the State Department. Thus the cacophony of *contra* voices echoed the diversity of Reagan bureaucratic perspectives on how to end the war, and on what conditions. By 1988 many of the more conservative members of the White House staff, Department of Defense, and other agencies had departed for other appointments, and leadership changes at the top in the CIA and the Department of Defense (from Casey and Weinberger to Webster and Carlucci) percolated changes down through their respective bureaucracies. Howard Baker also brought to the White House staff a perspective more attuned to cooperation with Congress than his immediate predecessor had shown. As a result, the prospect for movement toward some stability in El Salvador and progress in negotiating fora relative to Nicaragua (including the direct talks as well as the Contadora initiatives) seemed favorable.

These cases of U.S. involvement in Latin American civil wars are not digressions from the problem of defending Europe. To the contrary, they have direct implications—two-sided ones—for NATO alliance cohesion. The first implication is ideological: Europeans are unlikely to support U.S. uses of force in Central America or in the Caribbean, and even less likely to do so elsewhere in the Third World. European support for the

Sandinistas rankled the government in Washington and spilled over into disagreements about what to do about terrorism in Europe and in the Middle East. The U.S. role in Nicaragua appeared to Europeans as that of a counterrevolutionary (and therefore socially retrogressive) power, although the French role in Chad and the British role in the Falklands had involved the use of force to support the political status quo. U.S. opposition to liberation forces in Namibia and support for South African and indigenous efforts in Angola seemed reactionary to Europeans also.

The second implication of European-American differences over U.S. involvements in out-of-the-area wars is military: The United States is seen by Europeans as diverting its resources to prepare for interventions in places and circumstances less important to NATO alliance, or even U.S., security. From the standpoint of European skeptics, an ominous development is the emphasis in U.S. defense planning on the Southwest Asia–Persian Gulf theater of operations. Another ominous development from their perspective was the Department of Defense interest in developing light divisions for rapid deployment to remote areas, with the implication that war in Europe was of such low probability as to be a secondary planning contingency. Europeans are also very much aware that influential U.S. senators, congressmen, and other prominent officials and lay people have begun to propose reductions in U.S. peacetime military commitments to Western Europe. Further retrenchment in the Soviet military presence in Eastern Europe will vitiate consensus on trans-Atlantic security issues.

Consensus on a NATO response to war begun outside Europe is even more problematical. European members of NATO will want the protection of America's extended nuclear deterrent and its mobilization potential for deterring conventional as well as nuclear war in Europe. But they renege at "extending" the extended deterrent, and using NATO as a transmitter for doing so. Europeans balk at the "extended" extended deterrent not only out of obstinacy or nationalism but because they recognize that their conventional forces and diplomatic credibility, at least since Suez, are circumscribed outside Europe itself. If the Americans attempt to "play through" to the Middle East or Southwest Asia by way of Paris, Bonn, or London, then the Europeans are anchored indirectly to U.S. war aims, or the war aims of U.S. allies such as Israel.[70] The United States has little need to rely on allied European support for intervention in Latin America, but European opposition to such intervention is kindling for lighting domestic fires in the U.S. Congress, in the media, and among the public. If the United States expects to wage war outside Europe and to end it on terms that are not divisive of NATO, it will somehow have to isolate the

Soviets from those out-of-the-area conflicts (for risk of détente in Europe) and keep European perturbations from the U.S. home front.

CONCLUSION

The problem of conflict termination in Europe is compounded by the uncertainties of coalition warfare, by different superpower doctrines, and by the paucity of stopping points once war is underway in earnest. The Western emphasis on the threshold between conventional and limited nuclear war may be less important to the Soviets, who may prefer to distinguish between wars for small and large political objectives. Whether perceptions of limited objectives and limited means can be kept manageable may depend upon the fidelity of command and control under duress not previously experienced in combat. Subjected to high-intensity conventional or limited nuclear war, command systems may collapse into poor replicas of themselves, providing their owners with inappropriate or misleading information. The problem of U.S. strategic nuclear LNOs is even more prepossessing if it is supposed that reciprocal behavior is expected by the Soviet Union, that U.S. and Soviet C^3 systems will continue to operate with sufficient interpretive capacity to distinguish limited from total attacks, and that limited strategic options will not be viewed as lack of resolve. The superpowers' continuing vulnerability to attacks on their societies despite changes in force balances means that no defenses other than near-perfect ones can make the problem of conflict termination more controllable. And simplifying the problem for the U.S.–Soviet case by deploying defenses might complicate the problem of extending nuclear deterrence to U.S. allies. Thus, no escape is apparent from the difficult choices and trade-offs discussed in the following chapters.

NOTES

1. See Condoleezza Rice, "The Making of Soviet Strategy," Ch. 22 in Peter Paret, ed., *Makers of Modern Strategy: From Machiavelli to the Nuclear Age* (Princeton: Princeton University Press, 1986), pp. 648–76; and Kurt Gottfried and Bruce G. Blair, eds., *Crisis Stability and Nuclear War* (New York: Oxford University Press, 1988), Ch. 7.

2. Carl von Clausewitz, *On War*, edited and translated by Michael Howard and Peter Paret (Princeton: Princeton University Press, 1976). Of course, Clausewitz offers advice which is situationally dependent. In Chapter Two, on "Purpose and Means in War," he notes that in absolute (pure) war the enemy's fighting forces must be destroyed, the opponent's country occupied, and the will of the opponent broken. On the other hand, in real wars this is sometimes impractical from a policy standpoint: "Actual war is often far

removed from the pure concept postulated by theory." (ibid., pp. 90–91). See also his injunction that "since war is not an act of senseless passion but is controlled by its political object, the value of this object must determine the sacrifices to be made for it in *magnitude* and also in *duration*." (ibid., p. 92).

3. Mikhail Gorbachev, *Perestroika: New Thinking for Our Country and the World* (New York: Harper and Row, 1987).

4. See Stephen M. Meyer, "Soviet Perspectives on the Paths to Nuclear War," Ch. 7 in Graham T. Allison, Albert Carnesale, and Joseph S. Nye, Jr., *Hawks, Doves and Owls: An Agenda for Avoiding Nuclear War* (New York: W. W. Norton, 1985), pp. 167–205.

5. David N. Schwartz, *NATO's Nuclear Dilemmas* (Washington: Brookings Institution, 1983).

6. Michael MccGwire, *Military Objectives in Soviet Foreign Policy* (Washington: Brookings Institution, 1987), Ch. 2.

7. James M. McConnell, "The Soviet Shift in Emphasis from Nuclear to Conventional: The Mid-Term Perspective," Center for Naval Analyses (Alexandria, Va.: June 1983).

8. See the chapters on European peace movements in Walter Laqueur and Robert Hunter, eds., *European Peace Movements and the Future of the Western Alliance* (New Brunswick, N.J.: Transaction Books, 1985).

9. The seminal work was Herman Kahn, *On Escalation: Metaphors and Scenarios* (New York: Praeger, 1965).

10. See Richard K. Betts, *Nuclear Blackmail and Nuclear Balance* (Washington: Brookings Institution, 1987).

11. General-Major S. N. Kozlov, ed., *The Officer's Handbook* (Moscow: 1971), p. 62. Published under the auspices of the U.S. Air Force.

12. S. P. Ivanov, *The Initial Period of War* (Moscow: 1974). Translated and published under the auspices of the U.S. Air Force.

13. MccGwire, *Military Objectives in Soviet Foreign Policy*, pp. 40–42 and *passim*.

14. Christopher N. Donnelly, "Soviet Operational Concepts in the 1980s," in *Strengthening Conventional Deterrence in Europe: Proposals for the 1980s*, Report of the European Security Study (New York: St. Martin's Press, 1983), pp. 105–36.

15. William T. Lee and Richard F. Staar, *Soviet Military Policy since World War II* (Stanford, Cal.: Hoover Institution Press, 1986), esp. pp. 138–39.

16. U.S. Department of Defense, *Discriminate Deterrence*, Report of the Commission on Integrated Long-Term Strategy (Washington: January 1988), pp. 36–37.

17. Lynn Etheridge Davis, "Limited Nuclear Options: Deterrence and the New American Doctrine," in Christoph Bertram, ed., *Strategic Deterrence in a Changing Environment* (Montclair, N.J.: Allenheld, Osmun and Co., 1981), pp. 42–62.

18. Desmond Ball, "The Development of the SIOP, 1960–1983," Ch. 3 in Ball and Jeffrey Richelson, eds., *Strategic Nuclear Targeting* (Ithaca, N.Y.: Cornell University Press, 1986); Gottfried and Blair, *Crisis Stability and Nuclear War*, Ch. 4.

19. Desmond Ball, "U.S. Strategic Forces: How Would They Be Used?" *International Security* 7, no. 3 (Winter 1982-83), pp. 31–60; Gottfried and Blair, *Crisis Stability and Nuclear War*, Ch. 5.

20. Ball, "U.S. Strategic Forces," pp. 36–37.

21. James R. Schlesinger, Annual Defense Department Report, Fiscal Year 1975 (Washington: U.S. GPO, 1974), pp. 36, 38 in Ball, "U.S. Strategic Forces," p. 45. Emphasis added.

22. See Stephen M. Meyer, "The Soviet Theater Nuclear Force Posture: Doctrine,

Strategy and Capabilities," Ch. 7 in Jeffrey D. Boutwell, Paul Doty, and Gregory F. Treverton, eds., *The Nuclear Confrontation in Europe* (London: Croom, Helm, 1985), pp. 164–84.

23. See Paul Bracken, *The Command and Control of Nuclear Forces* (New Haven: Yale University Press, 1983); and Richard Ned Lebow, *Nuclear Crisis Management* (Ithaca, N.Y.: Cornell University Press, 1987).

24. Lt. Col. John G. Hines and Dr. Phillip A. Petersen, "The Changing Soviet System of Control for Theater War," in Stephen J. Cimbala, ed., *Soviet C3* (Washington: AFCEA International Press, 1987), pp. 191–219.

25. See Lt. Col. David M. Glantz, *August Storm: The Soviet 1945 Strategic Offensive in Manchuria* (Fort Leavenworth, Kans.: U.S. Army Command and General Staff College, February 1983), Leavenworth Papers No. 7.

26. Albert Wohlstetter and Richard Brody, "Continuing Control as a Requirement for Deterring," Ch. 5 in Ashton B. Carter, John D. Steinbruner, and Charles A. Zraket, eds., *Managing Nuclear Operations* (Washington: Brookings Institution, 1987).

27. On the importance of norms in Soviet operational planning, see John Erickson, Lynn Hansen, and William Schneider, *Soviet Ground Forces* (Boulder, Colo.: Westview Press, 1986), Ch. 4.

28. See Soviet Army Studies Office, U.S. Army Command and General Staff College, *The Soviet Conduct of War* (Fort Leavenworth, Kans.: U.S. Army Combined Arms Center, March 1987); and Donnelly, "Soviet Operational Concepts in the 1980s."

29. Chris Bellamy, *The Future of Land Warfare* (New York: St. Martin's Press, 1987), Ch. 7.

30. Bruce G. Blair, "Alerting in Crisis and Conventional War," Ch. 3 in Carter, Steinbruner, and Zraket, eds., *Managing Nuclear Operations*, pp. 75–120; and Scott D. Sagan, "Nuclear Alerts and Crisis Management," *International Security* 9 (Spring 1985), pp. 99–139.

31. Catherine McArdle Kelleher, "NATO Nuclear Operations," Ch. 14 in Carter, Steinbruner, and Zraket, eds., *Managing Nuclear Operations*, pp. 445–69.

32. Bracken, *The Command and Control of Nuclear Forces*, Ch. 5.

33. Ibid., p. 227.

34. For an excellent argument to this effect, see Bruce G. Blair, *Strategic Command and Control: Redefining the Nuclear Threat* (Washington: Brookings Institution, 1985), pp. 14–49.

35. Graham T. Allison, *Essence of Decision: Explaining the Cuban Missile Crisis* (Boston: Little, Brown, 1971), p. 138 discusses U.S. ASW activities during the crisis.

36. See Paul Bracken, "Accidental Nuclear War," Ch. 2 in Allison, Carnesale, and Nye, eds., *Hawks, Doves and Owls*, pp. 25–53.

37. Paul Bracken, "Delegation of Nuclear Command Authority," Ch. 10 in Carter, Steinbruner, and Zraket, eds., *Managing Nuclear Operations*, p. 367 ff.

38. Donnelly, "Soviet Operational Concepts in the 1980s"; P. H. Vigor, *Soviet Blitzkrieg Theory* (New York: St. Martin's Press, 1983).

39. For an excellent discussion of the difficulties in comparing NATO and Pact conventional strength and a review of some previous attempts, see International Institute for Strategic Studies, *The Military Balance, 1987–88* (London: IISS, Autumn 1987), pp. 226–34. This volume also contains a useful insert on NATO and Pact C^3 structures.

40. Bellamy, *The Future of Land Warfare*, Ch. 8.

41. John Hemsley, *Soviet Troop Control: The Role of Command Technology in the Soviet System* (New York: Brassey's Publishers Ltd., 1982).

42. U.S. strategic bomber modernization plans are described in Secretary of Defense Frank C. Carlucci, *Annual Report to the Congress: Fiscal Year 1989* (Washington: U.S. GPO, February 1988), pp. 236–39.

43. According to the U.S. Department of Defense, Soviet Bear-H bombers are capable of launching AS-15 nuclear armed cruise missiles (ALCM) up to 3,000 kilometers from their targets, and they frequently practice strike missions against North America. U.S. Department of Defense, *Soviet Military Power, 1988: An Assessment of the Threat* (Washington: U.S. GPO, April 1988), p. 51.

44. Ibid., p. 47.

45. Carlucci, *Annual Report to the Congress: FY 1989*, p. 232.

46. For development of one version of this idea, see Lt. Col. Fred J. Reule, USAF; Lt. Col. Harvey J. Crawford, USAF; Dr. Daniel S. Papp; and Major G. E. Myers, USAF, *Dynamic Stability: A New Concept for Deterrence* (Maxwell Air Force Base, Ala.: Air University Press, September 1987).

47. Ashton B. Carter, "Assessing Command System Vulnerability," Ch. 17 in Carter, Steinbruner, and Zraket, eds., *Managing Nuclear Operations*, pp. 555–610.

48. Remarks prepared for delivery by the Honorable Harold Brown, Secretary of Defense, at the Convocation Ceremonies for the 97th Naval War College Class, Naval War College, Newport, Rhode Island, Wednesday, August 20, 1980. According to Brown: "It is our policy—and we have increasingly the means and the detailed plans to carry out this policy—to ensure that the Soviet leadership knows that if they chose some intermediate level of aggression, we could, by selective, large (but still less than maximum) nuclear attacks, exact an unacceptably high price in things the Soviet leaders appear to value most—political and military control, military force both nuclear and conventional, and the industrial capability to sustain a war." (p. 7) For a critique of U.S. and NATO versions of countervailing strategy, see Robert Jervis, *The Illogic of American Nuclear Strategy* (Ithaca, N.Y.: Cornell University Press, 1984).

49. See, for example, U.S. Department of Defense, *Soviet Military Power, 1988*.

50. Leon Sloss and Marc Dean Millot, "U.S. Nuclear Strategy in Evolution," *Strategic Review* (Winter 1984), pp. 19–28.

51. See Louis René Beres, *Mimicking Sisyphus: America's Countervailing Strategy* (Lexington, Mass.: D. C. Heath/Lexington Books, 1983).

52. A two-layer defense system (boost phase and terminal) is illustrated in Robert H. Kupperman, Robert W. Selden, and Harvey A. Smith, *A Model of the Defense of Land-Based Missile Forces by a Multilayer Antimissile System* (Los Alamos, N.Mex.: Center for National Security Studies, Los Alamos National Laboratory, April 1987).

53. Paul H. Nitze, "On the Road to a More Stable Peace," U.S. Department of State, *Current Policy* 657, February 20, 1985.

54. MccGwire, *Military Objectives in Soviet Foreign Policy*, pp. 39–40.

55. See Stephen M. Meyer, "Soviet Nuclear Operations," in Carter, Steinbruner, and Zraket, eds., *Managing Nuclear Operations*, pp. 470–534.

56. See Paul K. Davis and Peter J. E. Stan, *Concepts and Models of Escalation* (Santa Monica, Cal.: RAND Corporation, May 1984), for a comparison of U.S. and Soviet concepts of escalation.

57. For pertinent scenarios, see Francis Fukuyama, "Escalation in the Middle East and Persian Gulf," Ch. 5 in Allison, Carnesale, and Nye, eds., *Hawks, Doves and Owls*, pp. 115–48.

58. See Edward Luttwak, *The Pentagon and the Art of War* (New York: Simon and Schuster, 1984), pp. 50–51.

59. Jeffrey Record, "Jousting with Unreality: Reagan's Military Strategy," *International Security* 8, no. 3 (Winter 1983-84), reprinted in Steven E. Miller, ed., *Conventional Forces and American Defense Policy* (Princeton: Princeton University Press, 1986), pp. 63–78.

60. A useful discussion is Joshua Epstein, "Horizontal Escalation: Sour Notes of a Recurrent Theme," *International Security* 8, no. 3 (Winter 1983-84), pp. 19–31.

61. John Ranelagh, *The Agency: The Rise and Decline of the CIA* (New York: Simon and Schuster, 1986), pp. 260–69.

62. For an argument in favor of pluralism and for the evolution of NATO away from American "hegemony," see David P. Calleo, *Beyond American Hegemony: The Future of the Atlantic Alliance* (New York: Basic Books, 1987).

63. Major General Chaim Herzog, *The War of Atonement: October 1973* (Boston: Little, Brown, 1975).

64. Ibid., Ch. 3, pp. 32–39 discusses the Egyptian deception campaign in 1973.

65. Ibid. *passim*; and Janice Gross Stein, Ch. 3 and Ch. 4 in Robert Jervis, Richard Ned Lebow, and Janice Gross Stein, *Psychology and Deterrence* (Baltimore: Johns Hopkins University Press, 1985).

66. Marvin Kalb and Bernard Kalb, *Kissinger* (New York: Dell Publishing Company, 1974), Ch. 17, pp. 509–540. This account is not uncontested and is not accepted unequivocally here.

67. Barry M. Blechman and Douglas M. Hart, "The Political Utility of Nuclear Weapons: The 1973 Middle East Crisis," *International Security* 7, no. 1 (Summer 1982), reprinted in Steven E. Miller, ed., *Strategy and Nuclear Deterrence* (Princeton: Princeton University Press, 1984), pp. 273–97.

68. Bruce G. Blair, "Alerting in Crisis and Conventional War," Ch. 3 in Carter, Steinbruner, and Zraket, eds., *Managing Nuclear Operations*, p. 95.

69. J. Bruce Amstutz, *Afghanistan: The First Five Years of Soviet Occupation* (Washington: National Defense University, 1986).

70. See Stephen J. Cimbala, "An Israeli Nuclear Deterrent: Implications for U.S.–Soviet Strategic Policies," Ch. 9 in Louis René Beres, ed., *Security or Armageddon: Israel's Nuclear Strategy* (Lexington, Mass.: D. C. Heath/Lexington Books, 1986).

PREGAME

2

First-Strike Stability and the State of Potential War

In the nuclear age, the time between the initiation of war and the ending of it may be too short to permit the supremacy of political control over military means. The surest path to the control of nuclear war is to prevent it. But one cannot depend only on the U.S. and Soviet nuclear blunderbusses to do this. The expectations of policymakers about how wars will end influence their willingness to begin them. And if policymakers imagine that relative advantage can be gained by striking first, even in desperation, the probability of a shattered peace rises accordingly.

Although, in the aftermath of many destructive wars, many people ask why the wars started, few have turned the question around and asked why peace ended. To do this in the contemporary era, first consider the problem of first-strike stability, which is a matter of keeping Soviet and U.S. nuclear arsenals leashed despite stressful political conditions or outbreak of actual war in Europe. Here, NATO leaders face a painful dilemma: The more securely deterrence of war in Europe is anchored to the U.S. strategic nuclear retaliatory force, the more deterring of Soviet adventurism NATO doctrine is thought to be; on the other hand, if faced with an actual crisis or wartime contingency, U.S. leaders would want flexibility, in part to avoid being pushed into prompt launch of strategic forces before other, less formidable options had been attempted.

This chapter outlines frequent assumptions about first-strike stability.

Parts of this chapter include material originally published in the author's *First Strike Stability* (Greenwood Press, 1990).

Then it suggests a three-part broadening of some traditional categories relative to first-strike stability, to show that simple models of preemption do an injustice to the complexity of crisis deterrence. Third, it opens a window on a theme central to this work: the inherent tension between requirements for first-strike stability between the Americans and Soviets, and requirements for U.S. "extended" nuclear deterrence of conventional or nuclear war limited to Europe.

THE STATE OF NATURE AND THE STATE OF WAR

A state of nature may be said to correspond to a state of ignorance and, therefore, innocence. Neither the benevolence nor the malevolence of the actors in the international system is assumed. Only after having been attacked can one state decide that another is hostile. But a state of nature can be modified by agreements among the participants to help one another under selected conditions. If a smaller unit in a global system is threatened by a larger one, it may turn for protection to a large state. There are no guarantees that such help will be provided; the larger state will provide help in the form of guaranteed assistance if it perceives the action to be in its self-interest. In a state of nature the concept of alliance is very fluid, and expedient.

An alternative hypothetical construct to describe an international environment is a state of war. A state of war is a condition in which the actors assume hostile intent on the part of those with the potential to do harm. Possessing the forces with which to destroy an opponent is almost tantamount to having the intent to do so. Prospective attackers will do the worst of which they are capable; prospective defenders, therefore, must arm to meet worst-case assessments. In the nuclear age a state of war implies a high degree of first-strike instability. Adversaries will launch nuclear forces at one another if there exists a perceived advantage for doing so, and if expected losses can be reduced to "acceptable" levels. Under conditions of mutual assured destruction by retaliation, arms races substitute for superpower involvement in nuclear war, but they do not remove the potential for first-strike instability driven by other factors.

The state of nature and the state of war are useful constructs that reveal some of the limitations of any nuclear deterrence doctrine that has among its objectives the promotion of first-strike stability. Conservative force planners operate on state-of-war assumptions: Whatever the opponent can do, he will. Therefore, arsenals are sized on worst-case expectations and contribute to an arms race and to crisis instability. Thus an assumed state of war with regard to the international threat environment results in the deterioration of a state of nature into a state of war. Inferences from arsenals to intentions feed back into the loop and create self-fulfilling prophecies.

Two examples will suffice. The United States alleged that the Soviet Union was opening a "window of vulnerability" against the U.S. land-based missile force with the deployment of fourth-generation Soviet ICBMs having improved accuracies. The Scowcroft Commission called this into question as a valid strategic proposition.[1]. However, the "window of vulnerability" problem led to deployment of MX missiles in fixed silos and in other modes not survivable without strategic warning, such as rail garrison basing. It also led to Congressional enthusiasm for the very costly, although putatively survivable, Midgetman.[2] The United States viewed the Soviet deployments as components of a potential first-strike threat, on the assumption that the international threat environment was a state of war. Instead, state-of-nature assumptions might have suggested that the Soviet ICBM program was a modernization designed to improve Soviet second-strike capabilities.

The Soviet view of U.S. SDI research and development was similarly motivated by state-of-war, and not state-of-nature, assumptions. Soviet political and military leaders warned that the United States intended to employ strategic defenses along with offenses as components of a first-strike capability.[3] The possibility that SDI was a product of U.S. fascination with technological innovation and presidential rhetoric was given less consideration. Reagan's offer to share defense technology with the Soviet Union was treated as insincere by both U.S. and Soviet commentators, who assumed that the president operated from devious motives. It is also possible that Reagan's expression of willingness to share technology was sincere, based on a congenital utopianism that periodically reasserts itself in American political life. Both Soviet and U.S. critics of the president assumed state-of-war motivations for his proposal, which in fact may have been prompted by state-of-nature assumptions. Reagan's later willingness to sign the INF treaty and to enter into START negotiations calling for 50 percent reductions in superpower strategic offensive forces proved to be based on state-of-nature assumptions that proved valid, to the dismay of the president's conservative critics.

FIRST-STRIKE INSTABILITY

First-strike instability can be likened to the problem of anticipating strategic military surprise. A putative attacker considers the forces available for surprise attack and those of the defender's forces that are likely to survive such attack. An analysis is then conducted to determine what the defender's surviving forces can do. If the consequences of the defender's retaliatory strike seem unacceptable, no premium is inherent in surprise. This very rational model of nuclear deterrence may be termed the force-based model and is an obvious component of any larger analysis.

However, the problem of surprise is more complicated than this.[4] Surprise can result from a variety of factors having to do with attacker incentives and defender vulnerabilities.[5] Studies of military surprise show that it has frequently succeeded in conventional warfare. Among the reasons for this are misplaced expectations and perceptions held by the victims of surprise. Intelligence failures play a part in this, but faulty decision making and misperception are more common.[6] Victims of surprise often deceive themselves by assuming a state of nature when a state of war exists. In a state of nature the two sides both have cooperative and conflictual motives; in a state of war at least one side has decided that aggression pays, or that war cannot be avoided sooner or later, and that striking now is preferable to waiting. Americans thought that the Japanese had some interest in the resolution of conflicting claims in the Pacific, even after the Japanese had decided to attack. Stalin expected Hitler to issue an ultimatum followed by a process of Soviet conciliation prior to any actual decision by the Nazi dictator to attack.[7]

In one form of nuclear surprise, either superpower takes a state of nature, in which there are mixed motives in avoiding nuclear war and in protecting vital interests, into a state of war by assuming unmixed hostility. Nothing less than the supposition that the other side no longer sees mixed motives as contributory to positive behavior would justify a nuclear first strike. Thus one plausible path to preemption is desperation.[8] We argue below that there are several possible varieties of preemption, and that not all have the same mix of causes. Desperation is less a kind of preemption than a motivational construct by which policymakers are induced to believe that all options short of war have been exhausted. This is almost never the case, however, and we must look for additional components to the problem of first-strike instability.

THE SOVEREIGNTY OF DETERRENCE

Preemption may be motivated by either the expectation of gain or the fear of loss.[9] The problem for the policymaker in a crisis is to know which set of motives might be influencing the opponent. Potential attackers motivated by fear of being surprised first need to be reassured that this is not the defender's intention; the priority for the defender is to avoid provocation. Potential attackers motivated primarily by some expectation of relative gain need to be reminded of the costs of war. The problem of deterrence versus provocation is a meaningful one, and has been since Hobbes' time. According to Hobbes, commonwealths come about in one of two ways: by institution and by acquisition. Commonwealths by acquisition result from war; those by institution, from the fear of anarchy and war that leads individuals to entrust the ultimate and decisive civil power to a sovereign who acts on behalf of all.[10] We can, by analogy, think of prospective attackers and defenders under the shadow of nuclear weapons as having a community of interest in preserving peace despite the temptation to obtain political objectives by the coercive power of nuclear threats.

Hobbes notes in the first section of *Leviathan* that humans are driven by their passions to seek values that jeopardize the common good and public order. He observes of the multitude that, "if their actions be directed according to their particular judgements, and particular appetites, they can expect thereby no defence, nor protection, neither against a Common enemy, nor against the injuries of one another."[11] Nations left to their own appetites will attack. One might think that nations armed with tools as terribly destructive as nuclear weapons would seek a sovereign power to represent and overawe them, as Hobbes recommended, as a solution preferable to nuclear anarchy. By the same token one might reason that nuclear surprise would never be preferable to an attempted attack. The first assumption has been disproved, but the second remains an article of faith in Western deterrence theory. The faith may be replaced.

Hobbes addresses the issue of whether individuals are necessarily social or anomic and selfish in a passage in which he disputes Aristotle's discussion of the social qualities of bees and ants. If insects can live together in cooperation for the common good, why cannot people? Hobbes provides six answers to this question; three are of special interest here. First, men are "continually in competition for Honour and Dignity" and, consequently, among them there arise "Envy and Hatred, and finally Warre."[12] Second, among insects "the Common good differeth not from the Private," whereas "man, whose Joy consisteth in comparing himselfe with other men, can relish nothing but what is eminent."[13] Third, nonhuman creatures do not see or think they see any fault in the administration of their common business, whereas "amongst men, there are very many, that thinke themselves wiser, and abler to govern the Publique, better than the rest; and these strive to reforme and innovate, one this way, another that way; and thereby bring it into Distraction and Civill warre."[14]

Hobbes' insight into human psychology cautions against the presumption that nuclear preemption can never be tempting. During the Cuban missile crisis, it was obvious that the strong egos of U.S. President John F. Kennedy and Soviet Premier Nikita Khrushchev were at the center of the dispute. Kennedy concluded that Khrushchev had evaluated him as easily intimidated, on account of his failure to provide full U.S. military backing for the Bay of Pigs invasion in 1961, and for other reasons. On the other hand, Raymond L. Garthoff, a participant in the Cuban crisis decision making and the author of an authoritative account of the episode, does not regard Kennedy's sense of personal humiliation or embarrassment as the key to U.S. decision making during the crisis. The perception that the balance of power would have been changed considerably to U.S. disadvantage was the most influential consideration for U.S. leaders, and the objective of removal of the Soviet missiles from Cuba was paramount in the prevention of that undesired outcome.[15] The U.S. and Soviet leaders, when they came to the brink of war, discovered that they had a limited community of interest in avoiding further escalation. Kennedy was determined to get the missiles out of Cuba, but he wanted also to give Khrushchev the time and wherewithal to make a considered, not a panicky, decision.[16] Khrushchev had run the risk of placing Soviet missiles in Cuba despite U.S. warnings in order to improve his prestige within the Soviet hierarchy, as a result of U.S. public revelations of U.S. nuclear superiority and Chinese remonstrances against the Soviet Union as a paper tiger.

The Cuban missile crisis of 1962 is often used to illustrate the barriers to preemption, and it cannot be doubted that the outcome was fortunate for both sides, compared to the costs and risks of nuclear war. With equal justice, it can be argued that the escape from the brink was fortuitous. Khrushchev's willingness to place missiles in Cuba was thought to have been deterred by U.S. public pronouncements and by the larger size and greater capability of U.S. strategic nuclear forces compared to Soviet. Neither U.S. declaratory policy nor Khrushchev's awareness of Soviet inferiority precluded deterrence failure with regard to the placement of Soviet missiles in Cuba. Kennedy was genuinely surprised by the Soviet leader's actions. While the Americans did not specifically threaten nuclear war except in response to the launching of Soviet missiles from Cuba against Western Hemisphere targets, the president took steps that created a plausible risk of nuclear escalation. Nor were these steps fully controllable by U.S. and Soviet policymakers. The U.S. implementation of the blockade around Cuba, and the use of coercive pressure by the U.S. Navy against Soviet submarines in the vicinity of the blockade, demonstrated that policymakers lacked a detailed grasp of unfolding events with high potential for escalation.

DETERRENCE AS CIVIL SOCIETY?

Human motivation may bring about preemption that is otherwise implausible on the basis of rational calculations or cost-effectiveness estimates. In the Cuban missile crisis, there were no objectives at stake for which the risk of nuclear war by either side was worth the cost, and especially not for the Soviet Union. Yet each leader perceived a significant probability of war, including nuclear war, if the crisis was not resolved in a short time. During the July 1914 crisis that preceded the outbreak of World War I, the czar and the kaiser alternated between outbursts of braggadocio and statements about the inevitability of war on the one hand, and desperate efforts to prevent war from happening on the other.[17] Prewar intelligence estimates on the part of leading Entente and Alliance powers were erroneous with regard to the importance of short war, rapid mobilization, and decisive offensives, and so contributed to misperceptions that preemption was the key to success, and being preempted to failure.[18] No systems analysis could have predicted the willingness of Hitler to attack the Soviet Union in 1941, or the Japanese to attack the U.S. fleet with such decisive impact the same year. Albert Wohlstetter showed during the 1950s that the purportedly invincible U.S. strategic bombing force was overly dependent on vulnerable forward basing, and therefore, like the fleet at Pearl Harbor, as much a target as it was a deterrent.[19]

The history of conventional deterrence is one of deterrence failure.[20] Nuclear deterrence is judged to be different. The consequences of even one failure of deterrence—given the costs—have created a Hobbesian commonwealth of mutual superpower interest in survival. No matter how much the two nuclear giants are pushing and shoving one another about, they will not allow the detonation of nuclear weapons by Americans against Soviets, or vice versa—or even against their vital interests outside their homelands. To do so would be to break the Hobbesian covenant that established the sovereign of mutual deterrence. This would be a breach of *propriety* in Hobbes' terms, which defines what goods men may enjoy and what actions they may do without injuring one another. The alternative is stark:

For before constitution of the Soveraign Power . . . all men had the right to all things; which necessarily causeth Warre: and therefore this Proprietie, being necessary to Peace, and depending on Soveraign Power, is the Act of that Power, in order to the publique peace.[21]

Propriety establishes the limits within which nuclear armed states, or the individuals who are contemplating the establishment of Hobbes' sovereign, can assert their interests without jeopardizing those of others. If either side builds forces that place at risk the other side's retaliatory capability, thus creating first-strike potential, it has broken the covenant of mutual deterrence. The other side is obligated to respond in kind, and may be motivated to do more. The Hobbesian covenant between nuclear-armed superpowers depends upon a balance of forces that is not actually precarious with regard to first-strike stability, and which is not *perceived* to be. Equally, it depends upon the willingness of both sides' leaders to forgo temptations to build forces for relative advantage, if that advantage is sufficient to confer a first-strike capability in fact. Each must maintain a second-strike capability but forgo any attempt for a first-strike capability. The combination of self-assertion and self-denial is made possible only by the assumption of a state of war, which would be obtained in the absence of the sovereign, nuclear deterrence.

Nor is this all. Deterrence may fail for reasons other than the acquisition by one side of a first-strike capability against the deterrent of the other. The difference between a state of nature (including that which has evolved into a civil society or commonwealth) and a state of war is also related to U.S. and Soviet intentions. In a crisis state-of-nature and state-of-war incentives will be mixed. The result will be a "prisoner's dilemma," in which one side's decision to avoid conflict could prove risky if the other took advantage of its generosity.[22] Each will guard against being returned to a state of war from a state of civil society or from a state of nature *under disadvantageous conditions*. Being the victim of a surprise attack "out of the blue" is equivalent to going from a potential state of war (with features of a state of nature) to an actual state of war. The victim of attack following a crisis, and therefore with a heightening of tension and some warning, is not fallen upon unexpectedly. The victim is already in an actual state of war, as opposed to a potential state of war, once the onset of crisis has underscored hostile intent. In the first case, the victim of nuclear surprise had no inkling of the opponent's interest in breaking the nuclear covenant. The most unexpected kind of "bolt from the blue" might not even be preemptive, but rather preventive, war, depending on the circumstances preceding the strike.[23] In the second case—of a crisis having preceded the outbreak of war—the commonwealth of mutual deterrence has already been placed in some doubt. Indeed, one party to the crisis may deliberately place the idea of mutual deterrence in doubt, as it threatens to wage war—and perhaps nuclear war—in order to get its way. The very onset of a crisis means that a state of nature under the sovereignty of mutual deterrence has already begun to transform itself into a state of war, in which no sovereign restrains aggression. However, it is not yet a state of war because the sovereign of deterrence has not yet been dethroned. Until the sovereign has been proved incompetent to preserve order, it is by definition due obedience and respect. And nuclear deterrence has proved remarkably durable, despite the warnings of some strategists that the balance of terror was delicate.

There are two sides to the durability of the sovereign of nuclear deterrence against crisis or arms-race disestablishment. The first is that it raises complacency on the part of national leaders and military strategists. U.S.–Soviet mutual deterrence has survived the fever charts of the cold war, détente, SALT, the ABM treaty, Afghanistan, and Vietnam, and other ups and downs. The longer it lasts, the more credible it seems. No one would argue that nuclear deterrence is not preferable to nuclear war, although some would argue that the Americans and Soviets do not have to be as dependent upon nuclear, as opposed to conventional, deterrence as they are. Complacency about the continuation of stable deterrence is not warranted, however. Contrary to the suppositions of some Western analysts, there is nothing automatic about mutual deterrence; the plethora of weapons on both sides and the damage that they can do in retaliation is not a guarantee that "civil society" will hold and that the "state of warre" can be contained under all conditions.

The second side to the durability of mutual deterrence is that it places undue emphasis on the balance of forces between the superpowers, to the comparative neglect of their decision-making processes, including their nuclear command and control systems. This is not necessarily true of nuclear deterrence theory, although it has been the case in policymaking and net assessment practice. Some recent studies have begun to remedy this deficiency in relative emphasis on force structures compared to command systems.[24] There is a great deal of knowledge about the technical characteristics of U.S. nuclear command systems, and more insightful studies are now appearing about the U.S. crisis management decision-making process.[25] The Soviet side is more opaque, but even there U.S. analysts are now beginning to understand the differences in Soviet command-system operations during peacetime, crisis, and wartime contingencies.[26] The next section attempts to describe some different kinds of preemption and their relationship to U.S. or Soviet decision-making processes, including superpower assumptions about whether they are in a state of nature (mixed motive) or a state of war (essentially conflictual) situation.

Before turning to that task, we must note that the durability of deterrence calls forth a logical paradox: The more secure it is, the more insensitive it is to perturbations at the margin, in the form of limited wars that would otherwise cause the superpowers to engage their interests. The paradoxical case is in Western Europe, where the superpower nuclear covenant has precluded even conventional war between NATO and the Warsaw Pact. This may attest to the fragility or the strength of deterrence, depending on how it is interpreted. Both sides may be so confident that deterrence is holding that neither seeks to challenge a vital interest of the other. On the other hand, both may be lacking confidence in the stability of deterrence to a degree sufficient that they will not seek to ignite even limited wars that could escalate into nuclear wars. The nuclear sovereign is intimidating because of both its predictability and its unpredictability: What is predictable is a high level of destruction should deterrence fail, and what is unpredictable is the ability of the sovereign to maintain deterrence at the center once it is destroyed at the periphery. The paradox has another face. Owing to stable deterrence, the superpowers might feel free to ignore the margins or, to the contrary, they might feel little risk in skirmishing at the edges. The stability-instability paradox thus allows for a more stable nuclear-deterrent relationship combined with a less stable conventional one, or with a more stable conventional one. Nuclear weapons contribute to conventional deterrence stability if conventional deterrence cannot be isolated from the impact of nuclear escalation. But if it can, or to the extent that it can, conventional deterrence may be more precarious, apart from the nuclear balance.

NATO's strategy for prevention of war essentially relies on a formula for dissuasion that combines these two features of predictability and unpredictability, of assured destruction and flexible response. But this requires a balancing act. European members of NATO feel that deterrence rests on the Soviet expectation of a prompt involvement of the U.S. strategic arsenal in any conflict. This is referred to as coupling, of U.S. strategic nuclear forces with NATO nuclear and conventional forces deployed in Western Europe. The United States, while not denying that NATO declaratory strategy couples the U.S. strategic nuclear arsenal to systems based in Europe, nevertheless interprets flexible response to provide for thresholds and firebreaks short of total war. These thresholds and firebreaks might confine war to Europe, decoupling the fates of the United States and West European members of NATO. This decoupling might also work the other way: Europeans might opt out of a war they felt had been provoked by the United States against the Soviet Union without sufficient cause.[27] NATO strategy relies on the indivisibility of nuclear sovereignty in order to invoke the U.S. strategic nuclear deterrent, and on the divisibility of it to maintain the option to create war controlling thresholds after deterrence has failed. On one hand the possible failure of superpower deterrence in increments is denied as a logical possibility, but on the other, it is asserted as the preferred condition.[28]

The divergence of the United States and NATO European members of the alliance are more matters of emphasis than they are disagreements about mission. The U.S.–Soviet differences with regard to the meaning of mutual deterrence are another matter. Both acknowledge the present condition as one of mutual deterrence, but the understandings held by Soviet and U.S. leaders and defense planners about the sources of insta-bility are very different.[29] Therefore the U.S.–Soviet deterrent relationship might be closer to a state of nature, and the NATO community to a civil society. Sometimes the differences of opinion within NATO push it closer to a state of nature, and sometimes the U.S.–Soviet relationship moves from a near state of nature into the area of civil society. In arms control, for example, the superpowers have developed a series of precedents and expectations that move in the direction of mutual sensitivity and depen-dency—that is, toward the attributes of a civil society. During the Reagan administration, on the other hand, U.S.–Soviet relations on Third World issues tumbled into the state-of-war category. U.S.–Soviet relations on nuclear strategy and arms control began in 1981 by moving toward the state of war, and then reversed during the second Reagan term to the point at which the U.S. president and the Soviet general secretary were discuss-ing reduction of nuclear weapons to absolute zero. Actually they had returned to a state of nature, but sounded for the purposes of publicity as if a civil society in the area of arms control and disarmament had been created (see Figure 2.1).

One difficult question is how we can have a sovereign in superpower relations and yet describe them as a state of nature or potential state of war. According to the logic of Hobbes and other contract theorists, the sover-eign goes together with civil society. This is not a contradiction but an allowance for change of context from domestic to international order. The sovereignty of nuclear deterrence as discussed here is a conditional one that prevails in one segment of the superpower relationship, and by mutual consent. Nuclear deterrence sovereignty is subsystem dominant, from a standpoint of the system as a whole. However, although it derives from the mutual consent of major actors over whom it then casts its shadow, nuclear deterrence cannot transcend the basically anarchic nature of international relations. Thus it is the sovereignty of a relationship instead of the sovereignty of a person, executive, or deliberative body.

Figure 2.1

```
Civil Society              State of Nature              State of War
-----------------------------------------------------------------------
          (NATO)                        (U.S.-Soviet)


                          (normal positions)
-----------------------------------------------------------------------
        (NATO)                                    (U.S.-Soviet)


                          (positions in 1981)
-----------------------------------------------------------------------
   (NATO)                   (U.S.-Soviet)


                          (positions in 1988)
-----------------------------------------------------------------------
```

*Illustration reflects the intra-NATO differences over INF modernization and arms control in 1981 as well as the deterioration of superpower arms control negotiations in Reagan's first term.

KINDS OF PREEMPTION

We have seen that first-strike instability is partly dependent upon the expectations that leaders have about the general threat environment: whether it is a state of nature, a state of war, or a civil society. There are at least two other dimensions to leaders' assessments of their opponents' intentions: the leaders' assumptions about the basic benevolence or malevolence of their prospective opponents, and their preferred policy options or "moves," given the assumptions about international threat environments and opponents' specific intentions. These sets of assumptions and expectations are not unrelated. An international environment of high threat, or one which is perceived to be so, invites further and related assumptions of potential opponents' specific and near-term malevolence. For example, the formation of the Triple Alliance and Entente preceding the outbreak of World War I made leaders more receptive to signals of specific and hostile intent. The Cuban missile crisis was preceded by gathering superpower tension over Berlin during the Eisenhower and Kennedy administrations. The Chinese entry into the Korean War was preceded by U.S. antagonism toward the new regime that took power in Beijing in 1949, and by the Chinese expectation that a U.S.–United Nations offensive which cast its net into North Korea might cross the Chinese border either deliberately or inadvertently.[30]

Levels of analysis are undoubtedly important here. The international "system" is the shorthand used by theorists to refer to those sets of processes that take place between states and to those structures that reach beyond the limits of state boundaries. This international political system is a subset of a larger international environment. We are pulling out of that very large matrix a small subset of processes and relationships, those related to the incentives of disincentives for preemption. A systems analysis, proceeding in a black-box–within–black-box fashion, could find determinants of crisis behavior, including incentives for preemption, at each of three levels of analysis: the system itself, the nation-state and its regime, and the decision-making process of individual actors. Historical case studies can be even more specific, down to the motivation constructs that bias individual leaders for or against war. There is no one right way to cut into this problem of multiple causation. It depends upon the interests of the investigator and the nature of the problem at hand. There are nevertheless tracks in the snow from those who have gone before, including many of the best-known scholars in the field of international relations and conflict studies. Without this work of several decades, the subject of preemption would be harder to isolate from the larger complex of international interactions. This includes the work of Kenneth Waltz and James N. Rosenau on levels of analysis; Alexander George on crisis management; Robert Jervis, Richard Ned Lebow, and Janice Gross Stein on the psychology of deterrence; Klaus Knorr and Patrick Morgan on surprise; and many others cited throughout this study. Despite this considerable scholarship, the problem remains elusive because there are no historical cases of preemptive attack by one nuclear armed state against another, in which the forces of the attacker and defender were comparable in size, diversity, and destructiveness.

The three dimensions—perceived international threat environment, specific expectations of actor hostility, and preferred policy options—are related to the decision for or against preemption. The following kinds of preemption are distinguished: anticipatory, reactive or retaliatory, and miscalculated. Anticipatory preemption is based on strategic warning of enemy intention to attack, although the attack is not yet underway. Reactive preemption involves a prompt launch of time-urgent forces in response to confirmed tactical warning of attack, although the exact nature of the attack and its purpose may not be fully known. Miscalculated preemption grows out of a process of misjudgment or misestimation. One side, fearing that the other is about to attack, decides to strike first in order to minimize the losses attendant to war. Anticipatory preemption has something in common with mobilization in cases where the options are restricted to total mobilization, or none. This was characteristic of the situation in July 1914, as perceived by Russian military leaders. Reactive preemption is a form of retaliation, although it is a form of preemption as well. True retaliation would wait to absorb the attack or at least until a significant portion of the attack had been completed. Miscalculated preemption can occur in response to strategic or tactical warning. Once the misjudgment has been made by country A and its forces have been launched in a mistaken preemption, the response by country B may be either retaliation or preemption. If it awaits the blow and then strikes back, B has retaliated. If B launches its nuclear forces in the expectation of a blow, on the basis of strategic or tactical warning, it has preempted.

The first kind of preemption—anticipatory—is prompted by an international threat environment of high tension and imminent expectation of war. The months of June and July 1914 in Europe provide one illustration; so, too, do the months preceding the Arab-Israeli wars of 1967 and 1973. In 1967, Israel preempted, convinced that Nasser was preparing a major attack since he had already undertaken several preliminary political and military steps that would logically precede such an attack. In 1973, Israel was cautioned by the United States not to preempt the Egyptians, and Israeli leaders felt overconfident of their ability to withstand any Arab attack.[31] With regard to the character of the international threat environment, in both cases it was supportive of incentives for preemption, on account of being heavily laden with signals of malice aforethought. One might argue, on the basis of Clausewitz's understanding of war as the continuation of political intercourse by other means, that there was one continuous war in Europe from the time of the first Balkan war until the end of World War I. In a similar fashion, it would be argued that the Israelis and Arabs actually fought a single war from 1948 through 1973, with the use of armed forces being alternated with other kinds of coercion.

Reactive preemption sounds oxymoronic. The terms *reaction* and *preemption* seem to contradict one another because our image of nuclear war has been conditioned by the importance of the distinction between first and second strike. Launch on tactical warning has therefore been described correctly as a capability necessary for deterrence. This is especially the case where war plans call for prompt destruction by the defender of the portion of the attacker's arsenal that has not already been launched as part of the first strike. For many years U.S. nuclear war plans have reportedly included a capability for prompt launch for just this reason. Launch on tactical warning is not necessarily easy to accomplish, however; forces must be kept in a state of readiness and control systems must function with high fidelity. The objective is to convince any prospective attacker that not only will high costs have to be paid for aggression, but they will have to be paid immediately. Nuclear strategists have laid particular stress upon this requirement for promptness as a component of deterrence, but it may apply to conventional deterrence as well. Samuel P. Huntington has noted that NATO has the theoretical option of *conventional retaliation*, immediately after the Warsaw Pact begins its attack, into Eastern Europe, withholding nuclear weapons for the deterrence of Soviet nuclear first use.[32] This more symmetrical response might not be as dissuasive for purposes of deterrence, but it makes the point that, from a policy standpoint, nuclear preemption is not mandated by NATO policy, only by its preferred declaratory strategy. And NATO declaratory strategy stretches to the limit, and perhaps exceeds, the category of preemption, since a nuclear first strike would not be undertaken *only* in response to the expectation of Soviet nuclear first use, but in response to conventional defeat. Nuclear first use of tactical weapons in the European theater is also not tantamount to a strategic preemptive attack, although it raises the risks of such an event in the minds of policymakers on both sides.

In the case of a direct U.S.–Soviet confrontation such as that in Cuba or elsewhere outside of Europe, much would depend upon the willingness and ability of either side to get its conventional forces into a position where they could serve as tripwires for further escalation. The U.S. assumption in the case of a Soviet invasion of Iran, at least during the reign of the Shah, was that U.S. forces would be deployed in that theater of operations without any expectation that conventional resistance alone could do the job. The role of U.S. conventional forces would be to present to the Soviet Union the burden of crossing two thresholds: direct fighting between U.S. and Soviet forces, and the possible U.S. use of tactical nuclear weapons if need be.[33] The threat of nuclear first use by the defender was implicit in the forward deployment of theater general-purpose forces whose resistance would create a heightened risk of local, and perhaps general, nuclear war. To some extent this is still the case for the U.S. Rapid Deployment

Force (now part of Central Command for the Southwest Asia–Middle East theater of operations).[34] Nuclear first use in such conditions, as in the European case, could lead through escalation into undesired strategic nuclear preemption.[35]

Escalation scenarios in the Persian Gulf and Western Europe illustrate a third possible form of preemption, one motivated by miscalculation. Miscalculated preemption is distinguished from reactive preemption in its degree of inadvertent, as opposed to deliberate, escalation. The U.S. and NATO declaratory strategy poses the deliberate threat of nuclear escalation should NATO conventional forces face defeat. The pace of escalation and the character of the scenario might confound leaders, but not the use of nuclear weapons. The expectation of strategic nuclear preemption would haunt deliberations in Moscow and Washington from the moment that war began. The case of U.S. intervention in Saudi Arabia or Iran is even more scenario-dependent upon the objectives of attackers and the willingness of the United States actually to commit its own combat forces to the region. The probability of a *direct* U.S.–Soviet shooting war in the Persian Gulf may be lower than it is in Europe, under assumed conditions of conventional deterrence failure in both places. However, the rules of engagement would be less obvious in the Gulf; the players and the rules have much more room to vary, with regard to taking sides and degrees of commitment. Thus the war in Europe might more likely lead to anticipatory or reactive preemption, while that which might begin in the Middle East would lead to preemption by miscalculation. For example, during the Arab-Israeli war of 1973, U.S. policy was pulled in several directions. The United States first acted to assist Israel in avoiding a significant military or political defeat as a result of Arab surprise. Then, as the momentum on the ground changed in favor of Israel, the Americans sought to obtain a cease-fire and to reassure the Soviets that the Israelis would honor it. Further, the United States wanted to avoid direct involvement of Soviet or U.S. forces, but it was unwilling to allow unilateral Soviet involvement without resistance. Thus the global military alert was implemented in order to signal to the Soviet Union that the risks of direct superpower conflict, including nuclear war, were not inconsiderable.[36] It is not entirely clear what the United States would have done if the cease-fire had collapsed and the Soviets had sent airborne or other forces into Egypt. The Soviet troop redeployments within the USSR and naval activities in the Mediterranean, together with changes in communications traffic and command procedures that the West was bound to notice, were designed to signal the seriousness of Brezhnev's intent not to allow the total collapse of Egypt's position.[37]

Figure 2.2
Level of Analysis

	Perceived Threat Environment	Leaders' view of Intent	Game Moves
Kind of Preemption			
Anticipatory			
Reactive			
Miscalculated			

The different kinds of preemption can be cross-matched with the dimensions of international threat environment, assumptions of state-specific hostility, and logical moves in an interactive game. These three dimensions crossed with the kinds of preemption yield a sixfold matrix, shown in Figure 2.2.

The causal dependency of preemption on clusters of variables within the categories of threat environment, leaders' view of intentions, and game moves makes the prediction of specific instances of preemption difficult. There are several conclusions that we can draw thus far. First, anticipatory preemption is most likely in a system marked by high levels of threat expectancy. High levels of threat expectancy would result from ideological heterogeneity, conflicts over system legitimacy, the mobilization of new resources by some actors that increase their military power relative to other actors, and a comparative deficiency of "regulatory" mechanisms in the system compared to those which promote conflict. These four attributes might be said to have characterized the European state system during the Napoleonic wars.[38] The marriage of nationalism and industrialism provided armed forces with substantial "force multipliers" in the nineteenth century. In the twentieth century the unexpected challenge to status quo actors came from the linkage of nationalism, peasant mobilization, and techniques of insurgency warfare, which pitted unconventional armed forces against the high technology and mechanized forces of Americans, Soviets, French, and others.[39]

Perceptions of specific hostility are insufficient by themselves to motivate preemption. Stalin did not preempt Hitler, the Americans chose not to strike first against Japan, and during the "Phony War" of 1939–40 the British and French declined to take the offensive against Germany.[40] John Mearsheimer refers quite correctly to the last case as an example of successful deterrence of the allies by the Germans.[41] A decision for nuclear preemption by one superpower against another would be even more difficult to take, unless and until the cities on either side were removed from their hostage condition. It would be difficult for military establishments to convince political leaders in either country that preemption was unavoidable unless tactical warning had already been received. Anticipatory preemption looks too much like preventive war or premeditated aggression. Reactive preemption would be countenanced as retaliation, but withheld, at least in the U.S. case, until more than one set of sensors had confirmed that a real attack was in progress. Preemption by miscalculation would be more likely to occur in a malign, as opposed to benign, threat environment. The United States is fortunate that the 1973 Middle East crisis occurred during a period of superpower détente. However, the Cuban missile crisis did not. An unfavorable psycho-milieu abetted by issue-specific hostilities could tip the scales toward preemption instead of against it.

GAME MOVES, DECISION ENVIRONMENTS, AND UNCERTAINTIES

Deterrence theory had its heyday in the 1950s and 1960s, when the future size and character of U.S. and Soviet strategic nuclear arsenals were matters of great uncertainty. The theory thus focused on the problem of instability and the possibility of first-strike incentives, for reasons that are obvious to most readers. Nowadays the U.S. and Soviet nuclear arsenals have reached a plateau of second-strike survivability and essential equivalence. Readers now ask why the problem of deterrence is so urgent. This places upon analysts the burden of showing how, in the presence of current and probable future superpower arsenals, any prospective attacker could calculate that aggression might pay. We leave aside for the moment the attacker who is not calculating, who is motivated by fear, paranoia, or other incentives for which the calculation of costs and gains is not relevant. Most leaders will make at least some crude calculations of gains and losses, and if they do, then calculations in favor of a first strike seem impossible. This raises the issue of game moves and the concept of game theory in which they are embedded.

The issue of games moves is one that derives from studies of game theory, dealing with the interdependency of decisions by competitors in various situations, including international conflict. Game theory provides useful illustrations of the kinds of interactions that can take place under carefully specified conditions. For example, an important contribution of game theory as used in economics and other decision sciences, and then applied to military strategy, has been to identify the minimax and maximin strategies. A minimax strategy identifies the opponent's best possible move and selects an option that minimizes the expected loss. A maximin strategy goes for the largest possible gain among all possible alternatives, assuming a high risk for the sake of a larger payoff.[42] The problem is to establish a payoff table that is (1) logically consistent across alternatives for a given state actor or individual decision maker; and (2) understandable by leaders of both sides in a crisis situation, so that side A understands the value hierarchies of side B, and vice versa. Game moves are thus not strictly deducible from logic except in very simple, and therefore uninteresting, cases.

An additional problem is that game value hierarchies are dependent upon the perceived threat environment and the expectations of specific hostility just discussed. If behaviors and perceptions in these two dimensions—of perceived general and specific threat—are pushing the contestants out of a state of nature and toward a state of war, then the estimation of the value hierarchies of one side by another will be complicated by additional "noise" confounding the intended "signals."[43] Changes in the threat environment, in terms of their potential to disrupt the value hierarchies of game participants, can be compared to plate tectonic movements in the earth's crust. Expectations of specific hostility can lead to game moves that reinforce an environment of pessimism. Further moves by the opponent, in reaction to these, create additional turbulence with regard to correct perception of options. Exits from the crisis begin to appear as out of reach or not worth the costs of yielding. One result of the reinforcement of negative specific threat assessments by the feedback from the opponent's (properly) negative responses is the phenomenon of bolstering. Bolstering occurs when a decision maker cannot find a preferred alternative, and is unable either to pass the decision along to someone else or to postpone it.[44] Bolstering is related to the tendency of policymakers and planners to "satisfice," or to choose the first acceptable alternative that comes along. This satisficing choice may be made under duress and with resentment, with the assumption that the decision maker cannot compromise further in subsequent rounds. Examples of bolstering appear frequently in decision-making situations involving competitive behavior. An obvious instance is the assumption by Stalin, despite repeated warnings, that Hitler would issue an ultimatum before attacking in 1941. Another is the case of Israeli and U.S. intelligence sources, which were surprised by the Egyptian and Syrian attack in October 1973. It was assumed that the Egyptians would not dare to go to war again until they had obtained air superiority vis-à-vis Israel. However, Egypt devised a strategy that was not dependent upon contesting the Israeli air force.[45]

DE-ESCALATION AND WAR TERMINATION

The kind of preemption chosen may influence the expectations of combatants about how to wind down a war or end it. Although de-escalation and termination are frequently discussed as if they were peas in a pod, they are very dissimilar. It may be possible to de-escalate a conflict long before it can be ended. Wars can start off with a bang and then diminish to a prolonged whimper. Or, the war can be ended before either side has had time or opportunity to adopt an explicit strategy of de-escalation. One side may not feel that it is worthwhile to reduce the costs of war while the fighting is still going on. Maintaining pressure on the opponent in the hope of an earlier victory or other war termination may be very appealing to politicians who feel the hot breath of the public on their necks, or otherwise fear the loss of their leadership positions.

As in war termination, the issue of de-escalation can readily succumb to a discussion of the mechanics—hotlines, the use of third-party intermediaries, and so forth. These are worthwhile topics but not the focus of the present discussion, which is more concerned with the relationship between how war starts and the way it is ended.[46] For example, the hypothetical worst-case "bolt from the blue" contains a built-in contradiction from the standpoint of preserving de-escalation and war termination options. The more successful the first strike is, the less likely it is that the victim can respond with a discriminate and controlled reaction. This is especially so if the nuclear first strike eliminates the opponent's central command structure. This fracturing of the command system will leave a disorganized and hydra-headed retaliatory force that will prevent optimization of the defender's targeting assignments. For this reason countercommand attacks seem militarily appealing. However, decapitation of the opponent's central command may be politically self-defeating, for want of any central processing unit to receive signals of de-escalation and termination.

In the case of superpower nuclear preemption (of which "bolt from the blue" is not in the strictest sense an exemplary illustration, for its provides an extreme rather than a typical case), anything less devastating than a "bolt from the blue" will leave the victim with even more survivable forces and with a larger expectation of fulfilling the requirements of targeting plans. If the attacker wants to communicate an intention to keep war within some political boundaries, it must somehow calibrate strikes against military targets while avoiding significant collateral damage to others. It would be difficult to write a U.S. or Soviet targeting plan that could walk this line between a militarily effective preemption and one dissuasive of further escalation. The most authoritative estimates show that even prompt fatalities from a "selective counterforce" attack by the United States against the Soviet Union, or by the latter against the former, will rapidly reach "unacceptable" levels.[47] The idea of controlled counterforce war fighting, followed by de-escalation and termination, is probably a chimera, which calls into question the political and military ancestry of this strategy.[48]

Although we should judge with proper skepticism the platitudes of U.S. declaratory policy about fighting nuclear war, it should be acknowledged that a preferable deterrent is one believable by the opponent. Since the Kennedy administration, U.S. policymakers have concluded that the credibility of U.S. deterrence strategy rests on the availability of plausible options capable of expressing firmness along with restraint.[49] The difficulty has been to draw the line between intra-war deterrence for de-escalation and war termination, and the threat to strike additional targets in order to coerce a surrender. Whether this distinction could be explained to the Soviet Union during a nuclear exchange remains doubtful. One would have to persuade the Soviet leadership that the state of war which had shattered the state of nature, with regard to the violation of nuclear taboos, was a temporary and expedient departure from the norm which we were earnestly trying to reestablish. Whether Humpty-Dumpty could be put back together again would depend very much upon the Soviet acceptance of a reconstructed state of nature within a state of war. This notion, of a state of nature within a state of war, might seem contradictory. It does so only because of the unprecedented character of a bipolar international system in which the sovereign of nuclear deterrence threatens to destroy itself, and the system with it, if war is unlimited. Therefore, even after war has begun, the requirements for deterrence remain important. Arguably, they are more important once war has begun than prior to it. However, the outbreak of war will have reduced faith in deterrence itself; the sovereign will have been compromised. A cease-fire and war termination will require the reestablishment of mutual confidence that deterrence will hold in the future, although it has failed at least once. Related to this, the incentives for policymakers to exercise control over military operations will increase as the war becomes more intense. Policymakers' capabilities to exert control may not keep pace with their incentives to do so.

The kinds of preemption and the levels of analysis discussed earlier might not make much difference if the war were sufficiently devastating. How the war began could be relevant to ending it only if both sides preserved enough attack-assessment capability and historical memory to modify their postattack plans accordingly. A limited nuclear war in which no more than tens of strategic nuclear weapons were used would leave open this possibility, but one involving hundreds or thousands of weapons exploding within the superpower homelands would not.[50] And even a limited strategic nuclear war, in which few weapons are exploded and their targeting is quite discriminate, will change forever the symbolism of superpower relationships and the perception of the international threat environment. The possibility of a future preemption, and a potentially more devastating one, will remain uppermost in the minds of U.S. or Soviet leaders after one event has happened.

In order to end a limited nuclear war, both sides would need to develop some notions about how and why it started. Getting from these initial assumptions to a mutually agreeable cease-fire and war termination would require leaders firmly in control of their military establishments throughout the crisis and war. If the war began as a result of miscalculated preemption by one side, the attacker might have difficulty convincing the defender that this was so, even if the nature of the miscalculation could be fully determined by the former. An anticipatory preemption would look much like a premeditated attack, with the risk of enraging the victim as a result of a nuclear Pearl Harbor. Moreover, it requires that the attacker play the game of selective and controlled first strike, which, in the event that such an unprecedented decision had been taken, the attacker might not prefer to do. There is at least a built-in logical contradiction between the willingness to take this awful step, despite all the inherent uncertainties, and a concomitant decision to limit it to a signal rather than a crushing blow.

ARMS CONTROL

Peacetime competition between superpowers in a state of nature which is a potential state of war (or an actual state of war, according to Hobbes, although not to all theorists) is more likely than actual war. Therefore arms races have in some sense become the substitute for war, in terms of providing indices of relative power and expected military performance. This makes arms control a form of deterrence as well as a way to accomplish its traditional objectives: improving crisis stability, increasing arms-race stability, and reducing the costs of war if deterrence fails. The superpower nuclear arms competition has been regulated by two SALT (Strategic Arms Limitation Talks) agreements, and the prospect of real reductions attendant to a START (Strategic Arms Reduction Talks) loomed large even before Ronald Reagan left the White House. What are the implications of future superpower arms negotiations for first-strike incentives and strategic stability?

We may understand arms control as one way to move from a state of nature toward a security community of limited auspices. Arms control agreements can limit the risk of war by reducing the temptation for preemption. They can also influence the size and character of arsenals over the long run, improving both crisis and arms race stability. Arms races can proceed even if first-strike stability is high. In that instance, they are likely to emphasize technological innovation in future generations of weapons instead of competitive near-term deployments.[51]

The most successful arms control agreement to date, with regard to its implications for first-strike stability, is the ABM treaty of 1972. This agreement precludes Soviet or U.S. national territorial defenses. By the logic of military deterrence preceding the nuclear age, this seems to contradict common sense. Prenuclear forces established deterrence by denial to the opponent of its objectives, be they territory, population, or economic values. Nuclear forces establish deterrence by their capabilities for retaliation. Therefore, preservation of each side's retaliatory capabilities is the essential prerequisite for the stability of deterrence. It follows that absolution from the effects of retaliation makes first strikes more likely.

U.S.–Soviet arms control agreements have made more progress with regard to nuclear than conventional weapons. The precedents of SALT I and II contributed to an atmosphere that made possible the Reagan–Gorbachev progress between 1986 and 1988 toward the conclusion of a START agreement. Reagan's successor was left with the task of concluding the agreement, but much of the underbrush had already been cleared. On the other hand, progress in the Mutual and Balanced Force Reductions Talks (MBFR) on reducing conventional forces in Central Europe was desultory since the talks began in 1973. Part of the difficulty in arriving at meaningful agreements in conventional-force reductions through MBFR was the limited geographical area that the talks encompassed; the so-called guidelines area included West Germany and Benelux for NATO and East Germany, Czechoslovakia, and Poland for the Warsaw Pact. A second difficulty was that the MBFR forum was restricted to force reductions per se. Qualitative issues having to do with the character of forces deployed on the Central Front, or behind it with the capability of rapidly reinforcing it, were left to other fora.

One of these other fora that emerged during Reagan's second term was the Conventional Stability Talks. The possibility that these talks might make faster progress than MBFR was increased with the apparent Soviet shift toward military-technical defensivism in doctrine and by several ambitious proposals by Gorbachev from 1986 to 1988. The most important departure from Soviet precedent came in Gorbachev's initiative at the 1988 superpower summit, in which he declared Soviet interest in removing disparities in conventional forces from the Atlantic to the Urals.[52] This broadens the focus from the narrow-gauge tracks to which MBFR was limited, and the Soviets have also indicated with regard to future negotiations a willingness to cooperate on establishing an agreed data base for the two sides' conventional forces. The Soviet objective is said to be a restructuring of the forces on both sides in order to eliminate their capabilities for surprise, short-warning attacks.[53] This is judged a desirable aim by NATO as well. The problem of conventional war in Europe escalating into superpower nuclear conflict is exacerbated by the capabilities that either NATO or the Pact might attribute to the other for conventional surprise attack.

The difficulty was that the two sides might focus on different kinds of systems as the source of conventional instability in Central Europe. NATO was obviously concerned with the forward-deployed tanks and artillery available to forward-deployed Soviet and Pact forces in East Germany, Poland, and Czechoslovakia. The Warsaw Pact considered NATO long-range strike aircraft a particular threat to the structure of its operational plans, especially if those aircraft were dually capable of carrying nuclear ordnance. The Soviet Union had been trying to get the inventory of U.S. "forward-based systems" deployed in Europe reduced since the onset of SALT I. Instead of cutting into NATO's inventory of dual-capable aircraft from the top down, the Soviets could use the conventional stability forum to negotiate for lower levels from the bottom up. Undoubtedly other trade-offs would be investigated, but whether they could reconcile the two disparate views of what constituted the most threatening capabilities for surprise remained uncertain.

A further difficulty was that stabilization via conventional-force manipulation would not necessarily lead to large, visible force reductions of the kind that developed a political appeal for NATO politicians. As Stephen J. Flanagan and Andrew Hamilton noted, "It is unlikely that conventional arms limitations would greatly reduce Western military requirements, given the demands of NATO's forward defense strategy."[54] NATO's forward defense–flexible response strategy dictated a minimum ratio of forces to space and a certain distribution of forces along the inter-German and German-Czechoslovak borders. NATO must also maintain a threshold of operational reserves, which are barely adequate or even deficient as of this writing. Nor is it clear that the Soviet Union can drastically reduce the numbers of divisions it has deployed in East Germany and Czechoslovakia while maintaining the cohesive wartime command and control required in its doctrine.[55] Although for either side increased stability might be correlated with reduced force, the correlation between stability enhancement and force reduction is not always positive.

This relationship between stability and force size must also be confronted by U.S. planners for the superpower START negotiations. Smaller U.S. and Soviet strategic nuclear forces are not necessarily more stable ones.[56] The large size of their arsenals, which SALT constrained but did not reduce, allowed for a redundancy that acted to guard against surprise attacks and disrupted command systems. The superpower START negotiations conducted thus far envision reductions to 1,600 strategic nuclear delivery vehicles for each side, 6,000 total force loadings (warheads),and a subceiling of 4,900 warheads on land- and sea-based ballistic missiles. Counting rules for bombers and air-launched strategic cruise missiles are apparently still being worked out, in the direction of counting bombers without ALCMs as equivalent to one warhead regardless of the other ordnance they carry.[57] There will be separate limitations on ballistic missile throw weight and a nominal 50 percent reduction in Soviet heavy ICBM launchers. Unresolved issues as of this writing included mobile ICBMs, proposed ICBM warhead sublimits, sea-launched cruise missiles, and, as noted, counting rules for ALCMs.[58]

Critics of the emerging START terms have charged that the agreement, if formalized according to its present auspices, would leave U.S. land-based missiles in fixed silos more vulnerable to first strikes than they are now. The ratios of Soviet accurate warheads to U.S. ICBM (silo-based) aim points would be even more heavily in favor of preemption than currently. Thus START could reopen the window of vulnerability debate that the Scowcroft Commission had diverted, by acknowledging that ICBMs alone were imperiled, but affirming the survivability of the strategic retaliatory forces as a whole.[59] The charge against START was premature in any case, since the United States would have options to redistribute ICBM warheads over more launchers by de-MIRVing. This was the idea behind the commission's endorsement of the Midgetman small, mobile single-warhead ICBM.[60] The START regime, as foreseen in 1988, would not place any serious constraint on superpower modernization plans, with regard to the replacement of older systems by newer.[61]

Also with regard to first-strike stability, counting rules envisioned for START would favor the deployment of bombers over other force components. This would be stabilizing in principle, since bombers are too slow for use as first-strike weapons compared to ICBMs or SLBMs. Future generations of bombers and ALCMs may pose more serious threats of surprise attack if air defenses are not modernized, especially in the U.S. case.[62] For the near term, the shift away from ICBM warheads and toward bomber-carried weapons seems to favor stability. On the other hand, the counting rules also favor bombers and bomber-delivered weapons over ballistic missile submarines and SLBMs. Submarines are the most survivable platform, and the trade-off of submarines for bombers adds less survivable platforms in place of more survivable ones. Taking into account alert rates for the various platforms, submarines carry some three-fourths of the alert and effective force.[63] A qualification to this concern arises from the deployment beginning in 1989 of Trident II (D-5) SLBM missiles with hard-target accuracies. The ability of sea-based missiles to threaten prompt destruction of hard targets is thought to detract from stability rather than to contribute to it.

The overall context of force survivability is the crucial one. START is unlikely to change the current condition of forces in excess of survivability and retaliatory strike requirements. As Walter Slocombe has noted, "neither side has any sort of plausible first-strike option, if first strike is understood to mean an attack that offers a reasonable chance of either limiting damage from retaliation, or even forcing the victim to an all-out spasm of revenge aimed at major cities."[64] Although the two-sided relationship between the Americans and Soviets will thus be unaffected by probable START outcomes, the problem of extended deterrence remains. Can U.S. strategic nuclear forces reduced to START-accountable limits provide for the limited nuclear options in support of less than total, but still substantial, compellent missions as implied in NATO declaratory strategy? Substantial U.S. strategic forces will remain even under START, but the process of superpower negotiation may spark some of the same anxieties that were provoked by SALT II in Europe. The concerns raised by West German Chancellor Helmut Schmidt in 1977 that SALT would codify U.S.–Soviet parity, and thus make more important theater nuclear and conventional-force balances between East and West, could be revisited after START. The direction taken in the INF negotiations toward the total elimination of land-based systems between ranges of 500 and 5,000 kilometers precludes the solution NATO adopted in response to the Schmidt challenge. Thus the reassurance that START would not leave Europeans without adequate insurance against deterrence failure may not be found in nuclear arsenals alone, but in conventional force improvements and stability negotiations.

Related to the post-START force balances is the balance of U.S. and Soviet strategic command, control, and communications (C^3) capabilities. These should remain as survivable as needed to guarantee assured retaliation. The U.S. C^3 system includes the strategic warning, communications, and force application and control needed to fulfill policy requirements. As these requirements have become more ambitious, the expectations for the C^3 system have increased as well. Nowadays it is expected to be much more secure against the side effects of limited attacks, even those directed at superpower homelands. Thus, U.S. and presumably Soviet forces are connected to national command authorities through systems that will not undergo deterioration precluding retaliation against the assured destruction target set. The superpowers' C^3 systems are also to provide for a larger menu of options from which policymakers can select, in order to provide for more discriminating responses appropriate to the circumstances.[65] Future technologies, some of which are near-term likelihoods and others for which the prognosis is less clear, could assist the C^3 systems in improving the accuracies of conventional and nuclear weapons of all ranges. Conventional weapons could then be tasked for some missions now assigned to nuclear, and nuclear weapon yields could be reduced significantly over the same mission profile, on account of accuracy improvements.[66] The possibility of strategic—that is, intercontinental range—weapons with conventional munitions being assigned some of the missions now allocated to strategic nuclear forces cannot be ruled out.[67]

A cautionary note is that, while post-START superpower forces and command systems can be expected to provide for first-strike stability about as well as they do now, complacency is unwarranted. The movement of C^3 systems and, perhaps later, weapons systems into space changes important components of the equation. Not all aspects of that can be gone into here. Crucial for stability is the preservation of the option of retaliation against whatever surprise attack is contemplated. Space-based defenses will be stabilizing if they protect retaliatory forces and destabilizing if they add uncertainty to the prospects for retaliation. A critical issue for stability is whether any C^3 or missile defense systems based in space can be maintained there at lesser cost than is required to knock them down. Systems that are easy to knock down invite attacks on themselves during a crisis, especially if, despite their vulnerability to defense suppression, they have some significant capability to intercept retaliatory strikes.[68]

However, the problem of vulnerability for space-based weapons or sensors can be overstated, as it has been for the terrestrial components of C^3 systems. Dedicated attacks, in which either side is willing to expend "diseconomical" numbers of attack platforms and weapons, will undoubtedly succeed against the C^3 systems deployed in space or on earth. The same can be said for most of the superpowers' strategic nuclear forces under present conditions, with the exception of those submarines on both sides that would be beyond the reach of even their opponents' best antisubmarine warfare. The point, especially pertinent under the assumption of arms control, is that excesses of weapons to overkill particular targets will be harder to come by. The C^3 and missile defense systems will be allocated only the numbers of hostile launchers and weapons their wartime value merits, and based upon optimization of targeting plans in which there are limits to redundancy.[69] Issues of scale are also important. The U.S. strategic command and control system, for example, is not designed for survival in the face of protracted, all-out nuclear exchanges against the Soviet Union. Nor need it be. As Charles A. Zraket has noted:

Short-term endurance to ensure positive control of weapons and selective retaliation is a feasible goal for the C^3I system. Long-term endurance and reliability in a large-scale exchange are impossible to achieve because of nuclear devastation of the environment due to direct effects and climatic phenomena and because the C^3I elements would probably be targeted heavily in such an attack.[70]

By the principle of Occam's razor, a BMD system with space-based components would not have to survive worst-case attacks against itself, but only plausible ones. This does not change the mission of BMD from the standpoint of stability, which is to support deterrence rather than transcend it. To remain in the state of nature and short of a state of war, as those philosophical categories apply to the problem of preemption, defenses and strategic C^3 systems need not meet heroic standards. They need only contribute to a situation in which first strikes "pay," are hard to make, and are difficult to justify.

The preeminent danger in deploying defenses is that, if they are wired incorrectly with C^3 systems or weapons platforms that are not fault tolerant, they could help provoke the very war they are intended to deter. A state of nature is one of potential hostility, as we have seen, but it is preferable to a state of war or the expectation of imminent attack. The balance between superpower first-strike uncertainties and retaliatory capabilities is such that a state of nature remains short of a state of war. Neither Americans nor Soviets can contemplate a first strike without unacceptable opportunity costs; neither side need fear, even under the most overbearing crisis conditions, a rational decision to strike. A rational decision is one that is taken in cool deliberation, in the expectation that benefits will exceed costs; *or* it is a decision made in desperation, in which leaders are wrongly convinced that preemption pays. In the second case, the decision is conditionally rational but not actually so. It is rational from the standpoint of a state of war, but not in relationship to the state of nature which it (unnecessarily) destroys.

CONCLUSION

First-strike stability is not guaranteed by the large and diverse superpower nuclear arsenals or by the promise of assured retaliation in response to aggression. Neither U.S. nor Soviet planners can assume that deterrence will hold if it is pushed hard by crisis-borne misperceptions, expectations of relative victory, or fears of imminent military and political defeat. Given the kinds of forces and command systems now deployed, neither NATO nor the Warsaw Pact could expect to exercise continuing control over wartime conventional-force operations—let alone nuclear—without risking expansion of the war into the U.S. and Soviet homelands. Nor has either side resolved the difficult trade-off between the certainty of a large and massive nuclear response as a peacetime deterrent, and the flexibility for smaller, more selective, but possibly less deterring attacks once war has begun. The next chapter looks at the problem of military stability specifically; Chapters 4 and 5 consider the Soviet view of these matters in some depth; and Chapter 6 considers whether new defensive technologies might lead to a new basis for superpower deterrence and crisis stability.

NOTES

1. President's Commission on U.S. Strategic Forces (Scowcroft Commission), *Report* (Washington: April 1983).

2. Jonathan E. Medalia, "Midgetman Small ICBM: Issues for Deterrence in the 1990s," in Stephen J. Cimbala, ed., *Challenges to Deterrence: Resources, Technology and Policy* (New York: Praeger Publishers, 1987), pp. 225–47.

3. According to Marshal Sergei Akhromeyev, then Chief of the Soviet General Staff: "Propaganda aside, the essence of the American Star Wars program boils down to the treacherous aim of giving the United States the potential to make a first nuclear strike at the Soviet Union with impunity and deprive it, by creating a national antimissile defense, of the opportunity to make a retaliatory strike." Akhromeyev, press conference following the Geneva summit meeting with President Ronald Reagan, November 21, 1985, quoted

in Arms Control Association, *Star Wars Quotes* (Washington: Arms Control Association, 1986), p. 115.

4. On the problem of nuclear surprise, see Richard K. Betts, "Surprise Attack and Preemption," Ch. 3 in Graham T. Allison, Albert Carnesale, and Joseph S. Nye, Jr., *Hawks, Doves and Owls: An Agenda for Avoiding Nuclear War* (New York: W. W. Norton, 1985), pp. 54–79. This is also discussed in Ch. 8, and in Cimbala, *Nuclear Endings* (New York: Praeger Publishers, 1989).

5. Klaus Knorr and Patrick Morgan, *Strategic Military Surprise: Incentives and Opportunities* (New Brunswick, N.J.: Transaction Books, 1983), contains a number of very useful case studies and theoretic discussions.

6. Patrick Morgan, "The Opportunity for a Strategic Surprise," Ch. 8 in Knorr and Morgan, *Strategic Military Surprise*, pp. 195–246.

7. See Barton Whaley, *Codeword Barbarossa* (Cambridge, Mass.: MIT Press, 1973).

8. I am indebted to Paul K. Davis for helping to clarify my thinking on these points, although he bears no responsibility for the argument. See Davis, *Studying First-Strike Stability with Knowledge-Based Models of Human Decisionmaking* (Santa Monica, Cal.: RAND Corporation, April 1989), R-3689-CC.

9. See Richard Ned Lebow, *Nuclear Crisis Management* (Ithaca, N.Y.: Cornell University Press, 1987), pp. 31–74.

10. Thomas Hobbes, *Leviathan* (New York: Washington Square Press, 1984), pp. 120–47. *Leviathan* was first published in 1651.

11. Ibid., p. 116.

12. Ibid., p. 117.

13. Ibid.

14. Ibid.

15. Raymond L. Garthoff, *Reflections on the Cuban Missile Crisis* (Second Edition) (Washington: Brookings Institution, 1989). See also Graham T. Allison, *Essence of Decision: Explaining the Cuban Missile Crisis* (Boston: Little, Brown, 1971).

16. A useful bibliography of the Cuban missile crisis literature is by Lieutenant Commander Michael N. Pocalyko, USN, *The Cuban Missile Crisis: A Short Bibliography, Naval History*, Summer 1988, pp. 57–58.

17. See Luigi Albertini, *The Origins of the War of 1914*, Vol. II, translated and edited by Isabella M. Massey (London: Oxford University Press, 1953), for historical detail on the crisis immediately preceding the outbreak of World War I. For perspective on brinkmanship and other crises, see Lebow, *Between Peace and War: The Nature of International Crisis* (Baltimore, Md.: Johns Hopkins University Press, 1981).

18. Ernest R. May, "Conclusions: Capabilities and Proclivities," in May, ed., *Knowing One's Enemies: Intelligence Assessment before the Two World Wars* (Princeton, N.J.: Princeton University Press, 1984), pp. 503–42.

19. Albert Wohlstetter, "The Delicate Balance of Terror," *Foreign Affairs* 37, no. 2 (January 1959), pp. 209–34.

20. John J. Mearsheimer, *Conventional Deterrence* (Ithaca, N.Y.: Cornell University Press, 1983).

21. Hobbes, *Leviathan*, p. 124.

22. For an analysis of Prisoner's Dilemma and suggested applications, see George H. Quester, *The Future of Nuclear Deterrence* (Lexington, Mass.: Lexington Books, 1986), pp. 31–33.

23. On the distinction between preemption and prevention, see Betts, "Surprise Attack and Preemption."

24. Desmond Ball, *Can Nuclear War Be Controlled?*, Adelphi Papers No. 169 (London: International Institute for Strategic Studies, Autumn 1981); Bruce G. Blair, *Strategic Command and Control: Redefining the Nuclear Threat* (Washington: Brookings Institution, 1985); Paul Bracken, *The Command and Control of Nuclear Forces* (New Haven, Conn.: Yale University Press, 1983).

25. Bruce G. Blair, "Alerting in Crisis and Conventional War," Ch. 3 in Ashton B. Carter, John D. Steinbruner, and Charles A. Zraket, eds., *Managing Nuclear Operations* (Washington: Brookings Institution, 1987), pp. 75–120.

26. Stephen M. Meyer, "Soviet Nuclear Operations," Ch. 15 in Carter, Steinbruner, and Zraket, eds., *Managing Nuclear Operations*, pp. 470–534.

27. For a discussion, see David N. Schwartz, *NATO's Nuclear Dilemmas* (Washington: Brookings Institution, 1983).

28. See Robert Jervis, *The Illogic of American Nuclear Strategy* (Ithaca, N.Y.: Cornell University Press, 1984).

29. Fritz W. Ermarth, "Contrasts in American and Soviet Strategic Thought," in Derek Leebaert, ed., *Soviet Military Thinking* (London: Allen and Unwin, 1981), pp. 50–72.

30. See Michael Doyle, "Endemic Surprise? Strategic Surprises in First World–Third World Relations," Ch. 4 in Knorr and Morgan, *Strategic Military Surprise*, pp. 77–110.

31. See Major-General Chaim Herzog, *The War of Atonement* (Boston: Little, Brown, 1975).

32. Samuel P. Huntington, "The Renewal of Strategy," in Huntington, ed., *The Strategic Imperative: New Policies for National Security* (Cambridge, Mass.: Ballinger Publishing Co., 1982), pp. 1–52.

33. See U.S. Congressional Budget Office, *Rapid Deployment Forces: Policy and Budgetary Implications* (Washington: Congressional Budget Office, February 1983).

34. Ibid.

35. Francis Fukuyama, "Escalation in the Middle East and Persian Gulf," Ch. 5 in Allison, Carnesale, and Nye, eds., *Hawks, Doves and Owls*, pp. 115–47.

36. Barry M. Blechman and Douglas M. Hart, "The Political Utility of Nuclear Weapons: The 1973 Middle East Crisis," in Steven E. Miller, ed., *Strategy and Nuclear Deterrence* (Princeton, N.J.: Princeton University Press, 1984), pp. 273–97.

37. Blair, "Alerting in Crisis and Conventional War," p. 95.

38. Herbert Butterfield, *Napoleon* (New York: Collier Books, 1962); Martin Van Creveld, *Command in War* (Cambridge, Mass.: Harvard University Press, 1985), pp. 58–102; Peter Paret, "Napoleon and the Revolution in War," Ch. 5 in Peter Paret, ed., *Makers of Modern Strategy* (Princeton, N.J.: Princeton University Press, 1986), pp. 123–42.

39. John Shy and Thomas Collier, "Revolutionary War," Ch. 27 in Paret, ed., *Makers of Modern Strategy*, pp. 815–62.

40. Jon Kimche, *The Unfought Battle* (New York: Stein and Day, 1968).

41. Mearsheimer, *Conventional Deterrence*, pp. 67–98.

42. Quester, *The Future of Nuclear Deterrence*, Ch. 2 applies game theoretical matrices to the problem of war causation.

43. Roberta Wohlstetter, *Pearl Harbor: Warning and Decision* (Stanford, Cal.: Stanford University Press, 1962).

44. Lebow, *Nuclear Crisis Management*, p. 128; see also Irving L. Janis and Leon Mann, *Decision Making: A Psychological Analysis of Conflict, Choice and Commitment* (New York: Free Press, 1977).

45. See Janice Gross Stein, "Calculation, Miscalculation, and Conventional Deterrence II: The View from Jerusalem," Ch. 4 in Robert Jervis, Richard Ned Lebow, and Janice Gross Stein, *Psychology and Deterrence* (Baltimore: Johns Hopkins University Press, 1985), pp. 60–88.

46. One of the most insightful discussions of the relationship between the causes of war and the reasons for peace, including the bringing of wars to an end, appears in Geoffrey Blainey, *The Causes of War* (New York: Free Press, 1973), esp. pp. 114–24.

47. Frank Von Hippel, Barbara G. Levi, Theodore A. Postol, and William H. Daugherty, "Civilian Casualties from Counterforce Attacks," *Scientific American* 259 (September 1988), pp. 36–40.

48. See Jervis, *Illogic of American Nuclear Strategy, passim.*

49. See Lawrence Freedman, *The Evolution of Nuclear Strategy* (New York: St. Martin's Press, 1981).

50. Ball, *Can Nuclear War Be Controlled?* See also Stephen J. Cimbala, *Nuclear War Termination: Concepts, Controversies and Conclusions* (Canberra, Australia: Strategic and Defence Studies Centre, Australian National University, June 1989).

51. For an assessment of U.S. arms control, see Albert Carnesale, *Learning from Experience with Arms Control: A Final Report*, submitted to the U.S. Arms Control and Disarmament Agency, John F. Kennedy School of Government, Harvard University, September 1986. Chapters 4 and 5 deal with SALT.

52. Robert D. Blackwill, "Specific Approaches to Conventional Arms Control in Europe," *Survival* 30, no 5 (September-October 1988), pp. 429–47, esp. pp. 429–31.

53. For pertinent sources, see Raymond L. Garthoff, "New Thinking in Soviet Military Doctrine," *Washington Quarterly* 11 (Summer 1988), pp. 131–58. Exemplary of new thinking is Vitaliy Zhurkin, Sergei Karaganov, and Andrey Kortunov, "Vyzovy bezopasnosti—staryye i novyye," *Kommunist* 1 (1988), pp. 42–50. See also Sergei Akhromeyev, "Doktrina predotvrashcheniya voyny, zashchity mira i sotsializma," *Problemy mira i sotsializma* 12 (December 1987), pp. 23–28. I am grateful to Dr. Harold Orenstein, Soviet Army Studies Office, for assistance in translating the Zhurkin et al. article and to Dr. James J. Tritten, U.S. Naval Postgraduate School, for calling it to my attention.

54. Stephen J. Flanagan and Andrew Hamilton, "Arms Control and Stability in Europe," *Survival* 30, no. 5 (September-October 1988), pp. 448–64.

55. M. A. Gareyev, *M. V. Frunze—voyennyy teoretik* (Moskva: Voyenizdat, 1985), published and translated as *M. V. Frunze, Military Theorist* (New York: Pergamon Brassey's, 1988), p. 214.

56. See Stephen J. Cimbala, "What Price Survivability? Progress vs. Perfection," *Armed Forces and Society* 13 (Fall 1986), pp. 107–24.

57. U.S. Arms Control and Disarmament Agency, *Arms Control Update*, January 1988, p. 1.

58. See Robert Einhorn, "The Emerging START Agreement," *Survival* 30, no. 5 (September-October 1988), pp. 387–401.

59. President's Commission on Strategic Forces, *Report, passim.*

60. Medalia, "Midgetman Small ICBM."

61. Walter Slocombe, "Force Posture Consequences of the START Treaty," *Survival* 30 (September-October 1988), pp. 402–8; and John D. Steinbruner, "The Purpose and Effect of Deep Strategic Force Reductions," Ch. 2 in *Reykjavik and Beyond: Deep Reductions in Strategic Nuclear Arsenals and the Future Direction of Arms Control* (Washington: National Academy of Sciences, 1988).

62. See David S. Sorenson, "Defending Against the Advanced Cruise Missile: The Ultimate Air Defense Nightmare?" in Cimbala, ed., *Strategic Air Defense* (Wilmington, Del.: Scholarly Resources, 1989), pp. 139–60.

63. Slocombe, "Force Posture Consequences of the START Treaty," pp. 405–6.

64. Ibid., p. 408.

65. See Commission on Integrated Long-Term Strategy, *Discriminate Deterrence* (Washington: U.S. GPO, January 1988).

66. Albert Wohlstetter, "The Political and Military Aims of Offensive and Defense Innovation," Ch. 1 in Fred S. Hoffman, Albert Wohlstetter, and David S. Yost, eds., *Swords and Shields: NATO, the USSR, and New Choices for Long-Range Offense and Defense* (Lexington, Mass.: Lexington Books, 1987), pp. 3–36.

67. Carl H. Builder, "The Impact of New Weapons Technologies," Ch. 8 in Cimbala, ed., *Strategic War Termination* (New York: Praeger Publishers, 1986), pp. 157–73.

68. See Michael Clarke, "Strategic Command and Control and the Militarisation of Space," Ch. 2 in Stephen Kirby and Gordon Robson, eds., *The Militarisation of Space* (Brighton, Sussex: Wheatsheaf Books Ltd., 1987), pp. 29–50.

69. For perspective on nuclear targeting issues, see Theodore A. Postol, "Targeting," Ch. 11 in Carter, Steinbruner, and Zraket, eds., *Managing Nuclear Operations*, pp. 373–406.

70. The difference between C^3 for flexible short-term endurance and that for long-term endurance is explained in Charles A. Zraket, "Strategic Command, Control, Communications and Intelligence," *Science* 224 (June 22, 1984), p. 1310.

3

Military Stability in Europe: Doctrines, Technology, and Forces

The search for stability in superpower political relations is marked by oscillations between optimism and pessimism that spill over into questions of armed suasion. Forces deployed by NATO and the Warsaw Pact in Europe serve many missions. They symbolize past decisions with regard to the outcome of World War II, and they embody future potential for destruction should World War III begin in Europe. Soviet forces deployed in Eastern Europe, and U.S. forces in Western Europe, announce the military bipolarity that underlies the conduct of international politics and diplomacy between the blocs. As the political climate becomes more propitious for East–West arms control, trade, investment, and other inter-bloc exchanges, the armed forces of NATO and the Warsaw Pact seem all the more anachronistic to some observers, and all the more necessary to others. NATO fears the sinking of its politics into complacency in the absence of obvious military threat; the Soviet Union fears a spillover of Westernization into Eastern Europe, with the potential for political revolution and military destabilization.

Military stability may be assumed to exist when political expectations, military doctrines, and force deployments create no incentives for offensively or defensively motivated attack. Military stability does not guarantee against inadvertent war or escalation (see Chapter 4). Finally, stability does not come about automatically as a result of force balances. There is a danger in assuming that conventional weapons of unprecedented lethality, assigned missions for which nuclear weapons were formerly tasked, will be self-deterring, as in the case of superpower strategic arsenals. These aspects of military stability in Europe—or the policies, military doctrines, and forces of the respective sides—receive specific consideration in the present chapter. The protean character of military stability argues against complacency with regard to avoidance of war, even under relatively favorable political climates in Europe.

THE MILITARY BALANCE AND DETERRENCE

The problem of conventional deterrence is not one that could be taken for granted even before conventional and nuclear weapons were deployed together by the major powers. History repeatedly records the failure of conventional deterrence, despite the presence of military balances which on their face should have discouraged prospective attackers. John J. Mearsheimer studied conventional deterrence failures and suggested that they had something to do with the attacker's strategy compared to the defender's strategic expectation. If the attacker contemplates the attainment of a rapid and decisive victory (*blitzkrieg*) for which the defender is judged to be ill prepared, then deterrence is likely to fail.[1] Conversely, if an exhaustive war of attrition is likely to follow on the heels of an attack, forbearance by the prospective attacker is more likely.

Mearsheimer's important insight called attention to the dimension of comparative strategy as an important variable in determining whether states choose to fight or avoid war. Jack L. Snyder studied the military doctrines of the major powers during the period preceding World War I and found that offensively minded doctrines contributed to optimistic expectations about war outcomes.[2] Richard Ned Lebow examined the crisis bargaining behavior of the powers in the July crisis of 1914 and elsewhere and found that this bargaining was influenced by military optimism and political fatalism, neither very well grounded in reality.[3] This mixture of military optimism and political fatalism turns up repeatedly as a contributor to the outbreak of wars that erupt unexpectedly or that take unanticipated turns once they have broken out.[4]

Despite the influence of situational factors, doctrinal optimism, and political fatalism, military establishments prior to the nuclear age believed that the military balance could be calculated with reasonable precision. Errors in judging the military capabilities and doctrine of the opponent were usually ascribed to faulty intelligence. Either the right intelligence was not gathered (failure of collection), it was improperly evaluated by the responsible agencies (failure of analysis and estimation), or it was incorrectly used or ignored by policymakers (failure of decision making and implementation).[5] The possibility also existed that at any of the various steps (collection, estimation, and decision making–implementation), enemy secrecy and deception muddled the assessment.[6] These were certainly obstacles to be overcome, but it was considered by most governments a matter of devoting sufficient resources to the task until the right amounts and kinds of information would dispel the fog of peacetime military and political assessment.

NUCLEAR WEAPONS AND THE MILITARY BALANCE

The arrival of nuclear weapons in the hands of the Americans and Soviets, and later others, changed the problem of military-balance assessment by changing the character of the uncertainties. Once numerous weapons of strategic range had been deployed by the superpowers, the possibility existed that neither the U.S. nor the Soviet homeland could survive an all-out war. This changed several other things, too: relations with allies, the importance of mobilization in war, and the possibility of winning a military victor of the "traditional" kind by defeating the opponent's forces on the battlefield.

Both NATO and the Warsaw Pact are based on the traditional, prenuclear assumption that larger states or coalitions can deter attacks against the smaller ones by extending the protection of their forces to include the states and territories of allies. The two alliances came about in different ways, by voluntary consensus in the case of NATO and by imposition of force in case of the Pact, but the underlying logic of deterrence in both cases was the prenuclear one. This might be called the logic of aggregation. Soviet or U.S. aggression against allies of the other—allies that might otherwise be vulnerable—would be deterred by the promise of a larger adversary automatically committed to rescue of the smaller.

However, this logic of aggregation operated differently in respect to the two alliance systems. The Soviet Union was already in Europe. Therefore, its logic of aggregation could be credible at the level of conventional forces deployed to fight in Europe at an early stage. For the Americans, the problem was more complicated. Following the abortive effort to establish the Lisbon force goals as an alliance commitment, NATO became dependent upon the threat of prompt use of theater nuclear weapons, and the eventual use of U.S. strategic nuclear ones if necessary, in order to deter attack.[7] Thousands of U.S. tactical and longer-range theater nuclear weapons were deployed in Western Europe during the 1950s and 1960s, and a large arsenal of these weapons remained two decades later. Eventually the Soviets also deployed nuclear weapons of tactical and theater range, and the Soviet ground forces were trained in the expectation that any war in Europe could go nuclear rather quickly.[8]

The deployment of strategic and theater nuclear weapons by both superpowers, and the development of independent nuclear arsenals by Britain and France, changed the relationship between the logic of strategy and the logic of alliance. Under prenuclear conditions the acquisition of additional allies and the deployment of more numerous weapons were considered eufunctional and stabilizing for deterrence. World War I demonstrated that this was not in fact so, but long after that war had ended military establishments continued to believe that more was better. Nuclear weapons changed this equation in an obvious way—so obvious that political leaders and military planners could hardly evade it. Now the starting point for calculation of a "favorable" military balance between the Americans and the Soviets was the degree of confidence held by both that they were not vulnerable to a disarming nuclear first strike. If either side suspected that any potential adversary might strike with surprise and virtually eliminate the defender's arsenal, then the temptation for preemption in a nuclear crisis might not be resisted. Thomas C. Schelling had referred to this temptation as the "reciprocal fear of surprise attack," in which the dynamics of crisis bargaining suggested to either side that it paid to jump the gun.[9]

It followed from this that the notion of a military balance of the traditional sort had been replaced by something qualitatively different.[10] True, defenders still had to persuade attackers that a surprise attack could not lead to rapid victory, as in prenuclear times. Now, however, two nuclear armed superpowers found that their large, diverse, and survivable arsenals (as they ultimately became) created common interests in preventing war's outbreak. These common interests in preventing nuclear war would be weighed equally by leaders and planners with any projected gains from actually fighting war. This applied to expected gains not only from any nuclear war, but also from wars between superpowers and their European allies in which nuclear weapons remained in the background. Skirmishing with conventional forces under the nuclear shadow could lead by the process of escalation into theater or strategic nuclear war itself.

Nuclear weapons, therefore, forced the superpowers to leash their political antagonisms and to modify their crisis-time behavior. This complicated U.S. relations with NATO European allies. The Americans could not appear to be too "trigger-happy" or the Europeans would be dragged into a war for which they had no political interest. Conversely, the U.S. strategic nuclear arsenal must not be seen by the Soviets as too remote a possibility to deter even conventional aggression. There was no way that NATO could have its cake and eat it at the level of operational planning, even if declaratory policy skated around the difficulty. Either more or less flexibility in nuclear options would have to be built into U.S. and allied NATO war planning. The alliance ultimately opted for more rather than less, but this raised delicate issues of "decoupling" of the U.S. strategic from the European theater nuclear arsenal.[11] The issue of decoupling was sensitive because the U.S. nuclear *deterrent* was wanted by Europeans and Americans, who preferred not to think very much about the consequences of nuclear dependence, once deterrence had failed.

Another aspect of the reliance upon nuclear instead of conventional deterrence was the impact upon mobilization as a factor in military force planning. Capacity for mobilization of industrial or other economic power for military purposes has been a principal criterion for separating major from minor powers in international relations since antiquity.[12] The side with superior resources did not always win wars, especially short wars, but superior resources that could be converted to military purposes frequently proved to be decisive for attaining favorable war outcomes in prolonged conflicts. Nuclear weapons made the issue of military-industrial mobilization seem less important, at least in the West. Now that entire societies could be destroyed in less than an hour, the problem of mobilization seemed anachronistic. A few strategic thinkers and military planners attempted to tie mobilization planning to nuclear survival in the form of civil defense preparedness. But this proved consistently unpopular with American opinion, and many U.S. policy elites remained opposed to civil defense as useless or, if useful, as provocative of Soviet distrust.[13] Mobilization would be relevant in an extended war in which both superpowers practiced nuclear avoidance, or in a limited nuclear war in Europe that left both U.S. and Soviet homelands untouched. In either case the fighting in Europe might be a first phase of a more geographically expansive conflict or one that became more extensive in time. The problem for Americans was that Europe could not be treated as a first, limited phase of a global war without creating divisive issues within NATO.

A third aspect of the shift to reliance upon nuclear weapons, with regard to the relationship between military balance and military strategy, was in respect to the new notion of victory. Conventional deterrence was thought to remain stable if no aggressor could contemplate the success of a *blitzkrieg* against an unwary defender.[14] However, it followed that, where and when such attacks could be contemplated, they might be launched. Further, once having been launched, they might provide victory according to prevailing definitions of victory: defeat of the opponent's armed forces on the battlefield, occupation of his territory, or the dethronement of his government. Once two superpowers had acquired diversified and survivable nuclear arsenals, precluding disarming first strikes, the prenuclear concept of victory became obsolete. One might still attain prenuclear standards of victory if war remained below the nuclear threshold, but if it did, then the cost of preserving that threshold during war was to make conventional war more attractive to the side better prepared for it.

During the Nixon, Ford, Carter, and Reagan administrations, the United States attempted to reconsider the notion of victory and how it might apply to nuclear war. Thinking on this point evolved in the direction of limited nuclear war, since total war seemed politically absurd and self-defeating. U.S. doctrinal developments throughout the 1970s and 1980s, with roots in McNamara's early formulations of city avoidance and counterforce, focused on the problem of attaining acceptable and favorable nuclear war outcomes. The "Schlesinger doctrine" embodied in NSDM-242 of 1974 was followed by the Carter administration's "countervailing strategy" of 1980 and the Reagan NSDD-13 and related defense guidance.[15] The assumption behind much of this thinking was that the Soviet Union would cooperate in limiting war to strikes outside U.S. and Soviet territory or, if necessary, to strikes against targets other than cities within those territories.

The dynamic aspects of the assumptions surrounding limited nuclear war concern us in the next section. The present question is how nuclear weapons changed the perception of the military balance, and thus the relationship between force balances and stability. The argument made by proponents of limited nuclear war was that the threat to wage limited war was more credible than total war. Threats of total war, especially against an opponent with survivable strategic nuclear forces, were believable, according to this logic, only in the extreme case of massive surprise attack against the U.S. or Soviet homeland. Even in these cases, it was judged by some U.S. strategists, war might still be controlled below the level of deliberate attacks against cities. McNamara had adumbrated this expectation, that even superpower strategic nuclear exchanges might be limited, in his Athens address to the NATO council in May 1962 and again in his Ann Arbor commencement address later that year.[16] When these ideas were "rediscovered" in the 1970s they were put to the task of preserving extended deterrence under conditions of nuclear parity, whereas McNamara had sought to exploit a military balance much more favorable to the Americans for intra-war deterrence.

McNamara was suggesting that a particular balance of military forces did not necessarily dictate how the war ought to be fought.[17] Superiority in numbers of launchers and nuclear charges did not necessarily allow for preeminence in crisis management, on account of the reciprocal fear of surprise attack. The dynamics of escalation control once nuclear weapons had been used were even more unfathomable than the management of crisis prior to nuclear first use. Contrary to the supposition widely held by U.S. nuclear strategists that essentially equivalent superpower nuclear force sizes practically guaranteed stability, in actual fact force sizes beyond the minimum required for assured retaliation were practically irrelevant. From this it did not necessarily follow that deterrence was stable at lower force levels than higher ones. Once the superpowers had embarked upon a crisis, stability prior to war would be based in part on their expectations about stability during it.

INTRA-WAR DETERRENCE

The notion that deterrence could be continued into war struck persons familiar with nuclear weapons and their effects as contradictory. Even very few nuclear weapons of moderate yield by the standards of the Soviet and U.S. arsenals of the 1980s would create great devastation. Further, the symbolism of using nuclear weapons in anger would be as likely to provoke unrestrained fury and psychological motives for revenge as it would be to induce restraint. The notion of nuclear restraint seemed to contradict common sense. It also seemed to contradict the requirements of an all-or-nothing strategy for NATO, putting the Americans into jeopardy along with the Europeans. A territorial sanctuary for North America was implied in notions for fighting a limited nuclear war in Europe.

The problem of limitations in war would not go away on account of the difference between the world of nuclear strategy and the world of actual policy-making in crisis and wartime. U.S. presidents from Kennedy through Reagan have expressed the desire for options other than massive and general nuclear war. And these options have been built into the U.S. SIOP and into NATO nuclear operational planning for the very reason that once war is on, the threat to fight unrestrained war is counterproductive. The dynamics of conflict in nuclear war, compared to conventional war in the prenuclear age, differ as much as the implications of conventional and nuclear military balances differed from one another, as noted above. Conventional deterrence depended primarily upon the expectation of successful denial, whereas nuclear force balances were toted up in terms of their survivable punishment capability. From this distinction followed the paradox, with regard to force balances, that a more favorable nuclear force balance—one allowing either superpower a first-strike capability— could actually bring about the war that nuclear deterrence was thought to prevent.

The same paradox—of apparent strength becoming actual weakness

relative to the accomplishment of policy aims—bedevils nuclear escalation control once war has actually begun. The paradox affects the conduct
of war at two levels, using the example of war in Europe. The first level
is that of conventional war being fought under the shadow of nuclear
weapons. The second level is activated once the nuclear threshold has been
crossed.

During conventional war between alliances led by superpowers armed
with nuclear weapons, the flow of events in the immediate theater of
operations takes a back seat to the expectations in Moscow and Washington about willingness to initiate nuclear war.[18] A decision reached on the
basis of fighting without nuclear escalation can only be tentative and
subject to renegotiation, owing to the as-yet-unexpended nuclear weapons
retained in NATO and Pact inventories. Conventional war in Europe is
thus the first step in a negotiated peace settlement in which the terms of
trade are only partly expressed by territory lost and military forces destroyed. The coercive power that remains under the control of U.S., allied
NATO, and Soviet military leaders is much more influential with regard
to war outcomes than preceding collisions between Soviet shock armies
and NATO forward-deployed forces.

The paradox of strength into weakness with regard to conventional war
fighting is that the side that is losing without nuclear weapons is strongly
tempted to initiate nuclear warfare. Therefore, rapid and decisive "victory"
at the conventional level opens the door to further bargaining about
whether this phase of combat ends the war or whether the "war" now goes
into another phase. The answer will not be obvious. How far Soviet forces
have advanced into West Germany, or U.S. and allied NATO into East
Germany and Czechoslovakia, will be pertinent to military planners but
not decisive for ending war by the calculation of policymakers. Cabinets
and ministers will be much more concerned with the destruction that has
so far been withheld than with that which has already taken place. The
expectation of coercive nuclear violence, as opposed to the continuation
of conventional war fighting, will determine whether U.S. or Soviet leaders
foresee acceptable war termination or continued political stalemate.

It cannot be assumed that conventional war fighting will remain constrained within the initial expectations set by policymakers, either. The
propensity of military establishments to strike at the flanks and rear of
opponents has suggested geographical war widening (now fashionably
described as horizontal escalation) to many planners and strategists as one
way around the dilemma of nuclear escalation. The U.S. maritime strategy

during the Reagan administration offered both geographical war widening (during a war that presumably was still conventional) and counterforce coercion (gradual attrition of the Soviet ballistic missile submarine force during the early stages of conventional warfare).[19] The concern with horizontal escalation leading to inadvertent nuclear war is genuine. Another concern is that the air-land battle being fought in Western Europe would involve conventional deep strikes against NATO and Pact logistical, command, and forces targets designed to cripple the timetable for reinforcement and sustainment of fighting forces. If the NATO and Warsaw Pact versions of conventional deep strike work successfully, the result may be marooned and isolated forces that are separated by islands of enemy troops and dissipated communications. This melee would not permit rapid war termination even without the use of nuclear weapons.[20]

To say that conventional high-technology warfare could be nearly as destructive as limited nuclear warfare misses the point, however. Conventional war can no longer be fought in the same way because nuclear weapons remain the ultimate arbiters of political fate as long as they are deployed in substantial numbers by potential antagonists. Conventional war in Europe is not an alternative to nuclear war but rather a potential detonator of nuclear war. That is why nuclear weapons have served to help deter both conventional and nuclear war; the first effect is more important than the second.[21] The contribution of nuclear weapons to the deterrence of conventional war is on account of the fear of escalation. If a clear line could be drawn in Europe by agreement between potential adversaries, so that one side allowed for fighting with conventional weapons exclusively and the other also permitted nuclear escalation, it would invite a conventional war. In fact, and in contrast to the viewpoint that nuclear weapons deployed in Europe or elsewhere serve only to deter the use of other nuclear weapons, nuclear deterrence spills over into conventional.

That nuclear deterrence also spills over into the prevention of conventional war is the positive side of the strength-into-weakness paradox that haunts force balances and escalation control in the nuclear age. The negative side is that lack of experience with nuclear weapons leaves policymakers with no historical points of reference once the nuclear threshold has been crossed. The establishment of stable expectations about the future course of war once nuclear weapons have been used is thus full of uncertainties. This difficulty is critical to the potential for the control of nuclear escalation, or for the potential for failure to do so. As Richard Smoke has noted, the crossing of certain thresholds establishes a saliency in the minds of the opponent's policymakers. However, not all saliencies are equally important with regard to the establishment of constraints upon fighting. The more important saliencies are those that, once having been crossed, create *expectation levers* resulting in qualitative shifts in leaders' perceptions about *future* escalation.[22]

For example, when the Germans, shortly before the outbreak of World War I, gave the Austro-Hungarians a blank check to discipline Serbia, the kaiser implied that this support was unconditional. He did not qualify his support with the admonition that, should Russia appear to be mobilizing in response to Austro-Hungarian suppression of Serbia, Germany would reconsider. Thus the Austro-Hungarians proceeded against the Serbians, whom they squashed temporarily. This, however, was a Pyrrhic victory, for the squashing of Serbia was not regarded by other major powers as an internal matter with regard to the contiguous empire of Austria-Hungary. Instead, it was viewed as exemplary of Austro-Hungarian willingness to court war among major powers, and it was further perceived that Germany was the *éminence grise* that was guiding the hapless Austro-Hungarians into war. This in turn cemented the alliance among France, Britain, and Russia, each becoming more wary of any further moves by the Austro-Hungarians or Germans (who in turn watched for any preemptive moves on the part of the Russians and French).[23]

World War I is almost too classical in its point-counterpoint during the July crisis of 1914, for few cases so perfectly exemplify the problem of conflict spiral, or amplifying feedback, without modulation or limitation. A more interesting, more ambiguous case occurred during the Korean War. MacArthur's landing at Inchon had turned the tide of battle, and the U.S.–United Nations forces now had the capability of recapturing lost territory and invading North Korea. The question of political aims was now paramount. Truman and his advisors, unable to reach a consensus *against* revising war aims to take advantage of battlefield developments, allowed MacArthur's forces to press toward the Yalu. How this would be perceived by China was uncertain. Truman and the U.S. Joint Chiefs of Staff issued orders to MacArthur that left him great discretion with regard to tactics and with respect to the interpretation of political and military intelligence. Thus, MacArthur conveniently assumed both (1) that the Chinese would not intervene in Korea in force, and (2) that if they did, their intervention would not be militarily consequential.[24]

Neither Truman nor MacArthur seems to have given sufficient weight to the crossing of a symbolic threshold (invading North Korea) and to the further approximation of crossing another (moving forces close to the border between China and Korea). President John F. Kennedy, during the

Cuban missile crisis of 1962, provided a contrasting example in recognizing the importance of political symbolism and its potential to shift expectations of future escalation. Kennedy chose as his initial reaction to the discovery of Soviet missiles in Cuba a "quarantine" that allowed for further escalation but provided Soviet Premier Khrushchev with the opportunity to withdraw without humiliation.

Had the United States chosen instead to bomb the missile sites in Cuba or to invade Cuba, Khrushchev would have been under strong pressure to demonstrate Soviet resolve, perhaps by moving against the U.S. and allied positions in West Berlin. However, events that occurred "off line" during the crisis were reminders that the superpowers, even when they both desire a safe exit from confrontation, can temporarily lose control over events. On the tense day before the crisis was finally resolved by Soviet acquiescence to Kennedy's demands, several incidents occurred that had been neither desired by policymakers nor expected by military planners. An American U-2 reconnaissance aircraft was shot down over Cuba and the U.S. pilot killed; apparently the Soviet-supplied surface-to-air missile (SAM) that downed the plane was fired despite Khrushchev's orders not to do so. And another American U-2 on an air-sampling mission over the North Pole strayed into Soviet air space, causing Soviet air defense fighter interceptors to scramble and Soviet military leaders to wonder whether this was the precursor to a preemptive bombing strike on the Soviet Union.[25]

Incidents of this sort happen frequently under normal peacetime conditions, when they are less apt to be noticed. On July 4, 1989, the pilot of a Soviet MIG-23 was on a training flight over Poland when he began to lose control of the aircraft. He bailed out after pointing the plane in a direction such that, given its altitude and location, it was expected to crash into the Baltic. Instead, the aircraft continued more than 500 miles westward, passing pilotless over the remainder of Poland, East Germany, West Germany, and the Netherlands, into Belgium, where it finally crashed. Soviet defense minister Yazov dryly commented that it seemed unusual that the plane had not been shot down over East European airspace before penetrating into Western territory. Soviet and East European officials issued no warning to the Germans, Dutch, or Belgians of the plane's impending approach. U.S. F-15 interceptors were scrambled from an air base in Holland but declined to shoot down the plane, explaining that its debris would be scattered widely over heavily populated areas in Germany and Holland. As it happened, the Soviet aircraft crashed into a populated area in Belgium, killing one person.[26] Soviet reasons for not alerting NATO are the subject of Western speculation. One plausible reason is that there existed no standard operating procedure (SOP) for doing so; no Soviet or East European officer is specifically tasked to notify NATO of accidental aircraft penetrations and the like.

An additional difficulty with the estimation of future expectations by national leaders, including those expectations specifically dealing with incentives for escalation, is the problem of ethnocentrism or national strategic culture. This causes many reverberations. One example is in the different national means or methods for estimating costs. During the Vietnam escalation, Americans sought to impose gradually increasing costs upon North Vietnam through airpower and upon the Viet Cong infrastructure (through search-and-destroy operations and political-psychological warfare). The assumption was that, beyond a certain threshold, North Vietnam would find it inexpedient to continue fighting; this decision, in turn, would lead to disintegration of the Viet Cong cadres. In fact, the approach of gradual escalation was descriptive of U.S. military technique, but not of North Vietnamese political evaluation of their stakes in the conflict. Further, the North Vietnamese political and military leadership was divided between "northern" and "southern" factions who sought various gradations of objectives. The U.S. descriptive knowledge of these factions and their relative power bases was minimal. Thus, U.S. efforts to use coercion to influence the North Vietnamese leadership were based on an assumption of consensus and unity that was unable to exploit intra–North Vietnamese differences.[27]

If adversaries calculate according to different metrics, then incommensurable results cannot send clear signals of intent to escalate or to de-escalate. Hitler judged correctly that Britain and France would not stand in his way if he wished to annex Austria and subjugate Czechoslovakia. He also judged that the British and French would stand aside if he attacked Poland; the latter judgment was incorrect. The judgment about Poland was perfectly logical on the basis of precedent behavior, but it misfired. It was equally logical for the Argentine leadership in 1982 to suppose that Britain would be unwilling, on the basis of recent precedent, to oppose militarily an Argentine occupation of the Falklands. This logical expectation was also disappointed. Stalin quite logically assumed that Hitler, following precedent, would issue an ultimatum to him before an actual attack began. The ultimatum would allow the Soviet ruler to stall for time to improve his forces for the day on which war proved unavoidable (estimated by the Soviets as sometime in 1942). Unfortunately for Stalin, war proved to be unavoidable on June 22, 1941.

Although the German invasion of the Soviet Union in 1941 is frequently studied on its own merits as a case of surprise attack, it also warrants examination as a case of escalation. Hitler had attained the temporary advantage with regard to the war against Britain and France. He failed to deliver the knockout blow against Britain and was forced to face the futility of plans for the invasion of Britain (Operation Sea Lion) in 1940. Having run out of actual opponents, he therefore turned to potential ones. The Soviet Union was a potential opponent, in terms of ideology and the potential for future competition for *lebensraum* in Eastern Europe. Hitler persuaded himself of the necessity for escalating the war into a war on two fronts, despite the conviction of some members of his military elite that a two-front war was a certain disaster. Hitler's previous successes in the West had been made possible by the German-Soviet nonaggression pact of August 1939. However, the German dictator had two hopes. The first was that rapid defeat of Soviet Russia would discourage Britain from continuation of the war. The second was that Japan might come into the war against the Soviet Union once it became clear that Hitler was on the verge of triumph.[28]

Hitler thus embarked on a military escalation in order to induce his opponents into a political de-escalation of war aims. This linkage was also attempted by the Germans during World War I. The example of unrestricted submarine warfare against enemy and neutral shipping is instructive. The political consequences of this move were ignored or assumed away in order to validate the choice from the standpoint of military advantage. It was thought necessary to interdict shipping to and from Britain in order to force economic disaster on its economy, thereby prompting London to sue for peace. However, the connection between economic strangulation and political or military incapacity to pursue war was a casual assumption based on mistaken hope.[29] In similar regard for military efficiency to the detriment of political objectives, the German general staff devised the Schlieffen Plan, which required attack through Belgium. This was guaranteed to bring Britain into the war, prolonging the fighting and at best making the victory expected for German arms more costly.

The parsimony of game theory and other rigorous descriptions of international conflict behavior contain a bias with regard to motives for escalation. Analytical models of conflict behavior assume that motives are identical and that the issue of outcomes depends upon the relative determination and bargaining skill of the contestants. But it cannot be assumed that, during international crisis or war, motives are symmetrical. They may not even follow from the same frame of reference with regard to history, culture, and politics. If we recall the misunderstandings about motives that characterized the leaders of Austria-Hungary, Germany, Russia, France, and Great Britain on the eve of World War I, we can expect the potential for misperception of aims in the more heterogeneous international system of today to be larger still. The U.S. intervention in Vietnam has already been noted as one example, although in a different context. Another is the U.S. perception of the revolution in Iran in 1978 and 1979. It was inconceivable to many in the Carter administration that Iranian clergy could exercise such strong political influence that they would serve as the catalysts for revolutionary outbreak. Further, it was inconceivable to many that once in power, the new regime would take the path of Islamic fundamentalism; after all, in the West religion had been "tamed" for centuries with regard to its role in politics. When the Ayatollah Khomeini proclaimed that the United States was the "Great Satan," many U.S. officials and journalists took this to be propaganda for the home front and not a true assessment of the leadership's world view. Later, the Reagan administration got itself involved in the Iran-*contra* scandal on the assumption that "moderates" in the Iranian leadership were prepared to support an arms-for-hostage trade to free Americans and others held in Lebanon by Shi'ite militias.

Another issue is whether the combatants have revisionist aims with regard to the basic structure of power and influence in international politics, or partial ambitions that can be accommodated within the basic system structure. The Napoleonic ambitions, both ideological and military, could not be accommodated by the international system of his day. Napoleon was suppressed, but the ideological forces let loose by his armies as they marched across Europe survived him. So, too, did Marx's armies of incendiary words about proletarian revolution; the force of his ideology survived the passing of the proletariat as a social force or a meaningful demographic focus. Today the writings of Marx, Engels, and Lenin remain as inspirations for many Western middle-class intellectuals, whose social positions are rather discrepant from those of the industrial revolution proletariat. When a genuine proletarian revolution of the doctrinal Marxian kind finally arrived, in Poland in the 1980s, the leadership of the Soviet Union and of the Polish Communist party declared that it was a revolt against the authority of a workers' state.

During the 1930s, the basic structure of the international system was contested by ideologies which proclaimed that the prevailing structure was illegitimate. Further, several proponents of these anti-systemic ideologies were prepared to do something to change the status quo: Germany, Japan, and Italy were the most noteworthy. Each of these revisionist actors perceived that the status quo powers were tired of war and sought to distance themselves from the bitter memories of World War I. Since it was perceived that a power vacuum had developed, those willing to take the initiative moved to fill it. When basic world views are at odds, the use of military force brings with it the banner of ideological imperialism. The contest becomes one of right versus wrong, and compromise, including the control of escalation during war, is not deemed a virtue when one is in combat with the devil incarnate. Churchill's descriptions of Hitler, as the Russians' of Napoleon, drew upon theological metaphors for political inspiration. This helped create the climate in which nothing less than total defeat of the enemy's armed forces was acceptable. The preferred ordering of postwar political outcomes is subject to disregard by antagonists who prefer to fight to the death of their societies, not just their armed forces, in the name of absolutist objectives and revisionist goals.

Imperial Japan in World War II is a case in point. Leon V. Sigal has done an exhaustive study of the problem of war termination in U.S.–Japanese relations.[30] It turns out, according to his analysis, that it may not have been necessary for the United States to drop atomic bombs, or to invade the Japanese home islands, in order to induce Japanese surrender. Contrary to the supposition of President Harry Truman and his advisors at the time, continuation of the conventional bombing campaign against Japan, and the effective economic isolation of the Japanese economy from outside help, might have sufficed to induce Japanese surrender. The question of how to induce Japanese surrender was not debated with regard to the avoidance of atomic use, but on the assumption that the bomb would be used if it became available in time. Organizational and bureaucratic politics within the U.S. government created a momentum for using the bomb against some suitable target, and these institutional prejudgments colored the deliberations about atomic bombing by higher-level officials, including cabinet officers. Nor were political inducements to Japanese surrender given consideration equivalent to the pressure which military escalation, with or without nuclear weapons, was assumed to exert. On the other hand, U.S. officials had justified skepticism about the possible formation of any consensus within the Japanese wartime leadership which favored negotiated peace over military defeat. The personal intervention of Hirohito was required to bring about a surrender even after Hiroshima and Nagasaki became the first targets of the nuclear age.[31]

During any future crisis or war in Europe, the potential for misperception of objectives and for the misunderstanding of cultural significance is enormous. The United States will have sufficient difficulty understanding the Soviet view of war and politics, and so too will the Soviet leadership with regard to the U.S. view of these matters. The mixture of national and cultural metaphors does not end there, however. NATO and the Warsaw

Pact each have a kaleidoscope of national military and political traditions, although those of the latter seem very subordinated in peacetime to the requirements of Soviet diplomacy. But war is another matter. The Soviet leadership must surely wonder, for example, whether its East European allies will join in any aggressive attack westward. If NATO gave evidence of planning to attack the Soviet Union, and this evidence were consensually believed among leaders from Warsaw to Sofia, then harmony would be the order of the day. But if it appeared that an aggressive war was being launched by the Soviet Union for aims that were not consensually held as desirable among Pact allies, the Soviet military offensive westward could be stopped by a soft political underbelly.[32] If the political softness with regard to Moscow's military aims lay in Sofia or in Belgrade, it might make little difference for the outcome of combat operations on the Central Front. But if the softness appeared in Poland or in East Germany, it would make greater odds.

Both superpowers have the disadvantage that they are structurally assumed to defend the status quo within their respective blocs. This makes them vulnerable to any change-oriented ideology that argues for a more pluralistic determinism of military and political history. Gorbachev has skillfully attempted to exploit this drift of postindustrial society toward political pluralism. This trend is judged by him as so pronounced that he is willing to reconsider the class basis of international conflict as a matter for debate, instead of as a historical truism.[33] If, however, the class-based model of the sources of international conflict is to be supplanted by a more complex model of social change and war causation, the Soviet leadership must embrace this newer model cautiously. Without the international class struggle and the class-based threat of imperialism, the Warsaw Pact in its present configuration seems less necessary. Therefore, the Soviet military elite will want to moderate the rate at which Gorbachev and advisor Aleksandr Yakovlev remove the international class struggle as the driving mechanism of world history. Further, under certain conditions including wartime, the class struggle argues for caution and for accepted finite military losses in order to persevere toward longer-term political goals. This was the decision made by Lenin that permitted the agreement at Brest-Litovsk, which Trotsky and others regarded as tantamount to humiliation and defeat. During war as well as before it begins, dyed-in-the-wool Marxists can be recognized by their conviction that all things are constantly undergoing change. This includes political conditions imposed by armed forces under the traditional rubric of victory. In allowing for the dialectical transformation of the Soviet system itself, both economically and politically, Gorbachev and his colleagues are simply following the original

Marxist script, minus its Leninist deviationism. This preeminence of the dialectic has implications for the Soviet view of nuclear war and stability more specifically, explored in the next section.

PARITY, STABILITY, AND SUPERIORITY

Since there are no single U.S. or Western definitions for the concepts of parity, stability, or superiority, it is no surprise that, as between Soviet and U.S. concepts, there is a wider gulf still.[34] One would do better to start with the Marxist model of historical change and to see how this is translated into military science and military art. Soviet military science is a conceptual frame of reference for understanding correctly the forces of change in history and their implications for present and future war.[35] There is no such thing as historical stasis. Military art, an important component of military science, thus includes the forces of change in strategy, operational art, and tactics. Dialectical laws govern the relationship between technology, military science, and military art. Three of the most significant are the law of the unity and struggle of opposites, the law of the negation of the negation, and the law of the transformation of quantitative change into qualitative.[36]

At the level of force structure and operational planning, the relationship between technology and strategy might be depicted as follows. A new technology becomes available and permits the adoption of a new weapons system by the armed forces. This, in turn, influences the concept of a military operation—how the forces will actually fight. A change in the concept of a military operation leads to changes in force structure, military organization, and training. The last set of changes has reciprocal effects on the development of new technology, and so the dialectical sequences begin again. One might diagram this as shown in Figure 3.1.

The Soviet view is conditioned by this paradigm but not necessarily consensual as between the military and political leadership, or within either group. Soviet military doctrine is that part of military science which has been adopted by the state as official policy.[37] Military science is a proper subject of debate until it has been established as military doctrine, and the debates are often vigorous. For example, the debates over the organization and training of the Red Army (RKKA) during the 1920s among Trotsky, Frunze, Gusev, and others were based on differences of opinion about military science in addition to the personal and careerist motives also evident.[38] The issues included the question as to whether the Soviet Union could provide for its defenses with a "people's army" or militia system as the basis of raising manpower or whether it required a

Figure 3.1
Reciprocal Effects

Technology   Operational Concept

            >   <

        Organization and Training

    Organization   Technology

            >   <

        Operational Concept

Operational Concept   Organization and Training

            >   <

        Technological Innovation

professional armed force based on universal military service. Presumably the officer corps would be professional in either case, although the voluntary cadre-militia system (favored by Trotsky) would undoubtedly have maintained less distance between officers and senior enlisted men than obtains in the Soviet armed forces of today.

There can be no more important issue than this. The relationship between the armed forces and the people is part of the essence of communism that sets it apart from capitalism. Whereas under capitalism the armed forces represent the ruling classes which exploit the masses, under communism the armed proletariat defends the revolution against enemies beyond Soviet borders and within them. Thus, it is of no small importance that the Great Patriotic War, thought to have resolved this issue once and for all, has not done so. Under Gorbachev the issue has come back into the public forum. Influential periodicals have run articles by field-grade Soviet officers and civilian analysts who favor a volunteer-militia system. They support their case with citations to Marx and Engels.[39] The Soviet military leadership as of 1989 had shown no interest in this concept, and several leaders expressed openly their criticism of it. Among those were Minister of Defense Dmitri Yazov and Chief of the General Staff Mikhail Moiseyev.[40]

This is not a detour from the subject of this third section of this chapter; to the contrary, it is immediately germane. How the Soviet armed forces are raised and trained has much to do with how well they can fight. In response to proposals for voluntary-militia systems of military manpower procurement, Soviet military leaders pointed to potential costs in excess of the present system and to the possibility of diminished effectiveness of the resulting forces. The problem of force components based on different nationalities was specifically noted as unresolvable in a territorially based militia system of recruitment. The first U.S. commander in chief would have sympathized with past and present Soviet critics of the militia concept. George Washington soon learned that militia could be usefully employed in a variety of ways, including local territorial defense, guerrilla warfare, and other missions other than set piece battles with regular forces. The Soviet definition of parity or stability must therefore provide, according to the dictates of Soviet military science, for forces capable of coming to grips with the standing, professional armed forces of NATO, if need be.

This might imply, under the prevailing circumstances of "reasonable sufficiency" as a guideline for military expenditures and force building, that the Soviet ground and tactical air forces in Central Europe would be reorganized or reduced in size. Arms-control agreements with NATO may well facilitate this, freeing resources for use in other than military sectors. While Gorbachev seems intent upon limiting the proportion of national product consumed by the armed forces, the Soviet General staff must have credible war plans and forces that are adequate for deterrence (*sderzhivanie*) or war prevention (*predotvrashchat'*) and for fighting successfully if war is deemed unavoidable. The war will by definition be a defensive war politically, but this does not exclude the conduct of an operational or operational-strategic counteroffensive. A recent article by Soviet analysts Kokoshin and Larionov describes four military postures by which the Warsaw Pact and NATO might establish future force structures and doctrines. The article makes the point that truly nonoffensive defenses at the conventional level may require that both sides give up the capability for strategic and operational counteroffensives.[41] However, the idea of taking nonoffensive defense to this extreme has more appeal among Western military professionals than among Soviet ones.[42] General Gareyev, in his celebrated *M. V. Frunze—Voyennyy teoretik* (M. V. Frunze— military theorist), made clear that the conduct of a decisive counteroffensive was an important requirement for fighting on the defensive.[43] And Kokoshin and Larionov, in an article on the Battle of Kursk and its lessons for contemporary military strategy, acknowledge the decisiveness of the counteroffensive that Soviet planners had prepared for the defeat of Operation *Zitadel* after German efforts to break through Soviet defenses failed.[44]

Any Soviet concept of parity or stability would recognize that the terms *offensive* and *defensive* apply to political intent as much as they do to military tactics and operations. Therefore, the Soviet political leadership as well as the General Staff may regard technologies and strategic concepts viewed in the United States as "defensive" in intent as having, from the Soviet perspective, the potential for offensive (meaning anti-Soviet) military exploitation. This is a fair summary of the Soviet declaratory position on the U.S. Strategic Defense Initiative (SDI) since President Ronald Reagan's call for research and development toward the possible deployment of missile defense in his speech of March 23, 1983. Forecasting the impact of future technologies on operational concepts and on defense organization is a requirement of Soviet military science in both the short and long term.[45] If the Soviets have accepted mutual nuclear deterrence as the basis of strategic stability, as some U.S. commentators have argued, then their objection to SDI is based on the assumption consistent with that of Western critics of SDI. Missile defenses when combined with improved offenses would allow the side with defenses to launch a first strike and to absorb the degraded retaliatory strike of its opponent. Thus, BMD (ballistic missile defenses) could be components of an offensive strategy to overturn mutual deterrence, despite the fact that those defenses are based on defensive (antimissile) technology.[46]

The problem of stability and parity in superpower nuclear forces at first glance seems more amenable to a simple solution than the problem of conventional parity and stability. Parity is the structural counterpart of the dynamic concept of stability in either case. Forces essentially equivalent in size and character should cancel each other out, favoring the defender and dissuading the attacker in all but desperate circumstances. Nuclear stability should, according to this logic, follow from the inability of either superpower to contemplate with plausible success the execution of a "successful" first strike, or one which denies to its opponent the opportunity for effective retaliation. For most analysts conventional stability has seemed harder to reckon with, since potential attackers can under some conditions expect to achieve their objectives in the form of territory or other tangible gains without suffering punishment out of proportion to the value of the objective sought.

That the problems of conventional parity and stability are complex is not doubted. But the preceding summary oversimplifies the problem of nuclear stability. Inability of the Americans or Soviets to contemplate in peacetime or during crisis the execution of a surprise first strike deters a deliberate all-out attack. Deterrence is not all of a piece, and nuclear deterrence failure is unlikely to occur as an all-or-nothing explosion of violence. During a short or extended crisis involving Soviet and U.S. allies in Europe, the Middle East, or elsewhere, deterrence will begin to erode at the margins as the allies of both superpowers are provided with military assistance and security guarantees against defeat. One side may then intervene to prevent a humiliating loss for its ally—say, the Syrians or the Israelis. This is what the Soviet Union threatened to do in 1973 as the military tide turned against Egypt in the October war: Brezhnev sent messages to Washington and moved military forces at various locations to send a signal that unilateral Soviet intervention was being seriously contemplated in Egypt. A U.S. global military alert followed.[47] The U.S. secretary of defense at the time, James R. Schlesinger, recalled in 1983 that during the Arab–Israeli war of 1973 "the Soviets introduced nuclear weapons into the Middle East and we did not overreact."[48] The U.S. global alert was described as precautionary and remindful to the Soviets of the risks inherent in placing Soviet forces into combat to rescue the Egyptian Third Army over U.S. objections.[49]

The gnawing away at deterrence during a crisis is a reminder that there are at least two different kinds of nuclear deterrence, as Patrick M. Morgan has noted. The first is general deterrence, which is the propensity for war avoidance characteristic of most states most of the time, and especially if their prospective victims are well armed. The second is specific deterrence, in which a particular combination of inter-state grievances and military vulnerabilities tempts at least one side to risk war.[50] This distinction is very useful, and one implication of it is that specific deterrence, of the kind pertinent to crisis stability, should be observable in use or not claimed to have been operative. A deterrent is not invoked until a specific threat of possible military action by one state against another has been made, and the second state, having been threatened, issues a rebuttal (if you do *x* as you have suggested, we will definitely do *y* and you will suffer the consequences). Following this distinction between general and specific deterrence, we can see that general deterrence is driven by "macro" variables such as the overall distribution of power in the international system and the ideological homogeneity or heterogeneity of the major actors. Conversely, specific deterrence is more responsive to "micro" variables, including the personalities of leaders, the perceptions and expectations of decision makers, and relative advantages in types of power, as in the contrast between land and naval forces.

The distinction between general and specific deterrence leads to two different kinds of rationalities for managing the arms race and preventing nuclear war. For general deterrence one wants to keep gross capabilities in check, and so to preserve mutual deterrence by threat of offensive retaliation against table-turning technologies that create highly competent national air and missile defenses. Specific deterrence, on the other hand, cannot be guaranteed by such rules of the road, and during any individual crisis leaders may see the prevailing balance of power as an obstacle to be overcome and not as an insurmountable barrier to action. In the case of Egypt's attack on Israel in 1973, Egyptian President Anwar Sadat decided to use military force to achieve a limited but important political objective. Having decided that some dramatic military moves would be necessary to restore respect for Arab armed forces, thereby furthering subsequent Egyptian political initiatives, Sadat and his advisors "designed around the scenario," as game designers say. They prepared for a rapid seizure of a strip of territory on the east bank of the Suez Canal and for a holding operation to deny Israel the option of taking it back by force without negotiation. Ultimately, the Israelis were able to dislodge the Egyptians and to throw back their Syrian allies, but not before accepting large losses of men and materiel and agreeing to a brokered peace settlement in which the United States would play a major part.[51]

Jack Snyder has illustrated the importance of military doctrine among those influential variables which contribute to the probability that deterrence will succeed or fail. Snyder studied the military doctrines of France, Germany, and Russia as they planned for the possibility of war prior to 1914.[52] One of his more interesting findings is that cognitive and organizational theories of decision making help explain choices among war plans that were otherwise unsuited to the international and strategic situation. The offensives of 1914 were attempted in the face of recent historical experience and technological constraints that favored the *defense*. Yet, as Geoffrey Blainey has noted, the expectations of cabinet ministers, military planners, and public opinion in the major autocracies and democracies alike was of a war that would be short and victorious.[53] Military doctrines and war plans favoring prompt strategic offensives at the outset of war were the result, according to Snyder, of the causal connections among rational plausibility, motivational biases, and doctrinal oversimplifications.[54] Among these motivational biases documented by Blainey was the expectation that, if military power failed to deliver a rapid and decisive victory, economic pressure would force one of the sides to quit the war before many months' duration.[55] Intra-war as well as prewar deterrence also failed on account of motivational biases and doctrinal legerdemain. A German approximation of modern operations analysis convinced the Kaiser's planners that submarine warfare would bring about British economic collapse in a short time. This assumption was then fed gratuitously into an estimate of the impact of U.S. entry into the war on England's side (superfluous, since the British would long since have capitulated).[56]

Another interesting implication of Snyder's study is that technology may favor a defensive strategy, but the planning process may nonetheless produce an offensive one. Much of the U.S. literature on nuclear strategy was fixated on the putatively offensive or defensive character of individual weapon systems, based on their speed, accuracy, lethality, and other indicators. The strategies or war plans within which these weapons were to be incorporated received less systematic scrutiny. Thus during most of Eisenhower's two terms the U.S. Strategic Air Command, under the direction of General Curtis LeMay, effectively implemented a doctrine of nuclear first strike (preemption) in response to Soviet conventional aggression against Western Europe.[57] And the U.S. Navy, under the aegis of Secretary of the Navy John Lehman and Chief of Naval Operations Admiral James D. Watkins, implemented a "maritime strategy" that called for prompt antisubmarine warfare (ASW) attacks against the Soviet fleet ballistic missile submarine (SSBN) force at the outset of conventional war.[58]

For many years Western analysts contended that the Soviet Union had an offensive military doctrine prejudicial to the stability of general and specific deterrence (or to basic stability and crisis stability). As previously noted, U.S. departures from assured destruction in declaratory policy after 1974 were designed to match the reality of war plans or employment policy. This policy had steadily drifted toward the accumulation of additional strategic nuclear warheads and the addition of further aimpoints on the National Strategic Target List, while, and despite, the conclusion of superpower arms control agreements that limited the number of launchers available to each side. The result was the paradox that more weapons were now available to be aimed at a smaller number of truly strategic targets.

Mutual assured destruction, which was the avowed U.S. declaratory strategy until 1974 and the basis of much U.S. arms control analysis then and now, was inconsistent with such a surplus of weapons to vital targets. The process of war planning had, by dint of organizational impetus and Air Force doctrinal preference, drifted into a search for counterforce preeminence in the 1970s, although U.S. declaratory policy at the presidential level favored arms reductions and mutual deterrence.[59]

Although the expansion of U.S. strategic target lists and weapons inventories was justified with reference to Soviet strategy favoring offensives and preemption, in fact the drift of Soviet strategy in the 1970s was in the opposite direction.[60] The large Soviet air defense system, Soviet deployment of a treaty-limited BMD system around Moscow, and the advent of fourth-generation ICBMs were construed as an attempt by the Soviet Union to establish a decisive superiority at the level of strategic nuclear weapons. This superiority might suffice to make possible a first strike that would destroy most of the U.S. ICBM force while withholding sufficient firepower to deter any U.S. retaliation against Soviet cities.[61] The purported "window of vulnerability" did not survive the scrutiny of the Scowcroft Commission in 1983, but what was most interesting about the U.S. "window" was the assumption that lack of prelaunch survivability for one leg of the U.S. strategic "Triad" could invite a Soviet attack against all of it. Soviet doctrine was thought to be so offensively oriented that it would fly in the face of the almost certain retaliation and subsequent societal destruction. Partisans of the "window" thesis might respond that, as prior to World War I, superpowers can entertain offensive doctrines for which technology is actually impermissive. Thus the argument about offensively oriented Soviet strategy was sometimes based on assumptions about Soviet strategic culture or military doctrinal biases, notwithstanding the realities of the nuclear balance.

Again, however, Soviet behavior contradicted the expectation of an offensively oriented military strategy. Unlike in the U.S. case, military strategy in the Soviet Union is strictly subordinated to the requirements of party policy. On the subject of party leadership of the armed forces, the Soviets do not equivocate: "The undivided leadership of the Armed Forces by the Party and its Central Committee is the objective law of their life and combat activities."[62] The Communist party's leadership of the armed forces "is expressed in the fact that its Central Committee is directly concerned with questions relating to their life and activities, determines the principal trends and challenges of their development, and takes care of the reinforcement of their fighting power, discipline and solidarity."[63] Thus there is no subsystem determinism or "servicism" in the formulation of Soviet military strategy comparable to the subsystemic influence of the U.S. armed services. The Soviet arms of service are certainly influential players in the policy- and strategy-making process, and individual military officers can become influential political actors on a broader canvas than the battlefield or war room (Zhukov, Ustinov, and others).[64] This influence does not permit autonomous strategy making, which remains the province of the General Staff under Party guidance with regard to military doctrine (*doktrina*).

Since at least 1977, Party policy has set down guidelines for the pursuit of sufficiency in nuclear armaments; superiority has been rejected as a meaningful and attainable military objective.[65] This stance did not preclude the attainment of favorable asymmetries with respect to certain aspects of the military balance, either conventional or nuclear, when those asymmetries seemed contributory to Soviet military strategy. As of the end of Reagan's second term, the Soviet Union remained well ahead of the United States in warheads deployed on modern ICBMs and in ICBM throw weight; in having deployed the only limited BMD system to defend its national capital; and in having tested and deployed a functioning antisatellite (ASAT) weapon system. The United States exceeded the Soviet capabilities in numbers of bomber-delivered weapons, submarine-launched ballistic missile (SLBM) warheads, and satellite-based reconnaissance ad communications pertinent to the missions of launch detection and attack characterization.[66] Western analysts of Soviet military policy did not agree whether the Soviet political or leadership accepted mutual deterrence as a necessary condition, or as a state of affairs that was, in addition to being a fact of life, desirable.[67] Soviet arms control initiatives since Gorbachev became general secretary have indicated not only an acceptance of mutual deterrence but also a turn toward a Soviet version of the concept of minimum deterrence. Gorbachev actually used the phrase "minimum deterrent" in a speech to the European Parliament at Strasbourg on July 6, 1989.[68]

With regard to stability, Soviet military writers sometimes use the term *stabilnost'* and at other times *ustoychivost'* to refer to this condition. The first of these terms does not derive from Russian, having instead been adopted from the English, and thus its meaning an be taken as approximating that of its English equivalent. *Ustoychivost'* as a noun refers to a condition of balance or firmness, related to the vert *ustoyat'*, to keep one's balance or hold one's ground. The term *stabilnost'* has become more frequent in recent Soviet writing, which may indicate a clearer Soviet understanding of the Western view if not necessarily an acceptance of it. However, it is very important to appreciate that, from the Soviet perspective, neither political nor military stability can be inferred from any particular distribution of force characteristics or force sizes. Stability or its absence results from the political intentions of states. If the capitalist world is fundamentally hostile, or entering its senescence and therefore subject to anxiety-driven attacks on the socialist community, then its military forces, however structured, are destabilizing. Although Gorbachev has offered various far-ranging proposals for arms control and even for complete nuclear disarmament, the Soviet military leadership has not necessarily changed its view of U.S. or allied NATO political objectives.

According to former Chief of the Soviet General Staff and Marshal of the Soviet Union Sergei Akhromeyev, now a top advisor to Gorbachev, the armed forces of the United States and NATO with each year acquire even more offensive shock character (*nastupatel'nyy, udarnyy kharakter*).[69] Washington is charged by Akhromeyev in 1987 with aggressive plans for the militarization of space and for the employment of weapons based on new physical principles. In the same article he characterizes the contemporary doctrine of the Warsaw Pact as emanating from "the reality of the nuclear-space era" and as "imbued with the spirit of the new political thinking" reflecting a new approach to security.[70] This doctrine is characterized by the Soviet leadership as fundamentally one of war prevention (*predotvrashchat'*). According to Soviet Defense Minister Dmitri Yazov, the first manifestation of the new political thinking on questions of war and peace in the nuclear age is the problem of defense and the guarantee of "equal security" (*ravnoy bezopasnosti*) for all states.[71] Marshal Akhromeyev noted that a special significance is attached to maintaining a balance (*ravnovesiya*) in strategic nuclear forces and that this is decisive (*reshayoshche*) for the management of the arms race.[72]

CORRELATION OF FORCES

The Soviet concept of the correlation of forces takes into account military as well as economic, political, and social factors. The military component is complicated in itself, for it includes not only the military force balance but also the comparative strategies of the superpowers. In his classic work *Narod, armiya, polkovodets* (The people, the army, the commander), M. P. Skirdo offers the following insight:

The experience of history and analysis of the present situation teach us that sober calculation of the correlation of forces between us and our adversary constitutes an important principle of leadership in a war. Correct calculation of the correlation of forces of the warring parties enables the political and military leadership to determine what is possible and impossible in the course of a war, to foresee the adversary's probable actions and to select the most effective methods and forms of armed struggle under various conditions.[73]

The military correlation of forces includes the revolution in military technology that is now in the process of amending, if not supplanting, the "revolution in military affairs" that took place during the nuclear age.[74] The Soviets feel the hot breath of Western technological innovation, which may be convertible into "space strike weapons" based on new physical principles or into new weapons for the accomplishment of strategic missions in a theater of operations *without relying on nuclear weapons*. Col. Gen. Gareyev called attention to this postnuclear revolution in military affairs in his critique of Marshal V. D. Sokolovskiy's *Voyennaya strategiya* (Military strategy) which was published in three editions in the 1960s. According to Gareyev, the Sokolovskiy volume provided "a profound and generally correct analysis" of theory and military strategy in view of the revolution in military affairs. However, he noted, "over more than 20 years not all the provisions of this book have been confirmed."[75]

It was formerly thought by Soviet commentators, according to Gareyev, that all wars would involve the use of nuclear weapons and that conventional war fighting was merely a prelude to the decisive nuclear exchanges. The present nuclear balance between the superpowers and their alliances has reached the point such that the massed used of these weapons would entail "catastrophic consequences" for both sides. At the same time, according to Gareyev, "there will be a greater opportunity for conducting a comparatively long war employing conventional weapons and primarily new types of high-precision weapons."[76] This statement by Gareyev is preceded by the phrase "as is assumed in the West," so that taken literally it is merely a summation of Western thinking that Soviet officers should pay attention to.

Some highly regarded Western analysts also think it points to a trend in Soviet thinking, and they draw some comfort for this view from Soviet sources. As early as 1982 Marshal N. V. Ogarkov, then chief of the General Staff of the Soviet Union, wrote of the development of a new Western military strategy of "direct confrontation" (*pryamogo protivoborstva*) and noted two important concepts inherent in that strategy, as perceived by him: "active countermeasures" (*aktivnogo protivodeystviya*) and "geographic escalation" (*geograficheskoy eskalatsii*).[77] (This Soviet perception of Reagan strategic concepts was noted in an earlier chapter.) It was clear that Obarkov expected active countermeasures and geographic escalation to be based on high-technology conventional weapons that were in the process of development in U.S. and allied

NATO weapons laboratories. Now Soviet armed forces fighting in the Western TVD and in other potential theaters of military action would have to be prepared for nuclear and conventional armed conflict that might be as destructive as nuclear conflict. In the same year as Ogarkov's *Always in Readiness to Defend the Fatherland* (Vsegda v gotovnosti k zashchite Otechestva) was published, M. M. Kir'yan's *Military-Technical Progress and the Armed Forces of the USSR* (Voyenno-tekhnicheskiy progress i vooruzhennye sily SSSR) appeared in print.[78] Both works were published by the military publishing house of the Soviet Ministry of Defense (abbreviated Voyenizdat in most Western references, for Voyennoye izdatel'stvo). Kir'yan's work was also sponsored by the military history institute of the defense ministry.

Kir'yan, although he acknowledges the importance of nuclear weapons and their potentially decisive role in combat, points to the impending development of new conventional weapons and associated means of command and control as factors that must be considered by future planners. Conventional armed forces are being improved in their ability to resist nuclear strikes and in their controllability in battle, in case they are tasked to fight in a nuclear environment. In addition, "efforts to improve the combat characteristics of this type of armament were also prompted by the possibility that in a future war military operations might have to be conducted without nuclear weapons."[79] Modern high-technology weapons depend for their effectiveness as much as do nuclear weapons on modern, highly automated, and potentially vulnerable means of command and control. As potential opponents have increased opportunities to exploit electronic countermeasures, it has become necessary, according to Kir'yan, to organize command and control on a new technical basis.[80] Complex, modern, automated systems of command and control should ensure operativeness, stability, covertness, and continuity in exercising command and control over troops and means of combat.[81] The introduction of automated command and control systems leads to "sharp reduction in the time and forces needed to organize an operation" and makes it possible to improve cooperation and coordination in combat operations by increasing the "stability of command and control" exercised over forces in combat.[82]

Improvements in command and control technology will not bring about this improvement in combat stability, however. The new weapons and methods of control will require changes in armed forces organization for combat. This recognition of the implications for Soviet armed forces organization and combat tactics of the micro-electronic revolution was apparent in their military-technical literature during the 1970s and picked up additional steam in the 1980s. Further, the impacts of the new weapons and control technologies also complicate the calculation of stability, parity, and correlation of forces between the sides. Now not only may the organization of forces for armed combat have to change, involving challenges to cherished principles of Soviet military art, but the very relationship between offense and defense may be redefined.

The first of these two issues is the relationship between new weapons and control technologies, on one hand; and the behavior and organization of combat forces on the other. Marshal Ogarkov noted in 1982 that the principal military operation that the Soviet armed forces could expect to have to carry out was the theater-strategic operation, or strategic operation in a theater of military action.[83] This has been brought about by the revolutions in military affairs, including the development of thermonuclear weapons, advances in electronics, weapons based on new physical principles, and qualitative improvements in conventional weapons.[84] Awareness of the dialectical process by which older weapons and approaches to combat are replaced by newer ones, according to Ogarkov, has never been more important than now, when principal weapons systems are "virtually renewed every 10–12 years."[85] A dialectical contradiction is especially manifest in the process of troop control (*upravleniye voyskami*):

In present-day conditions, where the potential adversary possesses weapons which make it possible to launch surprise attacks and execute swift maneuver and redeployment of troops, only a few weeks or even a few days can be allocated for preparation. Therefore, in conditions of increasingly more highly-dynamic combat operations and nontypicalness of combat situation, greater flexibility (*gibkost'*) and efficiency (*operativnost'*) of leadership are demanded of commanders and staffs than ever before.[86]

In a similar fashion, Kir'yan writes in 1982 of the impacts of new technology for weapons and command systems and of the interaction effects of improvements in one field upon the other. The increasing complexity and great dynamism of combat operations, according to Kir'yan, requires improvement in the controllability (*upravlyaemosti*) of formations and units on the battlefield.[87] Controllability is influenced by the troops' swiftness in reacting to changes in the combat situation and depends on the number of combat units and subunits, their mobility, and the technical and procedural methods used to control the troops when they are engaged in fighting. Even earlier, during the nuclear revolution in military affairs, it was found that commanders spent too much time passing information back and forth, making decisions, and disseminating the results of those decisions. This was for many reasons, among them a loss of command and control owing to overburdened multilevel chains of command.[88]

With the nuclear revolution having been supplemented by the revolution in electronics and communications technology, combat would move even faster, and the room for error in making decisions too slowly was even smaller. The Soviets had always believed, almost to the point of obsession, that time was of the essence in combat decision making, regardless of whether they were fighting on the operational offensive or defensive.[89] It is frequently and erroneously assumed in the West that Soviet military commanders and planners are obsessed with time only because they favor offensive military doctrines that stake everything on quick and decisive victories. The Soviet interest in time is much deeper in its philosophical and organizational roots. The Soviets have learned from Clausewitz and from their own experiences in war that the more time an operation takes to complete, the more things can go wrong.[90] This is why they are so concerned about combat stability or viability (*zhivuchest'*), sometimes translated as "survivability." The concept of viability in its broadest compass means that the sustainable cohesion of the Soviet forces, compared to their opponents' forces, will withstand the strain of combat.[91]

If the Soviets do a better job of maintaining combat viability than their opponents do, then Soviet commanders will be able to make the pertinent decisions about offensive *or* defensive operations in a timely manner. Timely decisions are those that can be completed within the time available before the opponent makes a move that prevents your making the move you had planned. To move within this "critical" time cycle, your control cycle must allow for observation, decision, and action (the old OODA loop) in a period of time shorter than the available critical time.[92] Under the impact of changing technologies and faster-moving operations, timely decision making and reaction become more difficult to accomplish.

One approach is to decentralize decision making by reducing the number of echelons through which orders have to pass. However, this may add unevenly to the span of control of certain commanders, who now must deal directly with too many subordinates.[93] To solve this problem, Soviet planners have turned to new technical methods designed to improve the "effectiveness of command and control" (*effektivnosti upravleniya*) while maintaining "unity of administrative and combat division" (*edinstva organizatsionnogo i boevogo deleniya*).[94] The possibility now exists that a modular approach to combat tasking may be necessary under the expected conditions of fluid combat patterns and organizational uncertainty. Organization of troops must provide, according to Kir'yan, for flexible reaction to the situation by creating an operational configuration (*operativnoye postroeniye*) that can be adapted to the prevailing conditions.[95] In some sense this is nothing new to Soviet military planners; since World War II their approach to combat has emphasized the use of combined arms and flexible tasking of subordinate units by commanders at the *front* and *army* level.[96] However, in the future this will not suffice, and decentralization of initiative down to the tactical level will somehow have to be amalgamated with the traditional Soviet propensity for centralized control.[97]

DEFENSE

The second issue, relative to the anticipated relationship between technologies for weapons and control and the organizational or operational aspects of armies, is the relationship between offense and defense. The Soviets' well-known interest in Clausewitz as a military theorist appeared not to extend to his dictum that defense is the stronger form of war. Soviet military operations below the level of strategic nuclear war were thought by many U.S. analysts to have a strictly offensive character. Defense was thought to be acceptable to Soviet commanders only temporarily, when it was forced upon them by unexpected events or by their own (temporary) military weaknesses. Recent changes in Soviet military doctrine have now added uncertainty and turbulence to this picture. A new center of gravity, variously described as reasonable or defensive sufficiency, has emerged in the literature contributed by leading Soviet political and military thinkers. According to the various logics of reasonable or defensive sufficiency, the future Soviet armed forces might be designed and operated for the conduct of defensive but not offensive operations at levels above the tactical.[98]

The implications of the electronics, communications, and conventional weapons (precision guidance) revolutions for the operational and operational-strategic defensive are not fully clear to Soviet planners. In their discussion of the essence of defensive combat, Reznichenko, Vorob'yev, and Miroshnichenko in 1987 summarized the traditional goals of defensive operations. Defensive operations include massing forces in some sectors while carrying out holding actions or limited incursions in others.[99] In addition, defensive operations serve to repel enemy counterattacks after a successful Soviet offensive. Covering the flanks and rear of advancing Soviet forces is accomplished through defensive operations. However, these are all very traditional missions associated with the use of defensive operations in support of an offensive military strategy. The implications of defensive sufficiency for future force structure and military operations may be more far-reaching. On both the offensive and the defensive, modern military forces have to take into account the new aspects of battlefield mobility, reconnaissance, and the almost instantaneous conversion of offensive into defensive operations and back gain.

The Soviet conceptual framework for military planning emphasizes the correct forecasting of the nature of future war.[100] Looking ahead to the latter 1990s and beyond, their military planners foresee an important impact on conventional warfare caused by technological developments in each of three areas: improved accuracy, greater lethality, and longer range.[101] The relationship between offense and defense will be affected by these developments. The range of the battlefield will be extended, and the rate at which people and material are used up will almost certainly increase. Helicopters used in conjunction with air- and space-based reconnaissance, together with precision weapons launched from land-based and airborne platforms, will create an air-land battle space of increased size and complexity.[102] Careful attention has been paid by Soviet forecasters to the NATO concepts for deep strike and to the U.S. Army planning framework known as AirLand Battle. U.S. military specialists, according to some Soviet analysts, have developed the concept of air-land operations with the purpose of destroying the enemy throughout the entire depth of his army's operational formation.

The most important technical development contributory toward this mission is the creation of high-precision weapons. In the view of "foreign specialists," according to Soviet writers, reconnaissance-strike or reconnaissance-fire complexes are the most effective form of precision weapon. High-precision weapons and reconnaissance systems are coordinated by automated control systems, which make it possible to conduct reconnaissance and destruction missions "practically in real time." The PLSS (Precision Location Strike System) and the Assault Breaker systems are described as exemplary of the capabilities of these proposed Western systems.[103]

The military potential of these and other reconnaissance-attack complexes interests Soviet planners on account of their potential impact on operations, and therefore on future decisions with regard to force structure (operative configurations). One implication of the combination of precision weapons with improved reconnaissance is that defenses may now have the same opportunity for surprise and decisiveness that was previously attributed to offenses only. The choice of the time of encounter has "ceased to be an exclusive attribute of the attacker," according to one Polish military analyst.[104] In the classical concept of Clausewitz, according to Colonel Stanislaw Koziej, the essence of the defense is to await the blow. The attacker chooses the timing and direction of attack, after which the defender can parry the blow. Future long-range weapons may change this relationship between defender passiveness and attacker activeness:

Now the defender, being able to reach the enemy at distant pre-battle positions, on march routes, and in assembly regions, does not have to only wait for the blow, i.e., for the strike. He himself can make the decision about the beginning of the battle. . . . The weaker can suddenly become the stronger. Therefore, the defender is not fated to a prolonged stay in the role of the weaker side; he can and should be prepared for a change in the conditions and type of operations being conducted, for crossing over from defender to attacker in case such a possibility arises.[105]

POLITICS

The correlation of political forces can hardly be separated from the balance of power (in the Western nomenclature) or from the correlation of military forces (in the preferred Soviet rendering). What the war is about and who has joined the battle, and on which sides, are decisive for the determination of military outcomes. The correlation of political forces is a complex issue because it requires military planners and political leaders to make estimates about intra-state and inter-state variables in order to forecast the intentions and capabilities of potential adversaries.[106] The decision-making process within another state can be as important a determinant of its foreign and military policies as the size of its weapons inventory or the program for military force modernization.[107] One of the asymmetries in Western and Soviet politico-military studies has been the comparative openness of Western national-security decision making. This has had the unfortunate by-product of "mirror imaging" Western values and decision criteria onto Soviet leaders in order to explain Soviet decisions retroactively, in the absence of hard-and-fast information about what actually happened.[108]

We cannot go into all aspects of the political correlation of forces here, nor cover comprehensively the problem of decision making. One example of decision making that is pertinent to the problem of future military balances in Europe is the question of comparative military doctrine. Jack Snyder's study of French, German, and Russian military doctrines prior to World War I revealed that they were the results of rational policy analysis, motivational biases, and doctrinal simplifications in operational and tactical content.[109] Barry R. Posen's study of comparative military doctrines noted that perceptions of the international balance of power and the organizational perspectives of military institutions interact in subtle ways to determine whether a state's military doctrines are offensive or defensive.[110] In addition, a nation's military doctrine reflects its degree of optimism or pessimism about the prospects for preserving peace or getting into war; its expectation of fatalism or perceived sense of control over events once engaged in war; and its flexibility in conducting campaigns and operations, including operations that might contribute to ending war. In short, military doctrines have pregame, midgame, and endgame aspects of which there is too little comparative study.

Current estimates of future balances of military power based on extrapolations of present trends could prove misleading. More than once the major powers of Europe have embarked on war that was expected to be short and destructive, only to experience one that was much longer and even more destructive.[111] Thanks in part to military doctrines that emphasized the offensive as the key to rapid and decisive military victory, at least three major powers in World War I plunged into an extended stalemate in the mistaken expectation that the first weeks or months of combat would tell the tale.[112] Compared to present expectations, future wars fought below the nuclear threshold might be intense *and* long, not intense and short. There is some indication that the Soviets have begun to take this possibility more seriously in their military writing and planning scenarios.[113] Michael MccGwire has noted that an important shift took place during the 1960s in the Soviet expectation about whether world war would automatically grow out of regional war in Europe or, if so, whether a global war had to be a nuclear war.[114] The Soviets subsequently established the avoidance of the nuclear devastation of the Soviet Union as a more important policy objective within their framework of military art and military strategic planning. It followed that future Soviet force structure could be based on the assumption of a greater likelihood for conventional war in Europe, followed by a second phase of global war remaining below the nuclear threshold (although not guaranteed to do so, since much depends upon what NATO or the Americans do).[115]

This new hierarchy of military objectives has been taken a step further by Gorbachev, who now avers that "Clausewitz's dictum that war is the continuation of policy only by different means, which was classical in his time, has grown hopelessly out of date. It now belongs to the libraries. . . . A new dialectic of strength and security follows from the impossibility of a military—that is, nuclear—solution to international differences."[116] Elsewhere in the same source Gorbachev notes that weapons of mass destruction have created an "objective limit" on class confrontation, although it would be wrong to "ignore the class heterogeneity of the forces acting in the international arena or to overlook the influence of class antagonisms" on international affairs.[117] This may suggest that more can be gleaned from the Soviet view of the political and economic correlation of forces between the blocs, with regard to predictions of the degree of military stability, than can be got from comparative measures of military balance or from force modeling exercises as they are frequently conducted in the West.[118] If the Soviet expectation is that Western societies lack internal cohesion, their economies are performing inadequately, and their political institutions fail to cast an aura of legitimacy for bodies politic, then military adventurism seems more tempting. On the other hand, if economic growth, political stability, and parliamentary-democratic legitimacy seem high in Western Europe, the prospects for destabilization through coercion or actual violence are more remote. The reverse of this is also true. If the economies, polities, and societies of Eastern Europe are seen as crumbling, the Soviet motivation to turn to military protectivism for the preservation of a political glacis is enhanced. Offensive military doctrines and war are born of desperation as much as they are of opportunism.

CONCLUSION

Military stability involves more than a balance of power or a series of force deployments. The components of military stability in Europe include all those factors contributory to political expectations, military doctrines, and force deployments which are conducive to war or preventive of it. Political expectations are in the largest sense the determining elements in this equation. Forces and doctrines that seem benign according to one constellation of political environments seem downright mischievous when that constellation is rearranged. Even with benign political environments and permissive military conditions, peace is not guaranteed. The process of making forces ready for deployment or combat can itself trigger sudden changes in the expectation of violence and subsequent loss of control. The problem of control is the subject of the next three chapters, which deal sequentially with the problems of escalation, command and control, and war termination, with emphasis on the Soviet view of these matters.

NOTES

1. John J. Mearsheimer, *Conventional Deterrence* (Ithaca, N.Y.: Cornell University Press, 1983).

2. Jack Snyder, *The Ideology of the Offensive: Military Decision Making and the Disasters of 1914* (Ithaca, N.Y.: Cornell University Press, 1984).

3. Richard Ned Lebow, *Between Peace and War: the Nature of International Crisis* (Baltimore: Johns Hopkins University Press, 1981).

4. Geoffrey Blainey, *The Causes of War* (New York: Free Press, 1973), Ch. 3.

5. See Richard Betts, *Surprise Attack: Lessons for Defense Planning* (Washington: Brookings Institution, 1982), esp. comments in Ch. 6 on defensive surprise as pertinent to NATO-Pact scenarios.

6. See Donald C. Daniel and Katherine L. Herbig, eds., *Strategic Military Deception* (New York: Pergamon Press, 1982); and Brian D. Dailey and Patrick J. Parker, eds., *Soviet Strategic Deception* (Lexington, Mass.: Lexington Books, 1987). See also M. M. Kir'yan et al., *Vnezapnost' v nastupatelnykh operatsiyakh velikoy Otechestvennoy voyny* (Surprise in offensive operations of the Great Patriotic War) (Moscow: Nauka, 1987), Ch. 1. This study contains numerous important references to other primary sources on the Soviet use of surprise and deception in World War II.

7. David N. Schwartz, *NATO's Nuclear Dilemmas* (Washington: Brookings Institution, 1983).

8. John Erickson, Lynn Hansen, and William Schneider, *Soviet Ground Forces: An Operational Assessment* (Boulder, Colo.: Westview Press, 1986), p. 55.

9. Thomas C. Schelling, *The Strategy of Conflict* (Cambridge, Mass.: Harvard University Press, 1960), pp. 207–29.

10. For more on this, see Robert Jervis, *The Illogic of American Nuclear Strategy* (Ithaca, N.Y.: Cornell University Press, 1984).

11. See Lawrence Freedman, "The Wilderness Years," Ch. 2 in Jeffrey D. Boutwell, Paul Doty, and Gregory F. Treverton, eds., *The Nuclear Confrontation in Europe* (London: Croom Helm, 1985), pp. 44–66.

12. Paul Kennedy, *The Rise and Fall of the Great Powers: Economic Change and Military Conflict from 1500 to 2000* (New York: Random House, 1987).

13. For comments on this and a résumé of recent U.S. government views on civil defense, see Federal Emergency Management Agency, *Recovery from Nuclear Attack* (Washington, D.C.: FEMA, October 1988).

14. Mearsheimer, *Conventional Deterrence*, Ch. 2.

15. Desmond Ball, "The Development of the SIOP, 1960–1983," Ch. 3 in Ball and Jeffrey Richelson, eds., *Strategic Nuclear Targeting* (Ithaca, N.Y.: Cornell University Press, 1986), pp. 57–83.

16. McNamara, quoted in Lawrence Freedman, *The Evolution of Nuclear Strategy* (New York: St. Martin's Press, 1981), p. 235.

17. Ibid., Ch. 16. See also Freedman, "The First Two Generations of Nuclear Strategists," Ch. 25 in Peter Paret, ed., *Makers of Modern Strategy* (Princeton, N.J.: Princeton University Press, 1986), pp. 735–78; Alain C. Enthoven and K. Wayne Smith, *How Much Is Enough? Shaping the Defense Program, 1961–69* (New York: Harper and Row, 1971).

18. The point is emphasized in Thomas C. Schelling, *Arms and Influence* (New Haven, Conn.: Yale University Press, 1966), p. 105ff.

19. Admiral James D. Watkins, USN, "The Maritime Strategy," *Proceedings of the U.S. Naval Institute*, January 1986, pp. 2–17; see also John J. Mearsheimer, "A Strategic Misstep: The Maritime Strategy and Deterrence in Europe," *International Security* 11, no. 2 (Fall 1986), pp. 3–57, for a critique.

20. Chris Bellamy, *The Future of Land Warfare* (New York: St. Martin's Press, 1987).

21. For an opposed view, see Robert S. McNamara, *Blundering Into Disaster: Surviving the First Century of the Nuclear Age* (New York: Pantheon Books, 1986).

22. Richard Smoke, *War: Controlling Escalation* (Cambridge, Mass.: Harvard University Press, 1977), Ch. 10, esp. pp. 268–77.

23. Luigi Albertini, *The Origins of the War of 1914*, Vol. II, translated and edited by

Isabella M. Massey (London: Oxford University Press, 1953); see also Snyder, *Ideology of the Offensive, passim.*

24. Michael Doyle, "Endemic Surprise? Strategic Surprises in First World–Third World Relations," Ch. 4 in Klaus Knorr and Patrick M. Morgan, eds., *Strategic Military Surprise: Incentives and Opportunities* (New Brunswick, N.J.: Transaction Books, 1983), pp. 77–110.

25. Important analyses and accounts of Cuba 1962 include Graham T. Allison, *Essence of Decision: Explaining the Cuban Missile Crisis* (Boston: Little, Brown, 1971); Elie Abel, *The Missile Crisis* (New York: Bantam Books, 1966). Meetings between U.S. and Soviet crisis decision-making participants in the 1980s have expanded significantly the archive of information about this confrontation, as have ongoing studies by the John F. Kennedy School of Public Policy, Harvard University. See McGeorge Bundy and James L. Blight, "October 27, 1962: Transcripts of the Meetings of the ExComm," *International Security* 12 (Winter 1987-88), pp. 30–92.

26. *Philadelphia Inquirer*, July 6, 1989.

27. See Phillip B. Davidson, *Vietnam at War* (Novato, Cal.: Presidio Press, 1988).

28. Albert Seaton, *The Russo-German War 1941–45* (New York: Praeger Publishers, 1971); see also Field Marshal Erich von Manstein, *Lost Victories* (Chicago: Henry Regnery Company, 1958).

29. Fred Charles Ikle, *Every War Must End* (New York: Columbia University Press, 1971), pp. 42ff.

30. Leon V. Sigal, *Fighting to a Finish: The Politics of War Termination in the United States and Japan, 1945* (Ithaca, N.Y.: Cornell University Press, 1988).

31. Ibid.

32. See P. H. Vigor, *Soviet Blitzkrieg Theory* (New York: St. Martin's Press, 1983).

33. Mikhail Gorbachev, *Perestroika: New Thinking for Our Country and the World* (New York: Harper and Row, 1987), Ch. 3–4, 6. I am indebted to Vernon V. Aspaturian for the opportunity to read a draft paper pertinent to this issue.

34. Peter H. Vigor, "Western Perceptions of Soviet Strategic Thought and Doctrine," Ch. 2 in Gregory Flynn, ed., *Soviet Military Doctrine and Western Policy* (London: Routledge, 1989), pp. 29–105.

35. See M. M. Kir'yan, *Voyenno-tekhnicheskiy progress i vooruzhennye sily SSSR* (Moscow: Voyenizdat, 1985).

36. Marshal N. V. Ogarkov, *Vsegda v gotovnosti k zashchite Otechestva* (Moscow: Voyenizdat, 1982), pp. 29–34.

37. Harriet Fast Scott and William F. Scott, *Soviet Military Doctrine: Continuity, Formulation and Dissemination* (Boulder, Colo.: Westview Press, 1988).

38. See Condoleezza Rice, "The Making of Soviet Strategy," Ch. 22 in Paret, ed., *Makers of Modern Strategy*, pp. 648–76.

39. Robert Arnett and Mary C. Fitzgerald, *Restructuring the Armed Forces: The Current Soviet Debate*, draft paper (1989) has been most helpful on this topic.

40. Ibid.

41. Andrey A. Kokoshin and Maj. Gen. Valentin Larionov, "The Confrontation of Conventional Forces in the Context of Ensuring Strategic Stability," *Mirovaya ekonomika i mezhdunarodnye otnosheniya* 6 (June 1988), pp. 23–31. I am grateful to Leon Goure and Mary Fitzgerald for pointing out pertinent sources.

42. A summary of European nonoffensive defense plans appears in Paul Rogers, "The Nuclear Connection," *Bulletin of the Atomic Scientists*, September 1988, pp. 20–23. Especially valuable in the same issue are Horst Afheldt, "New Policies, Old Fears,"

pp. 24–28, and John Grin and Lutz Unterseher, "The Spiderweb Defense," pp. 28–30. A critique of nonoffensive defense proposals is offered by Stephen Flanagan in the same issue, and by Josef Joffe, *The Limited Partnership: Europe, the United States and the Burdens of Alliance* (Cambridge, Mass.: Ballinger Publishing Co., 1987), Ch. 4, pp. 148–65.

43. M. A. Gareev, *M. V. Frunze: Military Theorist* (New York: Pergamon Brassey's, 1988), p. 160, notes that Frunze viewed the defensive not only as a necessary type of strategic action but also as one method for allocating forces efficiently over a broad front. The success of offensive operations on the main sectors could only be assured if defensive operations were conducted elsewhere. (This is a translation of the 1985 Soviet publication.)

44. A. Kokoshin and V. Larionov, "The Battle of Kursk in Light of Contemporary Defensive Doctrine," *Mirovaya ekonomika i mezhdunarodnye otnosheniya* 8 (1987), pp. 32–40.

45. See Jacob W. Kipp, *The Methodology of Foresight and Forecasting in Soviet Military Affairs* (Fort Leavenworth, Kans.: Soviet Army Studies Office, 1987); and Yu. V. Chuyev and Yu. B. Mikhaylov, *Prognozirovaniye v voyennom dele* (Forecasting in military affairs) (Moscow: Voyenizdat, 1975), U.S. Air Force Soviet Military Thought Series.

46. Raymond L. Garthoff, "Soviet Perceptions of Western Strategic Thought and Doctrine," Ch. 4 in Flynn, ed., *Soviet Military Doctrine and Western Policy*, pp. 197–328; Garthoff, "BMD and East-West Relations," Ch. 8 in Ashton B. Carter and David N. Schwartz, eds., *Ballistic Missile Defense* (Washington: Brookings Institution, 1984), pp. 275–329; Benjamin S. Lambeth, "Soviet Perspectives on the SDI," Ch. 2 in Samuel F. Wells, Jr., and Robert S. Littwak, eds., *Strategic Defenses and Soviet-American Relations* (Cambridge, Mass.: Ballinger Publishing Co., 1987), pp. 37–78.

47. Barry M. Blechman and Douglas M. Hart, "The Political Utility of Nuclear Weapons: The 1973 Middle East Crisis," *International Security* 7, no. 1 (Summer 1982), reprinted in Steven E. Miller, ed., *Strategy and Nuclear Deterrence* (Princeton, N.J.: Princeton University Press, 1984), pp. 273–97.

48. Schlesinger, in ABC News documentary drama, "The Crisis Game," quoted in Thomas B. Allen, *War Games* (New York: Berkeley Books, 1987), p. 235; see also Blechman and Hart, "The Political Utility of Nuclear Weapons," p. 278.

49. Blechman and Hart, "Political Utility of Nuclear Weapons."

50. Patrick M. Morgan, *Deterrence: A Conceptual Analysis* (Second Edition) (Beverly Hills, Cal.: Sage Publications, 1983), Ch. 2 and Ch. 3 distinguish general from specific or immediate deterrence.

51. Major-General Chaim Herzog, *The War of Atonement: October 1973* (Boston: Little, Brown, 1975).

52. Snyder, *Ideology of the Offensive*, Ch. 8.

53. Blainey, *The Causes of War*, Ch. 3, pp. 13–14.

54. Snyder, *Ideology of the Offensive, passim*; see also Michael Howard, "Men Against Fire: The Doctrine of the Offensive in 1914," Ch. 18 in Paret, ed., *Makers of Modern Strategy*, pp. 510–26.

55. Blainey, *The Causes of War*, p. 41, notes that expectations of a short war and of a victorious outcome go together in many leaders' estimates.

56. Ikle, *Every War Must End*, pp. 42–50.

57. See David Alan Rosenberg, "The Origins of Overkill: Nuclear Weapons and American Strategy, 1945–1960," *International Security* 7, no. 4 (Spring 1983), reprinted in Miller, ed., *Strategy and Nuclear Deterrence*, pp. 113–82.

58. Barry R. Posen, "Inadvertent Nuclear War? Escalation and NATO's Northern Flank," *International Security* 7, no. 2 (Fall 1982), reprinted in Miller, ed., *Strategy and Nuclear Deterrence*, pp. 85–112; Mearsheimer, "A Strategic Misstep," *passim*. For counterpoint, see Capt. Linton F. Brooks, USN, "Naval Power and National Security: The Case for a Maritime Strategy," *International Security* 11, no. 2 (Fall 1986), pp. 58–88. Capt. Peter M. Swartz has published several editions of the most comprehensive bibliography on U.S. maritime strategy; see, for example, the abbreviated version in the January 1986 issue of *Proceedings of the U.S. Naval Institute*.

59. See Desmond Ball, "U.S. Strategic Forces: How Would They Be Used?" *International Security* 7, no. 3 (Winter 1982-83), pp. 31–60.

60. However, Soviet reactions to the early Reagan nuclear strategy, as they understood it, were vehement. See Garthoff, "Soviet Perceptions of Western Strategic Thought and Doctrine," *passim*, and Garthoff, *Detente and Confrontation: U.S.–Soviet Relations from Nixon to Reagan* (Washington: Brookings Institution, 1985), pp. 1018–19. According to Garthoff, Soviet leaders saw the last years of the Carter military doctrine and the first years of Reagan defense policy as a continuous trend, in which the United States (from the Soviet perspective) "abandoned mutual deterrence based on parity and substituted a drive for superiority in war-waging capabilities in order to provide escalation dominance at all levels of nuclear and non-nuclear engagement." (Garthoff, *Detente and Confrontation*, p. 1019.) It is not without significance that the first chapter of Marshal Ogarkov's 1982 *Always in Readiness to Defend the Homeland* is entitled "Imperialism—the Source of Military Danger." In this chapter Ogarkov points specifically to the Reagan administration's "new military strategy" of "direct confrontation" (*pryamogo protivoborstva*) based on "active countermeasures" (*aktivnogo protivodeystviya*) and "geographical escalation" (*geograficheskoy eskalatsii*). Ogarkov, *Vsegda v gotovnosti k zashchite Otechestva*, pp. 15–16.

61. Paul H. Nitze, "Assuring Strategic Stability in an Era of Detente," *Foreign Affairs* 54 (1976), pp. 207–33.

62. General-Major S. N. Kozlov, ed., *Spravochnik ofitsera* (Officer's handbook) (Moscow: Voyenizdat, 1971). U.S. Air Force Soviet Military Thought Series (Washington: U.S. GPO, undated), p. 13.

63. Ibid., p. 15.

64. See Edward L. Warner III, "Defense Policymaking in the Soviet Union," Ch. 1 in Robert J. Art, Vincent Davis, and Samuel P. Huntington, eds., *Reorganizing America's Defense: Leadership in War and Peace* (New York: Pergamon Brassey's, 1985), pp. 3–36; and Stephen M. Meyer, "Civilian and Military Influence in the USSR," Ch. 2, pp. 37–61 in the same volume.

65. L. I. Brezhnev, "Outstanding Exploit of the Defenders of Tula," *Pravda*, January 19, 1977, cf. Garthoff, *Detente and Confrontation*, p. 771.

66. On comparative U.S. and Soviet capabilities, see Congress of the United States, Congressional Budget Office, *Modernizing U.S. Strategic Offensive Forces: Costs, Effects, and Alternatives* (Washington: Congressional Budget Office, November 1987), Appendices C and D; *Report of the Secretary of Defense Frank C. Carlucci to the Congress on Amended FY 1988/FY 1989 Biennial Budget* (Washington: U.S. GPO, February 18, 1988), pp. 25–26; *Report of the Secretary of Defense Frank C. Carlucci to the Congress on the FY 1990/FY 1991 Biennial Budget and FY 1990–94 Defense Programs* (Washington: U.S. GPO, January 17, 1989), pp. 13–17, 181–95; U.S. Department of Defense, *Soviet Military Power: An Assessment of the Threat* (Washington: U.S.

GPO, April 1988), pp. 44–67, 96–105; International Institute for Strategic Studies, *The Military Balance 1988–89* (London: IISS, Autumn 1988), p. 230, pp. 13–44.

67. On this see Garthoff, "Mutual Deterrence, Parity and Strategic Arms Limitation in Soviet Policy," Ch. 5 in Derek Leebaert, ed., *Soviet Military Thinking* (London: Allen and Unwin, 1981), pp. 92–125. The difficulty in establishing any consensus between U.S. and Soviet views of parity and equivalence is that there is often no consensus within the U.S. government per se, or among NATO allies. On the various possible meanings of parity and equivalence, see Richard K. Betts, "Elusive Equivalence: The Political and Military Meaning of the Nuclear Balance," Ch. 3 in Samuel P. Huntington, ed., *The Strategic Imperative: New Policies for National Security* (Cambridge, Mass.: Ballinger Publishing Co., 1982), pp. 101–40. U.S. politicians and analysts have used the terms *parity* and *equivalence* to convey any one or more of the following meanings: (1) both sides have *second strike countervalue* capabilities; (2) both sides can inflict retaliatory damage *unprecedented in history*; (3) both the Americans and the Soviets have *more than enough for the assured destruction mission*; (4) each superpower is capable of *extending deterrence to protect its allies* by virtue of its assured destruction and (depending on the analyst) other capabilities; (5) each side has enough retaliatory capability such that major and *politically unacceptable* damage to the attacker is guaranteed, regardless of the consequences of first strike.

68. *Philadelphia Inquirer*, July 7, 1989.

69. Marshal of the Soviet Union and Chief of the General Staff Sergey Akhromeyev, "Doktrina predotvrashcheniya voyny, zashchity mira i sotsializma," *Problemy mira i sotsializma* 12 (December 1987), pp. 23–28, this citation p. 24.

70. Ibid., p. 25.

71. Minister of Defense of the USSR D. T. Yazov, "Voennaya doktrina Varshavskogo Dogovora—doktrina zashchity mira i sotsializma," *Krasnaya zvezda*, July 28, 1987, p. 2.

72. Akhromeyev, "Doktrina predotvrashcheniya," p. 27.

73. Colonel (Polkovnik) M. P. Skirdo, *Narod, armiya, polkovodets* (The people, the army, the commander) (Moscow: Voyenizdat, 1970), U.S. Air Force Soviet Military Thought Series (Washington: U.S. GPO, undated), p. 89.

74. Scott and Scott, *Soviet Military Doctrine*, pp. 28–44; see also V. D. Sokolovskiy, ed., *Voyennaya strategiya* (Moscow: Voyenizdat, 1962). Subsequent editions appeared in 1963 and 1968. The various editions are compared in Harriet F. Scott, ed., *Soviet Military Strategy* (New York: Crane, Russak and Co., 1984).

75. Gareev, *M. V. Frunze*, p. 216.

76. Ibid.

77. Ogarkov, *Vsegda*, p. 16.

78. Kir'yan, *Voyenno-tekhnicheskiy progress*.

79. Ibid., p. 293.

80. Ibid., p. 282.

81. Ibid.

82. Ibid.

83. Ogarkov, *Vsegda*, pp. 34–35.

84. Ibid., p. 31.

85. Ibid.

86. Ibid., p. 26.

87. Kir'yan, *Voyenno-tekhnicheskiy progress*, p. 299.

88. Ibid.

89. See Nathan Leites, *Soviet Style in War* (Santa Monica, Cal.: RAND Corporation, 1982), pp. 87–135.

90. P. H. Vigor, *Soviet Blitzkrieg Theory* (New York: St. Martin's Press, 1983), Ch. 1.

91. C. N. Donnelly et al., *Sustainability of the Soviet Army in Battle* (The Hague: SHAPE Technical Center, STC CR-65, September 1986).

92. See D. A. Ivanov, V. P. Savel'yev, and P. V. Shemanskiy, *Osnovy upravleniya voyskami v boyu* (Moscow: Voyenizdat, 1977), pp. 167–68 and *passim*. See also the discussion of the relationship between "required time" and "available time" for the accomplishment of tasks of control in Colonel-General P. K. Altukhov et al., *Basis of the Theory of Troop Control* (Moscow: Voyenizdat, 1984). I am grateful to Jacob W. Kipp for calling this source to my attention. According to Army General Pyotr Lushev, now C-in-C of the Warsaw Pact Armed Forces, "the slightest blunder, or poor organization of the troop control system may be used by the enemy to uncover the concept of military operations, to launch preemptive attacks, and to foil a planned maneuver in an operation or battle." See Lushev, "Iskusstvo upravleniya voyskami," *Sovetskoye voyennoye Obozreniye*, January 1983, pp. 9–12.

93. Kir'yan, *Voyenno-tekhnicheskiy progress*, p. 299.

94. Ibid., pp. 299–300.

95. Ibid.

96. See Col. David M. Glantz, *Deep Attack: The Soviet Conduct of Operational Maneuver* (Fort Leavenworth, Kans.: Soviet Army Studies Office, April 1987). Of special interest with regard to Soviet experience in the third period of the Great Patriotic War is the conduct of the Belorussian campaign; see B. V. Panov, V. N. Kiselev, I. I. Kartavtsev et al., *Istoriya voyennogo iskusstva* (Moscow: Voyenizdat, 1984), Ch. 8, and John Erickson, *The Road to Berlin* (Boulder, Colo.: Westview Press, 1983), pp. 200–30.

97. John Hemsley, *Soviet Troop Control: The Role of Command Technology in the Soviet Military System* (London: Brassey's Publishers, 1982).

98. See Stephen M. Meyer, "The Sources and Prospects of Gorbachev's New Political Thinking on Security," *International Security* 13, no. 2 (Fall 1988), pp. 124–63; and Raymond L. Garthoff, "New Thinking in Soviet Military Doctrine," *Washington Quarterly* 11, no. 3 (Summer 1988), pp. 131–58.

99. Reznichenko et al. (1987), Ch. 1, part 2.

100. Soviet Army Studies Office, *Soviet Future War* (Fort Leavenworth, Kans.: Soviet Army Studies Office, Combined Arms Center, U.S. Army Command and General Staff College, 1987). See also Dr. Jacob W. Kipp, *Conventional Force Modernization and the Asymmetries of Military Doctrine: Historical Reflections on AirLand Battle and the Operational Maneuver Group* (Fort Leavenworth, Kans.: Soviet Army Studies Office, Combined Arms Center, U.S. Army Command and General Staff College, undated).

101. Soviet planning methodology emphasizes the mathematical modeling of pertinent operational indicators to the extent possible. See the discussion of Soviet approaches to calculation of the correlation of forces within a TSMA, and to calculation of the necessary forces for the main thrust sector within a multi-front operation, in Phillip A. Petersen and Notra Trulock III, "Equal Security: Greater Stability at Lower Force Levels," Ch. 5 in William B. Taylor, Jr., ed., *Beyond Burdensharing: Future Alliance Defense Cooperation* (Brussels, Belgium: U.S. Mission to NATO, Alliance Papers Proceedings No. 1, April 1989), pp. 61–92. Also important are Donnelly et al., *Sus-*

tainability, passim; John J. Yurechko, "Command and Control for Coalitional Warfare: The Soviet Approach," *Signal* 40, no. 4 (December 1985), pp. 31–44; and John G. Hines, "How Much Is Enough for Theater War? The Soviet Military Approach to Sufficiency of Conventional Forces in Europe," *NATO-Warsaw Pact Conventional Force Balance: Papers for U.S. and Soviet Perspectives Workshops* (Washington, D.C.: U.S. General Accounting Office, December 1988), Appendix X, pp. 224–61.

102. Reznichenko et al. (1987), Ch. 1, part 1.

103. Ibid.

104. Col. Stanislaw Koziej, "Anticipated Directions for Change in Tactics of Ground Troops," *Przeglad Wojsk Ladowych* (September 1986), pp. 5–9. Translated by Dr. Harold Orenstein, Soviet Army Studies Office, Fort Leavenworth, Kansas.

105. Ibid.

106. See Ernest R. May, "Conclusions: Capabilities and Proclivities," in May, ed., *Knowing One's Enemies: Intelligence Assessment before the Two World Wars* (Princeton, N.J.: Princeton University Press, 1984), pp. 503–42.

107. On decision-making processes, see Robert Jervis, Richard Ned Lebow, and Janice Gross Stein, *Psychology and Deterrence* (Baltimore: Johns Hopkins University Press, 1987); Lebow, "Decision Making in Crises," In Ralph K. White, ed., *Psychology and the Prevention of Nuclear War* (New York: New York University Press, 1986), pp. 397–413; Jervis, *Perception and Misperception in International Politics* (Princeton, N.J.: Princeton University Press, 1976); Alexander L. George and Richard Smoke, *Deterrence in American Foreign Policy: Theory and Practice* (New York: Columbia University Press, 1974); and Patrick M. Morgan, *Deterrence: A Conceptual Analysis*, Second Edition (Beverly Hills, Cal.: Sage Publications, 1983), Ch. 4 and 5.

108. Peter Vigor, "Western Perceptions of Soviet Strategic Thought and Doctrine."

109. Snyder, *Ideology of the Offensive*, esp. Ch. 8.

110. Barry R. Posen, *The Sources of Military Doctrine: France, Britain and Germany between the World Wars* (Ithaca, N.Y.: Cornell University Press, 1984).

111. Geoffrey Blainey, *The Causes of War* (New York: Free Press, 1973), Ch. 3.

112. Snyder, *Ideology of the Offensive, passim*.

113. See Phillip A. Petersen and Notra Trulock III, "Soviet Views on the Changing Context of Military Planning," *Journal of Soviet Military Studies* 1, no. 4 (December 1988), pp. 451–85.

114. Michael MccGwire, *Military Objectives in Soviet Foreign Policy* (Washington: Brookings Institution, 1987), Ch. 2 and Ch. 3.

115. Ibid.

116. Gorbachev, *Perestroika*, p. 141.

117. Ibid., pp. 146–48.

118. For a critique of these approaches with pertinent references, see Paul K. Davis, "The Role of Uncertainty in Assessing the NATO-Pact Central Region Balance," Appendix VII in General Accounting Office, *NATO–Warsaw Pact Conventional Force Balance*, pp. 112–52.

MIDGAME

4

Escalation and the Limitation of War: Western and Soviet Perspectives

This chapter compares Soviet and NATO doctrines with regard to the control of escalation and the limitation of war in Europe or globally. Two limitations confound comparative assessment of this type. First, the Soviet Union is in the midst of a major review of its military doctrine.[1] Academic analysts and policymakers attempting to determine the gist of Soviet military doctrine with regard to escalation, including nuclear escalation, are entering into a wilderness of mirrors. A second factor making any comparison between East and West tentative is that NATO speaks with many voices on this issue unofficially, regardless of the prevailing official policy.

These limitations are acknowledged, but the task of comparing Soviet and NATO assumptions about escalation is an urgent one. The calibration of force balances is now far ahead of the understanding of what makes crises slide downhill and wars spin out of policy control. We will look first into Soviet doctrine and then into that of NATO. In both cases the distribution of nuclear charges among general-purpose forces tasked also for conventional war creates obstacles to escalation control that may be insoluble. Nor is this all. A major issue throughout is the Soviet perception of NATO's ability to control its own nuclear dogs once they have been unleashed. The Soviet perception of NATO intent will be based on Soviet strategic culture. NATO must navigate between two dangers: Soviet fatalism that any nuclear use will automatically escape policy control and Soviet perceptions that NATO first use is a bluff born of desperation.

SOVIET DEFENSIVISM

The Soviet view of the relationship between force and policy is spelled out in military doctrine, which has various aspects. Military doctrine "consists of views officially adopted in the state and in the armed forces having to do with the nature of a potential war and means of conducting it, as well as the requirements stemming from these views relative to military development and preparation of the country and its armed forces for war."[2] The military doctrine of the Soviet Union is based on Marxist-Leninist principles that are commonly misunderstood in the West.[3] The Soviet Union is mandated to conduct the class struggle in its various forms. The class struggle is rooted in objective social conditions over which leaders have very little control. Gorbachev's declaratory policies have sometimes been interpreted as repudiations of socialism, the class struggle, and war altogether. Neither Gorbachev nor any other Soviet leader is in a position to do this.

The class struggle need not take the form of military aggression. The political leadership must assess the prevailing correlation of forces, including the political, social, economic, and moral forces. Only if these constellations are in place is war advised. As one Soviet writer notes:

The experience of history and analysis of the present situation teach us that *sober calculation of the correlation of forces between us and our adversary* constitutes an important principle of leadership in a war. Correct calculation of the correlation of forces of the warring parties enables the political and military leadership to determine what is possible and impossible in the course of war, to foresee the adversary's probable actions and to select the most effective methods and forms of armed struggle under various conditions.[4]

Sober calculation of the correlation of forces by the Soviet leadership under Gorbachev would result in the following inventory. First, the Soviet economy is lagging behind the leadership's expectations for its performance. Insufficient funds for future investment and for present consumption are available.[5] Soviet industry does not produce efficiently. Management is not tied to any system of reward for improved productivity and efficiency. Collectivized agriculture is such a failure that a series of disastrous harvests while Gorbachev held the party portfolio in that sector did nothing to delay his rise to general secretary. The Soviet economy is now being outperformed by some Third World countries, especially the NIC (newly industrialized countries) in which commercial enterprise flourishes.

Second, the Soviet armed forces have been studying very carefully their experiences during the Great Patriotic War, within some very new contexts. Two new contexts are important, and will be amplified later on. The first is the categorical rejection by the Soviet leadership since 1977 of the possibility of victory in nuclear war. In a widely reported speech at Tula, commemorating the sacrifices of persons in that city during World War II, Brezhnev declared that the Soviet Union did not seek to maintain nuclear weapons with the aim of attaining superiority or a first-strike capability.[6] The Tula speech was followed by other statements by Soviet political and military leaders that have continued to the present day. This is very much at variance with "traditional" Soviet thinking. Traditional Soviet thinking about nuclear weapons and nuclear war was that victory was possible, although losses were inevitable.[7] Degrees of preparedness for surprise and capability for damage limitation made a significant difference in war outcomes. Now preparedness for surprise and capacity for damage limitation are acknowledged as important in order to maintain a balanced force structure. They are also important for the preservation of the morale of the armed forces and the general population. Authoritative Soviet writers of the present day lay great stress on the importance of the morale factor in defense preparedness for come-as-you-are wars that the Soviet Union may have to fight.[8] However, there is no longer an expectation of victory, of suffering acceptable losses and prevailing in any meaningful political sense.

The newer Soviet appreciation of the military correlation of forces also has a second aspect. This is the revolution in military technology that includes the possible development of nonnuclear weapons of high lethality and great accuracy. The pertinent issue is not whether these weapons can be developed in the laboratories or can be field tested, for they have been. The issue is what difference they will make in strategy and operational art once they have been deployed. General M. A. Gareyev is among the Soviet authors who have called attention to this impending, postnuclear revolution in military affairs and its importance for Soviet planners. In his widely acclaimed *M. V. Frunze—Voyennyy teoretik* (M. V. Frunze—military theorist), which was awarded the Frunze prize for work in military history and theory, Gareyev critiques the authoritative *Voyennaya strategiya* (Military strategy) by V. D. Sokolovskiy. According to Gareyev, the volume edited by Sokolovskiy provided "a profound and generally correct analysis" of theory and military strategy in view of the nuclear revolution in military affairs.[9] A possible world war was still seen as a decisive clash between capitalist and socialist socioeconomic systems, as formerly.

But Gareyev also noted that a world war could begin with the employment of conventional weapons only. The assumption that any war between the major capitalist and socialist coalitions would inevitably involve nuclear weapons, be global in scope, and be short in duration was not necessarily valid. According to Gareyev:

Under present-day conditions, the outcome of a war depends significantly more than previously upon the quantity and effectiveness of the effort made at the very outset of the war. However, the strategic principle of the economy of forces as a whole survives, since it is difficult to assume a rapid war between major coalitions with their enormous potential.[10]

There is nothing new in the assertion that the Soviet armed forces should be *prepared* for war, either with or without nuclear weapons. But the expectation that war might be prolonged and conventional received impetus from political and technological sources. The Soviet reading of the U.S. defense program in the early 1980s was that the Reagan administration sought a global strategy of confrontation, based on the concept of horizontal escalation or geographical war widening.[11] This strategy was to be supported, in the Soviet view, by a U.S. buildup of its strategic and intermediate-range nuclear arsenals. The Soviets drew these conclusions from U.S. Department of Defense publications, presidential speeches, leaked Defense Guidance, and other sources.[12] (See the preceding chapter.)

This pessimistic Soviet view of U.S. strategy was all the more surprising in that it reflected a shift from the Soviet appraisal of the latter 1970s, when the party and military leadership concluded that the United States had accepted the growth of Soviet military power to a degree sufficient to establish an effective strategic parity. This appraisal was not unanimous within the Soviet party or military elite, for the concept of "military-strategic parity," as the Soviets call it, was as controversial in Moscow during the 1960s and 1970s as it was in Washington. While Brezhnev had to stand off those who were skeptical of SALT II and military détente, Carter, like Nixon before him, had to face skepticism that arms control would produce meaningful limitations or doubts that, even if it did, those limitations could be verified and enforced by treaty compliance.[13] The result in both capitals was the development of clear differences in emphasis between the sociopolitical and military-technical levels of analysis, in Soviet terms. The political leaderships continued to express interest in parity as a sufficient condition for both static and dynamic stability. But prominent Soviet and U.S. military leaders, and some European political ones, saw superpower bipolarity as insufficient to obtain dynamic (that is, crisis and escalation) stability, and some even saw U.S.–Soviet strategic nuclear parity as destructive of stability. This was one concern of former West German Chancellor Helmut Schmidt when he urged NATO to deploy new intermediate nuclear weapons in Europe in 1977. His concern was less with the static balance than with the enhanced potential for Soviet crisis coercion and wartime escalation dominance, assuming the two super-power arsenals would preclude each other's actual use.

The Soviet perception of U.S. military doctrine in the 1980s reflected more the U.S. declaratory strategy than the actual U.S. operational war plans. The Soviets saw no harm in exaggerating for effect the statements of President Reagan and Secretary of the Navy John Lehman, which paid dividends for the U.S. administration in congressional votes for expanded military budgets. It was those expanding budgets and the force structure that would result from them which concerned Moscow more than prevailing U.S. strategic doctrines. Marshal Ogarkov surely knew in 1982 that an effective strategic nuclear parity existed in static terms. The U.S. challenge to dynamic stability was a multipronged one and the Soviet General Staff was concerned with each facet: improving the U.S. strategic nuclear "triad"; conventional and theater nuclear force enhancements for American and, at American urging, allied NATO forces; and, after 1983, the U.S. Strategic Defense Initiative (SDI) research and development for ballistic missile defense. It is doubtful that Soviet planners, who think in longer ranges than Americans anyway, were all that surprised or alarmed by what they saw in U.S. declaratory policy. The Pershings and GLCMs could be negotiated out of Europe, although the Soviet strategy during Reagan's first term was ham-handed in the extreme. U.S. strategic nuclear forces might be increased in size, but the Americans could not obtain anything near to a first-strike capability (unless they perfected defenses—hence the Soviet concern over SDI). As for SDI, the Soviets were the acknowledged masters at *deploying* strategic defenses, although treaty-limited ones that provided partial rather than national territorial defense. This experience taught the Soviets painfully that the U.S. system, however, much was invested in it, could not preclude second-strike retaliation by Soviet offenses any time in the present century. Again, however, there was no harm in scoring propaganda points off SDI, especially since the U.S. defense and scientific communities were themselves divided over it.

The U.S. maritime strategy is also cast as a villain in Marshal Ogarkov's comments noted previously. But as in nuclear force structure expansion, so too in U.S. conventional force enhancement, structural growth was not accompanied by new strategic vision. Thus the threat to dynamic stability was less pronounced than Reagan critics in Washington and Moscow might suppose. The U.S. Navy was at pains to point out that its aggressive operational strategy was part of the *multilateral* war-fighting strategy for global war. It is doubtful whether U.S. naval strategists, as opposed to

Pentagon civilian ones, even used the term horizontal escalation. The Pentagon civilians were talking outside their force capabilities, in order to obtain an extra measure of declaratory deterrence by inducing Soviet uncertainties. The Soviets returned the favor by using U.S. declaratory deterrence as proof of malign intentions in arms control and political détente. Military planners on each side understood the nature of the game, but the public expressions had a life of their own. It was not until Gorbachev succeeded Chernenko and Reagan was into his second term that the public diplomacy of threat exaggeration was wound down in both capitals. When the dust had subsided, it became clearer that the Soviet perception of U.S. capabilities for global or regional war, conventional or nuclear, had not changed in essence. The Soviet perception included the assessment of the dynamics of war as well as the statics of the military balance. This steadiness of the Soviet dynamic assessment—the assessment of what Americans and NATO could actually do to them if war broke out—was the result of a long-range view of modern war, conditioned by Soviet historical military experience, careful assessments of the modern battlefield (see Chapter 2), and a coherent military doctrine at the level of operational art.

SURPRISE, THE OFFENSIVE, AND DYNAMIC STABILITY

The Soviet experience in World War II was mined for many lessons. Among them was the importance of avoiding surprise and of the decisive impact of the initial period of war. Nor have Soviet military writers downgraded surprise as an important factor in war. According to V. Z. Reznichenko, I. N. Vorob'yev, N. F. Miroshnichenko, and Yu. S. Nadirov, the element of surprise in combat operations "has long been the most important principle in the art of war."[14] Surprise is achieved by the use of new methods that the opponent does not expect, by covert concentration and large-scale use of new types of weapons unknown to the enemy, by misleading the opponent as to one's intentions, by delivering strikes where the opponent does not expect them, by the use of camouflage (*maskirovka*) and other measures to confound enemy reconnaissance, and by strict adherence to command and control procedures and communications security. The potential benefits from surprise can be decisive in the meeting engagement:

The element of surprise makes it possible to take the enemy unawares, to cause panic in his ranks, to paralyze his will to resist, to drastically reduce his fighting efficiency, to contain his operations, to disrupt his command and control, and to deny him the opportunity to take effective countermeasures quickly.[15]

Surprise is still important at the strategic and operational levels. In addition, commanders must demonstrate aggressiveness and decisiveness in the offensive. Aggressiveness and decisiveness in operations "predetermines the offensive as the main type of combat for our forces, since only an offensive that is conducted decisively, with high momentum, and in great depth, ensures the complete rout of the enemy."[16] Aggressiveness and decisiveness in the offensive are manifest primarily in attacking with nuclear weapons if they are used or, if not, with heavy fire and in "the swift advance of forces in combination with wide maneuver of personnel and equipment by land and air."[17]

It might be supposed that this emphasis on the importance of the offensive has diminished. The more recent edition of the authoritative *Taktika* (Tactics) by Reznichenko et al. gives no such indication. In the 1987 edition the authors note that offense is the "principal form" of battle. It has decisive significance for victory. Only decisive offense at a high tempo and to a great depth can guarantee the complete rout of the enemy's forces. This rout of enemy forces must be achieved in a short time by means of fire and maneuver carried out according to carefully laid down plans:

The goal of offense is attained by annihilating the enemy's nuclear and chemical weapons and his main groupings by means of strikes by missile troops, aviation and artillery fire, as well as through swift, deep advance of tank and motorized rifle subunits, units and formations interacting with aviation and airborne forces, through bold attainment of the enemy's flanks and rear, and, by encircling, dividing and defeating the enemy in parts.[18]

The later edition also emphasizes the importance of aggressiveness and decisiveness on the part of combat commanders in all situations:

High aggressiveness in a meeting engagement presupposes decisiveness and swiftness of reactions to a continually changing situation. A lack of information on the enemy cannot be used as an excuse for rejecting bold actions. Maximum aggressiveness aimed at seizing the initiative and at routing the advancing enemy *by means of like offensive actions* must be displayed constantly beginning from the moment when the vanguards and forward detachments engage the enemy in combat and nuclear and fire strikes are made against the advancing enemy grouping, and all the way until the enemy goes over to defense or retreats.[19]

In their discussion of the essence of defensive battle, Reznichenko, Vorob'yev, and Miroshnichenko (1987) summarize the traditional goals of defensive operations. These include the massing of forces and the combining of operations in some sectors while conducting holding actions or limited probes in others. Another goal of defensive operations is the repelling of enemy counterattacks following a successful Soviet offensive. Covering the flanks and rear of advancing Soviet forces is accomplished through defensive battle. Defenses were never sufficient by themselves to accomplish the defeat of the enemy; at some point, Soviet forces would have to take the offensive:

Consequently prior to the advent of nuclear weapons, defense was a special form of battle having the purpose of repelling an attack by superior enemy forces, inflicting significant losses on the enemy, holding occupied positions *and creating favorable conditions for going over to the offensive.* . . . The essence of the defense remains entirely the same today, assuming that combat operations are conducted only with conventional weapons.[20]

Conventional or Nuclear War?

The difficulty for Soviet planners is that, in the context of war in Europe, the assumption that combat operations will be conducted only with conventional weapons cannot be taken for granted. When combat operations involve nuclear weapons, the decisive strikes will be made by nuclear weapons. This entails obvious risks, but the Soviet assumption is that NATO will initiate nuclear strikes, or the planning for nuclear strikes, to which the Soviet Union must respond:

Preemptive nuclear strikes against the most important objectives of the enemy may be made during his preparations for attack in concentration areas, as his strike groupings approach the defenses, and during their deployment for attack from the line of march.[21]

Enemy pressure on Soviet defenses is expected to include nuclear strikes along with attacks from artillery, tank, and motorized rifle troops. Thus *"Osnovym sposobom dostizheniya tseley oborony yavlyatsya yadernyye udary"* (Nuclear strikes are a basic means of attaining the goals of defense).[22] However, the effects of nuclear weapons are not as precisely calculable as those of conventional weapons. Soviet writers acknowledge that "the most decisive" goal of the defense—breaking up an offensive being prepared by the opponent—can be achieved through the use of large nuclear strikes. But the use of nuclear weapons can prevent the attainment of other objectives of defensive operations:

It should be considered, however, that when nuclear weapons are employed, we cannot count on holding continuous positions with a high density of personnel and equipment. Attacking troops could create significant breaches in such positions with nuclear weapons, and strike deeply.[23]

The attacking side has the means to deliver weapons of mass destruction, including nuclear, and to deliver troops over great distances. Thus, even when going over to the defense without direct contact with the enemy, "troops must be constantly ready to recover from the enemy's use of mass destruction weapons, and to fight enemy troops dropped deep within the defenses."[24]

It might therefore be imprudent to preempt the opponent's first use of nuclear weapons if time and circumstances permitted the destruction of those weapons with conventional forces only. An important concept for the Soviets in this regard is the stability of the defense in its antinuclear aspects. This concept means attacking the enemy's nuclear weapons in the theater of military operations before he can use them, and protecting one's own forces and equipment from the enemy's nuclear attacks.[25] There are other implications of stability of the antinuclear defense that deserve mention. The first is withstanding the enemy's use of weapons of mass destruction other than nuclear. The second is resisting attack by high-precision weapons similar in range and destructive power to nuclear weapons.

On the offensive as well as when they must assume the defensive, Soviet planners are concerned about the evolution of NATO Follow-on Forces Attack (FOFA) and U.S. Army AirLand Battle Doctrine. The latter does not exclude the possible use of nuclear weapons early in the tactical battle, and FOFA calls for conventional deep strikes against mobile and stationary targets deep in the Pact operational depth.[26] The revolution in microelectronics may make possible the development of sensors and fusion centers that make the battlefield more transparent and the task of deception more difficult. Battlefield communications will become more rapid, and more attention will be paid to disruption of enemy communications or preservation of friendly ones.[27] The possibility of combined arms offensives using tanks and motorized rifle and heliborne forces will place unprecedented stresses on NATO and Pact defenses even without the use of nuclear weapons. The Soviet notion of the Western version of conventional deep strike is perceived through the conceptual lenses of lessons the Soviets have learned from their own exercises. As a 1987 article in the Polish journal *Zolnierz Wolnosci* (Soldier of freedom) explains:

Considerations of a theoretical nature which have lately been weighed ascertain that the appearance in the West of the concept of "forward defense" (literally, protruding lines) and the American theory of the "deep strike" which in norm documents has been ultimately formulated as the "air-land battle 2000," is only a part of the anticipated tasks which are intended to create conditions for penetration, maintenance of initiative, and execution of decisive strikes to assure success.[28]

The air strike in the first phase of the armed conflict in the European theater of war, according to the same author, can determine the subsequent course of military operations. His subject matter of immediate concern is air defense and the stresses to which it will be subjected by conventional deep strike. Accordingly, he and other Pact planners can expect that:

The conduct of "deep strike" will depend mainly on the strict isolation of the area of immediate combat activity, through the execution of deep raids, mainly with the help of tactical and winged rocket aviation, long range artillery strikes, use of radioelectronic warfare and *spetsnaz* means, and use of camouflage measures.[29]

In an article in the Polish military journal *Przeglad Wojsk Ladowych* (Ground forces review), Col. Stanislaw Koziej discusses the more important impacts of improved conventional weapons and means of command and control associated with them. He suggests that the formation of the theory and practice of air-land combat operations is "the most significant developmental tendency in modern tactics of ground forces."[30] One can find prototypes of modern air-land operations during World War II or even earlier. But the development of the modern version awaited the deployment of significant numbers of combat helicopters, especially the heavily armored versions. This adds another dimension to the capabilities of conventional forces:

The qualitative and quantitative development of helicopters and precision weapons significantly increases the role of the factor of mobility in tactical operations. One can anticipate that on the future battlefield, the function of mobility will broaden. It will not only manifest itself in the form of maneuver, but also as a component of the strike.[31]

Microelectronics and Military Strategy

Added to the deployment of precision weapons and helicopters in great numbers is the qualitative change in warfare brought about by the microelectronics and communications technologies. The opponent's command and control must be attacked and the command and control over friendly forces must not be interfered with, but both missions will have to be accomplished over a larger template. The growing complexity of force structures and the reduced time for making decisions, even in war without nuclear weapons, impede commanders' efforts to establish a clear view of the battlefield in its entirety. The battle for information is nonetheless decisive:

The struggle in the sphere of information ultimately boils down to the effect on the command and control system of the enemy (chiefly through his reconnaissance system). Winning this fight means the ability to steer the enemy in the direction of one's own plans and intentions. In the face of the growth in the effectiveness of strike means, the ability to steer the enemy, to impose one's will upon him, and to completely deceive him will have increasingly substantial significance for the course and results of combat operations.[32]

The combination of precision weapons, newer capabilities for desant operations, increased mobility all around, deep-raiding operations, and the information revolution will have profound influence on defenses as well as offenses. Precision weapons for deep strike, combined with accurate real time reconnaissance, may allow for the defenses the same opportunities for surprise and decisiveness that formerly could be obtained only by offenses. The choice of the time of encounter "has ceased to be an exclusive attribute of the attacker."[33] In the classical approach of Clausewitz, the essence of defense was to await the blow: The defender chose where and when to attack, imposing the conditions for beginning the battle. Now, according to the Polish military writer's assessment, which reflects some Soviet insights as well, "Future long-range precision means of striking ruin this design."[34] In a short period of time the correlation of forces may be changed:

Now the defender, being able to reach the enemy at distant pre-battle positions, on march routes, and in assembly regions, does not have to only wait for the blow, i.e., for the strike. He himself can make the decision about the beginning of the battle. . . . The weaker can suddenly become the stronger. Therefore, the defender is not fated to a prolonged stay in the role of the weaker side; he can and should be prepared for a change in the conditions and type of operations being conducted, for crossing over from defender to attacker in case such a possibility arises.[35]

DYNAMIC STABILITY AND STRATEGIC DEFENSIVISM

We have seen that the evolving Soviet view of operational art is compatible with the politico-military perspective of strategic defensivism. The Soviet view of strategic operations in a theater of military action (theater of strategic military action, or TSMA) includes a continuing awareness of the problem of surprise. Soviet forces must avoid being surprised either by the decision to wage war or by the operational and tactical methods used by opponents. Nevertheless, the possibility that some degree of surprise cannot be avoided, as to the specific time and place of attack, remains significant. As Gareyev concedes, mobilization by the defender cannot anticipate all the forms and methods of possible attack. And beyond a certain point, mobilization might provoke the very war that it is attempting to deter.[36] The conduct of military operations in the Western TVD/TSMA would be marked by a continuous flow of action in which offensive and defensive modes of battle, traditionally defined, would be commingled. Defense would be characterized by great *aktivnost'* (activeness) in all phases. The availability of new technologies for precision guidance, reconnaissance, and decision making makes an active defense as potentially disruptive of the opponent as an aggressive offense. The new technologies for conventional weapons and C^3 also enhance the importance of electronic support measures, countermeasures, and counter-countermeasures in all phases.[37]

These observations are important in charting the evolving Soviet view of superpower nuclear deterrence and strategic stability. Nuclear war could begin from a direct superpower confrontation, as in the Cuban missile crisis of 1962. But it could also break out as a result of escalation from conventional war in Europe or elsewhere.[38] Most important for the evolving Soviet view of strategic deterrence stability, war might break out by accident or inadvertence. In customary U.S. usage, accidental war is the result of an equipment breakdown or single technical error. Inadvertent war or escalation results from a process of mistaken judgment, in which a series of decisions and incidents compound one another into a cumulative disaster. Some writers have referred to accidental or inadvertent war as a generic description of the type.[39]

Defensive sufficiency provides a framework within which the Soviets can anticipate that the risk of deliberate nuclear war is being reduced, almost to the vanishing point. This is partly the result of the Soviets' having attained "military-strategic parity" with the United States in strategic and other nuclear weapons.[40] The attainment of parity and the disproportionate effects of nuclear weapons, relative to any political or military objective other than deterrence, suggest that the two superpowers need to acknowledge the futility of nuclear war. Even non-nuclear wars that are contained below the nuclear threshold, if they involve the forces of the superpowers and their allies, would be so destructive as to be pointless.

Few Attack Incentives

According to Vitaliy Zhurkin, Sergei Karaganov, and Andrei Kortunov, today "there is no single conflict in relations between East and West the solution of which could tempt one to resort to war." On the basis of "common sense," according to these authors, "it would be difficult to conceive of a sake for which Western armed forces could invade the territory of a socialist country."[41] Even a non-nuclear war on the European continent would lead to the "practical destruction of all civilizations on that continent."[42] In addition, "it would be impossible to imagine how a war in Europe could be contained on the non-nuclear level."[43] Traditional postulates of military strategy, according to these Soviet authors, must be reinterpreted on account of the "qualitatively different nature of the threat" that has come about in the present era. In their view:

In the past the level of sufficiency of the military power of the USSR on the European theater was based on the requirement of repelling any aggression and defeating any possible coalition of hostile countries. The task now is essentially formulated differently: to restrain, to prevent war itself.[44]

Strategic nuclear parity is acknowledged by these and other Soviet writers as an important factor for deterrence stability. A. G. Arbatov, A. A. Vasilyev, and A. A. Kokoshin noted in 1987 that stability had become one of the most important issues between the superpowers during the 1980s. Nuclear weapons are not an exception to the competition between offense and defense, but with nuclear weapons the competition takes "distinctive forms."[45] Traditionally armed forces protected a national economy and population from being taken over or destroyed by an opponent. The opponent had first to defeat the defender's armed forces before the economy and society were vulnerable. Although the mission of protecting the national economy and society remains, the method is different with nuclear weapons. Nuclear weapons prevent societal destruction not by blocking the opponent's armies but by posing the credible threat of retaliation. As the Soviet writers explain:

Successful attack and victory are impossible if the aggressor cannot prevent nuclear retaliation or at least reduce its force to an acceptable level. This is why the effectiveness of attack is measured primarily in terms of its ability to destroy the other side's nuclear weapons and the systems of their command and control in the absolute and relative respects. The strength of defenses, in turn, is reflected in the ability of strategic weapons to survive even a surprise attack and deliver a devastating retaliatory strike.[46]

Assured Retaliation and Stability

This endorsement of assured retaliation as the mechanism that underpins strategic stability is very much at variance with the view attributed to the Soviet Union by U.S. defense officials for several decades. This is true at two levels of Soviet military doctrine—the politico-military and the military-technical levels. From at least one Soviet perspective, strategic stability is not limited "to the approximate equality of the numerical features of the forces and weapons of the sides."[47] The military doctrines and strategic policy objectives of the two superpowers are also important. Although the Soviet view of strategic stability is less mechanistic than the American, there is convergence on the existence of a stable balance of strategic nuclear deterrence based on assured retaliation. This implies, again in contrast to the traditional view of conventional warfare in which offenses and defenses were mutually supportive, that national missile defense systems are destabilizing. According to Arbatov, Vasilyev, and Kokoshin:

The dialectics of the nuclear balance therefore put both offensive and defensive arms in an absolutely new light by radically changing their traditional role in the relationship between offense and defense. Broad-scale ABM systems could destabilize the strategic balance dramatically. Without these systems, the stability of the relative offensive nuclear forces of the sides in the presence of overall parity is augmented by the decline of the probable aggressor's ability to use a first strike to weaken the force of retaliation on absolute or relative scales or, in other words, by the enhancement of the reliability of the potential of each power for an adequate retaliatory strike.[48]

The objection is to "broad-scale ABM" and presumably excludes the ABM treaty limited system now deployed around Moscow. The reference to the stability-enhancing character of the inability of any first striker to weaken the force of retaliation absolutely *or relatively* casts an aspersion even on limited BMD systems. The impact of BMD systems on the stability of the balance is uncertain because, in the Soviet assessment, politico-military as well as technical factors must be taken into account. Among these qualitative factors are the prevailing military doctrines of the two sides and the qualitative impacts of drastic changes in force size, including those brought about by arms control. Arbatov et al. note that it is possible to imagine disruption of stable deterrence as a result of arms reductions instead of arms buildups, "for example, if this is accompanied by the increased vulnerability of more and more of the strategic weapons and command, control, and communications systems of one or both sides."[49]

Qualitative Factors

Increased concern on the part of Soviet analysts with the qualitative features of the military balance extends beyond the issue of force and command system vulnerability. Soviet writers have also expressed the view that the risk of inadvertent war is growing, even as the probability of deliberate nuclear or conventional aggression by the superpowers or their allies in Europe is decreasing. According to Zhurkin, Karaganov, and Kortunov, the possibility of a deliberate nuclear attack "is today as unlikely as the deliberate starting of a large-scale war in Europe." However, parity in itself "is no longer a war-preventing factor."[50] The concept of balance of forces and the concept of strategic stability "which more or less coincided in the past, have begun to diverge."[51] Thus:

The possibility of a random, unsanctioned outbreak of nuclear war and a fast and uncontrollable escalation of the crisis has increased. Therefore, an externally paradoxical situation is developing: the threat of deliberate nuclear aggression is diminishing, while the threat of war may be increasing.[52]

The Soviet concern with inadvertent war at the politico-military level is also evident at the military-technical level. According to Yevgeniy Velikhov, writing in 1988 as chairman of the Committee of Soviet Scientists for the Defense of Peace and Against the Nuclear Threat, there are significant risks of nuclear war growing out of technical failures. Velikhov attributes to a U.S. source the figure of 1,152 false alarms in the U.S. nuclear warning system between 1977 and 1984, "each one of which, had there been no system of checks and cross-checks, could have potentially led to a nuclear response to a nonexistent 'strike.'"[53]

This is obviously exaggerated, but the failures in the U.S. warning systems have been well documented. Few have led to serious incidents on account of the checks and balances institutionalized in peacetime. However, as Bruce G. Blair and other students of nuclear command and control have noted, in peacetime the command systems emphasize the prevention of accidental or unauthorized nuclear use, so-called negative control.[54] As a crisis began to develop and to intensify, levels of alert would rise and the emphasis in the standard operating procedures of the system would shift from negative to positive control. Positive control emphasizes the responsiveness of forces and command systems to authorized orders. As tensions mount the system shifts gradually from a "snooze alarm" status in which any warning would be greeted with almost instant disbelief, to a warning status in which small perturbations can trip the system into an assumption that war has begun.

Bureaucratic Forces

An additional risk is that in the process of raising levels of alert, different parts of the bureaucracy may understand what is happening from very different perspectives. A U.S. secretary of defense in the Eisenhower administration once called for an alert as an impromptu test of military readiness. The repercussions in terms of media reaction and possible response of the Soviet Union had not been carefully thought out, if they had been considered at all.[55] The raising of alert levels on both sides at the same time can have unexpected interaction effects. Simple errors that would be irrelevant under normal peacetime conditions become compound felonies when tensions increase, alert levels rise, and the intentions of adversary decision makers are uncertain. President John F. Kennedy and his advisors in the Executive Committee (ExCom) of the National Security Council experienced some of this tension and uncertainty as the Cuban missile crisis moved from the initial confirmation of MRBM (medium-range ballistic) missiles in Cuba by photographic intelligence to its final denouement. Several incidents during the crisis suggested that U.S. and Soviet policymakers were not fully familiar with the standard operating procedures and military doctrines of their respective armed services, and that this lack of familiarity with the implications of doctrines and procedures, under crisis conditions, complicated efforts to resolve the crisis.[56]

The first of these incidents was the effort by President Kennedy to establish a blockade line that would prevent Soviet or Soviet-chartered ships from bringing additional missiles into Cuba. The implementation of the blockade could not be left to U.S. Navy standard operating procedures. The president wanted to avoid inadvertent escalation or accidental outbreak of war. The Navy established an initial blockade line and was later forced to pull it back closer to Cuba, allowing several ships to pass through the blockade unchallenged. In addition, standard operating procedures for a blockade called for U.S. antisubmarine warfare forces to force to the surface any hostile submarines within the blockade zone or near it. A number of Soviet submarines, some of which may have been armed with nuclear weapons, were forced to surface in the Caribbean and Atlantic.

The second set of standard operating procedures that confounded analysts and policymakers during the crisis were the U.S. Air Force estimates of the likely success of a "surgical" air strike against missile installations in Cuba. Policymakers seemed to mean by this attacks against the surface-to-air (SAM) missile defense sites, or MRBM offensive missile construction sites, or both, while sparing collateral damage to the extent possible. The Air Force reported that this could not be done; significant destruction of surrounding property and persons was inevitable, and the loss of life by Soviet personnel could not be precluded. However, it later emerged during the crisis that the Air Force had answered the question it wanted to answer instead of the question policymakers thought they had asked. The Air Force had wanted to carry out the least surgical attack possible in order to guarantee maximum destruction of the offending Cuban and Soviet missiles and launchers. U.S. policymakers were told that this most comprehensive attack against the most threatening military targets could not be sparing of collateral damage. The policymakers did not ask whether lesser but still adequate attacks could do so.

A third set of procedures and decision-making incidents involved the Soviets. They installed defensive and offensive missiles in Cuba in exactly the same patterns that were used to construct them in the Soviet Union and in Eastern Europe. No effort was made to camouflage the SAM sites despite the suspicious activity with regard to the construction of offensive missile installations nearby, and the concealment of offensive missiles themselves was lackadaisical compared to customary Soviet deception practices. In addition, the construction of SAMs and MRBMs was not coordinated: Military strategic considerations would have dictated finishing the air defense installations before beginning construction of the MRBM launchers.[57] The Soviet diplomatic efforts were uncoordinated and confused; Soviet Ambassador to the U.S. Dobrynin denied that there were offensive missiles in Cuba at the same time that Khrushchev was admitting as much to a visiting U.S. businessman. Finally, the Soviet leadership sent two completely different messages one day apart about its terms for resolving the crisis. The first message was far more conciliatory, and the second demanded tougher terms for the removal of Soviet missiles from Cuba, including the removal of U.S. Jupiter missiles from Turkey. Here misfortune had intervened to create a spoiling point in the super-power negotiations. President Kennedy had ordered the State Department to have the Turkish missiles removed, but the Turks had balked and the State Department postponed further confrontation until tempers cooled. The missile crisis caught the United States with obsolete Jupiter missiles deployed in a position where they might have been attacked easily, thus tempting preemption if the crisis seemed to be slipping beyond control. There is some recent evidence provided by McGeorge Bundy, the president's national security advisor during the Cuban crisis, and Harvard University's James L. Blight that Kennedy might have agreed to remove the missiles from Turkey if that step were necessary to avoid war.[58]

Inadvertent or Deliberate Crisis?

Given Khrushchev's decision to place Soviet missiles in Cuba despite clear U.S. warnings, one can question whether the crisis was as inadvertent as some observers and participants have supposed. Khrushchev may have calculated that, even if caught before the missiles were operational, he would be forced to bargain diplomatically for an eventual quid pro quo, such as the removal of Turkish missiles. He may also have calculated that at most a political and propaganda showdown, devoid of military confrontation, was in the offing once the buildup could no longer be concealed. He may have been urged by Soviet military leaders to reverse the apparent image of second best in strategic nuclear forces, following the U.S. confirmation of Soviet inferiority by satellite reconnaissance. Finally, the symbolism of putting Soviet missiles so close to U.S. shores may have intrigued the ebullient Soviet premier. It would show his Politburo colleagues that his policy of downsizing conventional forces for nuclear was not bluff, and his Chinese competitors for influence in the socialist world that he was not a paper tiger.

Richard Betts has also suggested that Khrushchev may have seen some symmetry in the U.S. position in Cuba and the Soviet one in Berlin during the crises of the late 1950s.[59] The U.S. effort in Cuba was to destabilize a regime friendly to the Kremlin but located geographically within the foreign policy preserve of the Americans. The Soviet effort in Berlin was to squeeze out the Western powers from an enclave that was within East German territory or the extended Soviet security zone. Thus both the Soviets and the Americans had a problem of "extended deterrence" of aggression, as they saw it, against an allied city or regime vulnerable to rapid destruction and encirclement by hostile forces. Both cases were ones of deterrence because, on the basis of purely military calculations without taking into account nuclear weapons, the Soviets could easily have crushed resistance in Berlin, and the Americans in Cuba. Prior to the nuclear age neither enclave would have endured, as the Americans showed as early as the Spanish-American war, and as the Soviets demonstrated in their sphere of influence in Eastern Europe wherever the allies had no presence.

What deters the superpowers in these cases, however, is not the certainty that nuclear war will result. It did not result from any of the Berlin crises, nor from the confrontation over Cuba. What deters more of these kinds of crises is the uncertainty that war might begin as a result of a process over which both sides gradually lost control. This uncertainty is what Schelling referred to as "the manipulation of risk" based upon threats that leave the outcome to chance as well as to management.[60] If war were certain and its consequences absolutely calculable in advance, it would never begin unless leaders had lost their senses. What makes war possible, including nuclear war, is the absence of any calculus for predicting the rate of escalation from conventional into nuclear war, and the ensuing consequences. There are two parts to this dynamic—one involving changes in the intentions and priorities of individual actors as the crisis deepens or the fighting continues, and the other of the reciprocal impact of each side's behavior on the other's perceptions. U.S. actions may be signaling to the Soviets intentions that we really do not intend, but they have inferred from events that happened accidentally, or according to standard operating procedures which are now mistimed. An example occurred during the Cuban missile crisis, when an American U-2 strayed accidentally into Soviet air space and Soviet air defense fighters scrambled to meet it. U.S. fighter planes from Alaska were sent to escort the U-2 back to safety.[61] This incident was later noted by Khrushchev as a possible cause of inadvertent war, and Kennedy reacted with ironic black humor: "There is always some so-and-so who doesn't get the word."[62]

NATO STRATEGY AND DYNAMIC STABILITY

The preceding discussions are not intended to exaggerate the danger of war between superpowers in the nuclear age, but to establish a baseline against which the future development of NATO strategy may be considered. If the evolving Soviet view is as suggested, with enhanced sensitivity to inadvertent war and escalation, then there are implications for NATO strategy and doctrine that need thinking through. There are several areas in which this thinking might be done. The discussion here emphasizes the control of escalation and the relationship between NATO and Soviet approaches to that task. Other, and equally valid, perspectives might be taken, including conventional force modernization, arms control, unambiguously defensive defenses, or no first use.[63] The focus on escalation and its control, relative to the interaction between Soviet-Pact and U.S.–NATO doctrines, grows out of the preceding review of an increased Soviet emphasis on inadvertent nuclear and conventional war as opposed to deliberate nuclear aggression by either side.

The conceptual model of escalation implicit in NATO strategy is a progression from direct defense with conventional forces, through escalation to theater nuclear war, ending in strategic nuclear exchanges if necessary.[64] NATO declaratory strategy of "flexible response" calls for the use of nuclear weapons for a variety of purposes if necessary. Americans and Europeans, broadly speaking and allowing for intra-European divergence on some matters, take contrasting views of the relationship between escalation and deterrence. Further, within the U.S. defense and foreign policy community, there are contrasting views as well.[65]

The first divergence, between U.S. and notional "European" views, is the difference between coupling and firebreaks. The U.S. view is that the firebreak between conventional resistance and nuclear escalation is a meaningful distinction, both before and after deterrence has failed. Europeans are more skeptical. They tend to view the relationship between conventional denial forces and nuclear escalation as a seamless web. Any suggestion that escalation from conventional to nuclear war might occur less than automatically sends to the Soviet Union a signal that conventional war is feasible, and possibly winnable.

Political or Military Disagreements?

Both points or view can be overstated, and have been from time to time in partisan and heated transatlantic debates. As Josef Joffe has noted, debates about strategy within the NATO alliance are only nominally about matters of nuclear theology. They are actually debates about power and position, about relative degrees of influence within alliance policy-making.[66] Nevertheless, the differences in doctrinal center of gravity are important. They were important enough for French strategists to go their own way, with de Gaulle's encouragement, in the 1960s, and contributory to the French withdrawal from the alliance military command structure.

The problem of coupling is the obverse of firebreaks. Coupling is both political and military. Political coupling of the U.S. defense policy and program to the defense of Europe is manifest in the deployment of more than 300,000 U.S. forces there, and in the commitment of some 60 percent of the U.S. general-purpose forces budget to the defense of NATO Europe. This coupling is one of the complications in superpower arms control agreements as applied to Eastern and Western Europe. Military coupling is created by the presence of U.S. divisions and corps close to the inter-German border, where they would be subject to immediate attack, encirclement, and destruction if the Pact began an offensive.

Nuclear weapons provide coupling and create the incentive to establish firebreaks. They provide coupling on account of the linkage among U.S. and allied NATO conventional forces deployed in Western Europe, U.S. nuclear weapons also deployed there, and U.S. strategic nuclear forces. However, the deterrent effect of these weapons lies in their potential to do great damage with unprecedented speed, and the non-nuclear members of NATO are entirely dependent upon the Americans for nuclear deterrence of a power with its own nuclear arsenal. Therefore, firebreaks between conventional and nuclear first use, and between limited and massive theater uses, become important in force and strike planning. NATO has a nuclear operations plan that is "de-conflicted" with the U.S. Single Integrated Operational Plan (SIOP) for strategic nuclear targeting.[67] This plan allows for very selective and limited uses of nuclear weapons according to the inclinations of policymakers and force commanders. The variety of options and packages may be more of an exercise than a practical reality that can be pulled off in the exigent circumstances.

The tension between Europeans and Americans over coupling and firebreaks does not reside mainly in diverse theories of deterrence. It is rooted in the problem of indivisible risk.[68] For the U.S. nuclear deterrent to extend beyond basic deterrence of attacks against North America, the United States must credibly threaten to initiate nuclear war in order to avoid conventional defeat. From the European perspective, the Soviets should not perceive any meaningful firebreak between NATO's imminent conventional defeat and nuclear first use in Europe. But from the U.S. perspective, it might not be so obvious that nuclear use is called for. The defeat of NATO armies in Europe by conventional aggression does not mean that the United States has been knocked out of the war. Pushing Americans off the continent of Europe only opens the door to a prolonged struggle between Americans and Soviets for global stakes. What is left of Western Europe becomes a pawn in the power struggle between the global giants. This scenario has occurred to Soviet planners since at least the establishment of U.S.–Soviet strategic nuclear parity.[69]

European Perspectives

The European members of NATO, therefore, and especially the non-nuclear ones, will seek to strengthen coupling and to erode firebreaks, especially those between conventional war and nuclear escalation. The Americans and perhaps the NATO nuclear powers, France and Britain, might be more interested in preserving firebreaks and thresholds, and not only after the first use of nuclear weapons in the European theater of operations. For the British as for the French a key threshold is crossed when Pact nuclear weapons are exploded near their borders or within them. This leaves the U.S. deterrent as a residual threat that may be called into question later, but the credibility of the British or French retaliatory force, under the hypothetical just noted, is immediately jeopardized. Attacks on French and British territory would certainly call forth some nuclear response, and the two powers' targeting priorities are from all appearances counter-city and other countervalue.[70] Even limited nuclear strikes with tactical weapons near the French border by Pact armies crossing Germany would probably result in French retaliation with land-based or air-delivered nuclear weapons against the invaders. The French have been deliberately vague about this, of course. The French SSBN force would undoubtedly be withheld for the most drastic situation. The British SSBN force is coordinated with NATO but use is subject to final unilateral determination by the prime minister of Great Britain.

The tension between firebreaks and coupling is only one part of the intra-NATO divergence on escalation. This first divergence is structural and, as noted, based more on politics than on deterrence theory. It reflects important differences in assumed risk during conventional or theater nuclear war in Europe. The second divergence in assumptions about escalation within NATO is dynamic rather than structural. It has to do with the expectations of various parties about how escalation can be controlled after war has started. This has two facets, of course: escalation control after conventional war has begun but before nuclear escalation has occurred, and control of escalation after nuclear first use.

The dynamics of escalation control are nowhere spelled out explicitly in NATO strategy documents. But we can infer that there are two broadly contrasting theories by which NATO planners expect to manage the control of escalation. These are risk-assuming and force-dependent approaches. The first approach is based on arguments and assumptions about intentions, motivations, and decisions of adversaries during wartime. The second approach counts on force superiority to deter escalation and force inferiority to invite it.

Force-Dependent Approach

The force-dependent approach appeals to military planners, especially to those who equate larger forces with improved deterrent credibility. The U.S. debate over the modernization of theater nuclear forces from 1979 through 1983, which also carried over into NATO Europe, had a force-oriented center of gravity.[71] The assumption was that the Soviet SS-20 force modernization had somehow to be matched. The force-oriented perspective of planners on INF modernization was also given unintended support from arms controllers. Instead of counting upward toward higher levels, their proposals focused on counting downward toward eventual reductions. These reductions were achieved under the INF treaty signed by Reagan and Gorbachev in December 1987.

Conclusion of the INF treaty led to euphoria in the same citadels wherein previously there had been despair. When NATO, following its "two-track" decision of 1979, began to deploy Pershing II and GLCM over much European political protest in December 1983, the Soviets walked out of arms-reduction talks. Arms control seemed dead and was so pronounced by U.S. academics, policy analysts, and bureaucrats. Once firmly in control, Gorbachev saw the advantages of public arms-control diplomacy skillfully engineered. He not only agreed to partial reductions along the lines of Reagan's original "zero option" but offered to go one better by destroying shorter-range as well as intermediate-range ballistic missiles (ground launched). The result was that all land-based ballistic missiles with ranges of 500 to 5,500 kilometers were included in the INF eliminations. Whereas the U.S. had proposed the zero option as a way of putting the onus on the Soviets, in the expectation that it would be unacceptable for them to trade in something actually deployed for a NATO "perhaps," the Soviets played back on the U.S. keyboard. The Reagan administration was caught up in its own checkmate. The administration then made vice into virtue—according to INF skeptics such as Henry Kissinger; former Supreme Allied Command, Europe (SACEUR) Bernard Rogers; and Richard Nixon—by treating the agreement as militarily advantageous for the West. According to the critics, it was not. It would remove modernized NATO theater nuclear forces and leave the Soviets with a favorable force advantage in conventional arms. Thus, during the INF debate leading up to the first "572" deployments, during the arms negotiations once resumed, and during the INF treaty aftermath in 1988, the currency of pro- and anti-agreement debate was mostly of the force-dependent variety.

The risk-inviting logic of escalation management was more implicit in the INF debate, attaining periodic visibility on a somewhat elliptical orbit. The risk-inviting logic said that the so-called theater, or long-range theater, nuclear force balance was not so significant. More important was the presence of any U.S. nuclear weapons in Europe, of whatever range, lethality, and survivability. These technical parameters were important, especially survivability. But the primary political importance of U.S. and other NATO nuclear weapons is, according to risk-inviting logic, that they present to the Soviets a risk the Soviet Union cannot calculate. Instead of posing a force which can deny Pact attackers their objectives (by conventional defenses against conventional attack, or by superpower attritive firepower in theater nuclear war), the risk-inviting approach contends that certainty of defeat is less important than uncertainty of mutual destruction.

Manipulation of Risk

The risk-inviting logic borrows from Schelling's discussion of the notion that two sides can get into a war or, once in war, into a larger one without necessarily intending to do so.[72] The logic of war, as Clausewitz once so profoundly explained it, tends toward increasing levels of violence and diminished political control over operations.[73] Once conventional war has begun in Europe, it will no longer be a "conventional" war at all. The primary concern of the two superpowers will be how to contain that war short of the nuclear threshold or, having failed to do so, how to prevent its escalation into attacks on each other's homelands. It is this fear of a process that gets out of control, of an escalatory process gone berserk, which is counted upon to deter war and, if deterrence fails, to limit it.

The risk-inviting logic of escalation control borrows something from "rationality of irrationality" theories, as they were known in early years of deterrence theory. These were related to the notion of brinkmanship, of making plausible threats to create a dangerous situation that would compel the other side to back down from the brink or raise the ante. The notion of brinkmanship was mostly applied to crisis management, but its extension into war, for the firebreak between conventional defense and nuclear escalation, was easily imagined.[74] The problem with U.S. versions of crisis management by brinkmanship was that the theory of coercive diplomacy was not cleanly separated from the brute fact of coercion per se. The difference between intimidating the opponent from further escalation by virtue of one's own superior forces, compared to persuasion of the opponent that even marginally better outcomes for him were not acceptable, was insufficiently clear. The lack of clarity spilled over from theory and planning with regard to U.S. strategic nuclear forces, applied in the case of two-sided U.S.–Soviet conflict, to the multilateral template of NATO.

The choice between the "harder" and "softer" forms of risk-inviting behavior was difficult for planners to translate into force structure in a multinational forum. As noted earlier, some planners saw Pershing II and GLCM as force-structure enhancements from the perspective of force dependency. The issue was the size of the NATO inventory relative to that of the Pact. For others, the risk-inviting framework was employed to evaluate the "572" deployments, which implied that the symbolism of military and political coupling was more important than force size. The problem was that the risks could not be shared equally. The Europeans had to accept the deployment of missiles of greater range—up to 2,500 kilometers for the GLCMs and, in the case of Pershing II, one capable of arriving at time-urgent targets in the Soviet Union with unprecedented speed. The Soviet need to preempt these weapons during crisis or conventional war fighting was acute. NATO had deployed nuclear weapons capable of making strategic strikes into Soviet territory, not on U.S. soil. This was not unprecedented, of course, and the furor over Pershing II and GLCM was reminiscent of the controversy surrounding the deployment of U.S. Thor and Jupiter IRBM in the 1950s.[75] Chancellor Adenauer, who normally followed the U.S. lead on alliance issues, would have nothing to do with IRBMs deployed on West German soil. This was to turn Germany and NATO non-German NATO forces deployed in West Germany from a deterrent into a target, in his judgment. The judgment was not mistaken. Had the Cuban missile crisis deteriorated into war in 1962, the Turks would have learned the hard way what Adenauer had perceived years earlier. Turkey would certainly have been subjected to Soviet coercion about the missiles, if not to outright attack.

Carter and Escalation Control

The Carter administration wavered between force-dependent and risk-provoking logics of escalation control in its development of "countervailing strategy."[76] The administration favored deployment of 200 MX missiles in a mobile "racetrack" basing scheme, Trident II SLBM modernization, and other force enhancements without which the U.S. arsenal would be subjected, in the Carter view, to Soviet crisis or wartime blackmail. The MX was justified as a requirement for attacking time-urgent hard targets such as missile silos and command bunkers. It was not clear why the United States would want high lethalities against missile silos if it was assumed that the Soviet Union was striking first and the Americans second. Prompt destruction of command bunkers would disrupt the Soviet system of control and communications, but this was undesirable unless the United States planned not to attempt any restoration of intra-war deterrence. The notions of bargaining for war termination and of destroying the Soviet politico-military command structure were logically inconsistent.[77] The public expositions of countervailing strategy offered by Secretary of Defense Harold Brown drew upon force-dependent and risk-inviting logics, and upon both variations of the risk-inviting mode.

In his remarks at the Naval War College, Newport, Rhode Island, in August 1980, Brown noted that successful deterrence involved shaping the Soviet view of what a war might mean. He sought to explain how the United States might define more carefully the purposes for which strategic forces are employed, while maintaining essential continuity with the force-employment policies of his predecessors. Thus Brown noted that P.D. (Presidential Directive) 59, which laid down the U.S. strategic doctrine, was "*not* a radical departure from U.S. strategic policy over the past decade or so."[78] This was an explicit reference to the "Schlesinger doctrine" that was publicly explained by the former Secretary of Defense James R. Schlesinger in January 1974.[79] The Schlesinger doctrine, or formally NSDM (National Security Decision Memorandum) 242, attempted to define more selective and limited options for the use of U.S. strategic forces that were less massive in size and blunt in character than those previously existing in the SIOP.[80] The continuity with NSDM 242 intended by Brown was that he hoped to reaffirm the absence of interest in any so-called nuclear war fighting doctrine, which might mistakenly suggest that the United States expected to prevail in an extended nuclear war of attrition. The United States was building war-fighting capabilities in order to improve deterrence.

The difficulty was that the United States was leading a coalition, not just speaking for itself. War-fighting capabilities sounded provocative whether their intended purpose was improved deterrence or something else. McNamara had faced this dilemma in explaining publicly what appeared to be a contradictory strategy on account of the different emphases given to its declaratory and operational casts. His "counterforce" and "city avoidance" strategies, when explained in public, sounded to European and Soviet audiences like first-strike and war-fighting postures.[81] Schlesinger had got caught in this same entrapment—between the exigencies of employment policy and the requirements of declaratory policy—in explaining NSDM 242. Now it was Brown's turn. The improved U.S. capabilities for war fighting were required in order to maintain credible deterrence against the Soviet Union. The Soviet leadership had a different view of nuclear war than the United States and its allies. Successful deterrence required, according to Brown, influencing the Soviet view of wins and losses in a direction favorable to U.S. and allied interests, even after war had broken out.

The Soviet view of nuclear war apparently envisioned scenarios in which their losses would prove to be acceptable and those of the United States not. As Brown noted:

We must have forces, contingency plans, and command and control capabilities that will convince the Soviet leadership that no war and no course of aggression by them that led to use of nuclear weapons—on any scale of attack and at any stage of conflict—could lead to victory, however they define victory.[82]

Which Soviet View?

Of course, the Soviet view being described here was not the Soviet view, but the U.S. view of a Soviet view that was already in the process of being changed (see my previous remarks). By the midpoint of the Carter administration Soviet leadership had begun to proclaim publicly that nuclear superiority was meaningless, and that nuclear war had no outcome that corresponded to victory in the traditional understanding of that term. Nevertheless the Carter administration stewed for several years in studies on nuclear policy that were caught up in intra-administration divisions between hawkish and dovish factions. The presidential campaign of 1980 and the Soviet invasion of Afghanistan in December 1979 allowed the hawkish version of preferred U.S. nuclear employment policy to prevail in public expositions.

Brown not only laid down the conceptual foundations of countervailing strategy. He also attempted to specify, insofar as one could do so in public, its operational character. He noted that the U.S. policy would continue to emphasize plans and policies for the selective use of strategic nuclear forces. Brown now looked through the glass darkly, as Schlesinger had. He resolved that the United States could use discriminating, but still adequately punitive, strikes in order to deter the Soviets from escalating an aggression they had already started. As he explained:

It is our policy—and we have increasingly the means and the detailed plans to carry out this policy—to ensure that the Soviet leadership knows that if they chose some intermediate level of aggression, we could, by selective, large (but still less than maximum) nuclear attacks, exact an unacceptably high price in the things the Soviet leaders appear to value most—political and military control, military force both nuclear and conventional, and the industrial capability to sustain a war.[83]

The "means" referred to were improvements in U.S. strategic command, control, and communications (C^3) that were in progress or had been made, including command-post exercises in which high officials including President Carter had, for the first time in many years, rehearsed postattack control procedures.[84] The detailed plans were modifications to the SIOP that allowed for selective, regional, and limited nuclear options in addition to massive ones.[85] The definition of "intermediate" aggression was left unspecified but it presumably referred to a Warsaw Pact invasion of West Germany and/or the Low Countries. Undoubtedly some thought had been given to the Persian Gulf as well, but for present purposes the European scene is the focus of interest. In that instance, the United States would respond with "selective, large (but still less than maximum)" strikes from strategic nuclear forces, presumably into Western Europe in order to stop the Red Army, and perhaps into Eastern Europe against its rear echelons and other targets. The intended effect was both dissuasion of further aggression and punishment for offenses already committed. The assumption was that the attack had been premeditated and that NATO conventional resistance would be inadequate for more than a delaying action. How selective, large, but not yet massive attacks from U.S. strategic forces were to be viewed as limited was not explained, and seemed especially eccentric as a view of the *Soviet* view of escalation.[86]

Conventional Force Constraints

The threatened use of U.S. nuclear forces or NATO theater nuclear forces to halt a conventional invasion was an acknowledgment that the lowest rung of the NATO deterrence ladder—conventional forces—was inadequate for actual defense, and that therefore it might be insufficient for deterrence. It was the Soviet conventional buildup that actually threatened deterrence stability if that stability was force dependent, not the prevailing nuclear force balance. The United States under Carter did invest in improved general-purpose forces for NATO. However, this was considered insufficient since the Soviets could still, according to the Carter administration, dominate any process of escalation. The Soviet view of nuclear war was that, under some favorable conditions which U.S. forces might permit, it could be won, or at least lost in a tolerable way. This U.S. view of the Soviet view further supposed that the addition of improved U.S. counterforce capabilities and command systems would improve deterrence *and* the control of escalation if deterrence failed. For if the new forces and command system improvements did not improve the actual capability to control escalation and terminate the war, then they added nothing meaningful to peacetime deterrence. Brown made clear that war termination had not been neglected as a planning consideration:

In our planning we have not ignored the problem of ending the war, nor would we ignore it in the event of a war. And, of course, we have, and we will keep, a survivable and enduring capability to attack the full range of targets, including the Soviet economic base, if that is the appropriate response to a Soviet strike.[87]

The difficulty was in connecting the paradigm for war termination with a consistent theory of escalation control and a plausible mechanism for bringing about de-escalation.[88] The Soviets could be forgiven for missing the point. Some U.S. analysts argued that the Soviets *did* get the point and that this is what deterred them.[89] The evidence cited was the Soviets' own investment in prompt, hard-target counterforce capabilities (modernized ICBMs), air defenses, and potential improvement in antisubmarine warfare (ASW) capabilities that, if unanswered, left U.S. forces putatively vulnerable to future, if not current, Soviet threats.[90]

The pertinent question was one of increments, relative to the incentive structure that would dissuade the Soviets from continuing a war they would otherwise have stopped. The incremental improvement in escalation control, for purposes of de-escalation and war termination, offered by the countervailing strategy was not apparent to most NATO governments, nor to their parliaments and publics. The countervailing strategy was campaign rhetoric and force building, encapsulated in a modernized version of the "Schlesinger doctrine." The modernized version justified the MX as a weapon that would be used in an effective, yet selective, way in order to reestablish deterrence instead of contributing to further escalation. The Carter basing scheme emphasized survivability against future versions of the MIRVed Soviet ICBM threat, but the Reagan administration quickly returned to silo basing for the first 50 MX (now Peacekeeper). The Carter administration bequeathed to Reagan a set of weapons in development and a rationale based on presumed versions of the Soviet strategy that were inconsistent with actual Soviet strategy. The Reagan program carried this heritage forward.

Reagan and Carter Similarities

The logic of both Carter and Reagan planners was that the capability to disarm whatever silos remained after a Soviet first strike would supplement basic deterrence. It would also reinforce extended deterrence, since the expected loss of their remaining silos, following a Soviet first strike and a U.S. retaliation, would keep the Soviets from attacking Western Europe. Third, should deterrence fail and the Soviet conventional offensive appear to be succeeding, then U.S. ICBMs could be used in a selective and discriminating way in order to reestablish deterrence and end the war. Meanwhile, NATO was to go along with U.S. strategic force modernization by improving the balance of long-range theater nuclear forces. The LRTNF (long-range theater nuclear forces) modernization partook of a force-building or force-dependent logic, in order to match Soviet SS-20 deployments or to induce a symmetrical withdrawal, and of a risk-inviting rationale, by attempting to couple the U.S. strategic deterrent more securely to the NATO TNF. The U.S. countervailing strategy did likewise. It sought to close the gap between Soviet and U.S. modernized ICBM capabilities ("prompt hard-target counterforce") while preserving control over the escalation that would come from using these capabilities in conjunction with improved command and control systems.

The difficulty was that the competition in risk taking implied in U.S. strategy, for basic or extended deterrence, was dependent on more credible command and control systems than NATO could count on. The situation with regard to the U.S. strategic nuclear command system was problematical enough. The problem was not whether a basic "assured destruction" retaliation could be launched against the Soviet Union in the event of an unprovoked and massive strike against North America. This deterrence objective had been fulfilled for some time. The more demanding case was whether the U.S. strategic nuclear C^3 system could provide for retaliation against a comprehensive target set that included prompt and slow counterforce, countervalue, and other targets.[91] The U.S. strategic nuclear command system could provide for massive retaliation or flexible response, but it was unclear whether it could provide for massive *and* flexible response. The command system might lack sufficient endurance for attacking the comprehensive targets set provided in the SIOPs developed under the Carter PD-59 and the equivalent Reagan policy guidance.[92]

One might reasonably question whether the limitations in the U.S. command system mattered, given the force redundancy of U.S. and Soviet arsenals relative to their societal vulnerabilities. The destruction of the attacker's cities even after the defender absorbed the most destructive attack remained unavoidable. The relevancy of the command system was twofold. First, it influenced perceptions of U.S. capabilities, including the expectations of organizations within the U.S. military establishment. Pessimism about the capacity of the organizations in question to fulfill their operational requirements might suggest to operators that a blunt and massive response to any aggression was the only choice in which they had confidence. Policymakers in search of less than massive options might be told, as the Air Force told President Kennedy during the Cuban missile crisis, that a surgical strike was not feasible. That the feasibility was later confirmed was of little use to the president, who believed otherwise when it mattered most.

Second, the U.S. strategic nuclear command system is fettered to the NATO European one. The credibility of U.S. extended nuclear deterrence is dependent upon both ends of the transatlantic link. Important components of U.S. strategic command and control are based in NATO Europe. Others such as reconnaissance and communications satellites might be under attack shortly after conventional war had broken out in Europe. Soviet interest in denying U.S. naval forces the use of overhead reconnaissance, and in using Soviet electronic and radar ocean reconnaissance satellites of their own for sea-based counterforce targeting, is apparent.[93] Apart from their connections to U.S. strategic command and control, NATO C^3 systems are subject to self-induced confusion and possible preemptive destruction with conventional weapons. The mixture of NATO and national command channels on which the alliance would rely in wartime argues for chaotic communication and widespread misunderstanding of plans, situation reports, and enemy intentions. The number of fixed command centers, SIGINT (signals intelligence) installations, and other C^3 targets, without which NATO command and control would be immobilized, is well within the range of Soviet limited nuclear options, and may be vulnerable to conventional deep strike without nuclear escalation.[94]

The politics surrounding any "NATO" decision to escalate assume that the core nuclear states (United States, Great Britain, and France) can find common ground with the non-nuclear members, especially the Federal Republic of Germany, on issues of high politics as well as operational ones. Once war has begun in Europe, or even before when crisis management seems insecure, the unequal risks being assumed by the various member states of NATO will become paramount concerns. This is already apparent.

INF Treaty

The U.S.–Soviet INF agreement of December 1987, for example, now raises the delicate issue of modernization for the remaining NATO theater nuclear forces. These include demolition munitions (land mines), air-delivered weapons, surface-to-surface missiles, and nuclear artillery rounds. NATO has already undertaken unilateral withdrawals of TNF systems in 1979, pursuant to the "two track" INF decision, and in 1983 under the alliance agreements reached at Montebello. The first decision reduced the NATO inventory by some 1,000 nuclear charges and the second, scheduled for completion in 1988, by another 1,400. The INF treaty meanwhile called for elimination of all land-based systems with ranges from 500 to 5,500 kilometers. The remaining short-range nuclear forces were to be modernized according to a plan to be drawn up by then-SACEUR Rogers. This plan included stipulations for modernized 155 mm and 203 mm artillery rounds, a Lance follow-on with extended range (since aborted), and a possible air-to-surface tactical missile (TASM) derived from SRAM IV.[95] The objective of NATO SRF modernization as defined by the NATO Nuclear Planning Group was to improve survivability and accuracy of the remaining weapons, while removing those that were obsolete or dangerous.

These modernization plans remain in abeyance, and for some of the same reasons that would complicate nuclear use and escalation control in wartime. The problem of unequal risk in TNF modernization means that the West Germans are worried about being "singularized"; TNF weapons remaining after eliminations pursuant to the INF treaty would be mostly based in, or designed to explode in, Germany. West German political parties have closed ideological ranks to object to deployment of a Lance follow-on; the objections forced West German Chancellor Helmut Kohl to get the United States and other alliance partners to defer the issue for further study; finally FOTL was canceled in May 1990.[96] The Bush administration finally obtained West German and British agreement to a proposed acceleration of East-West conventional-force reductions and a temporary deferral of SRF modernization until after the next West German elections.

On the other hand, other alliance members, including some nuclear armed ones, insist upon TNF modernization as necessary in order to maintain deterrence under reduced nuclear-, and perhaps conventional-, force inventories in Europe. Already there are objections to INF on the grounds that it preserves Soviet force advantages in conventional weapons deployed in Europe or capable of attacking Europe. Further, prominent U.S. politicians, including President Bush's vice-president, have suggested that START might be held up until conventional-force reductions in Europe are agreed to.[97] The West Germans will almost certainly have to go along with some kind of modernization, although for domestic purposes the issue of singularity will somehow have to be dealt with. The INF solution was to spread the deployments among other members of the alliance. This made sense because the systems in question were of longer range and not designed for early use. The short-range systems are likely to be used early in war if at all. They and the C^3 systems on which they depend are priority targets for Pact conventional offenses. There is considerable risk of two sorts for NATO: The conventional war may have progressed beyond the point where SRF are useful before nuclear release can be granted (although the United States could grant release to its forces through its own chain of command separately, with the attendant political complications), or vulnerable SRF may invite nuclear preemption that would not otherwise occur. The forward basing of nuclear artillery and short-range missiles trades off deterrence by viability for deterrence through competition in risk taking. Specifically, NATO is raising the risk of inadvertent escalation in order to deter conventional war.

This strategy implies that NATO C^3 is at least as survivable and flexible as that of the Pact. Competition in risk taking is a strategy that is thought through under peacetime assumptions and then applied to a wartime environment. NATO's collage of military doctrines, national force deployments, and C^3 systems must remain cohesive in the face of unprecedented stress or its risk-acceptant strategy will be turned against it. Escalatory brinkmanship is self-defeating for the side that has less survivable and supple command and control systems, few survivable theater nuclear forces, and conventional forces that are themselves in need of modernization. Further, the START regime may reduce the U.S. strategic nuclear arsenal to some 6,000 warheads, creating additional pressure for theater nuclear and conventional forces to fulfill their missions in a self-sufficient way. The modernization of theater nuclear and conventional forces will require order of magnitude improvements in capabilities for precision guidance, reconnaissance and surveillance, and battle management in order to fulfill the tasking set by NATO commanders in the 1990s. The Soviet modernization set in train by Gorbachev will doubtless result in a smaller, but more supple, Soviet and Pact force opposite the Western TVD. NATO's capability to preserve its political cohesion during crisis or war may be under more stress in the 1990s than in the 1980s; increasingly dependent on communications and electronics technology, the Western alliance will face an opponent whose own strategies and tables of organization and equipment are also undergoing substantial recasting.

CONCLUSION

The avoidance of inadvertent conventional war is as important as the fear of nuclear conflict, since the first can lead directly to the second. It needs recalling, though, that conventional deterrence is not the same as nuclear deterrence. Conventional deterrence is based upon the capability to deny a prospective attacker his objective, preferably at an acceptable cost to the defender. Nuclear deterrence is based primarily on the credible capacity of the defender to punish the attacker by imposing unacceptable costs on the society of the latter. Although both denial and punishment capabilities exert influence in both cases, the relative emphasis is clear. Where conventional and nuclear deterrence are commingled in the same force structure and policy guidance, a potential contradiction is created. Only a plausible theory of escalation control can resolve the tension between the requirements of conventional and nuclear deterrence imposed on the same template of states, decision makers, forces, and doctrines. The next chapter pursues the theme of control into its implications for the conduct of war on a theater scale with strategic significance.

NOTES

1. See Stephen M. Meyer, "The Sources and Prospects of Gorbachev's New Political Thinking on Security," *International Security* 13, no. 2 (Fall 1988), pp. 124–63; and Raymond L. Garthoff, "New Thinking in Soviet Military Doctrine," *Washington Quarterly* 11, no. 3 (Summer 1988), pp. 131–58. A timely Soviet statement in a Western forum is that of Colonel General Makhmut Gareyev, "Soviet Military Doctrine: Current and Future Developments," *RUSI Journal*, Winter 1988, pp. 5–10.

2. M. P. Skirdo, *Narod, armiya, polkovodets* (The people, the army, the military leader) (Moscow: 1970). U.S. Air Force Soviet Military Thought Series (Washington: GPO, undated), p. 98.

3. B. Byely et al., *Marksizm-leninizm o voyne i armii* (Marxism-Leninism on war and the army) (Moscow: Progress Publishers, 1972). U.S. Air Force Soviet Military Thought Series (Washington: GPO, undated).

4. Skirdo, *Narod, armiya, polkovodets*, p. 89.

5. Central Intelligence Agency and Defense Intelligence Agency, *Gorbachev's Economic Program: Problems Emerge* (Washington: March 24, 1988).

6. Brezhnev's comments at Tula in 1977 are noted in Raymond L. Garthoff, *Detente and Confrontation* (Washington: Brookings Institution, 1985), p. 771.

7. Skirdo, *Narod, armiya, polkovodets*, and Byely, *Marksizm-leninizm, passim.*

8. Marshal A. A. Grechko, *Vooruzhennye sily sovetskogo gosudarstva* (The armed forces of the Soviet state) (Moscow: 1975), Ch. 4, Ch. 6. U.S. Air Force Soviet Military Thought Series (Washington: GPO, undated).

9. M. A. Gareyev, *M. V. Frunze—Voyennyy teoretik* (Moscow: Voyenizdat, 1985), translated as M. V. Frunze—Military Theorist (New York: Pergamon Brassey's, 1988), p. 216.

10. Ibid., p. 217.

11. Marshal N. V. Ogarkov, *Vsegda v gotovnosti k zashchite Otechestva* (Always in readiness to defend the Fatherland) (Moscow: Voyenizdat, 1982), p. 15.

12. Ibid., p. 16.

13. Raymond L. Garthoff, *Detente and Confrontation: American-Soviet Relations from Nixon to Reagan* (Washington: Brookings Institution, 1985), Ch. 21.

14. V. G. Rezhichenko, I. N. Vorob'yev, N. F. Miroshnichenko, Yu. S. Nadirov, *Taktika* (Tactics) (Moscow: Voyenizdat, 1984), Ch. 1, part 5, "The Basic Principles of Conducting Modern Combined Arms Combat."

15. Ibid.

16. Ibid.

17. Ibid.

18. V. G. Reznichenko, I. N. Vorob'yev, N. F. Miroshnichenko, *Taktika* (Tactics) (Moscow: Voyenizdat, 1987), Ch. 1, part 2, "Essence and Forms of Modern Combined Arms Combat."

19. Ibid., Ch. 1, part 4, "Basic Principles of Modern Combined Arms Combat."

20. Ibid., Ch. 6, part 1, "The Essence of Defensive Battle." Emphasis added.

21. Ibid. According to the Voroshilov Lectures, in a nuclear war "decisive importance" is given to the timely delivery of initial strategic nuclear strikes by strategic nuclear forces and by the nuclear delivery means of the fronts and fleets. Moreover, it cannot be excluded that "the strategic action of the Armed Forces in a theater of strategic military action would terminate following initial massive nuclear strikes" in cases where "the strategic initiative is seized by our Armed Forces and, as a result of nuclear strikes, the

major imperialist countries are ousted from the war, because the restoration of their armed forces and industry requires a long time." Ghulam Dastagir Wardak, compiler, and Graham Hall Turbiville, Jr., general editor, *The Voroshilov Lectures: Materials from the Soviet General Staff Academy*, Vol. I (Washington: National Defense University Press, 1989), pp. 254, 237.

22. Ibid.

23. Ibid.

24. Ibid.

25. Ibid., Ch. 6, part 2, "Typical Features of Modern Defensive Battle and Requirements Imposed on Defense." In an important article on the battle of Kursk from the perspective of contemporary Soviet doctrine, Kokoshin and Larionov note that, at the outset of the Second World War, the Soviet high command was preoccupied ("carried away") with the idea of carrying the war immediately into the enemy's territory. Thus "the possibility of conducting operations in their own territory was for all intents and purposes excluded. This had an extremely adverse affect on the preparation of not only defense, but also of theaters of military operations in the depth of their own territory." See A. Kokoshin and V. Larionov, "The Battle of Kursk in Light of Contemporary Defensive Doctrine," *Mirovaya Ekonomika i Mezhdunarodnyye Otnosheniya (MEMO)*, No. 8 (August 1987), pp. 32–40. In *M. V. Frunze*, Gareyev attempts to reconcile Soviet lack of preparedness for strategically defensive operations in June 1941 with the correctness of Soviet military theory in general. He notes that "the most important provisions of Soviet military-theoretical thought were affirmed" but "it would be wrong to assert that all the provisions of our military theory were irreproachable and had been completely worked out prior to the war." It turned out that "not all questions could be foreseen with sufficient scientific reliability" because one of the most difficult issues facing the Soviet high command was "the organization and conduct of the strategic defensive." As a result, "The underestimation of the defensive and the incorrect assessment of the changing character of the beginning period of a war had more severe consequences than is sometimes depicted in military literature." *M. V. Frunze*, Ch. 3, Part 3, "The Further development of Military Art," *passim*. See also S. P. Ivanov, *Nachal' nyy period voyny* (The initial period of war) (Moscow: Voyenizdat, 1974), esp. Ch. 11. I am grateful to Peter Adams for the Kikoshin-Larionov reference.

26. See Joel S. Wit, "Deep Strike: NATO's New Defense Concept and Its Implications for Arms Control," *Arms Control Today*, November 1983, pp. 1, 4–9; and Daniel Goure and Jeffrey R. Cooper, "Conventional Deep Strike: A Critical Look," *Comparative Strategy* 4, no. 3 (1984), pp. 215–48.

27. Chris Bellamy, *The Future of Land Warfare* (New York: St. Martin's Press, 1987), Ch. 7.

28. Col. Witold Pokruszynski, "There Is No Room for Surprise," *Zolnierz Wolnosci*, April 14, 1987, p. 3.

29. Ibid.

30. Col. Stanislaw Koziej, "Anticipated Directions for Change in Tactics of Ground Troops," *Przeglad Wojsk Ladowych*, September 1986, pp. 5–9. Translation for this and footnote 28 by Dr. Harold Orenstein, Soviet Army Studies Office, Fort Leavenworth, Kansas.

31. Ibid.

32. Ibid.

33. Ibid.

34. Ibid.

35. Ibid.

36. See Richard Ned Lebow, *Nuclear Crisis Management* (Ithaca, N.Y.: Cornell University Press, 1987), Ch. 2.

37. See John Erickson, "Soviet Cybermen: Men and Machines in the System," *Signal*, December 1984, reprinted in Stephen J. Cimbala, ed., *Soviet C3* (Washington: AFCEA International Press, 1987), pp. 82–88.

38. Fen Osler Hampsen, "Escalation in Europe," Ch. 4 in Graham T. Allison, Albert Carnesale, and Joseph S. Nye, Jr., *Hawks, Doves and Owls: An Agenda for Avoiding Nuclear War* (New York: W. W. Norton, 1985), pp. 80–114.

39. Paul Bracken, "Accidental Nuclear War," Ch. 2 in Allison et al., eds., *Hawks, Doves and Owls*, pp. 25–53.

40. See Raymond L. Garthoff, "Mutual Deterrence, Parity and Strategic Arms Limitation in Soviet Policy," Ch. 5 in Derek Leebaert, ed., *Soviet Military Thinking* (London: Allen and Unwin, 1981), pp. 92–124.

41. Vitaliy Zhurkin, Sergey Karaganov, and Andrey Kortunov, "Security Challenges: Old and New," *Kommunist* 1 (January 1988), pp. 42–50.

42. Ibid.

43. Ibid.

44. Ibid.

45. A. G. Arbatov, A. A. Vasilyev, and A. A. Kokoshin, "Nuclear Weapons and Strategic Stability," *SShA: Ekonomika, politika, ideologiya* 9 (September 1987), pp. 3–13.

46. Ibid.

47. Ibid.

48. Ibid.

49. Zhurkin, Karaganov, and Kortunov, "Security Challenges."

50. Ibid.

51. Ibid.

52. Yevgeniy Velikhov, "Call for Change," *Kommunist* 1 (January 1988), pp. 51–53.

53. Ibid.

54. See Bruce G. Blair, *Strategic Command and Control: Redefining the Nuclear Threat* (Washington: Brookings Institution, 1985), for background and Blair, "Alerting in Crisis and Conventional War," Ch. 3 in Ashton B. Carter, John D. Steinbruner, and Charles A. Zraket, eds., *Managing Nuclear Operations* (Washington: Brookings Institution, 1987), pp. 75–120.

55. Scott D. Sagan, "Nuclear Alerts and Crisis Management," *International Security* 9 (Spring 1985), pp. 99–139.

56. For the discussion below, see Graham T. Allison, *Essence of Decision: Explaining the Cuban Missile Crisis* (Boston: Little, Brown, 1971); Alexander L. George, "The Cuban Missile Crisis, 1962," in Alexander L. George, David K. Hall, and William E. Simons, *The Limits of Coercive Diplomacy* (Boston: Little, Brown, 1971), pp. 86–143; McGeorge Bundy and James L. Blight, "October 27, 1962: Transcripts of the Meetings of the ExComm," *International Security* 12, no. 3 (Winter 1987-88), pp. 30–92; Elie Abel, *The Missile Crisis* (New York: Bantam Books, 1966). Extremely valuable on Soviet decision making and on the aftermath of the crisis that extended until November 20 is Raymond L. Garthoff, *Reflections on the Cuban Missile Crisis* (Washington: Brookings Institution, 1989).

57. Allison, *Essence of Decision*, pp. 110–11. See Leon Sloss, "Impact of Deception on U.S. Nuclear Strategy," Ch. 20 in Brian D. Dailey and Patrick J. Parker, eds., *Soviet*

Strategic Deception (Lexington, Mass.: Lexington Books, 1987), pp. 431–48, as well as the chapters in the same volume by William R. Graham and William R. Harris, for background on deception.

58. See the Bundy-Blight article, fn. 56.

59. Richard K. Betts, *Nuclear Blackmail and Nuclear Balance* (Washington: Brookings Institution, 1987), pp. 108–23.

60. Thomas C. Schelling, *Arms and Influence* (New Haven: Yale University Press, 1966), Ch. 3.

61. Abel, *Missile Crisis*, pp. 172–73.

62. Ibid., p. 173.

63. See Joseph S. Nye, Jr., Graham T. Allison, and Albert Carnesale, eds., *Fateful Visions: Avoiding Nuclear Catastrophe* (Cambridge, Mass.: Ballinger Publishing Co., 1988).

64. A NATO conceptual model of escalation is described in Paul Bracken, *The Command and Control of Nuclear Forces* (New Haven: Yale University Press, 1983), pp. 131–34.

65. For a résumé, see David N. Schwartz, *NATO's Nuclear Dilemmas* (Washington: Brookings Institution, 1983).

66. Josef Joffe, *The Limited Partnership: Europe, the United States and the Burdens of Alliance* (Cambridge, Mass.: Ballinger Publishing Co., 1987), treats this issue superbly.

67. See Desmond Ball and Jeffrey Richelson, eds., *Strategic Nuclear Targeting* (Ithaca, N.Y.: Cornell University Press, 1986).

68. Joffe, *Limited Partnership.*

69. Michael MccGwire, *Military Objectives in Soviet Foreign Policy* (Washington: Brookings Institution, 1987), Ch. 4.

70. See the chapters by Lawrence Freedman and David S.Yost in Ball and Richelson, eds., *Strategic Nuclear Targeting.*

71. For background, see Leon V. Sigal, *Nuclear Forces in Europe: Enduring Dilemmas, Present Prospects* (Washington: Brookings Institution, 1984).

72. Schelling, *Arms and Influence.*

73. Carl von Clausewitz, *On War*, edited and translated by Michael Howard and Peter Paret (Princeton: Princeton University Press, 1976).

74. See Richard Ned Lebow, "The Deterrence Deadlock: Is There a Way Out?" in Robert Jervis, Janice Gross Stein, and Richard Ned Lebow, *Psychology and Deterrence* (Baltimore: Johns Hopkins University Press, 1985), pp. 180–202.

75. See Timothy Ireland, "Building NATO's Nuclear Posture: 1950–65," Ch. 1 in Jeffrey D. Boutwell, Paul Doty, and Gregory F. Treverton, eds., *The Nuclear Confrontation in Europe* (London: Croom Helm, 1985), pp. 5–43.

76. See Walter Slocombe, "The Countervailing Strategy," *International Security* 5, no. 4 (Spring 1981), in Steven E. Miller, ed., *Strategy and Nuclear Deterrence* (Princeton: Princeton University Press, 1984), pp. 245–54. For a critique of countervailing strategy, see Robert Jervis, *The Illogic of American Nuclear Strategy* (Ithaca, N.Y.: Cornell University Press, 1984).

77. Statement by Lt. Gen. Brent Scowcroft, in ESD/MITRE Corporation, *Strategic Nuclear Policies, Weapons and the C^3 Connection* (Bedford, Mass.: MITRE Corporation, October 13–14, 1981), pp. 93–98.

78. Remarks prepared for delivery by Hon. Harold Brown, Secretary of Defense, at the U.S. Naval War College, Newport, Rhode Island, August 20, 1980, p. 6.

79. See Desmond Ball, "Counterforce Targeting: How New? How Viable?" *Arms Control Today* 11, no. 4 (February 1981), reprinted with revisions in John F. Reichart and Steven R. Sturm, eds., *American Defense Policy* (Baltimore: Johns Hopkins University Press, 1982), pp. 227–34.

80. Ibid.

81. Lawrence Freedman, *The Evolution of Nuclear Strategy* (New York: St. Martin's Press, 1981), Ch. 16.

82. Brown, see n. 78, p. 6.

83. Ibid., p. 7.

84. Peter Pringle and William Arkin, *SIOP* (New York: W. W. Norton, 1983), pp. 21–41.

85. See Desmond Ball, "The Development of the SIOP, 1960–1983," Ch. 3 in Ball and Richelson, eds., *Strategic Nuclear Targeting*, pp. 57–83; and Kurt Gottfried and Bruce G. Blair, *Crisis Stability and Nuclear War* (New York: Oxford University Press, 1988), Ch. 4.

86. Soviet concerns with regard to nuclear crisis management and escalation are discussed in Stephen M. Meyer, "Soviet Nuclear Operations," Ch. 15 in Carter, Steinbruner, and Zraket, eds., *Managing Nuclear Operations*, pp. 470–534.

87. Brown, see n. 78, p. 7.

88. On de-escalation, see Colin S. Gray, "Strategic De-escalation," Ch. 5 in Stephen J. Cimbala and Joseph D. Douglass, Jr., eds., *Ending a Nuclear War: Are the Superpowers Prepared?* (New York: Pergamon Brassey's, 1988), pp. 60–78.

89. See, for example, Jonathan Samuel Lockwood, *The Soviet View of U.S. Strategic Doctrine* (New York: National Strategy Information Center, 1983).

90. See the editions of *Soviet Military Power*, the public version of DOD's threat assessment, during the Reagan years.

91. Ashton B. Carter, "Assessing Command System Vulnerability," Ch. 17 in Carter, Steinbruner, and Zraket, eds., *Managing Nuclear Operations*, pp. 555–610.

92. Blair, *Strategic Command and Control*, Ch. 7.

93. U.S. Congress, Office of Technology Assessment, *Anti-Satellite Weapons, Countermeasures and Arms Control* (Washington: GPO, September 1985), p. 4.

94. Desmond Ball, *Controlling Theater Nuclear War*, Working Paper No. 138 (Canberra, Australia: Strategic and Defence Studies Centre, Research School of Pacific Studies, Australian National University, October 1987).

95. See Jesse James, "Tactical Nuclear Weapons: From the Halls of Montebello, to the Shores of Triple Z," *Arms Control Today*, December 1988, pp. 19–24.

96. Ibid.

97. *Arms Control Today*, December 1988, p. 25.

5

Control and Military Operations: Soviet Perspectives and Implications for NATO

The Soviet view of command and control is related to the Soviet view of war.[1] War is a political act designed to fulfill the political objectives of the party leadership. It has no goals, no objectives, no significance in and of itself. Thus the purpose of fighting cannot be divorced from the means for doing so. The Soviet command and control systems are part and parcel of this philosophy of war. The Soviet military elite is under the control of the Communist party of the Soviet Union, for the purpose of waging war if necessary. The Soviet leadership would prefer to accomplish its objectives without war. Thus one mission of the military in peacetime is to cast a shadow that follows Soviet diplomacy. Soviet diplomats speak with the knowledge that behind them stands the military power of their armed forces, which, if necessary, will be tasked to accomplish to same mission but in a different way.

The distinction between command and control is important in Western military thought and practice. Command is the leadership of forces in combat and peacetime in order that their objectives can be accomplished in the most effective and efficient manner.[2] Control is the monitoring of subordinates' behavior to accomplish the requirements of command.[3] In practice, there is overlap between command and control, but the missions are still judged to be distinct. The Soviet view is that command and control are inseparable. They are two halves of the same whole, as are war and peace.[4] Command is the responsibility of the commander. Control is also the responsibility of the commander. Control is both operational and ideological, in the Soviet view. Operational control means that subordinate commands understand their orders and effectively carry them out. Ideological controls ensure that the loyalty of commanders from the bottom to the top of the chain of command is secure.[5]

MYTHS ABOUT SOVIET COMMAND AND CONTROL

There are many myths about Soviet command and control for the conduct of military operations. Three examples are: (1) that the Soviet system is inflexible; (2) that Soviet technology is greatly inferior to Western; and (3) that the Soviet empire in Eastern Europe is less likely to fall apart under the stress of war than is the Western alliance.

As to the first item, alleged Soviet inflexibility, this contention results from a Western misperception of Soviet military strategy, operational art, and tactics. All are derived from military doctrine, which is the party-prescribed, authoritative policy for the conduct of war and, in peacetime, for the development and training of armed forces.[6] Military doctrine has two aspects: the socio-political and the military-technical. The socio-political aspects of military doctrine determine what wars the Soviet Union is prepared to fight, who the enemy is, and what the stakes are. Military-technical aspects of doctrine are concerned with the means and methods of fighting wars, including the necessity to make available to the armed forces the most modern means for doing so.[7] One should remember that the Soviets as Marxists believe that the strength of an economy lies in its scientific principles of organization and in its material base. The socio-political level of military doctrine, however important it is, is insufficient by itself to determine Soviet strategic, operational, or tactical objectives, or the means for attaining them. Soviet forces that go into war as anything less than the technological equals of their adversaries are in danger of losing, according to Marxist doctrine and the priorities of Soviet military planners.[8]

The second myth—the Soviet scientific, technological, and industrial advantage—is a strong one, related to the first myth. The postindustrial age surely challenges the ways and means of organizing the economy to bring to fruition the next stage of the scientific-technical revolution in military affairs. One stage the Soviets already have surmounted: the development and deployment of nuclear weapons. One recalls predictions in the 1940s that it would take the Soviet Union until the mid-1950s to detonate its first atomic weapon. The nuclear "revolution in military affairs" was quickly perceived by the Soviet elite and incorporated into their long-range planning for force structure, research and development, and operational art. By the end of the 1960s and against predictions of the U.S. Department of Defense and the U.S. intelligence community, the

Soviet Union had caught up with the United States in the numbers of delivery vehicles for launching strategic nuclear weapons. Today it maintains an essential parity with the United States in strategic nuclear forces, which it has every intention of maintaining.

The Soviets recognize that the revolution in military affairs has now taken another turn, away from total dependency on nuclear weapons for fighting major wars.[9] This revolution is fundamentally a revolution in information and electronics, including technology for remote sensing, precision aiming, and data processing. Future generations of artificial intelligence and other decision aids will provide commanders and military planners with options for conducting battles of unprecedented spatial breadth and depth.[10] The Soviet theory of deep operations, which has roots that go as far back as the czarist armies and that was developed most intensively in the 1930s by Tukhachevskiy and others, now depends upon the application of this second, postnuclear revolution to Soviet military art.[11] It is in one sense a "negation of the negation" in Marxist philosophy. The brooding omnipresence of nuclear weapons is now qualified by the development of smart, high-lethality non-nuclear weapons that can be tasked to accomplish missions formerly assigned to nuclear forces.

However, this second evolutionary step—toward improved non-nuclear capabilities for the accomplishment of strategic objectives in a theater of military operations—does not do away with nuclear weapons or their importance in Soviet strategy. Nuclear weapons remain as the *ultima ratio* if the issue cannot be decided by the conventional clash of arms. They also provide the Soviet armed forces with the means of counter-deterrence, in order to prevent NATO and U.S. first use of nuclear weapons except in the most desperate circumstances.[12] Thus the postnuclear and nuclear revolutions in military affairs will provide for the Soviet armed forces in the future a diverse panoply of options short of total war, and below the nuclear threshold.

The third myth is the cohesion of the Warsaw Pact compared to that of NATO. Even before the dramatic events of 1989 this was the problematical factor for Soviet planners. An important aspect of this issue is whether the Soviets anticipate a long or short war, a regional or a global one (Figures 5.1 and 5.2). In the case of a conventional war fought entirely in Europe, and preferably in Western Europe from the Soviet standpoint, the cohesion of the Warsaw Pact might be stressed at its periphery but would remain strong at its core. Now even more than prior to the demise of Ceaucescu, the southern flank of the Warsaw Pact is undependable. Unification of Germany and the expulsion of Soviet troops from Hungary and Czechoslovakia all but eliminate offensive Pact military options

Figure 5.1
Soviet Theaters of Strategic Military Action

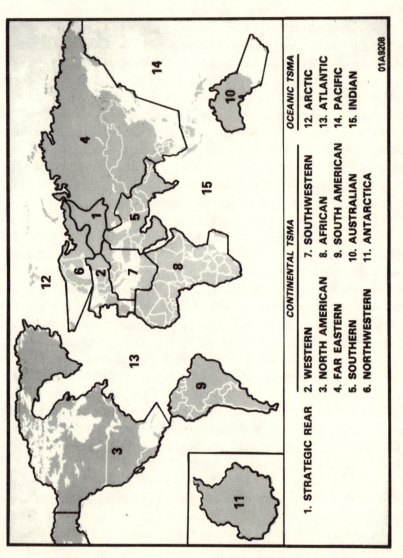

CONTINENTAL TSMA

1. STRATEGIC REAR
2. WESTERN
3. NORTH AMERICAN
4. FAR EASTERN
5. SOUTHERN
6. NORTHWESTERN
7. SOUTHWESTERN
8. AFRICAN
9. SOUTH AMERICAN
10. AUSTRALIAN
11. ANTARCTICA

OCEANIC TSMA

12. ARCTIC
13. ATLANTIC
14. PACIFIC
15. INDIAN

01A9208

Source: U. S. Department of Defense. See also John G. Hines and Phillip A. Petersen, "NATO and the Changing Soviet Concept of Control for Theater War," Ch. 3 in Stephen J. Cimbala, ed., *The Soviet Challenge in the 1990s* (New York: Praeger, 1989), pp. 65–118. For an updated Pentagon assessment, see *Washington Times*, March 12, 1990, p. A6.

against NATO based on short warning. The fate of CENTAG (Central Army Group) and NORTHAG (Northern Army Group) does not depend on what Rumania does, but on the decisions of East Germany, Poland, and Czechoslovakia, as well as Soviet ones. The forces of East Germany, Poland, and Czechoslovakia may act on behalf of national and strictly defensive goals, not according to Soviet wishes.[13] A war begun by the Soviet Union against the West for no apparent reason (apparent, that is, to the ruling elites in Eastern Europe) might lead to dissension and perhaps open revolt within the Bloc. But a war begun under such auspices is improbable. Causes for the outbreak of war will almost certainly be more ambiguous, or they can be made to seem ambiguous. Thus the responsibility for the outbreak of war will be placed on the shoulders of NATO, however wrongheaded this seems from NATO's standpoint.

The Soviets do not like to wage war against opponents who will offer strong resistance. Thus they will be reluctant to undertake a war in Western Europe unless NATO is showing signs of pluralistic disintegration. The class struggle in Europe, in Soviet parlance, should have progressed to the point at which the Red Army and its Warsaw Pact allies can topple the hollow shell of capitalism. Unless the Western political and economic systems are already rotting from within, they may not be vulnerable, in the Soviet expectation, to a push from without. The war must take place in an atmosphere in which NATO, and not the Pact, offers a divided house; otherwise, the war will be postponed until a more favorable time appears, or be forgotten altogether. This willingness to base war plans to some extent on political developments within the countries of prospective opponents is a derivative of Marxist doctrine and an expedient in maintaining alliance solidarity in the East. If NATO is divided and uncertain about its objectives, and especially if some members of NATO can be made to believe that NATO has provoked the crisis as much as the Soviets have, the Warsaw Pact has every opportunity to maintain its crisis and wartime cohesion.

Western observers often place their bets, for disruption of Soviet war plans and the prevention of a cohesive Pact offensive westward, on developments in Poland. Poland is certainly a serious concern to Soviet planners. The second strategic echelon must be got to the front through Poland. If the supplies and reinforcements can be interdicted by NATO, that is trouble enough. If they are interdicted by the Poles themselves, that is worse. Poland or at least its political and military leadership must be on board the Soviet war plan before the fact. One can assume that the Soviets know this; therefore, they will not embark upon war if the situation in Poland precludes their doing so. Of course, events may get out of hand,

Figure 5.2
European Theaters of Strategic Military Action

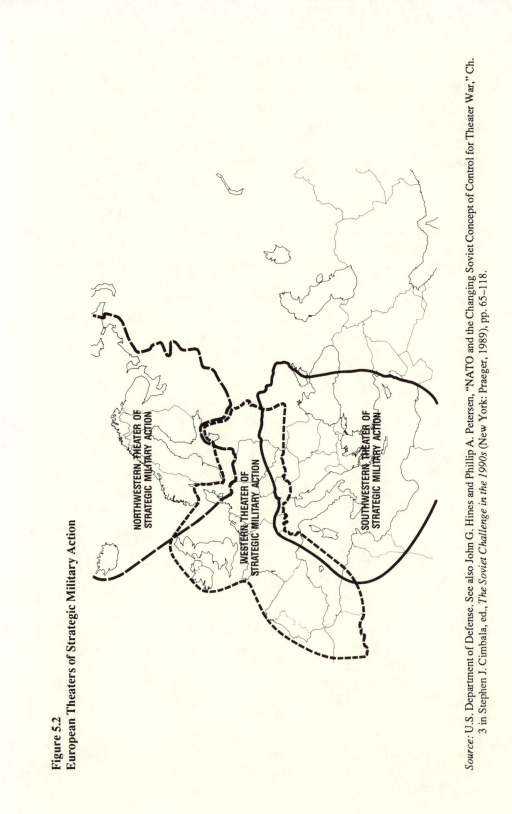

NORTHWESTERN THEATER OF
STRATEGIC MILITARY ACTION

WESTERN THEATER OF
STRATEGIC MILITARY ACTION

SOUTHWESTERN THEATER OF
STRATEGIC MILITARY ACTION

Source: U.S. Department of Defense. See also John G. Hines and Phillip A. Petersen, "NATO and the Changing Soviet Concept of Control for Theater War," Ch. 3 in Stephen J. Cimbala, ed., *The Soviet Challenge in the 1990s* (New York: Praeger, 1989), pp. 65–118.

and a crisis within Poland may spread outward to East Germany and then into West Germany, thus provoking East–West war by inadvertence. This is a popular Western scenario for the outbreak of war in Europe.[14] From the Soviet perspective, it has little chance of happening. The Soviet leadership, recognizing that war must fulfill a political aim or it is pointless, would back down from any war in which they could not assume a buttoned-down strategic rear, including the operational-strategic rear in Eastern Europe. Either Poland is on board or the war is off. Faced with the imminent reunification of Germany in 1990, Soviet and Polish military planners saw a virtue in the preservation of the Soviet military presence in Poland for defensive, not offensive, motives.

SOVIET OPERATIONAL ART

The Soviet expectation is that a war for strategic objectives in a theater of operations would have several phases.[15] The first phase would involve the paralysis of the political will to resist, and would be accomplished in peacetime. This paralysis need not last forever. It is sufficient if confusion reigns in the camps of the Soviets' potential opponents long enough for the Soviets to prepare their opening campaigns. During this preparatory phase, planning would include diplomatic initiatives for the disruption of NATO political cohesion in peacetime. The ideal achievement prior to the start of war would be to keep the United States in a state of indecision or uncertainty until the Soviets had actually begun military operations against Western Europe. Modern reconnaissance and intelligence systems make this no easy task. On the other hand, the Soviet intelligence services will have, as a result of their penetration of military and political institutions through Europe, accurate knowledge of those issues likely to be most divisive and of the ways in which to manipulate them.

This exploitation of potential differences among West Europeans within NATO, or between the U.S. and European branches, extends from the preparatory into the crisis phase. In this second phase, it becomes obvious that the possibility of war is no longer remote. Western military forces may be placed on alert. NATO capitals will be humming with activity. Thus the crisis phase must be managed so that war does not break out at an inopportune time for the Soviet Union.[16] Two things must be accomplished in this phase: NATO must be kept off balance and guessing with regard to the likelihood of any attack; and the nuts and bolts of the Soviet war plan must be put into place before war breaks out. This will include the command and control components of the strategic operation. During this phase if not before, the requirements for *zhivuchest'*, or sustainability

Figure 5.3

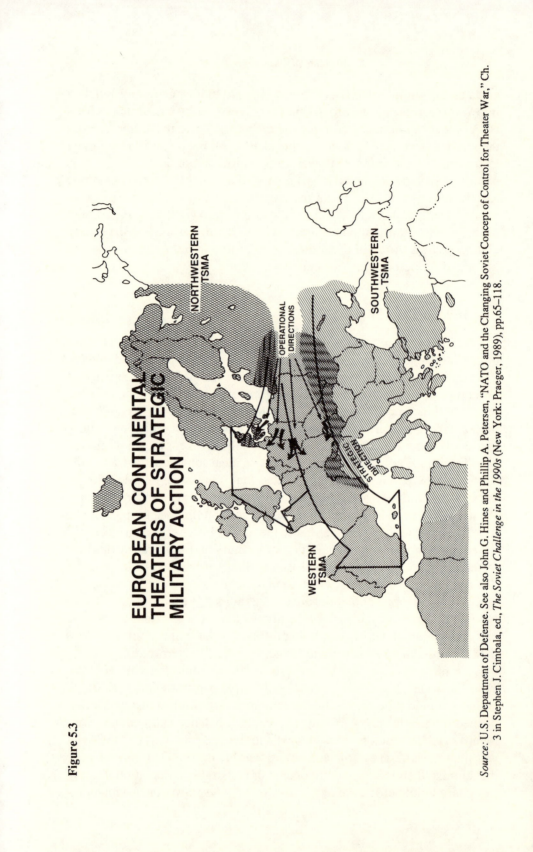

EUROPEAN CONTINENTAL
THEATERS OF STRATEGIC
MILITARY ACTION

NORTHWESTERN
TSMA

OPERATIONAL
DIRECTIONS

STRATEGIC
DIRECTION

WESTERN
TSMA

SOUTHWESTERN
TSMA

Source: U.S. Department of Defense. See also John G. Hines and Phillip A. Petersen, "NATO and the Changing Soviet Concept of Control for Theater War," Ch. 3 in Stephen J. Cimbala, ed., *The Soviet Challenge in the 1990s* (New York: Praeger, 1989), pp.65–118.

in its most inclusive sense, must be assured. Also during this phase, Soviet forces of special designation (*spetsnaz*) may be moved into critical areas within Western Europe, supplementing the preparatory work already completed by agents in place, in order to create time-urgent threats to vital NATO targets at the very outbreak of war, or even slightly before it.[17] These targets would include NATO political and military leadership, command centers, communications nodes, nuclear weapons storage sites, and other vital links in the chain of command and control. Soviet preparations to jam or otherwise disrupt NATO communications channels will also be exercised during the crisis phase, so that they can be activated rapidly once war begins.

The third phase is the outbreak of war itself. Here we must distinguish the preferred Soviet war plan from the way in which the war might actually proceed. The preferred Soviet war plan prior to 1989, according to the U.S. analysts who have closely studied Soviet literature and Soviet exercises, was for a rapid and decisive conventional offensive that closes off NATO's capability for nuclear escalation, disrupts its operational cohesion throughout the depth of the theater of operations, and maintains a tempo sufficient to force the West to withdraw to militarily indefensible positions, and then to surrender occupied territory.[18] The immediate objectives of the ground and tactical air campaign on the Central Front would be West Germany, the Low Countries, and parts of Norway and Denmark (see Figure 5.3). Britain and France would be excluded on account of their nuclear arsenals. A modified plan would seek to occupy most of West Germany while making it clear that the Soviets' political aim did not extend into the conquest of any other territory, especially not French territory. The Soviets would seek in this first phase of the war to dissuade or prevent NATO from nuclear escalation; to occupy significant portions of West Germany in order to establish a fait accompli with regard to future negotiations; to raise the threat of disestablishment of the governing bodies of the occupied territories, and to incorporate those territories into East Germany and Czechoslovakia, unless NATO forbears from continuing the war and especially from nuclear escalation.

A Soviet conventional offensive of this type calls for significant capabilities in firepower and maneuver. An air offensive would have to precede and prepare the way for the success of the ground offensive across the inter-German border. This air offensive might include prompt attacks from Pact short-range ballistic missiles (SRBMs) against NATO airfields, air defense installations, command and control centers, and other targets whose early destruction would increase the vulnerability of NATO's rear assets to follow-on destruction.[19] The air offensive would also include several waves of attacking aircraft—the first to clear paths through surviving air defenses and to attack targets of opportunity, and the second to accomplish key components of the counter-air and air defensive missions. Soviet frontal and strategic aviation in these waves of attacks would attempt to (1) destroy and degrade NATO forward and rearward air defense and C^3 capabilities, (2) destroy runways and aircraft shelters in order to prevent reconstitution of NATO tactical aircraft after their initial sorties, and (3) identify potential breakthrough points of vulnerability for Soviet first-echelon ground forces whose forward detachments would, simultaneously with the onset of the air offensive, be pushing across the FLOT (forward line of troops).

Soviet tactics in the ground offensive would follow a standard operational template but also be adapted to the situation at hand. Forward detachments would attempt to penetrate NATO defenses at the inter-German border along as many as six to ten separate axes of advance. These might meet with different rates of advance and success. Those that succeeded would be reinforced. The High Command of Forces in the TVD would decide within a very short time which axes of advance were most promising. Operational maneuver groups would be tasked as deep-raiding forces to exploit the potential for breakthrough in these sectors.[20] Where developments had proceeded most favorably, from the standpoint of Soviet commanders, forward detachments would have penetrated into NATO's tactical depth and disrupted the cohesion of its defenses. This tactical success would be meaningful, in the view of Soviet military planners, only if it were followed up by exploitation forces that turned tactical into operational, and operational into strategic, success.

The OMG (operational maneuver group) has become a highly visible, and controversial, symbol of Soviet military art in the West. It was a modern version of an old idea, open to misunderstanding. It was in part an adaptation of the Soviet experience with mobile groups in World War II to modern conditions, and in part a reflection of long-standing Soviet, and Russian, interests in deep operations.[21] However, and somewhat inconsistently with Soviet precedent, it was also a daring concept that creates significant risks of failure, should the timing of commitment, tasking, and structure of the OMG prove to be inappropriate. In addition to the problem of greater risk should planning prove inaccurate, there is also the greater challenge to command and control inherent in the use of OMGs, especially at *front* level. An army-size OMG is going to be a heterogeneous force composed of tank, motor rifle, heliborne assault, and other components that will appear in its final form only after it has *erupted within the rear of its opponent's defenses.*[22] In other words, it may be clear on paper and in peacetime exercises what is desired by higher level commanders, but in wartime the chaos attendant to getting the OMG into the right place, at the right time, may be substantial. The other side to this, from the standpoint of "Blue looking at Red," is that NATO may have difficulty deciding where exactly the OMG is located or what exactly it is composed of. An OMG that has not yet been launched on its preferred trajectory is an inchoate force-in-the-making, and its composition may alter as it worms its way through the resistance of NATO defenses, which can be assumed to extract some costs even under the most unfavorable (for NATO) conditions.

But we are focusing on the Soviet problem of command and control, not the NATO one (see Figure 5.4). The Soviet problem will, as we have seen, require the identification of the most attractive axes of advance into NATO depth. Then the exploitation-raiding forces must be shot into the bolt before NATO can preempt their arrival, either by destroying the inchoate OMGs on their launching pads or by preparing an unwelcome reception for them at their intended destinations. Given the preservation of sufficient NATO command and control throughout its operational depth, these unwelcome receptions could turn the OMG into a confused and isolated force surrounded by unfriendly natives. Thus, to take maximum advantage of OMG and other specially tasked raiding forces, Soviet commanders must attack NATO's command and control via the air operation, and prior to the arrival of the OMG in NATO's tactical or operational depth.[23] The NATO forward defenses and their limited operational reserves will be attempting to seal off the punctures created by Soviet forward detachments and the follow-on forces of the first operational strategic echelons. If the forward defenses can hold a line that is bending but not breaking, and if the Soviets can be prevented from disrupting NATO's rearward cohesion as a result of counter-air, counter-C^3, and counter-nuclear deep strikes, then the potential for the successful use of OMGs will be very limited. There is also, from the standpoint of Soviet planners, the difficulty of coordinating the combined air and ground components of the OMG. The Soviets practice combined arms, and it is deeply embedded in their operational philosophy and practice. However, absent the immediate collapse of NATO's forward defense within days, the Soviets will be hard pressed to coordinate the combined use of air and ground components of army- and division-level OMGs against the kind of forces NATO will be able to direct against them. Given a continuation of present political and miliary trends in Eastern and Central Europe, the prospects for NATO defenses appear decidedly optimistic.

The command and control battle to establish the OMGs in NATO's

Figure 5.4
Wartime Command Systems of Opposing Forces in Central Europe

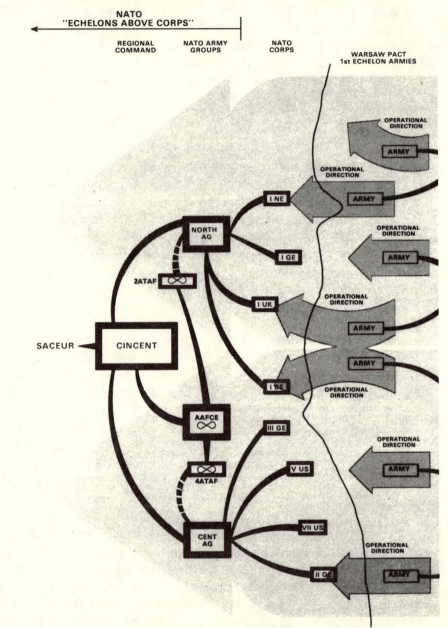

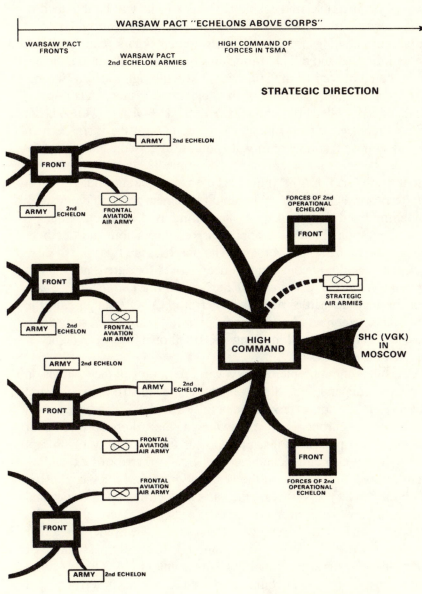

WARSAW PACT "ECHELONS ABOVE CORPS"

WARSAW PACT
FRONTS

WARSAW PACT
2nd ECHELON ARMIES

HIGH COMMAND OF
FORCES IN TSMA

STRATEGIC DIRECTION

ARMY 2nd ECHELON

FRONT

ARMY 2nd ECHELON

FRONTAL
AVIATION
AIR ARMY

FRONT

ARMY 2nd ECHELON

FRONTAL
AVIATION
AIR ARMY

ARMY 2nd ECHELON

ARMY 2nd ECHELON

FRONT

FRONTAL
AVIATION
AIR ARMY

FRONTAL
AVIATION
AIR ARMY

FRONT

ARMY 2nd ECHELON

FORCES OF 2nd
OPERATIONAL
ECHELON

FRONT

STRATEGIC
AIR ARMIES

HIGH
COMMAND

SHC (VGK)
IN
MOSCOW

FRONT

FORCES OF 2nd
OPERATIONAL
ECHELON

STRATEGIC DIRECTION

Source: U.S. Department of Defense. See also John G. Hines and Phillip A. Petersen, "NATO and the Changing Soviet Concept of Control for Theater War," Ch. 3 in Stephen J. Cimbala, ed., *The Soviet Challenge in the 1990s* (New York: Praeger, 1989), pp. 65–118. For an updated assessment, see *Washington Times*, March 12, 1990, p. A6.

operational depth, and so to disrupt and destroy the cohesion of NATO's defenses, will also have to take into account the effect of NATO deep strikes into the Soviet second echelon. These attacks will be intended to disrupt the forward movement of reinforcements, and to destroy fixed and mobile targets including bridges, rail transshipment points, road junctions, and the various road and rail platforms on which stocks of equipment and troops are being moved from the Soviet Union through Eastern Europe. There is some misunderstanding of the objectives of this NATO operational subconcept, called Follow-on Forces Attack (FOFA).[24] FOFA is not designed to replace, or to preclude, robust defense at the inter-German border. It does not substitute for forward defense against the Pact first-echelon forces, because these are the most immediately dangerous, and because the politics of NATO precludes the voluntary surrender of West German territory. FOFA is designed to complement forward defense by providing improved sensors, deep-strike munitions, and fusion centers to allow the attack on fixed and mobile targets throughout the depth of Eastern Europe to the Soviet border.[25] The purposes are twofold: to raise the nuclear threshold by conventional deep strike, for deterrence, and to destroy reinforcements *without which* the Soviets must *adjust their game plan* for the forward battle. And ideally, from NATO's standpoint, the Soviets would be forced to adjust their plan in "real time," something which NATO planners have long contended their own forces can do better than the Soviets can.

FOFA is not without problems, however. First, some of the systems on which it would depend, including conventional deep-strike missiles and airborne sensors, are not yet developed or fully tested.[26] Second, the Soviet strategy for war in Europe will certainly include the prompt destruction of those sensors and platforms that provide for the possibility of prompt attacks on their reinforcing echelons. This creates the risk of expanding the depth of Soviet offensives at the very outset of war. Such expansion is already the Soviet propensity on the basis of doctrine, but the doctrinal impulse would now be reinforced by the expedient pressure of NATO's marriage between high technology and deep strike. The Soviet version of high technology mated to deep strike could be absolutely destructive of NATO's plans for the operational defensive, unless NATO adds to its operational reserves *and* can count upon the use of French territory and the probable early commitment of French forces to the forward battle in West Germany.[27]

Third, to the extent that the Soviets assume that FOFA is going to succeed, they have additional incentives to develop and deploy theater ballistic missile defenses (ATBMs) and to improve the mobile surface-to-air (SAM) defense systems that will accompany their forces into combat. The West has these options too, but it also has political impediments to seeing these systems actually put into place. Moreover, the potential deployment of ATBMs and improved air defenses by both sides may create a high-technology stalemate rather than a low-technology one. There is, for the Western side, the additional possibility that even theater ballistic missile defenses, let along Soviet strategic ones, might diminish the credibility of limited strategic options, disallowing the possibility of sub-SIOP nuclear strikes as a deterrent to Soviet nuclear escalation.[28]

FUTURE ISSUES

Soviet planning for future war in Europe must address the following issues, among others. First, will the technology spinoffs from SDI lead to improvements in NATO high-technology conventional defenses that trump current and future Soviet war planning? Second, can the Soviets exercise their command and control systems in wartime with the expectation of cooperation on the part of their formerly Communist allies in Eastern Europe? Third, can the Soviets assume that any war in Europe, whether begun by them deliberately or resulting from crisis mismanagement and inadvertent escalation, will be conducted without the use of nuclear weapons? There are no easy answers to these questions.

The first question obviously troubles Soviet planners and accounts for some of their anxiety about SDI. They can depend upon the ABM treaty as a vehicle for limiting U.S. territorial defenses unless the U.S. government chooses to abrogate the treaty. But theater ballistic missile defenses are not precluded by the ABM treaty. Nor are innovations in other technological areas, including the use of lasers in ground forces' operations, precluded. SDI research and development, as seen by the Soviets, may lead to technological offsets to their superior forces in being on the Central Front. On the other hand, it should be remembered that what the West invents, the Soviets can emulate or functionally duplicate with some other system. The Soviets do not lag behind the West in basic research, but rather in applications of it to systems engineering and operations research. The lags are also less pronounced in the military sector than in others.[29]

The second question—of maintaining command and control in wartime—is of critical importance for the Soviet military, and has several parts. The Soviets must disrupt NATO's cohesion even while they preserve their own. This implies fast-moving operations in three dimensions that deny the initiative to NATO at all stages. It also implies a three-dimensional "battle of the ether" for the control of information and intelligence: electronic support measures (ESM), electronic countermeasures (ECM), and electronic counter-countermeasures (ECCM).[30] This tripartite electronic warfare will depend upon who has the better technology, and who has the better concept. Open-source literature would argue, as of the moment, that NATO and the United States in particular have the better technology but the Soviets have the superior concept.[31] It takes delving into the actual outcomes of exercises to referee this. However, one can infer from open sources that the Soviets are not standing still with regard to technology or the concept of information war (radio-electronic combat, reflexive control, and so forth). Therefore NATO must improve its technology and command concepts while trying to understand the Soviet concept and how it is evolving. NATO must also do something about Soviet SIGINT penetration of its secrets in peacetime and the capability for doing so in wartime.[32] If things remain as they are now, there is the significant possibility that NATO plans and movements will be known before they are implemented and, if so implemented, defeated. For the moment, the largest uncertainty for Soviet military planners is the political unreliability of formerly Communist allies in Eastern Europe and especially the uncertain political status of East Germany.

The third question is whether any war in Europe could be conducted for very long without the introduction of nuclear weapons into the battle. Related to this is the question whether, once they are used, their use can be contained. The first thing to say about this is that NATO Europeans and Americans have genuine differences of opinion about escalation. Europeans prefer to present to the Soviet Union the prospect of prompt escalation to nuclear warfare, in the interest of deterrence of any war. Americans are understandably more interested in firebreaks, thresholds of intra-war deterrence, and the possibility of gradations in conventional, or even nuclear, war fighting.[33] A large literature has been devoted to this topic, but it is more informative with regard to force structure and deterrence doctrine than regarding command-control issues.

The first part of the third question is the feasibility and desirability of keeping war below the nuclear threshold. It might seem self-evident that this is so, considering the potential destructiveness of nuclear war compared to conventional. But it must be remembered that the primary objective of NATO is deterrence. The firebreak between conventional and nuclear war cannot be so distinct that deterrence is eroded and the Soviets emboldened to challenge NATO below the nuclear threshold. Related to the theoretical issue of a clear and sharp distinction between conventional and nuclear war is the perception of Soviet doctrine held by Western analysts. It is now appreciated by U.S. and other NATO Western observers that the Soviets have long since departed from an early doctrinal expectation of one variant war. They now anticipate that war in Europe might include an extended conventional phase, or even be conducted entirely without the use of nuclear weapons.[34] Further, and most untraditionally for the Soviets in the nuclear age, there is some evidence of increased capability for, and declaratory interest in, the selective and graduated use of nuclear weapons in order to obtain military objectives in a theater-strategic operation.[35]

This is not necessarily good news for NATO. Were the Soviets to become much more optimistic about containing war below the nuclear threshold, or about fighting a limited nuclear war in Europe without extending it into superpower homelands, deterrence might weaken. Here we see the clash between two theories of deterrence and, contrary to standard accounts, both Western and Soviet writings borrow from both genres. The first genre is the absolutist argument that nuclear deterrence is indivisible. In this view, the Soviet Union will disbelieve the U.S. pledge of extended deterrence unless the U.S. and NATO force structure is configured so that NATO's options are nothing or massive retaliation. The second genre is the relativist position, which argues that the capability for graduated and selective nuclear response is more dissuasive of aggression because the putative aggressor will find it more believable. In a way, both theories are statements of important truths about deterrence. It can fail drastically or gracefully, all at once or in stages. It has never failed in Europe since nuclear weapons were deployed there, so hypothetical arguments seem to cancel one another out.

But not entirely. NATO must ask to whose advantage it is to accept positions on the relativist side of the scale as opposed to the absolutist. The absolutist position is militarily dubious but politically acceptable to NATO parliaments and publics. The relativist position is militarily more defensible, especially if deterrence fails, but may contribute to the very failure of the deterrence it aims to prevent. Herein lies the paradox if not the irony. The absolutist position—that the seamless web of deterrence cannot be broken apart and threatened in increments—ironically assumes a very fragile balance of terror, for if the balance of terror between superpowers were stable it would not be risky to subdivide it into increments of more, or less, feasible use. Conversely, the implications of the relativist position are that the balance of terror must be very stable. Otherwise the threat to wage nuclear war in installments can never be credible, because the jump from small to large exchanges will be almost automatic.[36]

The first aspect of this issue—of feasible conventional or limited nuclear war fighting in Europe—was the feasibility or desirability of such a doctrine and force posture. The second aspect is the availability of command, control, and communications (C^3) for extended conventional or nuclear war fighting. No one can deny that NATO has made and is making significant improvements in its C^3; more can certainly be expected by the 1990s. So are the Soviets. The question is whether command-system improvements can offset the expected disruption and destruction to which they will be subjected in the event of war in Europe at any time in this century. It would seem a safe hypothesis that the lethality of modern conventional weapons has increased at least as much as the survivability of communications and other control assets.[37] This could change if the superpowers and their alliances continue to base more of their important communications and control assets in space, while at the same time forgoing the deployment of very competent, long-range antisatellite weapons (ASATs). Absent arms control agreements of this type, it would appear that the improvements of C^3 technology cannot be guaranteed to be any more survivable in the future, against conventional high-technology or nuclear attack, than they are now.

In addition, the Soviet conventional war plan calls for destruction of NATO C^3 assets as early in war as possible, in order to preclude the defender's capability for nuclear escalation.[38] Many of these command, control, and communications assets destroyed in attacks with conventional weapons are also relied upon for the conduct of theater or strategic nuclear war. Either theater or strategic ballistic missile defenses might serve to protect C^3 in Europe or in North America, and so preclude the prompt destruction of command systems. On the other hand, the deployment of theater or strategic defenses introduces complications with regard to U.S. domestic politics, transatlantic arms control policies, and possible Soviet reactions, including the potential for BMD deployments of their own.[39] One argument for defenses that protect command centers and communications is that C^3 systems are subject to degradation more rapidly than forces, which may be used up over a longer period of time. A partial disruption of a command system might ripple through the system and result in faulty decisions all along the line. On the other hand, command systems can be made to degrade gracefully, as in the case of packet-switching techniques or distributed data processing and communications networks. SDI or ATBM systems might utilize distributed design networks in order to offset the possibility of rapid, as opposed to gradual, degradation. The theater ballistic missile defenses would have to degrade more gradually than the C^3 systems they protected; otherwise, they would contribute to systemic defense failure of the weapons platforms themselves.

SOVIET DEFENSIVISM

Recent pronouncements at party conferences and Warsaw Pact conclaves, and in military and party publications, have raised the issue of whether Soviet military doctrine is evolving in the direction of a declaratory and operational defensivism. If so, what are its implications for NATO strategy and operations, including command and control, and for Soviet strategy and command systems? Some of this has already been alluded to. *Perestroika* might contribute to the development of enhanced-technology force multipliers that could make Soviet operational art that much more formidable. On the other hand, the Soviet planner must fear that NATO could potentially afford to deploy more of this technology than the Pact, provided NATO were committed to doing so. These microeconomic and intermediate operational-strategic impacts of *perestroika* are significant, but the most interesting political possibility is that of a revision of Soviet aims and objectives.

The Soviet interest in strategic defensivism is nothing new. There is a long-standing belief based on Soviet military experience that the strategic defensive can be combined with an assertive and offensively minded operational art. This the Soviets have learned from Clausewitz, and from their own experience. The relationship between offense and defense is always dialectical, never static. Thus "defensive sufficiency" does not preclude the preparedness for retaliatory counteroffensives of the most decisive kind, and at the earliest opportunity. This is made clear by Gareyev in his widely acclaimed discussion of Frunze as a military theorist.[40] Nor is this all. Defensive sufficiency can be adopted by the Soviets, in their view, only if the capitalist world cooperates. That is the point of ventilating their debates about it. If the capitalists will not cooperate, in the form of arms-control agreements that leave the Soviets no worse off with defensive sufficiency than without it, then the Soviets cannot implement a restructured force-development program. This is more than the old arms-race idea, which has been questioned by astute analysts for many decades. The Soviets may be racing with themselves. They are caught on the horns of a dilemma: In order to modernize their economy for the long run, they must, in the short run, reallocate some resources to consumption and investment, especially the latter, and away from defense. All modern industrial societies face this macro-allocative choice among consumption, investment, and government spending, but the choices the Soviets must make over the next several decades are especially problematic.

In the next century the Soviet military and political leadership could well be faced with economic and technological backwardness comparable to that of present-day Third World countries.[41] This would have ominous implications for the Marxist world view. It would also have ominous implications for the Soviet military, which has been arguing for some time, with Marshal Ogarkov in the lead, for modernization of Soviet conventional, high-technology forces and command systems.[42] However, the economic and technological modernization cannot be accomplished by the Soviet leadership without devolution of political and economic initiative contrary to the Stalinist canon. Hence it is no accident that another campaign of de-Stalinization is underway in Moscow, accompanied by another campaign of de-Brezhnevization. For the collectivism of Stalin is only one half of the legacy that stands in the way of devolution, preceding or accompanying modernization. The other "ism" standing in the way of progress is immobilism. This is by far the greater danger. The Soviets can recreate the memory of Stalin to suit the stylistic needs of current public relations; the generations that can recall the experiences of the Great Patriotic War are now passing the torch to younger cadres. It will be harder to overcome the inertia of large planning bureaucracies and party hierarchies that have become dependent upon the routinization of mediocrity for their survival. Andropov's efforts to regenerate this system from the top reveal the difficulties of fighting an entrenched system of "mediocracy."

So, too, in the armed forces. It is one thing to tell commanders that they will be provided with computers and other decision aids in order to carry out even more faithfully the operational and strategic designs of the higher levels. It is quite another thing to expect tactical innovation and operational creativity under the stress of combat to evolve a Soviet version of *auftragstaktik*, in which subordinates are given a broad mission statement and left to their own wits with regard to its implementation. This will demand not only improved C^3 technology but a new Soviet strategic culture, and this culture will have to be rooted in cultural change more broadly defined. One implication is that the non-Russian and non-Slavic nationalities will have to be brought up to an educational par with their fellow citizens if the Soviets expect to maintain armed forces of their current sizes and geographical deployments, relative to those of their potential opponents. It may well be that the trade-off in the 1990s and beyond will have to be between larger armed forces, which are less well equipped and trained, and a smaller force that has the latest technology and is more dependable across the board. This would be consolation if it were not for the apparent need for NATO to face the same set of decisions.

It is also not clear whether the Soviet interest in high-technology conventional modernization, in response to assumed NATO and U.S. interest, is motivated by feelings of presumed inferiority. As Leon Goure has noted, some Western enthusiasm for the development of conventional high-technology weapons "is based on an ethnocentric bias—on faith in perpetual U.S. technological superiority over the Soviet Union."[43] The eventual impact of the postnuclear revolution in military affairs is not yet clear, and by imitating Western innovations at less cost, the Soviets can have their cake and eat it, too. In addition, the enthusiasm of U.S. NATO allies for high-technology–deep attack reconnaissance-strike complexes may wither if they perceive them to be provocative to the Soviet Union and dissuasive of Soviet interest in arms control. Last, there is the problem of the considerable expense needed to get some of the technologies off the drawing board onto the battlefield and to provide ammunition and spare parts to sustain them on the modern battlefield.[44]

All of this suggests that war in Europe, if it remained below the nuclear threshold, might very well occur in two phases. The first phase would involve rapid and fluid engagements in which forces moved over broad fronts and used up most of their better divisions and equipment. Then the second phase might continue with degraded and comparatively primitive C^3, reserve forces, and attrition tactics.[45] Sustainability would become the more important for as long as the fighting continued without negotiation or escalation. Arguably, neither side is very well prepared for this extended battlefield. Not only might the duration and cost of fighting be extended, compared to prewar expectations, but the very concept of fighting might degenerate into a grinding endurance contest bereft of clear doctrinal and political guidance.

THE DEEP BATTLE: HISTORICAL ANTECEDENTS, CURRENT ISSUES

The Soviet expectation of a two-phased battle beneath the nuclear threshold, should it be realized, should call to their attention the study of their own experience in the Great Patriotic War. There they learned the importance of the strategic and operational rear.[46] The Soviets were caught unprepared during the early stages of the war for the conduct of deep offensive or defensive operations, and their doctrine was woefully out of touch with their capabilities. The reestablishment of the doctrine whose development had begun under Tukhachevskiy and Triandafillov in the 1920s, and which had fully matured in the 1930s only to run up against Stalin's purge, was insufficient by itself to provide the wherewithal for the successful operations of 1944 and 1945 on the Eastern front. The Soviet armed forces that were surprised by Hitler on June 22, 1941, also lacked the proper equipment, training, and doctrine for the conduct of deep operations on the theater-strategic scale, covering several fronts and moving hundreds of kilometers in three dimensions. Despite these early setbacks, by 1945 the Soviet armed forces had established themselves as masters of operational maneuver on a strategic scale, in a theater of operations of unprecedented depth and variability. The grandeur of sweeping operations over wide expanses of territory, of the kind conducted in the Vistula-Oder, Jassy-Kishinev, and Belorussian offensives, was contrapuntal to the smash-and-grab of street and house-to-house fighting in Stalingrad and Berlin. Nowadays the discussion of AirLand Battle and the "reconnaissance-strike complexes" in the defense literature exhibits only partial awareness of the precursor problems that Soviet commanders had to solve under fire. From the Soviet perspective, the operation that most successfully demonstrated their ability to move large forces across vast distances, to surprise the opponent, and to conduct rapid and decisive theater-strategic operations was the Manchurian campaign of 1945.

According to an authoritative study of the Manchurian campaign by Col. David M. Glantz, subsequent Soviet military studies emphasize a number of lessons that, in their judgment, should be learned from the Soviet Union's experience in that theater of operations. The importance of surprise and deception was affirmed, although the affirmation was somewhat delayed in the expression, on account of Stalin's insistence on the primacy of "permanent operating factors" in war, surprise excluded. The long-standing Soviet emphasis on combined arms combat was also affirmed. Other techniques used by the Soviets in Manchuria may have special pertinence for contemporary military planners, especially if they are Soviet ones. First, forces should be echeloned in an imaginative way, with reference to the character of the defense. A single-echelon formation across a broad front may suffice to break the grip of a defense not yet fully organized.[47] Second, forces should be committed in carefully timed phases. In Manchuria, "relentless hammering destroyed Japanese equilibrium and accelerated Japanese collapse."[48] The contemporary application might be that rapid penetrations on multiple axes of advance into the tactical and operational depth of the enemy formations would preclude the use of tactical nuclear weapons.[49] Third, it is advisable to lead with forward detachments at every command level. Soviet forward detachments in Manchuria, and in operations against the Germans noted earlier, moved rapidly into the depth of enemy defenses, disrupted the cohesion of those defenses, and accomplished critical, time-urgent objectives that kept the momentum of the offensives going. The description by Glantz of the Soviet experience in Manchuria is informative for students of contemporary operational art:

> The Soviets used armor-heavy forward detachments of every size to drive deep into Japanese positions. With limited combat power forward, Soviet main force units could advance almost unhindered. Each detachment worked in a manner similar to an awl, boring a hole into hard wood and preparing the wood for subsequent penetration by a screw. Punctured in numerous sectors, the Japanese defense lost all coherence and never regained it.[50]

The Soviets of today feel that the modus operandi of the Manchurian offensive and their other successful operations is informative, but not definitive, of the possibilities for combat under contemporary conditions. Many things have since changed. Among these are the means for attaining fire superiority over the enemy and the preservation of command and control over larger distances and in the face of attacks by more accurate, longer-range conventional and nuclear weapons. The pressure of time weighs heavily on Soviet commanders as never before. According to Soviet analysts, NATO armies have established fire norms that require the destruction of particular numbers of targets within prescribed time intervals: A battalion must destroy 250 targets in ten minutes and a division over 2,000 targets in several hours (if possible, or a day at most).[51] To prevent the enemy from carrying out these missions, he "must be forestalled in opening fire, the fire initiative must be seized as quickly as possible and firmly held, effective use of available weapons must be ensured, and the enemy must not be allowed to make full use of his weapons."[52] This is more complicated now than formerly. During the Great Patriotic War, the job of attaining fire superiority over the opponent was essentially a mission assigned to artillery. Future commanders will have to make use of a broader array of factors:

> Today, successful counter-battery bombardment does not ensure fire superiority. The first thing that must be done is to reveal and annihilate the enemy's offensive nuclear weapons, his tactical missiles, long-range artillery, especially that firing nuclear ammunition, and reconnaissance-strike complexes. It is also important to disrupt the antitank, antipersonnel and antiaircraft fire plan and to disorganize the enemy's troop and fire command and control system.[53]

Figure 5.5
Command Subordination in Wartime

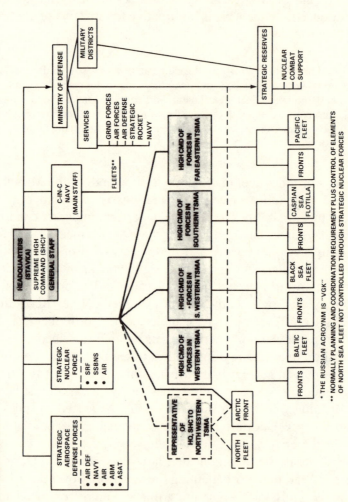

Source: U.S. Department of Defense. See also John G. Hines and Phillip A. Petersen, "NATO and the Changing Soviet Concept of Control for Theater War," Ch. 3 in Stephen J. Cimbala, ed., *The Soviet Challenge in the 1990s* (New York: Praeger, 1989), pp. 65–118. For an updated assessment, see *Washington Times*, March 12, 1990, p. A6.

Of course, one must maintain the coherence of one's own command and control system while disrupting that of the enemy. In modern combined-arms combat this will be extremely complicated. There are a number of reasons for this increased difficulty of preserving command system cohesion. First, the battlefield situation will be marked by frequent transitions from one form of battle to another. Second, growth of the spatial scope of modern operations results in wider dispersal of troops and, consequently, of command posts. Third, the vulnerability of command posts and command-control-communications infrastructure to destruction by the enemy has increased. The use of high-precision weapons, sabotage, and radio-electronic combat against command posts can be anticipated. Finally, the volume of troop command and control measures has increased, but the time for their accomplishment is constantly decreasing.[54] This last pattern might be called the "Phillips curve" of Soviet (and, for that matter, Western) military command and control, by analogy to the controversial macroeconomic hypothesis that one must have either inflation with higher employment or deflation with lower employment. One can imagine two curves—of the volume of troop control measures and the speed with which forces can act—gradually reaching a point at which additional volume overloads the system and brings it to a standstill. This is not a hypothetical situation in military affairs. Martin Van Creveld has analyzed the U.S. command system performance in Vietnam and argued that the communications channels were so confounded with system overload and mismatched protocols that the command system cannibalized itself.[55]

The Soviet remedy for this vulnerability and complexity of command systems on the modern battlefield is to require that command systems be stable, continuous, efficient, and covert (see Figure 5.5). Stable command and control implies that command systems must maintain their cohesion and perform their missions despite any enemy pressures. Continuity of command and control means that superiors must constantly monitor the performance of their subordinates, maintain the command-control infrastructure necessary to execute plans, and be ready to adapt to changed conditions, including destruction of important parts of the command system itself. Efficiency (*operativnost'*) of command and control is especially significant. It means that command and control measures must be implemented within the time necessary to accomplish the mission and to forestall enemy operations. If command organs are slow to react to developing events, "orders given previously may turn out to be inconsistent with the real situation on the battlefield."[56] The fourth attribute required in command systems is covertness, which is dictated by three related factors: the larger role played in modern operations compared to earlier ones by surprise; the greater potential of enemy reconnaissance owing to modern technical systems; and the likely use of long-range precision weapons by the opponent against any detected command nodes.[57]

The conditions of the modern battlefield also imply that the training of commanders must be such that they can exercise initiative and determination within the context of the overall plan of operations. Combat operations that do not develop in a uniform way

increase the significance of the independence of units and subunits operating in isolated sectors, of the initiative of commanders of all ranks, and of support to intervals, flanks and the rear of friendly troops. . . . All of this makes it necessary to train the troops to carry out combat missions in the face of extremely swift and abrupt changes in the situation, and commanders and staffs to react competently to changes in the situation in minimum time, displaying decisiveness, initiative, creativity and independence.[58]

Associated with initiative and decisiveness is aggressiveness. Aggressiveness and decisiveness are important in meeting engagements in which the enemy's fire and maneuver plans may change swiftly:

High aggressiveness in a meeting engagement presupposes decisiveness and swiftness of reactions to a continually changing situation. A lack of information on the enemy cannot be used as an excuse for rejecting bold actions.[59]

The high tempo of offensive operations is necessary to keep pressure on the opponent and, if the opponent is NATO, to preclude NATO use of nuclear weapons:

The uninterrupted conduct of battle at a high tempo creates unfavorable conditions for the enemy's use of mass destruction weapons. He cannot accurately determine targets for nuclear strikes; moreover he is compelled to frequently move his nuclear attack resources.[60]

There is another reason for the insistence upon *operativnost'* and the maximum exploitation of time. The more time elapses from the start of a military operation until it has been concluded, the more things can go wrong. This point is emphasized by Clausewitz in his exceptional discussion of the things that make "war on paper" differ from actual war, including "friction." Friction is the sum total of forces that make the outcomes of battle and war differ from those intended war plans.[61] As Clausewitz has explained in a passage more often quoted than applied successfully:

Everything in war is very simple, but the simplest thing is difficult. The difficulties accumulate and end by producing a kind of friction that is inconceivable unless one has experienced war.[62]

The dilemma for the Soviet planners is this: Either the planner must advise an attack from a standing start against NATO forces in order to reduce the defender's warning time and response capability (less possible after completion of the reductions announced by Gorbachev in 1988), or the planner may advise waiting in order to improve the readiness and sustainability of Soviet and other Pact forces. Either way there is a trade-off. A short-warning attack, according to Soviet assessments of the early 1980s, was a high-risk, potentially high-payoff strategy, counting on incompetent NATO response to warning and inadequate mobilization. However, the force ratios for such a venture are razor thin. The Soviets and their Pact allies, especially the Soviet forces in East Germany (as long as it exists as a separate state), which would provide the spearhead of the attack against the Central Front, would have to conduct a very rapid and highly destructive set of meeting engagements against NATO in West Germany, the Low Countries, and/or the NATO allies and neutrals on the Baltic littoral. It is not insignificant that the Pentagon expresses both pessimism about NATO's potential for being caught unaware and optimism about the difficulty facing Soviet military planners. In the 1988 edition of *Soviet Military Power*, the following assessment is offered:

NATO's forward-defense strategy requires sufficient time for its ground forces to move forward and prepare defensive positions prior to a Pact attack. Depending on how a war began, there may not be time to capitalize on the inherent military advantages of defensive operations. NATO's FOFA concept is highly dependent on fielding enough survivable, long-range systems to engage the Pact's follow-on forces, as well as maintaining the command, control, communications and intelligence (C^3I) fusion to engage them in a timely way. To date, NATO's inventory of those types of systems is uncomfortably low.[63]

According to the U.S. Department of Defense in 1988, the Pact's now enfeebled theater-strategic operational concept "still seeks a quick, conventional victory over NATO," and the probable overall objectives of the concept are "to destroy NATO's surviving nuclear capabilities, destroy large groupings of NATO ground forces, and quickly reach the English Channel ports to prevent reinforcement and resupply."[64] On the other hand, recent changes in Soviet doctrine suggest a concern that "they may no longer be able to defeat an opponent totally in a short, rapid, offensive campaign lasting several weeks." Instead, a future campaign "may be a succession of operations and campaigns conducted over an extended period, due, in part, to the enormous resources of present-day coalitions."[65] The Soviets, at least in their military doctrinal writings, have acknowledged that a conventional war under modern conditions might be a protracted rather than a short one.[66]

There is a second kind of uncertainty in addition to these operational ones: the problem of nuclear escalation. Any war in Europe raises this possibility, even if the Pact forces have objectives that stop far short of an effort to "reach the English channel ports," which they surely will. An effort to reach the English channel ports must involve Pact forces in war on French territory, and the French dispose of "pre-strategic" and strategic nuclear forces. Therefore the Soviets must reckon that their crossing of the French border may bring down upon their heads the destruction of Moscow, Leningrad, and Kiev; and by the 1990s the French and British strategic nuclear deterrents, submarine based, could destroy many more together. Therefore a "conventional" war plan must at least initially exclude attacks against France, although the French are now considering the "enlarged sanctuarization" of allies via their nuclear deterrent and may have committed elements of their FAR (Rapid Action Force) to prompt forward deployment into West Germany in the event of war.[67]

CONCLUSION

The Soviet command system is the product of its concept of operational art and vice versa. Neither can be fully understood without reference to the other. If the command system is treated as a "dependent variable," then it can be said to have philosophical-doctrinal causes and organizational-bureaucratic causes. This is an extremely complicated matrix through which Western concepts cannot easily be compared to Soviet ones. Speaking broadly, the NATO command systems (the plural is important) seem more designed for crisis management, including the prevention of accidental war and inadvertent escalation, than does the Soviet. The Soviet system is certainly concerned with preventing unauthorized use, but once war seems possible it is more concerned with enabling a smooth transition from peacetime to wartime operations. In theory so are the NATO systems, but the cumbersome procedures by which corps commanders request and obtain nuclear release suggest that when it is necessary it will be too late. NATO has other release channels, including U.S. and allied national ones, but the emphasis at the NATO Council and U.S. presidential levels remains that of nuclear containment, for good reasons. The Soviets are aware of this. Therefore, if war begins in Europe, their theater-strategic offensive will aim to neutralize NATO's capability to resort to nuclear use and its willingness to do so. Efforts to disrupt NATO C^3 and to preserve Soviet C^3 are an important part of this.

The implications of strategic defensivism for the Soviet operational maneuver plan in case of war in Europe are not fully fleshed out. Significant changes in the socio-political level of military doctrine are underway. Whether these will take deep root in the military-technical aspects of doctrine is an open question. The Soviet command system will find that its adaptive capabilities are least stressed in normal peacetime conditions or if the Soviet Union is subjected to a "bolt from the blue" attack. In the first case standard operating procedures are all that is needed; in the second, they are all that time permits. In between lie zones of uncertainty in which the system must improvise from the top, including crisis management during periods of tension.[68] Soviet confidence in doing so will be based on the preparations they have made beforehand. Above all, the calculations made by Soviet planners will emphasize sustainability and combat capability in their most comprehensive forms, including the capabilities of command systems to support operational norms and political objectives.[69] Only if these calculations seem favorable is war feasible, if at all.

NOTES

1. Harriet Fast Scott and William F. Scott, *Soviet Military Doctrine: Continuity, Formulation and Dissemination* (Boulder, Colo.: Westview Press, 1988), esp. Ch. 2; see also Col. B. Byely et al., *Marksizm-leninizm o voyne i armii* (Marxism-Leninism on war and army) (Moscow: Progress Publishers, 1972), U.S. Air Force Soviet Military Thought Series.

2. Martin Van Creveld, *Command in War* (Cambridge, Mass.: Harvard University Press, 1985).

3. See Jon L. Boyes and Stephen J. Andriole, eds., *Principles of Command and Control* (Washington: AFCEA International Press, 1987), for a collection of representative and authoritative views.

4. John Hemsley, *Soviet Troop Control: The Role of Command Technology in the Soviet System* (New York: Brassey's Publishers Ltd., 1982). See also Army General P. Lushev, "The Art of Command and Control," *Sovetskoye voyennoye obozreniye*, January 1983, pp. 9–12. According to General Lushev, "Command and control is the goal-directed activity of commanders, staffs, and political elements to maintain formation and unit combat readiness at the level of contemporary requirements and to train them for military operations and successful execution of missions in battle through effective employment of available forces."

5. Major General S. N. Koslov, ed., *Spravochnik ofitsera* (Officer's Handbook) (Moscow: Voyenizdat, 1971), U.S. Air Force Soviet Military Thought Series (Washington: GPO, undated), esp. Ch. 2.

6. Phillip A. Petersen and Notra Trulock III, "A 'New' Soviet Military Doctrine: Origins and Implications," *Strategic Review* 16, no. 3 (Summer 1988), pp. 9–24.

7. Military doctrine, *voyennaya doktrina*, is "a nation's officially accepted system of scientifically founded views on the nature of modern wars and the use of armed forces in them, and also on the requirements arising from these views regarding the country and its armed forces being made ready for war." Military doctrine has two aspects: the

socio-political and military-technical. See General-Colonel A. I. Radziyevskiy, ed., *Dictionary of Basic Military Terms* (Moscow: Voyenizdat, 1965), U.S. Air Force Soviet Military Thought Series, p. 37. See also Raymond L. Garthoff, *Detente and Confrontation: American-Soviet Relations from Nixon to Reagan* (Washington: Brookings Institution, 1985), p. 776.

8. Col. Gen. N. A. Lomov, ed., *Scientific-Technical Progress and the Revolution in Military Affairs* (Moscow: Voyenizdat, 1973), U.S. Air Force Soviet Military Thought Series, pp. 28–29.

9. Soviet Army Studies Office, *Soviet Future War* (Ft. Leavenworth, Kans.: U.S. Army Combined Arms Center, Command and General Staff College, April 27, 1987).

10. V. V. Druzhinin and D. S. Kontorov, *Concept, Algorithm, Decision: Decision Making and Automation* (Moscow: Voyenizdat, 1972). U.S. Air Force Soviet Military Thought Series. See also Col. Y. M. Bondarenko, "Nauchno-tekhnicheskiy progress i upravleniye voyskami," *Kommunist vooruzhennykh sil* 10 (Moscow: May 1973), pp. 27–33. Translated and published under the auspices of the U.S. Air Force in *Selected Soviet Military Writings, 1970–75* (Washington: GPO, undated), reprinted as "Scientific-Technical Progress and Troop Control," in Stephen J. Cimbala, ed., *Soviet C³* (Washington: AFCEA International Press, 1987), pp. 73–81.

11. See Condolezza Rice, "The Making of Soviet Strategy," Ch. 22 in Peter Paret, ed., *Makers of Modern Strategy* (Princeton: Princeton University Press, 1986), pp. 648–76.

12. The counterdeterrent role of Soviet nuclear forces is emphasized in Samuel P. Huntington, "The Renewal of Strategy," in Samuel P. Huntington, ed., *The Strategic Imperative: New Policies for National Security* (Cambridge, Mass.: Ballinger Publishing Co., 1982), pp. 1–52.

13. See statement of Edward L. Warner III, Rand Corporation, to U.S. Senate Armed Services Committee, January 24, 1990, for an updated assessment of Soviet and Warsaw Pact force potentials.

14. As noted in Fen Osler Hampsen, "Escalation in Europe," Ch. 4 in Graham T. Allison, Albert Carnesale, and Joseph S. Nye, Jr., *Hawks, Doves and Owls: An Agenda for Avoiding Nuclear War* (New York: W. W. Norton, 1985), pp. 80–114.

15. Christopher N. Donnelly, "Soviet Operational Concepts in the 1980s," in *Strengthening Conventional Deterrence in Europe: Proposals for the 1980s*, Report of the European Security Study (New York: St. Martin's Press, 1983), pp. 105–36; Lt. Col. Yu Chumakov, "Swiftness and Continuity of Attack," *Voyennyy vestnik* 1 (1983), pp. 22–26.

16. On Soviet nuclear crisis management, see Stephen M. Meyer, "Soviet Nuclear Operations," Ch. 15 in Ashton B. Carter, John D. Steinbruner, and Charles A. Zraket, eds., *Managing Nuclear Operations* (Washington: Brookings Institution, 1987), pp. 470–534.

17. Joseph D. Douglass, Jr., "What Happens If Deterrence Fails?" *Air University Review*, November-December 1982, pp. 2–17, esp. pp. 5–6.

18. John G. Hines and Phillip A. Petersen, "The Warsaw Pact Strategic Offensive: The OMG in Context," *International Defense Review*, October 1983, pp. 1391–95; Charles J. Dick, "Soviet Operational Concepts: Part I," *Military Review* 65, no. 9 (September 1985), pp. 29–45. For revised assessment in terms of 1989–90 events, see Warner, statement to Senate Armed Services Committee.

19. Hines and Petersen, "The Warsaw Pact Strategic Offensive"; also Phillip A. Petersen, *Soviet Air Power and the Pursuit of New Military Options* (Washington: GPO, undated), esp. pp. 5–12, pp. 53–56.

20. C. N. Donnelly, "The Soviet Operational Maneuver Group: A New Challenge for

NATO," *International Defense Review* 15, no. 9 (1982), pp. 1177–86; Soviet Army Studies Office, *The Soviet Conduct of War* (Fort Leavenworth, Kans.: Combined Arms Center, U.S. Army Command and General Staff College, March 30, 1987; Warner, statement to Senate Armed Services Committee.

21. See Col. David N. Glantz, *Deep Attack: The Soviet Conduct of Operational Maneuver* (Fort Leavenworth, Kans.: Combined Arms Center, U.S. Army Command and General Staff College, April 1987).

22. Chris Bellamy, *The Future of Land Warfare* (New York: St. Martin's Press, 1987), pp. 113–21; Donnelly, "The Soviet Operational Maneuver Group," *passim.* See Lieutenant General V. G. Reznichenko et al., *Taktika* (Tactics) (Moscow: Voyenizdat, 1984). According to Major General I. N. Vorob'yev, during the modern, fast-moving offensive operation, the enemy's offensive nuclear weapons, reconnaissance-strike complexes, tanks, infantry-fighting vehicles, self-propelled artillery, fixed-wing aircraft, helicopters, anti-air weapons, and airborne assault forces must be neutralized or destroyed. "Since these and other targets crucial to the integrity of the defense are mainly located deep behind enemy lines, the attacking forces should try wherever possible to pressure the entire combat formation of a defensively deployed enemy by means of simultaneous aggressive operations." Ibid., Ch. 2, part 3, "Combat Tasks." According to Reznichenko, among the more important means of achieving surprise in combat are "the covert concentration and unanticipated large-scale use of new types of weapons and combat equipment unknown to the enemy," "delivering strikes where the enemy does not anticipate them," "strict adherence to requirements concerning secrecy in command and control, communications security, and security procedures." Ibid., Ch. 1, part 5, "Basic Principles of Conducting Modern Combined Arms Combat."

23. Dennis Gormley, "Emerging Attack Options in Soviet Theater Strategy," Ch. 4 in Fred S. Hoffman, Albert Wohlstetter, and David S. Yost, eds., *Swords and Shields: NATO, the USSR, and New Choices for Long-Range Offense and Defense* (Lexington, Mass.: Lexington Books/D. C. Heath, 1987), pp. 87–122.

24. Gen. Bernard W. Rogers, "Follow-on Forces Attack (FOFA): Myths and Realities," *NATO Review*, December 1984, pp. 1–8.

25. For assessments of deep strike and FOFA, see Jacquelyn K. Davis, "Europe's Edgy Approach to Strategy," *Air Force Magazine*, December 1985, pp. 82–88; Joel S. Wit, "Deep Strike: NATO's New Defense Concept and Its Implications for Arms Control," *Arms Control Today* 13, no. 10 (November 1983), pp. 1, 4–7, 9; Daniel Gouré and Jeffrey Cooper, "Conventional Deep Strike: A Critical Look," *Comparative Strategy* 4, no. 3 (1984), pp. 215–48.

26. Richard D. DeLauer, "Emerging Technologies and Their Impact on the Conventional Deterrent," in Andrew J. Pierre, ed., *The Conventional Defense of Europe: New Technologies and New Strategies* (New York: Council on Foreign Relations, 1986), pp. 40–70.

27. See Diego A. Ruiz Palmer, "Between the Rhine and the Elbe: France and the Conventional Defense of Central Europe," *Comparative Strategy* 6, no. 4 (1987), pp. 471–512.

28. Kevin N. Lewis, "Implications for Strategic Offensive Force Modernization," Ch. 3 in Samuel F. Wells and Robert S. Litwak, eds., *Strategic Defenses and Soviet-American Relations* (Cambridge, Mass.: Ballinger Publishing Co., 1987), pp. 79–100.

29. According to the U.S. Department of Defense, the Soviets, "although lagging the West in technology, frequently field systems that are sufficiently well engineered to meet or exceed the combat capabilities of Western counterpart systems." U.S. DOD, *Soviet*

Military Power: 1988, An Assessment of the Threat (Washington: GPO, April 1988), p. 149. See the comparisons of U.S. and Soviet systems technologies across a variety of strategic and tactical forces, ibid.

30. Bellamy, *The Future of Land Warfare*, Ch. 7, pp. 243–73.

31. John J. Yurechko, "Command and Control for Coalitional Warfare: The Soviet Approach," in Cimbala, *Soviet C³*, pp. 17–34.

32. Desmond Ball, *Soviet Signals Intelligence (SIGINT): Vehicular Systems and Operations* (Canberra, Australia: Research School of Pacific Studies, Australian National University, February 1988, Reference Paper No. 159).

33. Josef Joffe, *The Limited Partnership: Europe, the United States, and the Burdens of Alliance* (Cambridge, Mass.: Ballinger Publishing Co., 1987), Ch. 2, pp. 45–92.

34. General I. V. Shavrov, "Osnovy i soderzhanie voennoi strategii" (Principles and Content of Military Strategy), Lectures from the Voroshilov General Staff Academy in *Journal of Soviet Military Studies* 1, no. 1 (April 1988), pp. 30–53. Introduction by Graham H. Turbiville, Jr., pp. 29–30.

35. John G. Hines, Phillip A. Petersen, and Notra Trulock III, "Soviet Military Theory from 1945–2000: Implications for NATO," *Washington Quarterly* 9, no. 4 (Fall 1986), pp. 117–37.

36. This is against prevailing, and important, U.S. views. See Robert S. McNamara, *Blundering into Disaster: Surviving the First Century of the Nuclear Age* (New York: Pantheon Books, 1986); and Albert Wohlstetter, "The Political and Military Aims of Offensive and Defensive Innovation," Ch. 1 in Hoffman, Wohlstetter, and Yost, eds., *Swords and Shields*, pp. 3–36.

37. See Donald Cotter, "Potential Future Roles for Conventional and Nuclear Forces in Defense of Western Europe," in European Security Study, *Strengthening Conventional Deterrence in Europe*, pp. 209–53.

38. C. N. Donnelly et al., *Sustainability of the Soviet Army in Combat* (London: Royal Military Academy Sandhurst, 1986).

39. For a compendium of views on the implications of strategic or theater ballistic missile defenses for NATO, see Sanford Lakoff and Randy Willoughby, *Strategic Defense and the Western Alliance* (Lexington, Mass.: Lexington Books/D. C. Heath, 1987), especially the chapters by David S. Yost and Pierre Lellouche.

40. Col. Gen. M. A. Gareev, *M. V. Frunze—Voyennyy Teoretik* (M. V. Frunze—military theorist) (New York: Pergamon-Brassey's, 1988), p. 192: "M. V. Frunze considered it essential to skillfully combine the offensive and defensive as the main forms of combat not only on the strategic scale, but also the operational-tactical one. In giving preference to the offensive as the basic type of combat operations, he demanded the careful elaboration of the questions of modern defense, considering that this should be employed when an offensive was disadvantageous or impossible." Modern Soviet defensive doctrine stresses defenses in depth but in the form of clusters of strongpoints instead of continuous belts. Army second-echelon divisions, although occupying defensive positions, will have as their major task counterattacks against enemy forces which penetrate forward defenses. See John Erickson, Lynn Hansen, and William Schneider, *Soviet Ground Forces: An Operational Assessment* (Boulder, Colo.: Westview, 1986), p. 103.

41. Seweryn Bialer, *The Soviet Paradox: External Expansion, Internal Decline* (New York: Knopf, 1986).

42. Marshal N. V. Ogarkov, *Istoriya uchit bditel'nosti* (History Teaches Vigilance) (Moscow: Voyenizdat, 1985).

43. Leon Goure, "A 'New' Soviet Military Doctrine: Reality or Mirage?" *Strategic Review* 16, no. 3 (Summer 1988), pp. 25–33, citation p. 30.

44. U.S. Congress, Congressional Budget Office, *U.S. Ground Forces and the Conventional Balance in Europe* (Washington, Congressional Budget Office, June 1988), Appendix D, pp. 101–14.

45. Bellamy, *The Future of Land Warfare*, Ch. 8, pp. 274–302.

46. Graham H. Turbiville, Jr., "Logistics: Sustaining Theater Strategic Operations," in *Journal of Soviet Military Studies* 1, no. 1 (April 1988), pp. 81–107.

47. Lt. Col. David M. Glantz, USA, *August Storm: The Soviet 1945 Strategic Offensive in Manchuria* (Fort Leavenworth, Kans.: U.S. Army Command and General Staff College, Combat Studies Institute, February 1983), p. 186.

48. Ibid., p. 187.

49. Ibid.

50. Ibid., p. 186.

51. V. G. Reznichenko, I. N. Vorob'yev, and N. F. Miroshnichenko, *Taktika* (Tactics) (Moscow: Voyenizdat, 1987), Ch. 4, part 6, "Destruction of the Enemy by Fire."

52. Ibid.

53. Ibid.

54. Ibid., Ch. 2, part 1, "Principles of Command and Control of Troops."

55. Martin Van Creveld, *Command in War* (Cambridge, Mass.: Harvard University Press, 1985), Ch. 7, pp. 232–60.

56. Reznichenko, Vorob'yev, and Miroshnichenko, *Taktika*, Chapter 2, part 1, "Principles of Command and Control of Troops."

57. Ibid.

58. Ibid., Ch. 1, part 3, "Characteristic Traits of Modern Combined-Arms Combat"; see also Colonel N. Kireyev, "The Employment of Tank Subunits and Units in the Penetration of Enemy Defense," *Voyenno-Istoricheskiy Zhurnal* 2 (February 1982), pp. 42–51, in *Selected Readings in Military History* II, pp. 139–49.

59. Reznichenko, Vorob'yev, and Miroshnichenko, *Taktika*, Ch. 1, part 4, "Basic Principles of Modern Combined-Arms Combat."

60. Ibid.

61. Carl Von Clausewitz, *On War*, edited and translated by Michael Howard and Peter Paret (Princeton: Princeton University Press, 1976), Book One, Ch. 7, pp. 119–21. In the next chapter Clausewitz identifies danger, physical exertion, intelligence, and friction as "the elements that coalesce to form the atmosphere of war" and in their restrictive effects "they can be grouped into a single concept of general friction." The only "lubricant" against this general friction is combat experience. Ibid., p. 122.

62. Ibid., p. 119.

63. U.S. Department of Defense, *Soviet Military Power: An Assessment of the Threat, 1988* (Washington: GPO, April 1988), p. 117.

64. Ibid. The Soviet preference for obtaining their objectives without the use of nuclear weapons is as evident as is the difficulty of providing a road map for doing so as long as NATO remains nuclear armed. Therefore, when discussion gets down to the nitty-gritty of operations, the shift to conventional emphasis is less pronounced. Reznichenko in 1984 noted that the influence of nuclear weapons on combined arms combat was becoming "increasingly significant," although "however powerful nuclear weapons are, it is not possible to accomplish all tasks in combat by means of them alone." Fire by conventional weapons "is an important means of completing the enemy's rout in

a nuclear war, and the main means of defeating him while conducting combat operations without the use of nuclear weapons." Reznichenko et al., *Taktika* (1984), Ch. 1, part 2, "The Weaponry Employed in Modern Combined Arms Combat," and part 3, "The Nature and Forms of Modern Combined Arms Combat."

65. *Soviet Military Power: 1988*, p. 74.

66. Soviet command arrangements, however, facilitate rapid transition from nonnuclear to nuclear operations. See U.S. Army, FM 100-2-1, *The Soviet Army: Operations and Tactics*, Ch. 3 and Ch. 4 (Washington: Headquarters, Department of the Army, July 1984), and Erickson, Hansen, and Schneider, *Soviet Ground Forces*, pp. 26–27. On trends in Soviet doctrine, see Petersen and Trulock, "A 'New' Soviet Military Doctrine?" and Jacob W. Kipp, *Conventional Force Modernization and the Asymmetries of Military Doctrine: Historical Reflections on AirLand Battle and the Operational Maneuver Group* (Fort Leavenworth, Kans.: Soviet Army Studies Office, U.S. Army Combined Arms Center, 1987).

67. See Ruiz Palmer, "Between the Rhine and the Elbe."

68. On this see Meyer, "Soviet Nuclear Operations," pp. 524–25.

69. Donnelly et al., *Sustainability of the Soviet Army in Battle, passim.*

ENDGAME

6

Strategic Defense and
Conflict Termination

Recent strategic debates have revolved around contending paradigms, or conceptual frameworks, of mutual assured destruction and mutual assured survival. Mutual assured destruction asserts that stable deterrence rests upon the certainty that the defender can retaliate against the attacker's society, even after absorbing a first strike. M.A.D. is predicated on the superiority of offenses over defenses.[1] Mutual assured survival is the antithesis of mutual assured destruction. It provides that defenses superior to offenses can improve deterrence and limit damage if deterrence fails.[2] President Reagan's speech of March 23, 1983, called for research to determine whether deployment of U.S. strategic defenses would be feasible in the near or long term.[3]

Adherents of mutual assured destruction and mutual assured survival have disagreed about many things. Central to their disagreements is the concept of stability. Stability in the deterrence lexicon takes three forms: crisis, arms race, and basic (or deterrence) stability.[4] Crisis stability means that neither side is tempted to strike first for fear of enemy preemption. Arms race stability reduces incentives to deploy new generations of more capable weapons. Basic or deterrence stability implies that neither side has anything close to a first-strike capability against the forces of the opponent.

Parts of this chapter include material originally published in Stephen J. Cimbala and Joseph D. Douglass, Jr., eds., *Ending a Nuclear War* (Pergamon Brassey's International Defense Publishers, 1988).

Seen from the perspective of mutual assured destruction, defenses are destabilizing if they can protect populations. Protecting populations from retaliatory destruction undermines the credibility of the deterrent, in this view, because those populations are the "hostages" that make deterrence work effectively. Know that both sides' cities and economies are subject to almost certain destruction after any conceivable first strike, neither side will initiate war. Indeed, assured destruction strategists, including former Secretary of Defense Robert McNamara, argued that U.S. forces should be sized against "greater than expected" threats in order to make certain that retaliation would exceed any level the opponent might find acceptable.[5]

The attitude of assured destruction theorists toward defenses for U.S. strategic forces and their associated command, control, and communications (C^3) is more ambivalent. Some M.A.D. proponents feel that defending retaliatory forces improves stability because it complicates the opponent's first-strike calculations. Others are suspicious that the Reagan Strategic Defense Initiative (SDI) will deploy point defenses for missile silos and other targets only as a way station toward eventual deployment of comprehensive defenses for the entire country.[6]

As can be anticipated, the position of assured survival theorists is more supportive of defense deployments to improve stability. They contend that defenses will protect the U.S. strategic deterrent by complicating Soviet attack calculations. The initial stages of ballistic missile defense (BMD) might be deployed to protect the U.S. land-based missile (ICBM) force, for example, which now appears vulnerable to Soviet preemption.[7] Later stages could be deployed along with equivalent Soviet defenses and a build-down of both superpowers' strategic offenses.[8] Robust defenses and diminished offenses would make for a more stable world than one which now relies upon the guaranteed destruction of both sides' populations, according to mutual assured survival theorists.

Both assured destruction and assured survival reflected the state of technology available for offenses and defenses. Assured destruction was formulated during the 1960s and emphasized in U.S. arms-control policy during the 1970s, when defensive technologies seemed immature and incompetent compared to offenses. Assured survival has been given a rebirth in the 1980s owing to the conviction of former president Ronald Reagan and others that improved defense technologies may make possible protection of U.S. forces, society, or both in the near and distant future.[9] Neither of these conceptual frameworks was entirely convincing, or deficient, by itself.

ASSURED DESTRUCTION AND ASSURED SURVIVAL: VIRTUES AND VICES

Assured destruction had the virtues of simplicity in concept and apparent success in practice. Although we can never know with certainty whether deterrence really "worked" unless and until it fails, strategic stability based on mutual vulnerability seemed to U.S. policymakers to be working. The superpowers had not come close to war since the Cuban missile crisis of 1962. Both had developed large and diversified deterrents seemingly incapable of being eliminated by the surprise attack.[10] Moreover, it seemed to some observers that the Strategic Arms Limitation Talks (SALT) agreements had codified a shared understanding of deterrence based on mutual vulnerability. The Soviets might not *prefer* to base deterrence on mutual vulnerability, but they might have to acknowledge that their society was vulnerable to U.S. countervalue (against cities and society rather than military forces, or counterforce) retaliation.[11]

Whatever its apparent virtues, assured destruction lost adherents during the 1970s as the Soviet buildup of offensive forces placed the land-based portion of the U.S. strategic deterrent in imminent jeopardy.[12] Even before President Reagan's speech of March 23, 1983, dissatisfaction with assured destruction was widespread within the U.S. strategic and defense community. Most notably, SALT I had been based upon an expectation by the United States of future U.S.–Soviet offensive arms reductions, which did not in fact occur.[13] Assured destruction also received only qualified support within the U.S. defense establishment. Former secretary of defense James R. Schlesinger explained in 1974 that the Nixon administration required strategic forces that could be used with selectivity and flexibility against a variety of targets and in a variety of circumstances other than all-out war.[14] The Carter administration also indicated that assured destruction by itself was felt insufficient for deterrence, especially in cases other than direct Soviet attack against the U.S. homeland. The promulgation of PD-59 (Presidential Directive 59) in 1980 called for flexible targeting and escalation control, as had its predecessor NSDM-242 during the Nixon administration. In addition, PD-59 and other Carter guidance called for capabilities to fight protracted nuclear war if need be.[15]

It was also the case that assured destruction (with flexible targeting amendments) provided little consolation if deterrence failed. Damage limitation would be based upon the U.S. capability to retaliate with offensive forces after absorbing a Soviet first strike, and attack the remaining Soviet forces before they could be used. The capability was not judged great by some analysts, nor was it evaluated optimistically by the U.S. government. And, to accomplish damage limitation without defenses, U.S. forces might have to be launched early and after ambiguous warning, rather than being permitted to "ride out" the attack.[16]

Assured survival also had apparent virtues and vices. Its virtues lay in the potential it held for the superpowers to escape their dependence on maintaining large, diverse, and possibly redundant offensive forces. Populations could be protected in the event deterrence failed; at least partial protection seemed more humane than total vulnerability. Assured survival also seemed more consistent with the Soviet view of deterrence than assured destruction or assured vulnerability. Despite the ABM treaty, some U.S. experts doubted that the Soviet Union really acknowledged mutual societal vulnerability as a reliable basis for deterrence. Rather, the Soviets had always sought to defend their homeland with all resources possible.[17] Soviet interest in restraining defenses was temporary, in the view of assured survival proponents, until the Soviet Union could catch up to Western technology and deploy equivalent or superior systems of its own.[18]

The problems with assured survival were also noted by scholars and political disputants. First, assured survival might make the probability of conventional war in Europe greater. If both superpowers defended their homelands and not the territories of their allies, the Soviet Union might be tempted to exploit the sword of its conventional forces behind a shield of BMD that denied escalation to NATO. (Even Soviet deployment of theater ballistic missile defenses complicates NATO conventional deterrence, as we will note later.) Second, assured survival was a technological risk. It would be based on systems that could not be tested "realistically" in the absence of war. Third, assured survival might call for so much U.S. spending on defenses that offensive nuclear force modernization, and conventional forces, would suffer.

WAR TERMINATION: A MISSING ELEMENT

Critics of assured destruction and assured survival succeeded in punching holes in each other's theories. But they both overlooked one limitation common to both. Neither assured destruction (however amended) nor assured survival explained what to do to stop a U.S.–Soviet strategic war after it began. In fact, PD-59, as noted above, apparently contemplated the prospect of a protracted war between U.S. and Soviet forces without providing a clear recipe for war termination.[19] The omission of war termination from assured destruction and assured survival strategies, except by implication, was not trivial. If the U.S. cannot describe how a war can be ended, in terms of meaningful policy objectives, it has not embarked on war at all. It has instead begun a process of destruction for no purpose.

It is no wonder, however, that assured destruction and assured survival have said very little about war termination. The reasons are that the difference between fighting for war termination and fighting for destruction are very great. The former involves the subtlety of the connection between war and policy, with which the public is often impatient. Fighting for destruction or revenge is something that an angered populace, Congress, and media can relate to viscerally. As Col. Harry Summers has noted with regard to the Vietnam War, U.S. prosecution of the war was handicapped because the public mood was never stirred into a war fever that would have galvanized public support for the U.S. military intervention.[20]

A second reason why war termination has been neglected in U.S. strategic thought is that policymakers have lacked the apparent capabilities to pursue it. The missing capabilities included both strategic forces that could be used flexibly and command and control capabilities that could survive early attacks and provide for "postattack" continuity of control over the use of strategic forces. Although the flexibility of U.S. strategic offensive forces was improved by the Nixon-Ford and Carter programs, the improvements were insufficient to provide much confidence in war termination. The corequisite C^3 capabilities were missing. Desmond Ball, Bruce Clair, and Paul Bracken have all catalogued the deficiencies of the U.S. strategic C^3 system in the past and present (through the mid-1980s).[21] Past and present conditions provide for little postattack survivability and no endurance for key components of the U.S. C^3 infrastructure, including fixed command posts, communications connectivity, and the commanders themselves. Even small but well-designed Soviet attacks against the C^3 system could preclude a coherent U.S. retaliation; Bruce G. Blair notes that the destruction of fixed land-based U.S. strategic command and control "is a Soviet prerogative."[22]

U.S. strategy for nuclear war cannot continue this apparent neglect of war termination concepts or capabilities. No single study can remedy all deficiencies. Both assured destruction and assured survival theorists need to spell out how war termination fits into their models. If it does not, a problematical connection between war and policy is apparent.

Assured destruction and assured survival provide some implicit answers to the issue of war termination. They are not entirely convincing. The two paradigms are understandably more concerned about preventing war than they are about limiting war after it begins. Concern with war termination does not preclude emphasis on war prevention; instead, it reinforces the healthy caution against getting into war at all. War termination insists upon forcing to the forefront questions about what it is that we want to accomplish during a war. How will the U.S. postwar position be improved, compared to its prewar position (or its postwar position if we do not fight)? If the question cannot be answered clearly, the war may be a mistaken enterprise for us.

Assured destruction assumed by implication that war would be terminated when a certain level of societal destruction had been reached on both sides. What that level of counter-societal destruction would be is uncertain and has rarely been quantified even hypothetically. But former secretary McNamara and his Pentagon associates did try. They estimated that a U.S. retaliation would have to be capable of destroying one-quarter to one-third of the Soviet population, and one-half to two-thirds of its industrial capacity, in order to deter the Soviet Union.[23] The implication is that this was the level of destruction that U.S. forces would be prepared to inflict if war actually broke out.

A level of destruction equal to or greater than the level of destruction postulated by these assured destruction theorists would undoubtedly terminate the war, but what war? Long before assured destruction levels were reached, U.S. and Soviet forces could be exhausted or destroyed, populations reduced to primitive standards of living, and governments probably toppled.[24] This was not war but revenge. It is clear that Secretary McNamara recognized this, and that if war actually occurred U.S. forces could not *initially* attack cities. Rather, the initial retaliatory strikes would be against Soviet strategic forces and other military targets, in order to create incentives for the Soviets to spare U.S. cities. McNamara noted that "to the extent possible" the United States planned to conduct nuclear war in the same way as conventional war, sparing cities and attacking military targets until this became impossible or imprudent.[25] Although McNamara later backed away from this "city avoidance" strategy as *declaratory* policy, U.S. targeting plans continued to place emphasis upon counterforce rather than countervalue destruction.[26]

Thus, the implicit war termination strategy in assured destruction *operational* policy was to avoid city attacks and to hope that the opponent would do the same. The same implicit war termination strategy marked the Nixon-Ford and Carter policies. Although the lexicon of declaratory policy changed from assured destruction in the Kennedy-Johnson years to "essential equivalence" under Nixon-Ford and "countervailing strategy" under Carter, operational policy evolved more gradually. The Reagan administration assumed office to inherit a policy of assured destruction modified by flexible targeting, escalation control (by reciprocal targeting restraint), and "countervailing" capabilities to respond to Soviet aggression at the corresponding level of provocation.[27]

Assured survival, like assured destruction, treated war termination as a peripheral issue. The assured survival model assumes that both superpowers have defenses (eventually) that are much more competent than their offenses. In that case, attacking the defense makes no sense for either side. It is also assumed, per the administration's "strategic concept" as explained by Ambassador Paul H. Nitze, that these very competent defenses must, in the U.S. case, be both survivable and "cost effective at the margin."[28] This last condition means that it must cost the Soviet Union more than a dollar of investment in offensive force improvements to offset each dollar spent on U.S. defenses.

If war broke out, defenses under assured survival could contribute to war termination by limiting the damage absorbed by either side's forces, society, and government. This last entity assumes special importance in war termination. Preserving the opponent's command structure, to the extent that we can communicate with some accountable authority on the other side, is important if war termination is to be realized. But this presents a dilemma for our defense posture under mutual assured survival. Attacking a well-defended opponent might prove hopeless if our effort is to disrupt his military potential as rapidly as possible. If deployed, Soviet BMD would presumably be used in defense of many of their strategic forces. Thus, U.S. offensive forces (especially if they are built down as defenses are built up) might not be adequate to penetrate Soviet defenses protecting their strategic forces.

Under such conditions—Soviet defenses providing substantial protection to their offensive forces—the United States might need to attack the Soviet command structure to preclude further coordinated strikes by them. A presumed inability to destroy Soviet forces might be compensated for by a concentration of remaining U.S. forces in salvos designed to destroy the Soviet High Command and its control over forces and society. Such countercommand attacks might become more tempting and apparently "cost-effective" in an environment of protected retaliatory forces and societies. Of course, if the superpowers' defenses were nearly perfect and offenses incapable of more than token penetration, then true defense dominance and deterrence could hold. But defenses are unlikely to become almost perfect unless innovation in offenses stands still; superpower past behavior does not make the hypothesis of offensive inertia seem plausible.

Space-based components of BMD could complicate the problem of war termination in a special way. The United States and the Soviet Union might become more dependent upon space-based defenses and spaceborne warning and attack assessment. These defenses and warning satellites could then become vulnerable to the missile defenses of the opponent. The possibility of mutual vulnerability of defense systems in space replacing the mutual vulnerability of societies on earth is a very real one. In that eventuality, war might occur very rapidly as the mutual destruction of warning and missile defense systems invited both sides to launch full-scale preemptive attacks on earth. The decision to go to war with early and indiscriminate attacks might seem the only logical one in the face of "blinded" warning sensors and denuded defense systems.

WAR TERMINATION AND EXTENDED DETERRENCE

Thus far we have been discussing the issue of war termination as it might apply to direct U.S.–Soviet conflicts isolated from involvement by alliance partners. Necessary to this point, that discussion must now be supplemented by recognition of U.S. alliance commitments to the defense of NATO Europe. Those commitments create already apparent mismatches between our military forces and U.S.–NATO political objectives, with serious implications for war termination.

Most probably, U.S.–Soviet nuclear conflict would begin after conventional war in Europe, or following superpower clashes somewhere else which then escalated into war in Europe.[29] Assuming for the moment a Soviet "standing start" attack on the Central Front against NATO, alliance declaratory policy calls for "flexible response" in meeting conventional aggression with conventional forces.[30] However, NATO is committed to escalate the conflict by using theater-based nuclear forces of short, medium, and longer range, and if necessary by employing U.S. strategic nuclear forces in selective strikes against targets in Europe and elsewhere.

There was some disagreement prior to 1989 about whether NATO conventional forces could withstand a Soviet-Pact attack without nuclear weapons with the objective of swallowing up West Germany and/or the Low Countries.[31] John J. Mearsheimer makes a persuasive case that, from static indicators alone, one cannot conclude that NATO forces are deficient or that they would be defeated easily.[32] Charles J. Dick argues that more dynamic and unpredictable factors, including Soviet doctrine for operational art, create a significant probability of a successful Soviet offensive, given any advantageous surprise against slow-reacting NATO defenses.[33] Peter H. Vigor has created a surprise-attack scenario for Soviet planners, based on examinations of their military doctrine historical war experience.[34] William W. Kaufmann has contended that, with incremental improvements such as permanent fortifications and improved operational reserves, the Central Front can be defended with high probability of success by NATO conventional forces.[35]

Although these assessments conflict, they deal with only one part of the problem: the conventional war between ground and tactical air forces. Infrequently addressed in assessments of the conventional balance are the expected performances and missions of the U.S. and Soviet navies.[36] Yet the U.S. "maritime strategy," as promulgated by former Secretary of the Navy John Lehman and Admiral James N. Watkins, assumed that the U.S. Navy would have a decisive role to play early as well as later in a conventional war in Europe.[37] It also has important implications for war termination. The assumption of the U.S. maritime strategy is that aggressive prosecution of attrition against the Soviet navy, wherever it may be found and including its home ports and naval air bases, will contribute to ending the war on terms favorable to NATO.[38] This will come about, it is assumed, not only by bottling up the Soviet surface and subsurface maritime force north of the GIUK (Greenland, Iceland, and United Kingdom) gap in order to protect transatlantic sea-lanes of communication, but also by a full-court press against the Soviets in the Norwegian and Barents seas. Attacks against Soviet nuclear-armed attack submarines (SSN) and strategic ballistic missile submarines (SSBN) are not precluded in the early stages of conventional war.[39]

When all of this is combined, it appears that the NATO land-sea-air conventional strategy calls for holding the line as close to the inter-German border as feasible with ground and tactical air forces, while squeezing the Soviet periphery with U.S.–NATO maritime forces. For this strategy to accomplish its objectives, which we will assume means getting the Soviets to say "uncle" without escalating to nuclear use, several assumptions must be fulfilled. First, NATO ground and air defense forces cannot be caught by strategic (at the theater level) as opposed to tactical surprise. Strategic surprise might occur if, for example, NATO political leaders failed to react to warning indicators and to authorize responsive alerts for fear of provoking, rather than deterring, the Soviets.[40] Second, NATO must maintain control of its own air space and eventually dominate air space over the Pact side of the battle on the Central Front.[41] Third, and paradoxically, the Warsaw Pact must hang together for the Soviet Union to perceive its self-interest in terminating, as opposed to escalating, the war. Potential disintegration of the Pact would pose a challenge to Soviet values of the "reversing of history" that could preclude, rather than assist, war termination. Of course, we are speaking of these effects on the assumption that the Western objective is war termination rather than dissolution of the

Soviet empire in Europe; one of the difficulties of terminating (even) conventional war in Europe is how to make certain that the Soviet Union knows the difference.

For these favorable conditions to emerge, NATO must plainly deter Soviet first use of nuclear weapons and the possible expansion of that use into full-scale theater and strategic nuclear exchanges. NATO's policy story for accomplishing termination of war in Europe, under these conditions, would be more credible if U.S. strategic and NATO theater nuclear forces were superior to those of their Soviet counterparts. Alas, they are either equivalent or inferior, measured by such indicators as survivability, countermilitary potential, accuracy, and redundancy.[42] Thus there is little reason for the Soviets to withhold escalation if they fear they are losing the conventional war. To redress these imbalances at the top and middle of the NATO "Triad," the United States and its allies might improve strategic and theater offensive forces, or deploy defenses, or both. We have already discussed the issue of BMD and some of its implications for U.S.–Soviet bilateral deterrence. Defenses complicate matters even more when they are considered within the context of "flexible response" strategy and NATO's commitment to forward defense.

Not all aspects of the relationship between strategic and theater defenses and flexible response can be discussed here. But one is immediately apparent for the agenda of policymakers. The Soviet Union, independently of whatever the NATO alliance decides to do, may itself deploy theater or strategic defenses. Initially these defenses would be unlikely to provide comprehensive protection for the Soviet or East European population, nor would they need to. hey might be tasked for protection of time-urgent military and command, control, and communications (C^3) targets in the European theater, including nuclear-weapons storage sites and launchers. Limited theater ballistic missile defenses (ATBM, for antitactical ballistic missile defenses) would provide for the Soviet Union strong counterweight to the NATO declaratory Follow-on Forces Attack strategy of deep attack with high-technology "smart" weapons against Pact second-echelon targets.[43] With a capability to nullify NATO counteroffensive deep strikes against their reinforcing echelons, the Soviets would not necessarily need a rapid, conventional *blitzkrieg* offensive to defeat NATO without using nuclear weapons. Their more traditional World War II tactics would do quite nicely.[44]

Nor is this all. The Soviet Union could internet theater ballistic missile defenses based in Europe or in the western USSR with strategic defenses for its retaliatory forces and command centers. There is some concern on the part of Pentagon officials that the Soviets may be planning to do exactly that, whether or not the United States deploys SDI.[45] Even comparable defenses on the NATO side would not necessarily restore the *status quo ante*, as is often assumed in scenarios of bilateral BMD deployments. NATO's conventional deterrence depends upon a subtle blend of denial and punishment capabilities, the former mostly conventional and the latter mostly nuclear. By deploying a theater ballistic missile defense system equivalent to one deployed by the Soviets, NATO would restore equity to the punishment capabilities of the two sides, but not to their comparative denial capabilities. The reason why denial capabilities would still favor the Pact is that NATO's conventional deep-attack operations would no longer be viable; the Pact would not have to win quickly to win without using nuclear weapons, as is now assumed.

SOVIET DOCTRINE

Thus far, it has been argued that war termination has been a neglected element in mainstream and alternative deterrence theories, and in actual operational planning to the extent that we can determine.[46] There is a lack of connection between U.S. declaratory policy about escalation control of theater or strategic nuclear warfare, and the absence of capabilities for extended war without which no adversary can be compelled to come to terms. It may be that those capabilities are not within the technical and policy reach of either superpower for uncontrolled "spasm" exchanges, and even "limited" nuclear wars can involve substantial collateral damage.[47] Nevertheless, it would be imprudent to assume only the worst case and then to make it the sole possible outcome by default. U.S. nuclear strategy is forever complicated by the paradox that, although no one can guarantee that nuclear war can be controlled, this is not equivalent to proving that it cannot be.

In practice rather than in theory, U.S. expectations for controlled nuclear war fighting and war termination bear some relationship to Soviet doctrine and behavior. The problem is to define the character of that relationship. Does war termination even figure into the Soviet "calculus" of nuclear war? There are daunting issues of style and substance to decipher here. One can argue from the perspective of Soviet doctrine that has appeared in the statements of political and military leaders, from their force deployments, or from their assumed targeting requirements.[48]

Soviet declaratory doctrine involves assumptions about military art at the levels of strategy, operational art, and tactics.[49] Soviet military doctrine has been described as applicable at two levels or within two frames of reference. The first is the primary political guidance to the armed forces about the kinds of wars they will have to fight, the identification of threats to Soviet security and enemies of the state, and the ideological frame of reference within which the politico-military struggle can be expected to occur.[50] The second level is the military-technical level and has a more operational cast, describing probable measures of preparedness and actual war-fighting objectives and tactics. This multivariate character of Soviet doctrine creates anomalies, at least from the standpoint of Western audiences. Soviet party leaders, including former general secretary Leonid Brezhnev, began in the mid-1970s to declare that nuclear war was unthinkable and calamitous for either of the prospective superpower combatants. Speaking on behalf of the Soviet leadership, Konstantin Chernenko in 1981 made the statement that "It is criminal to look upon nuclear war as a rational, almost legitimate continuation of policy."[51] In his noted January 1977 speech at Tula, Brezhnev said that the Soviet Union was not "striving for superiority in armaments with the aim of delivering a 'first strike.'"[52]

However much their political leadership might disclaim the desirability of nuclear war in public pronouncements, the Soviets perceive that, despite their efforts, war might happen. Should war be forced upon them, in their judgment, their military power would be employed to destroy the armed forces, command centers, and war-supporting industry of their opponents.[53] Moreover, Soviet military leaders are charged with being prepared to carry out these missions under even the most stressful conditions of a U.S.–Soviet nuclear exchange. Soviet doctrine provides that their forces be able to preempt if enemy attack is detected or judged imminent, but they are also prepared for launch under attack or retaliation after being struck first.[54]

The Soviet view of history is different from the U.S. one. This difference is so basic and fundamental that the temptation for Americans to "mirror image" their perceptions onto Soviets is a seductive trap.[55] As close students of Clausewitz interpreted through the conceptual lenses of Lenin, the Soviet leadership believes that its system is historically predestined to triumph over its capitalist opponents. History, however much it might be helped along from time to time, is inexorably moving in directions favorable to the final victory of socialism. This world historical vision of Soviet theoreticians provides a conceptual framework within which a positive, flexible foreign policy can be adapted to the changing tides of circumstance. The Soviets know the general direction in which they are headed, however many detours (in their judgment) may be required to get there.

If the Soviet perspective on war follows from this world historical view, then war between the United States and its NATO allies and the Soviet–

Warsaw Pact coalition cannot be trivialized. It will be a decisive global struggle in which both sides will use not only their strategic and theater nuclear forces but also their general-purpose (conventional) and special forces as required. The possibility of such a war's having a prolonged conventional phase prior to the introduction of nuclear weapons is not precluded.[56] However, this can be misunderstood as a Soviet preference for a protracted conventional war, rather than the first use of nuclear weapons by them in order to bring about victory. No such doctrine has been promulgated by the Soviet military leadership, and it would be most un-Leninist of them to abjure the use of weapons of mass destruction, either nuclear or chemical, if those weapons were thought to be decisive. On the other hand, the Soviet Union is prepared for the possibility of protracted war if need be, including protracted conventional war.[57] The Soviets did, after all, fight the classical protracted conventional war in the Great Patriotic War, albeit after the war was forced upon them by the Nazis and in defense of their homeland. Whether they fought in retaliation or assumed the role of aggression, Soviet leaders would be cognizant of their opponents' conceptual framework and of the possibility for exploiting it. As Robert Bathurst has noted:

Thus, the Soviet language of war does not begin where the American does, with a breach of legality, or end where it does with a military defeat. It begins with the exacerbation of class warfare (which emerges often as the warfare of political parties) and ends with nothing less than the transformation of society. The last Soviet battle does not take place when the missiles have ceased to fly, but when the revolutionary executions against the wall have stopped.[58]

Of course, the Soviets are not unaware of the differences between nuclear and conventional war, and their pronouncements make very clear their concern about the effects of nuclear war on their society. This is among the reasons for their very substantial civil defense program. Although Western observers are prone to disregard its importance, Soviet civil defense has objectives that are not apparent by mirror imaging. The program is not designed primarily for the survival of Soviet citizens in general, but for survival of the political and military leadership.[59] The Soviet Union has made far more extensive commitments to the protection of its leadership than has the United States or its allies. Certainly the Soviets have every motivation to do this, for U.S. nuclear weapons employment policies are thought to include options for targeting the Soviet command structure, including the highest levels of party and state leadership.[60]

The concept of escalation control is more a Western than a Soviet reference. Western writing tends to distinguish escalation control from escalation dominance. Escalation control refers to the limitation upon deliberate or inadvertent growth in the scope or destructiveness of a conflict. Escalation dominance is the ability to impose escalation control on terms favorable to one side because its opponent would lose more than it would gain from expanding the conflict.[61] For the Soviets, once they were involved in a conventional or theater nuclear war against the West, escalation dominance would be imposed if possible and negotiated only under duress. Apparently the Soviets do recognize the possibility of a threshold between the theater and strategic nuclear levels of conflict, under the very scenario-dependent condition that their homeland is not under attack.[62] The problem of escalation control with the objective of war termination, from the Western perspective, is that the Soviet Union, having crossed the threshold of war with the West in the first place, would be hard pressed to justify this exertion without bringing about some change in the postconflict military and political balance of power. Even if the Soviet homeland were somehow not attacked, Eastern Europe would have absorbed very destructive blows from NATO conventional and/or theater nuclear forces. The possibility of revolt within the contiguous empire that separates the Soviet Union from the West would be considered seriously by Soviet planners. Indeed, this might be among the most restraining preattack forces in favor of deterrence instead of war.

STRATEGIC DEFENSIVISM, *PERESTROIKA*, AND THE CHANGING SOVIET VIEW OF INTERNATIONAL POLITICS

A broader compass must now be brought to bear on the subject of contending paradigms and mutual superpower deterrence. We have seen that the supporting structure of mutual deterrence was under attack in the United States during the Reagan administration, offering the view that deterrence based on retaliation can be circumvented by technology. It has been noted as well that this great leap over deterrence is suspiciously regarded by America's NATO European allies, U.S. critics of the Strategic Defense Initiative, and the Soviets. This last disregard might seem to contradict traditional Soviet interest in defense of the homeland, their treaty-limited BMD deployments already in place, and the synergistic relationship between offense and defense that is so much a part of their military-historical heritage.[63]

Soviet skepticism about SDI is partly based on fears that a less than totally effective U.S. BMD system could absorb a ragged retaliatory strike, thus denying them the option of assured retaliation. Skepticism is also based on the more realistic fear of U.S. technological competition across the board, including SDI spillovers into the modernization of sensors, fusion centers, and more accurate munitions for conventional deep strike.[64] Directed energy-weapons technologies such as lasers and kinetic kill vehicles may become useful on the terrestrial battlefields of the 1990s or beyond. The management of electronic warfare, including electronic support measures (ESM), electronic countermeasures (ECM), and electronic counter-countermeasures (ECCM) in the high-technology environment of the 1990s will stress Soviet capabilities for the development of information systems and command technology.[65] The potential for technological encirclement by the combined innovation of the United States, the European Community, and Japan presents the Soviet leadership with significant dilemmas and hard policy choices.

Gorbachev has indicated since his assumption of the position of general secretary in 1985 that he is prepared to set priorities and to make hard choices.[66] In international relations this means that he must soften the harder edges of the U.S.–Soviet arms competition in order to reduce the burden that this places on the Soviet economy. In domestic politics, he must preside over the redistribution of political and economic power among Soviet party bureaucrats, military professionals, intelligentsia, and other constituent factions of the Soviet body politic. These factions will welcome leadership in favor of change that does not bite too hard into their respective shares of resources or esteem. If the reforms of *perestroika* become too threatening to one or more constituencies, however, resistance will be felt and the ability of the leadership to maintain its forward momentum may be compromised. Gorbachev must walk the line between modernization of the economy that is acceptable within the framework of progressive socialism, and modernization that would threaten the very foundations of socialism itself.[67]

The concerns of the Soviet leadership, while valid, should not be misperceived or exaggerated. The Soviet Union has substantial resources and strong capacity for innovation in science and technology, provided the capacity is systematically applied. The success of the Soviet space program during the 1980s, compared to the difficulties of the American, shows this. On the other hand, a far-sighted leadership, with regard to the uncertainties attendant to world political developments, must act prudently to propel the correlation of forces in a direction more favorable to the Soviets' domestic and foreign-policy objectives. This means a restructuring of Soviet foreign-policy objectives, which is bound to influence their military doctrines and expectations about how wars start and how they might be concluded.

The declaratory doctrine of most contemporary interest to Western

audiences is the notion of strategic defensivism. As explained by
Gorbachev and other high-ranking leaders, and as endorsed by the Warsaw
Pact in official policy directives, the official position is that Soviet armed
forces now have as their main mission the prevention of any war, nuclear
or conventional. This is connected to Gorbachev's arms-control policies,
which call for the gradual dismantling of superpower nuclear arsenals, the
withdrawal of superpower nuclear weapons from Europe, and the restructuring of the U.S.–Soviet arms race into something approximating a
security community.[68] The military aspects of this doctrine are referred to
as either "reasonable sufficiency" or "defensive sufficiency," depending
upon whether the Soviet officials involved are military professionals (who
prefer defensive sufficiency) or others.[69]

The real issue is how much difference this declaratory doctrine might
make in actual Soviet force structure and force-employment policy over
the long term. Some U.S. skepticism is obviously warranted, if only
because changes in force structure will have to have the concurrence of
the Soviet military leadership. The Soviet military leadership has an
obvious interest in not being technologically outflanked. Therefore, it can
be expected to support force modernization and may well be inclined to
trade off some force size as a reciprocal. However, the Soviet military
leadership is unlikely to go as far in this direction, on account of their
institutionalized distrust of the Americans and NATO, as the more arms-
control–oriented sections of the Soviet party bureaucracy. The inertial
drag of sunken costs, in weapons systems and force structures already
committed or planned, will also limit the velocity with which economic
reorganization can be translated into a trade-off between improved force
modernization and smaller force size.

Much U.S. and Western interest has focused on the possibility of troop
reductions within the guidelines encompassed by the CFE (Conventional
Forces in Europe) negotiating forum, which called as of early 1990 for
U.S. and Soviet forces to be limited to 195,000 each in Central Europe.
Meanwhile the discussion of "operational" arms control proceeded in the
larger CSCE (Conference on Security and Cooperation in Europe), em-
phasizing confidence-building measures instead of arms reduction per se.
Essentially, the confidence-building measures are designed to provide
mutual advance notification by NATO and the Warsaw Pact of military
exercises that involve more than a certain number of forces. Also involved
in CSBM (confidence and security-building measures) agreements is the
acceptance by both sides of the right to inspect one another's force
structures and to observe one another's exercises under certain conditions.
The idea is that, even before force-structure reductions can be agreed to,

the mutual fear of surprise attack can be moderated by allowing both sides to be reassured of absence of hostile intent. The objective is also to improve crisis stability in the event that the political atmosphere should deteriorate. CSBMs are regarded as the archetypical "positive sum game," in that they are mutually advantageous and involve no substantial risks and vulnerabilities should they prove ineffective or irrelevant. Neither side would want war to break out accidentally or to escalate inadvertently.[70]

Force reductions in the NATO guidelines will be tougher to come by, but they are by no means precluded. The Soviet model of defensive sufficiency is compatible with the reduction of both sides' capabilities for conventional surprise attack and deep strike. This might stabilize conventional deterrence under the nuclear threshold, but if the nuclear threshold became indistinct, on account of nuclear force reductions, the incentives for conventional cuts would be reduced. NATO will be hard pressed to demonstrate that the Soviets are so accommodating that both nuclear and conventional forces can be reduced simultaneously. Even mutual conventional-force reductions will take place in a technological environment permissive of significant force modernization, although at perhaps reduced levels. Qualitative and quantitative conventional-force reductions or limitations may have to be coordinated. It may matter more what kinds of forces are reduced or pulled back from the inter-German border than it does how many. Heavy tank and motorized rifle or mechanized infantry divisions may have to be replaced in the forward areas by straight-leg infantry divisions that have comparatively smaller capabilities for offensive, surprise, and deep attack. However, even this raises serious questions of "how" the qualitative aspects of reductions can be managed while preserving NATO's requirements for interoperability of command systems and C^3 equipment or protocols. The problem of command-system survivability and integrity may be exacerbated by force reductions instead of improved by them. The Pact will have fewer forces with which to attack NATO C^3 targets, but there will be fewer nodes to attack. The ratio of attacker incentive to potential vulnerabilities of NATO C^3 is already too precarious, according to some expert assessments.[71]

Discussion of the practical difficulties attendant to conventional-force reductions or stability enhancements reveals the irrelevance of grandiose debates about replacing deterrence with preclusive defense. Long before deterrence could ever be supplanted, the superpowers will be forced to modernize their conventional-force structures and the industrial bases that underlie them. The choice is between force and industrial-base modernization during a period of "defense transition" on one hand, and the continuation of assured retaliation and the modernization of conventional arsenals within the existing framework on the other. This also brings in by the back door the question of what kind of conventional war the super-powers are preparing to fight, or to deter. The Soviets were thought by NATO planners prior to 1989 to be biased toward a fast-moving, *blitzkrieg* offensive that would (preferably) catch NATO less than fully deployed and prepared. If they cannot win the short war and must persevere into a longer, and probably global, conventional war, can the Soviet military count on their economy to sustain them? The argument that the Soviet economy in peacetime coughs up 14 to 15 percent of GNP to support defense, as opposed to other needs, is insufficient to predict what it could do under the stress of even a short war. Norman Stone has shown that, contrary to conventional wisdom, the Russian economy did not stagnate during World War I. Economic growth exploded, as did inflation; the problem was not insufficient growth or production but the management of it and its inflationary side effects.[72] By peacetime standards of economic mismanagement prior to Gorbachev, the Soviet economy would not make it through the stresses of a global and extended war. This recognition, which the present Soviet leadership has acknowledged, feeds backward from the strategic rear to the front. If the protracted war cannot be sustained, then the shorter war must be won at all cost. But if it is not, what then?

It could be argued that a "fortress Soviet Union" strategic defensivism would be compatible with improved ground forces for extended war and limited BMD deployments to preclude U.S. first strike.[73] This would provide counterdeterrence to the U.S. strategic nuclear deterrent and remove from the latter its potential for use in compellent missions against targets in the Soviet Union or in Eastern Europe. However, the limitation of the Soviet economy remains; in this vision just proposed, it must somehow provide for the canopy of a Soviet "Star Wars" while sustaining economic endurance in case the war extends for weeks or months. With or without its own version of SDI, the Soviet Union must expect that its options exclusive of a rapid and decisive conventional victory are very limited. And even with the best-case scenario for a Soviet *blitzkrieg* in Western Europe, excluding nuclear escalation, the United States remains undivested of its potential for a return to the continent with liberating forces. Only the sinking of the U.S. and allied navies by the Soviet navy can preclude that, and the balance at sea would have to shift drastically before such a hypothetical possibility became probable.

Assuming the defense transition envisioned by the Reagan administration does not materialize and that defenses, if deployed, are deployed to protect retaliatory forces and command centers, they would serve the purpose of reinforcing deterrence by retaliation, not supplanting it. This leaves the issue of conventional deterrence and force stabilization in Europe about where it is now. The nuclear-conventional coupling under assured retaliation places the burden of force reduction and stability enhancement on the alliances' military doctrines for conventional warfare. Absent a preclusive national territorial defense for the Americans or Soviets, West Europeans remain linked to the U.S. strategic deterrent by shared commitment and vulnerability. The proposition is often advanced that a "Star Wars" defense will make the United States bolder in defense of allies under attack, but this proposition assumes no Soviet defenses or no new look at alliance commitments once defenses are deployed. In fact, NATO Europeans would look again at the U.S. commitment once Americans were protected behind an antinuclear defense shield. They would recognize that whatever declaratory policy said, the United States could in fact selectively disengage from any war in Europe.[74] In addition, the British and French strategic deterrents are placed in jeopardy by very competent theater missile defense systems for Eastern Europe that might have overlapping, expandable capabilities for strategic BMD.[75] And the British and French deterrents are more than jeopardized, perhaps negated altogether, by a BMD system that provides reliable protection for the national territory of the Soviet Union.

A safe assumption, in view of the above, is that the land and tactical air battles of the future fought in Europe, if deterrence fails, will take place in several phases with or without a defense transition having occurred in U.S.–Soviet relations. The first phase would involve rapid encounter battles and meeting engagements on a fluid landscape that may well prove inconclusive after the first days or weeks. If so, and if nuclear escalation is meanwhile avoided, a second stage of the war would set in, one in which lower technology and higher manpower intensive warfare grind across irregular frontages mapped by degraded command, control, and communications systems.[76] These are big "ifs." Neither side would be prudent to plan on keeping nuclear weapons out of war in Europe, but either might prefer to if its conventional war plan were going well. The objective for the "winner" of this first sortie would be to stabilize the front at an advantageous time and place, arrange some sort of cease-fire, and then negotiate on the basis of "what's mine, is mine" and so forth. The question would be the balance of incentives for the opponent to compromise or escalate. This balance cannot be known ahead of time, and it is difficult to see how it would be much affected by strategic defenses unless they were nearly perfect, and so precluded credible threats of escalation to the top of the ladder.

NOTES

1. An argument for this position appears in Spurgeon M. Keeny, Jr., and Wolfgang K. H. Panofsky, "MAD Versus NUTS: Can Doctrine or Weaponry Remedy the Mutual Hostage Relationship of the Superpowers?" *Foreign Affairs* 60, no. 2 (Winter 1981-82), pp. 287–304.

2. Keith B. Payne, *Strategic Defense: "Star Wars" in Perspective* (Lanham, Md.: Hamilton Press, 1986).

3. "President's Speech on Military Spending and a New Defense," *New York Times*, March 24, 1983, p. 20.

4. Leon V. Sigal distinguishes among strategic (which we have termed *basic* or *deterrence stability*), crisis, and arms race stability. See Segal, *Nuclear Forces in Europe: Enduring Dilemmas, Present Prospects* (Washington: Brookings Institution, 1984), p. 9.

5. Greater-than-expected threats provided a basis for defining prelaunch survivability requirements very conservatively. See Alan C. Enthoven and K. Wayne Smith, *How Much is Enough? Shaping the Defense Program, 1961–69* (New York: Harper and Row, 1971).

6. See Leon Sloss, "The Strategist's Perspective," Ch. 2 in Ashton B. Carter and David N. Schwartz, eds., *Ballistic Missile Defense* (Washington: Brookings Institution 1984), pp. 24–48, for important distinctions about strategic contexts pertinent to this issue.

7. Useful technical discussion appears in Barry R. Schneider, "Soviet Uncertainties in Targeting Peacekeeper," pp. 109–34 in Schneider, Colin S. Gray, and Keith B. Payne, eds., *Missiles for the Nineties* (Boulder, Colo.: Westview Press, 1984).

8. Keith B. Payne and Colin S. Gray, "Nuclear Policy and the Defensive Transition," *Foreign Affairs* 62, no. 4 (Spring 1984), pp. 820–42.

9. James C. Fletcher, "Technologies for Strategic Defense," *Issues in Science and Technology* 1, no. 1 (Fall 1984), pp. 15–29.

10. Congress of the United States, Congressional Budget Office, *Modernizing U.S. Strategic Offensive Forces: The Administration's Program and Alternatives* (Washington: GPO, May 1983).

11. Raymond L. Garthoff, "Mutual Deterrence, Parity and Strategic Arms Limitation in Soviet Policy," in Derek Leebaert, ed., *Soviet Military Thinking* (London: Allen and Unwin, 1981), pp. 50–69.

12. Paul Nitze, "Assuring Strategic Stability in an Era of Detente," *Foreign Affairs* 54 (1976), pp. 207–33.

13. Lawrence Freedman, *The Evolution of Nuclear Strategy* (New York: St. Martin's Press, 1981), p. 357.

14. Lynn Etheridge Davis, "Limited Nuclear Options: Deterrence and the New American Doctrine," in Christoph Bertram, ed., *Strategic Deterrence in a Changing Environment* (Montclair, N.J.: Allenheld, Osmun and Co., 1981), pp. 42–62.

15. Desmond Ball, "Counterforce Targeting? How New? How Viable?" *Arms Control Today* 22, no. 2 (February 1981), reprinted with revisions in John F. Reichart and Steven R. Sturm, eds., *American Defense Policy* (Baltimore: Johns Hopkins University Press, 1982), pp. 227–34. See also Kurt Gottfried and Bruce G. Blair, *Crisis Stability and Nuclear War* (New York: Oxford University Press, 1988), Ch. 5.

16. U.S. dependency upon strategic warning for execution of the SIOP is alleged by William R. Van Cleave, "U.S. Defense Strategy: A Debate," in George E. Hudson and

Joseph Kruzel, eds., *American Defense Annual 1985–86* (Lexington, Mass.: D. C. Heath, 1985), pp. 21–24.

17. On Soviet military strategy and wartime objectives, see Robert P. Berman and John C. Baker, *Soviet Strategic Forces* (Washington: Brookings Institution, 1982), pp. 27–37. See also Joseph D. Douglass, Jr., and Amoretta M. Hoeber, *Soviet Strategy for Nuclear War* (Stanford, Calif.: Hoover Institution Press, 1979), pp. 14–33.

18. For an assessment, see Sayre Stevens, "The Soviet BMD Program," in Ashton B. Carter and David N. Schwartz, eds., *Ballistic Missile Defense*, pp. 182–220.

19. Christoph I. Branch, *Fighting a Long Nuclear War: A Strategy, Force, Policy Mismatch*, National Defense University, National Security Affairs Monograph Series, 1984 (Washington, D.C.: Ft. McNair).

20. Harry G. Summers, Jr., *On Strategy: A Critical Analysis of the Vietnam War* (New York: Dell Publishing Co., 1984), pp. 33–43. Originally published by Presidio Press, 1982).

21. Desmond Ball, "Can Nuclear War Be Controlled?" *Adelphi Papers*, no. 169 (London: International Institute for Strategic Studies, Autumn 1981); Paul Bracken, *The Command and Control of Nuclear Forces* (New Haven: Yale University Press, 1983); Bruce G. Blair, *Strategic Command and Control: Redefining the Nuclear Threat* (Washington: Brookings Institution, 1985).

22. Blair, *Strategic Command and Control*, p. 187.

23. Fred Kaplan, *The Wizards of Armageddon* (New York: Simon and Schuster, 1983), pp. 317–19, notes that McNamara and his associates estimated a requirement for 400 survivable megatons on each leg of the Triad.

24. Stockholm International Peace Research Institute, *Nuclear Radiation in Warfare* (London: Taylor and Francis, 1981); William Daugherty, Barbara Levi, and Frank von Hippel, "The Consequences of 'Limited' Nuclear Attacks on the United States," *International Security* 10, no. 4 (Spring 1986), pp. 3–45.

25. Lawrence Freedman, *The Evolution of Nuclear Strategy* (New York: St. Martin's Press, 1981), p. 235.

26. Ball, "Counterforce Targeting," *passim*; and Kaplan, *Wizards of Armageddon*, p. 319.

27. Leon Sloss and Marc Dean Millot, "U.S. Nuclear Strategy in Evolution," *Strategic Review*, Winter 1984, pp. 19–28.

28. Paul H. Nitze, "On the Road to a More Stable Peace," February 20, 1985, U.S. Department of State, *Current Policy*, no. 657.

29. Fen Osler Hampsen, "Escalation in Europe," in Graham T. Allison, Albert Carnesale, and Joseph S. Nye, Jr., eds., *Hawks, Doves and Owls: An Agenda for Avoiding Nuclear War* (New York: W. W. Norton and Co., 1985), pp. 79–114.

30. This is according to MC 14/3 adopted in 1967. For background, see David N. Schwartz, *NATO's Nuclear Dilemmas* (Washington: Brookings Institution, 1983), pp. 136–92.

31. For an overview of this issue, see William P. Mako, *U.S. Ground Forces and the Defense of Central Europe* (Washington: Brookings Institution, 1983).

32. John J. Mearsheimer, *Conventional Deterrence* (Ithaca, N.Y.: Cornell University Press, 1983), pp. 165–88.

33. C. J. Dick, "Catching NATO Unawares: Soviet Army Surprise and Deception Techniques," *International Defense Review* 19, no. 1 (1986), pp. 21–26.

34. P. H. Vigor, *Soviet Blitzkrieg Theory* (New York: St. Martin's Press, 1983).

35. William W. Kaufmann, "Nonnuclear Deterrence," Ch. 4 in John D. Steinbruner and Leon V. Sigal, eds., *Alliance Security and the No First Use Question* (Washington: Brookings Institute, 1983), pp. 43–90.

36. An exception is Kaufmann. See his *A Reasonable Defense* (Washington: Brookings Institution, 1986), pp. 72–75.

37. U.S. Naval Institute, *Proceedings*, January 1986, includes the official statement of U.S. maritime strategy by Admiral James D. Watkins, USN, pp. 3–17.

38. According to Admiral Watkins, the objective of U.S. maritime strategy is to contribute to "war termination on favorable terms." See Watkins, "The Maritime Strategy," p. 3.

39. Watkins, "The Maritime Strategy," p. 11.

40. Richard K. Betts, *Surprise Attack: Lessons for Defense Planning* (Washington: Brookings Institution, 1982), pp. 153–257, discusses the problem of surprise relative to NATO.

41. European Security Study, *Strengthening Conventional Deterrence in Europe* (New York: St. Martin's Press, 1983), p. 201.

42. Anthony H. Cordesman, "Theater Forces," in Joseph Kruzel, ed., *American Defense Annual* 1986–87 (Lexington, Mass.:D. C. Heath and Co., 1986), pp. 89–119.

43. See Joel S. Wit, "Deep Strike: NATO's New Defense Concept and Its Implications for Arms Control," *Arms Control Today* 13, no. 10 (November 1983), pp. 1, 4–7, 9.

44. Steven Canby refers to Soviet World War II tactics as "steamroller" tactics. See Canby, "The Alliance and Europe—Part IV: Military Doctrine and Technology," *Adelphi Papers,* no. 109 (London: International Institute for Strategic Studies, Winter 1974-75), p. 10.

45. U.S. Department of Defense, *Soviet Strategic Defense Programs* (Washington: GPO, October 1985). Released by the Department of Defense and Department of State.

46. An exception is Albert Carnesale et al., *Living with Nuclear Weapons* (New York: Bantam Books, 1983), pp. 149–50, and earlier writings by Thomas Schelling, Herman Kahn, and Fred C. Ikle.

47. William Daugherty et al., "The Consequences of 'Limited' Nuclear Attacks on the United States," *International Security* 10, no. 4 (Spring 1986), pp. 3–45.

48. A useful compendium is Derek Leebaert, ed., *Soviet Military Thinking* (London: Allen and Unwin, 1981).

49. On the formulation of Soviet military doctrine as applied to nuclear war, see Col. M. P. Skirdo, *The People, the Army, the Commander* (Moscow: 1970), pp. 98–108.

50. Raymond L. Garthoff, *Detente and Confrontation: American-Soviet Relations from Nixon to Reagan* (Washington: Brookings Institution, 1985), p. 780.

51. Garthoff, *Detente and Confrontation*, pp. 778–79.

52. *Pravda*, January 19, 1977. I am grateful to Mary C. FitzGerald, Center for Naval Analyses, for this reference.

53. Army General S. Ivanov, "Soviet Military Doctrine and Strategy," in *Selected Readings from MILITARY THOUGHT 1963–1973*, selected and compiled by Joseph D. Douglass, Jr., and Amoretta M. Hoeber (Washington: GPO, undated), p. 27; and Maj. Gen. V. Zemskov, "Characteristic Features of Modern Wars and Possible Methods of Conducting Them," in Douglass and Hoeber, ibid., p. 49.

54. William T. Lee and Richard F. Staar, *Soviet Military Policy Since World War II* (Stanford, Calif.: Hoover Institution, 1986), p. 28.

55. For appropriate summations of the differences and relevant cautions, see Fritz W.

Ermarth, "Contrasts in American and Soviet Strategic Thought," in Leebaert, ed., *Soviet Military Thinking*, pp. 50–69.

56. Joseph D. Douglass, Jr., and Amoretta M. Hoeber, *Conventional War and Escalation* (New York: Crane, Russak and Co., 1981), argue: "Should a war in Europe, in particular, or against the United States anywhere, begin with a conventional phase, Soviet operations planning would be conducted with the possible sudden transition to nuclear operations as *the* primary consideration" (p. 7, italics in original).

57. Scott and Scott, *The Soviet Control Structure*, pp. 122–24 and *passim*.

58. Robert Bathurst, "Two Languages of War," in Leebaert, ed., *Soviet Military Thinking*, p. 31.

59. Scott and Scott, *The Soviet Control Structure*, *passim*.

60. Desmond Ball, "Targeting for Strategic Deterrence," *Adelphi Papers*, no. 185 (Summer 1983), pp. 31–32.

61. Herman Kahn, *On Escalation: Metaphors and Scenarios* (New York: Praeger, 1965), pp. 3–9.

62. Stephen M. Meyer, "Soviet Perspectives on the Paths to Nuclear War," in Graham T. Allison et al., ed., *Hawks, Doves and Owls: An Agenda for Avoiding Nuclear War* (New York: W. W. Norton and Co., 1985), pp. 167–205, esp. pp. 185–86. However, a Soviet decision about nuclear escalation would take place in an unfamiliar environment in which military imperatives might suggest preemption as the least miserable of options (Ibid., pp. 199–201).

63. Jacob W. Kipp, *Conventional Force Modernization and the Asymmetries of Military Doctrine: Historical Reflections on AirLand Battle and the Operational Maneuver Group* (Fort Leavenworth, Kans.: Soviet Army Studies Office, U.S. Army Combined Arms Center, 1987).

64. See the discussion in Col. Stanislaw Koziej, "Anticipated Directions for Change in Tactics of Ground Troops," *Przeglad Wojsk Ladowych* (Ground Forces Review), September 1986, pp. 5–9; Captain Leon Turczynski, "Microcomputers in the Decision Process of the Commander and Chief of Technical Services," *Przeglad Wojsk Ladowych*, August 1986, pp. 117–19. I am grateful to Harold Orenstein for these references.

65. John Erickson, "Soviet Cybermen: Men and Machines in the System," *Signal*, December 1984, reprinted in Stephen J. Cimbala, ed., *Soviet C³* (Washington: AFCEA International Press, 1987), pp. 82–88.

66. Mikhail Gorbachev, *Perestroika: New Thinking for Our Country and the World* (New York: Harper and Row, 1987).

67. See Seweryn Bialer, *The Soviet Paradox: External Expansion, Internal Decline* (New York: Knopf, 1986).

68. For an elaboration, see Seweryn Bialer, "'New Thinking' and Soviet Foreign Policy," *Survival* 30, no. 4 (July-August 1988), pp. 291–309.

69. Raymond L. Garthoff, "New Thinking in Soviet Military Doctrine," *The Washington Quarterly* 11, no. 3 (Summer 1988), pp. 131–58.

70. The distinction between accidental and inadvertent war or escalation is explained in Paul Bracken, "Accidental Nuclear War," Ch. 2 in Graham T. Allison, Albert Carnesale, and Joseph S. Nye, Jr., *Hawks, Doves and Owls: An Agenda for Avoiding Nuclear War* (New York: W. W. Norton, 1985), pp. 25–53.

71. Desmond Ball, *Controlling Theater Nuclear War*, Working Paper No. 138 (Canberra, Australia: Research School of Pacific Studies, Australian National University, October 1987).

72. Norman Stone, *The Eastern Front, 1914–1917* (New York: Charles Scribner's Sons, 1975), esp. Ch. 13.

73. See Stephen M. Meyer, "Soviet Nuclear Operations," Ch. 15, in Ashton B. Carter, John D. Steinbruner, and Charles A. Zraket, eds., *Managing Nuclear Operations* (Washington: Brookings Institution, 1987), pp. 470–534, esp. p. 523.

74. Stephen Kirby, "The Military Uses of Space and European Security," Ch. 9 in Stephen Kirby and Gordon Robson, eds., *The Militarisation of Space* (London: Wheatsheaf Books/Lynne Rienner, 1987), pp. 173–99.

75. See David S. Yost, "Strategic Defenses in Soviet Doctrine and Force Posture," Ch. 5 in Fred S. Hoffman, Albert Wohlstetter, and David S. Yost, eds., *Swords and Shields: NATO, the USSR, and New Choices for Long-Range Offense and Defense* (Lexington, Mass.: Lexington Books, 1987), pp. 123–58. According to Yost:

In contrast to the widespread Western view that the probable levels of destruction that would be entailed in any future European war would make the political outcome irrelevant, the Soviets appear to have given attention to achieving specific military and political results. The Western emphasis on prewar deterrence differs from the Soviet preoccupation with being prepared for combat and war termination. Soviet strategic planning places great emphasis on the results of "theater-strategic" campaigns, even in the context of possible intercontinental war. From the Soviet perspective, victory in a NATO–Warsaw Pact conflict would be meaningful to the extent that the European region could be kept intact and made to serve Soviet purposes.

Ibid., p. 141. This assessment is correct with the proviso that the Soviets must preferably confine war below the nuclear threshold or, if nuclear, below the threshold of intercontinental nuclear exchanges.

76. According to a Polish military writer:

The possibilities of fighting against means of air attack under conditions of strong radioelectronic interference is the next essential requirement which will have great significance in the future. Currently, activity in the presence of radioelectronic interference should be considered as something normal. *The lack of such interference during the execution of activity should cause alarm* . . . the efficient use of radioelectronic interference reduces air defense effectiveness—for the time being by almost 40 per cent—which is not without significance while conducting combat activities on an operational-strategic scale.

Colonel (Professor) Witold Pokruszynski, "There Is No Room for Surprise," *Zolnierz Wolnosci* (Soldier of Freedom), April 14, 1987, p. 3. See also Phillip A. Petersen and Major John R. Clark, "Soviet Air and Antiair Operations," *Air University Review*, March–April 1985, pp. 36–54.

7

Ending War in Europe: Conclusions and Uncertainties

The purpose of this chapter is to offer some conclusions about the problem of war termination in Europe. Readers who have come this far have recognized that getting policymakers to take seriously the problem of war termination, given the assumed low probability of war in Europe, is sufficiently imposing. There is also the theoretical difficulty of isolating the more significant conceptual issues and variables from the lesser ones.[1] Further, strategies for the deterrence of nuclear war and for the fighting of a conventional war under the shadow of nuclear weapons are commingled. The Soviet view of deterrence, escalation, and war termination, so different from the Western one, poses additional difficulties. Yet perseverance with the question, however difficult, is dictated by its importance. If the most important problem is preventing the outbreak of war in Europe, the second most important is limiting it and ending it should it occur.

The probability that any of these wars, once begun, could be terminated in a rational way is unknown. As Gregory Treverton has noted, a "classic" literature on this subject appeared during the 1960s and suggests some general propositions that might apply to war termination in Europe:

1. Termination planning must be in place before war begins.
2. Communication with the opponent must be continued during the fighting (although communication need not be direct).
3. Thresholds, pauses, and prominent features can be exploited in order to increase the probability of successful termination.
4. Some (perhaps substantial) forces should be held as intra-war deterrents and not used immediately.

5. The fog of war makes agreements difficult to verify; thus cooperative measures, including unilateral gestures, might be necessary while fighting continues.[2]

The same requirements presumably might apply to a U.S.–Soviet direct nuclear exchange, whether it grew out of regional war or not. These requirements are process oriented. They impose obligations on U.S. and Soviet, or NATO and Pact, decision-making processes that may be as important as force-structure requirements or nuclear war-fighting strategies. Simply put, deliberate war termination requires that U.S. and Soviet adversaries, and their alliance partners, be able to make the most difficult kinds of decisions under unprecedented stresses. Further, national or bloc leaders must be able to enforce these decisions down the chain of command to far-flung military forces with fractured communications and uncertain organizational cohesion. Even if we assume that once war begins the bloc partners will follow at the behest of their Soviet and U.S. leaders, which is a large assumption, important obstacles remain to prevent war termination under conditions acceptable to both sides.

If nuclear war termination under conditions that are mutually acceptable to both superpowers is unattainable, three basic alternatives remain. Either the Soviet Union attains its objectives and the United States or NATO no longer resists, or the reverse outcome applies, with Soviet leaders yielding to the objectives of the Americans and the West. A third alternative is that both sides lose so much, by virtue of damage to their societies, that neither attains any meaningful political objectives. Once nuclear detonations on U.S. or Soviet homelands exceed several tens of weapons, the likelihood of this third outcome is very strong. This makes the case for avoiding nuclear war as imperative as any political imperative can be.

Nevertheless, NATO declaratory policy and U.S. vital interests make it apparent that there are conditions under which the United States would be willing to engage in nuclear war against the Soviet Union. And it is not determined how such a conflict would turn out. It could *conceivably* be terminated well short of a mutually destructive exhaustion of superpower nuclear arsenals. The fact that outcomes short of holocaust are conceivable does not make them probable. Nor should conceivable outcomes be treated as equally desirable in policy planning. The apparent opposite is also true: that intermediate outcomes are difficult to conceive of does not make them inconceivable.

Despite the foregoing observations, there are reasons why a conventional war in Europe might be limited below the nuclear threshold. And there are other reasons why a limited nuclear war in Europe would not necessarily expand into a general nuclear war. These reasons are worth reviewing.

First, the use of military forces has something to do with the policy objectives for which they are fighting. Surely this will be recalled in Moscow, where there are many devotees of Clausewitz. Given the potential destructive power of U.S. and Soviet strategic nuclear arsenals, there is no point (if there ever was) to "unconditional surrender" or other absolutist statements of policy objectives. In a nuclear war, unconditional surrender is a formula for mutual suicide, of nations and of their inhabitants. Policy objectives must therefore be formulated with a sharper end, and these should be thought through before any war begins.

For example, if Soviet forces cross the inter-German border and proceed to move against Frankfurt, what is NATO's political objective, from which its military objective is presumably derived? Is it to annihilate the Soviet forces in West Germany where they were, or to push them back across the border? And in either case, what is the political objective that corresponds to this military objective? The temptation among U.S. officials might be to punish the Warsaw Pact in some ways for having committed "aggression" against the defenders; U.S. history is replete with such morality-of-revenge tales. However, revenge is a poor policy objective, even near to the next election. In this instance it risks escalation that cannot be controlled by NATO to its advantage. So NATO will somehow have to make clear that its political objectives are limited, and perhaps commensurate with Soviet ones, whereas its *staying power* and *military potential* are superior to theirs.

The last statement implies that NATO must not lose its identity as a defensive *political* alliance, even in wartime when it might have to undertake operational and tactical *military* offensives. The same applies to the United States in a two-way confrontation with the Soviet Union—for example, in Cuba in 1962. President Kennedy chose the blockade or "quarantine" because it was a military operation that suggested specific political objectives, tied to the possibility of intimidating escalation if Khrushchev did not comply. What the United States wanted was the removal of the Soviet missiles from Cuba. There was no demand for Castro to resign or to be deposed. Nor was there an effort by the Americans to impose "horizontal escalation" on the Kremlin by attacking at some other point on the compass where Soviet vital interests might be threatened. The Kennedy administration kept the political issue to the specific point: withdrawal of the missiles from Cuba.

Kennedy's advisors (the ExComm, or Executive Committee of the National Security Council) also avoided being sucked into a closure of de-escalatory alternatives in face of escalatory ones. This almost happened as a result of the two very different messages received by Kennedy from the Soviet Union on October 26 and 27, and following several incidents on October 27 that seemed to point toward deterrence failure in the near term.[3] One of these incidents was an off-course American U-2 spy plane that strayed into Soviet territory, and the other was the shooting down of a similar reconnaissance aircraft over Cuba.[4] The second incident was especially ominous because it was clear to U.S. intelligence that the plane had been shot down by Soviet surface-to-air missiles (SAMs) that were now operational. And some U.S. authorities suspected that the Cubans had control over SAM launches. Had the United States stuck to its original plan, formulated the preceding Tuesday, it would have responded to the downing of the U-2 by taking out the offending SAM site with conventional air strikes, risking the killing of Soviet personnel. However, President Kennedy demurred at the brink—preferring to resist the temptation to even the score, so to speak, at the tactical or operational level—in order to preserve the hope of attaining U.S. strategic objectives, which were to remove the Soviet missiles from Cuba without war.

The blockade was an exercise in coercive diplomacy of the kind that we have been discussing throughout. But the "success" of the crisis for the United States was in many ways a near miss. Some of Kennedy's intimate advisors were disappointed that the U-2 downing over Cuba did not provide the pretext for an air strike or even an invasion; an opportunity to get rid of Castro and to demonstrate U.S. resolve to the Soviets had been missed, in their view.[5] On the other hand, President Kennedy was apparently more impressed with Khrushchev's determination, or recklessness, than were his advisors. Or Kennedy might have felt more vulnerable to the same fates that drove the major powers over the bring in World War I. Here the issue was not preemptive mobilization followed by a conflict spiral, as in World War I, but preventive conventional war that might escalate into nuclear war.[6]

Kennedy resisted a temptation to which others had fallen victim. The opportunity for an operationally advantageous campaign is so attractive that the costs of continued fighting, if the campaign fails to end the war, are not fully considered. This mistaken inference, or omitted reasoning, was characteristic of German and Japanese planning in World War II. Hitler could not resist the opportunity to attack the Soviet Union in 1941, although his strategic objectives would have been better served by continuing the nonaggression pact and fighting on one front, against England. And after Japan attacked Pearl Harbor on December 7, 1941, Hitler gratuitously declared war on America. Admittedly this would have come anyway, but Hitler accelerated the date on which England acquired a guarantee against eventual defeat, since there was not the faintest hope that Germany could defeat the United States in an extended war. The Japanese attack against Pearl Harbor, as is well known, was a brilliant tactical and operational coup; its military planning was impeccable. However, the Japanese refused to confront the full implications of a protracted war against the United States. Their military objectives simply absorbed their political ones. Roberta Wohlstetter's classic study of Pearl Harbor, on the topic of Japanese long-range military estimation, makes the following observation:

The Japanese did have the material for making some relevant long-range predictions. The intelligence estimates released by USSBS (United States Strategic Bombing Survey), for example, show that their assessment of our war potential in aircraft manufacture, shipbuilding, and rate of training of the necessary crews was much more accurate than our own for 1941, 1942, and 1943. The relation between this material and the decision to take on the United States as an opponent is simply not explicable in rational terms.[7]

If Soviet leaders have studied the history of World War II as carefully as one would think, they have drawn several lessons from the experience of their German and Japanese adversaries. First, under the right conditions, lightning campaigns like that in Manchuria in 1945 can pay large dividends. Second, one should not get entangled in an extended war against a foe superior in economic and military potential. Third, the command and control of military operations must be adapted to the unique circumstances of the theater of war, the capabilities and objectives of the opponent, and one's own objectives and capabilities.

In the case of the Manchurian campaign, the Soviet Union can be said to have applied all these lessons correctly. The Japanese Kwantung army was overwhelmed by a three-front combined arms offensive along a 5,000-kilometer frontline in six days.[8] Although the Japanese forces had serious technological weakness and numerical inferiority, Soviet analyses of this campaign have attributed their victory to the surprise, speed, depth, and strength of their offensive. And Soviet studies of the Manchurian campaign have also noted that they were concerned about being trapped into a protracted war, and devised solutions specifically to avoid this potential problem.[9] Although the basic concept of operations proved to be sound, this did not eliminate difficulties in the execution, including deficient tactical intelligence, lack of basic supplies, and a fragile troop-control network.[10]

The third lesson—that command and control of operations had to be adapted to local circumstances—was evident in the Soviet command organization for the Manchurian campaign. Forces in the Far East and Trans-Baikal regions were grouped into a unified command under Marshal

A. M. Vasilevsky. The shuttle arrangements used earlier in the war, in which coordinators from Moscow would be sent to control multifront operations on behalf of Headquarters, Supreme High Command (STAVKA), was discarded. The geographical size and diversity of the theater of war dictated the creation of a new Far East Command with overall responsibility for land, sea, and air operations in the Far East and Trans-Baikal regions.[11] This unprecedented arrangement was not without its apparent frictions, but in the event Soviet military historians have judged that it was appropriate to the commanders' and policymakers' requirements.

The Manchurian campaign provided a textbook case of the effectiveness of strategic surprise against a less well-equipped foe. Soviet Marshals would be loath to assume that this illustration could be transposed into a strategic (or theater-strategic, in Soviet terminology) offensive against Western Europe. The Kwantung army in Manchuria was doomed in the long run. The Soviet Union had concluded its war against Germany in the west. It was a matter of time until the superior Soviet war potential crushed the nearly defeated Japanese, who were also being battered by the United States and its European allies. However, although not transferable to the European template of today in literal terms, the Manchurian campaign suggests to Soviet planners the limitations of any proposed initiative in Europe. It suggests to them that such an offensive with the objective of conquering West Germany and/or the Low Countries is not in the cards, unless some very favorable conditions come together unexpectedly:

1. The societies of Western Europe begin to come apart as a result of their own domestic instabilities and contradictions.
2. Elements within those societies appeal to the Soviet Union for "fraternal" socialist assistance to parties or forces obviously prepared to seize power, and seemingly with credible means to do so.
3. The United States, for reasons of being deterred or for other causes, is likely to stay out of the war beyond absorbing the casualties to those of its divisions already stationed in West Germany.
4. If no. 3 is unlikely, the U.S. intervention is limited to conventional war waging and does not cross the nuclear threshold; and the rest of NATO Europe so forbears, including France.

The coming together of these contingencies is highly improbable if not impossible. But many wars have started from seemingly improbable or impossible causes. What we have been saying is that for the Manchurian campaign to provide a model for what the Soviets might want to accomplish in present-day Europe, the appropriate operational methods (operational art, in Soviet terms) must be mated to the appropriate policy objectives. The appropriate objectives, for the Soviet Union with regard to Europe, would have to include the Sovietization of the parliamentary-democratic regimes located there. Skirmishing with NATO ground and tactical air forces, however invigorating an exercise, is not an end in itself.

The last sentence is stated somewhat facetiously, out of exasperation. For years U.S. and allied NATO war games, as well as academic and think-tank analyses, have been concocting detailed scenarios for war in Europe. These scenarios rarely take into account the reasons why the war is supposedly being fought in the first place, or the architectonic Marxist character of Soviet foreign-policy objectives. The Soviets of today are not (merely) interested in winning battles over pieces of territory; they are not modern-day replacements for Frederick the Great. Soviet foreign-policy objectives, and therefore Soviet politico-military strategy, reflect partially and imperfectly the influence of Marxist historicism and Leninist adaptation to it. As we have seen, this filtration process separates those who think of war as an end in itself, as something self-sufficiently glorious and nationally enriching, from those who understand that war has specific, and limited, utility.

For Soviet Marxists, this utility is that war is part of the midwifery of revolution. Societies ripe for revolution owing to basically indigenous failures can be given a helpful push at a timely moment. And Lenin's deviation from Marx even allowed that this timely push could come about in a society not *theoretically* prepared for it. "Theoretically" here has two applications, one objective and one subjective. Viewed objectively, pre-capitalist societies should be premature laboratories for a proletarian revolution, regardless of the state of political consciousness of their peoples. Viewed subjectively, the peoples themselves may not be prepared with proper revolutionary ardor and education. More than once Marx and Lenin admitted that revolutionary intellectuals would have to lead the proletariat, even when the objective social conditions were permissive, into the promised land.

Now for Marxist Soviet members of the Politburo to contemplate these objective and subjective requirements for extending the proletarian revolution to Western Europe, they must conclude that the proper conditions are far from having been fulfilled. Western Europe is not ripe for revolution, at least not by revolutionary working-class movements. A feeling of déclassé alienation is widespread among the well-educated middle class, but this phenomenon is not restricted to Western Europe, nor to Europe. Nor does it present the Soviet Union with material that can be exploited to turn the societies of Western Europe into socialized paradises. To the contrary, the Soviet Union must see that the trends are going against any hopes that they may have of a nineteenth-century–style working class uprising.

To be sure, the Soviet Union can exploit divisions within Western democratic polities, but these divisions are not necessarily signs of weakness that would be contributory to a Soviet victory in war. There is a great deal of difference between the cohesion of democracies during peacetime and wartime, assuming something as momentous as a war in Europe would be. In peacetime, parliamentary-democratic regimes are divided houses and disputation rules the day. In wartime, they are apt to become mobilized monsters, unforgiving and ultrademanding of punishment against any presumed aggressor. One can imagine that the Dutch and the Belgians might demur in a crisis of very ambiguous origin, and there is some risk that an ambiguous crisis could spill over into war in Europe. But if the crisis truly arose from misunderstanding and not from an attempted conquest of NATO European territory, the Soviet Union would have as many incentives to terminate the fighting as would NATO. On the other hand, the Soviet Union could not turn a presumed crisis growing out of misperception or inadvertence into a full-scale war without making its intentions clear very soon. At the point at which it became clear that a full-scale war was on, the Dutch, Belgians, and everybody else in NATO would be getting on board, for they would have no other realistic option.

Soviet planners, then, would have to assume that the conditions are not ripe for the plucking of Western Europe, meaning that the class struggle is not in the proper phase and the peoples are not properly indoctrinated with the secular religion of Marxist deliverance. If war broke out, the Soviet Union could expect resistance instead of willing subjection. Given these unfavorable portents in West European domestic politics, Soviet leaders would have to expect that any conflict not terminated quickly would become a protracted conventional war, to their ultimate disadvantage, or escalate into a nuclear war, even more disadvantageous. So there is some strong incentive on the Soviet side to get the fighting stopped in the short term, whatever the putative causes that started it. As we have just been saying, there is one exception to this, and that is the unlikely circumstance that the class struggle in Europe is so advanced (from the Soviet standpoint) that the policy objective of conquering and occupying one or more West European countries is now appealing. Actually, the class struggle in Marxist terms is more advanced in Eastern than in Western Europe, if Polish Solidarity is any indication. One has to wonder how the Kremlin would deal with the occupation of Western Europe on a permanent basis without also subduing the United States, where the class struggle is hopelessly retrograde.

Another incentive for the Soviet Union to terminate any war in Europe shortly after it begins, and prior to nuclear escalation, also relates to the class struggle—in this case the international class struggle, of which the Kremlin claims undisputed leadership. However, the disputant in Beijing also lays claim to the same papacy, and would undoubtedly see a war between the Warsaw Pact and NATO as an opportunity from which to benefit even by inaction. The first problem for the Soviets here is that they would be taxed into fighting a two-front war if the Chinese decided to intervene. But even if Beijing stayed out, it would benefit at Soviet expense. Of course, the Soviet Union might win a conventional war in Europe, provided the United States did not intervene. But regardless, Moscow would still have the problem of facing the Americans eventually. And the Americans, seeing Europe imperiled, would now open their war chests and embark on a sustained military buildup of the kind that Moscow could never hope to match. The Soviet Union would be hard pressed to run a protracted war-machine building contest with the United States after the latter had opened the spigot of war production. Such a postwar (in Europe) production race would at long last demonstrate the superior economic competency of capitalism. Meanwhile, the Soviet Union would have fewer resources to devote to containment of its potential Chinese adversaries. A war in Europe, if stalemated or lost, could turn the Soviet Union into the world's second most important Marxist power. For some Soviet leaders past and present, and certainly for Brezhnev, playing second fiddle to Beijing would be the worst outcome of all.

So, contrary to the supposition of pessimists, there is in the Soviet lexicon some hopeful indication that, should war in Europe get started, it might be important to terminate it quickly. Granted, a Soviet attack is unlikely in the first place, but we assume here nonetheless that this event, however improbable, has begun. And we further assume that the Soviets' interest in deliberate and purposeful war termination thereafter is not precluded by their ideology or prewar plans (admittedly, this assumption is open to challenge). This means that if NATO too sought to bring about a purposeful end to the fighting, there might be a meeting of the minds at some salient threshold, either before nuclear weapons were used or before very many were used against certain kinds of targets. A number of these salient points have been suggested by theorists. One dividing line is between no use of nuclear weapons and first use by either side. Another is between selective, constrained uses of battlefield nuclear weapons once authority for their use has been delegated, and continuous and sustained employment with the objective of destroying the opponent's capacity for theater nuclear war.[12] Still another is the line between attacks on Soviet and U.S. homelands with nuclear weapons, and regional uses of nuclear weapons by the superpowers outside Europe but with potential spillover to Europe.[13] Albert Wohlstetter and Richard Brody suggest an interesting variation on the theater versus strategic threshold, illustrating the complexity of observing distinctions under fire. The Soviet Union might strike at a restricted number of military bases in the United States during a conventional war in Europe, in order to prevent U.S. reinforcements from crossing the Atlantic.[14] This would be limited war on the U.S. strategic homeland, perhaps comparable to the scenarios in which the United States fires "limited" strategic strikes against Soviet oil refineries or conventional forces north of Iran.

However, to say that policy objectives of the Soviet Union and NATO during conventional or theater nuclear war in Europe would be *permissive* of war termination is not to prove that the mechanisms for doing it would be in place when and where needed. The "mechanisms" have to do with the doctrines, organizations, and equipments of the two sides' forces as they pitch forward into battle. The fog of war would be immense, even in the first few hours of contact between Pact and NATO forces in West Germany. Intelligence systems would be dumping large amounts of data onto fusion centers that might not be able to collate the material, even if they survived deliberate attacks. Both sides might be tempted to attack space-based as well as ground-based photographic and electronic reconnaissance assets, including satellite-based ones. Lacking a clear picture of the battlefield, corps commanders might have to proceed by "dead reckoning," according to rehearsed standard operating procedures that had now become irrelevant.

This last point, about the vulnerability of command systems to information overload or direct attack, is obviously going to be exploited by the Soviet Union, with consequences for efforts to terminate war. This brings us to the topic of Soviet operational art, and requires that we say something about the Soviet style of war and its implications for war termination in Europe.

The first implication we have already seen: that the vulnerability of NATO theater command systems will be a temptation to Soviet attackers. But where does exploitation of that NATO vulnerability fit into Soviet strategy, and what, if any, are the Soviet command and control vulnerabilities? The larger issue of Soviet operational art for war in Europe has been studied by Western experts, including C. N. Donnelly of the United Kingdom and John Hines and Phillip A. Petersen of the U.S. Department of Defense.[15] The Soviets have also written a great deal about their own military operations and theories of war, and much of this literature is now readily available in Western libraries.[16] Some notion of how the Soviet Union would attack Western Europe, in the event that this option somehow presented itself as attractive (but see above), can be gleaned from these and other sources.

In general, the Soviet approach to military operations in a continental theater of military operations such as Western Europe would emphasize the accomplishment of five basic missions or functions: penetration; exploitation and encirclement; disruption; deception; and pursuit. Penetration is the piercing of the front-line defenses that NATO has deployed forward in West Germany in eight corps sectors. Soviet advance detachments and combined arms armies in the first echelon would attempt to make penetrations in depth during the first day or days of fighting. However, this penetration is temporary unless it is exploited, and the exploitation is to be accomplished by Operational Maneuver Groups (OMGs) when the moment is ripe. OMGs are tank heavy, specially tasked units at army or front level that exploit the most promising initial penetrations of the opponent's forward defenses. These and adjunct raiding forces will move rapidly into the opponent's operational depth in order to frustrate his effort to reinforce his forward defenses, maintain communications, and preserve organizational cohesion in his fighting units.[17] At the same time that these operational raiding forces are exploiting deep penetrations into the defender's rear, rapid encirclement of the defender's forces is taking place. This encirclement is really a three-dimensional envelopment of the defender's ground and tactical air forces, brought about by combined arms air and ground offensives. The "air" offensive includes the early use by the Soviet Union of ground-to-ground short-range ballistic missiles, designed to destroy NATO air defenses, runways, and other lucrative targets and thereby pave the way for follow-up destruction by Soviet Frontal Aviation against other NATO fixed and mobile targets. And, of course, among those targets will be NATO command systems, nuclear weapons storage sites, and nuclear-capable delivery vehicles.

Disruption of the opponent's command systems and organization cohesion we have already noted. Deception, or *maskirovka* (the Soviet generic term), adds another dimension, and involves both tactical and operational deception on small and large scales. The STAVKA plan Uranus by which the Soviets eventually prevailed at Stalingrad during World War II illustrates the successful use of operational-level deception.[18] Repetition of such a feat of concealment might be thought impossible under conditions of modern reconnaissance, but the Soviet interest in deception is considerable, and the U.S. capacity for observation not invulnerable to destruction. For approximately one year following the American *Challenger* space shuttle disaster, the United States had a single modern reconnaissance satellite (KH-11) in orbit.[19] The United States does not depend upon low-orbiting satellites for tactical warning of Soviet missile launches, but it does depend on close-look satellites like KH-11 (and its near-term successor, KH-12) for detailed evidence of Soviet noncompliance with arms control agreements and other authentication of intelligence information. As Paul B. Stares has recently shown, the U.S. ASAT that was undergoing testing during the Reagan administration, and the Soviet ASAT which was already operational, would each threaten significant numbers of the other's satellites that performed vital peacetime and wartime missions.[20] The U.S. Navy is particularly interested in negating the Soviet RORSAT and EORSAT (radar ocean reconnaissance and ELINT ocean reconnaissance) satellites early in a global or regional conventional war, in order to prevent prompt Soviet detection and destruction of carrier battle groups.

Moreover, the Soviet view of deception is not that it is an aggregate of measures in themselves. It is instead a way of thinking about the conduct of war itself. Active and passive deception is something that competent commanders and planners just "naturally" do. Now tactical deception, such as the deployment of individual dummy tanks or formulations, is something that Western planners are familiar with. But Soviet *maskirovka* includes an entire menu of approaches to anticipating the intelligence and decision-making cycles of the opponent. The latter is then allowed to believe that he has in fact discerned the applicable Soviet plans when he has not, or is thrown off balance by an attack along more than one axis of advance.[21] The illustrations of *maskirovka* are seemingly endless and the point is not to multiply illustrations, but to advance the notion that the Soviet conduct of war is embedded with the concept of deception in its active and passive forms.[22] Thus a Soviet attack on NATO might be preceded by a large military exercise that continued into a different, and more sinister, phase. The Soviet Union might, if it feared an outbreak of war for which its military leaders judged it unprepared, go through a demonstrative "mobilization" in Eastern Europe and the Western Soviet Union designed to intimidate U.S. and West European officials and their publics. In this regard, the Soviet civil defense program has been cited as providing them with an active defense asset that the United States, by comparison, lacks in comparable scope and effectiveness. Others have said the Soviet program would not actually provide very much protection in the event of nuclear war, but that it adds to the Soviet prewar deterrent. Few have noticed the possibility that the Soviet civil defense program may in addition have a deception component, not unlike the impressive bomber aircraft that overflew the reviewing stands in Moscow during parades in the 1950s (impressions of a larger than actual force were created by repeatedly overflying the stand with the same few planes). American have difficulty understanding the Soviet civil defense programs on account of the former's assumption that the purpose of civil defense is population protection. Instead, the primary purpose of the Soviet civil defense system may be to protect the political and military leadership from all but attacks specifically against them.

Pursuit, as a component of Soviet operational methods, is the following up of a defender when he is on the run. Defensive forces moving backward from their initial defense positions and attempting to regroup would be hard pressed to reconstitute a movable fire base, to reestablish survivable command and control, or to take the offensive against the flanks of advancing Soviet armored divisions. Assuming at least a standoff in the counter-air battle over Western Europe, these Soviet armored divisions would be provided with some substantial close air support and mobile artillery that would prove to be very destructive to forces undergoing regroupment. In this regard NATO has set itself up for additional difficulties by lacking the echelons-above-corps grasp of the fog of war that the Soviet Union will have, in all likelihood, as a result of its intermediate commands (TSMA, for theater of strategic military action, or formerly TVD) between Front and Supreme Headquarters.[23] Nor should it be forgotten that a critical component of the pursuit, deception, and disruption missions will be the probable use of Soviet *spetsnaz* (forces of special designation, including but not limited to "special operations" as used in U.S. nomenclature).[24] They will certainly conduct commando raids against NATO political and military targets, and perhaps even preemptive strikes if the Soviets decide that war is unavoidable. But they will also be a moving finger that can be used to pinpoint vulnerable civilian and military command centers, warning systems, and communications networks *à la carte*. As NATO corps sectors move to reestablish their command and control systems under the duress of Soviet operational maneuver by their conventional ground and air armies, special designation forces will be eating away from within at the NATO command and communications infrastructure.

What all of this amounts to is summarized very concisely by the U.S.

Army Combined Arms Center, Soviet Army Studies Office, at Fort Leavenworth, Kansas, in its paper *The Soviet Conduct of War*:

Forces within the theater of war (TV) will seek to achieve rapid victory by conducting successive *front* operations without pause in the theater's TVDs (TSMAs). A first strategic echelon will consist of combat-ready forces (fronts) within the TVD (TSMA) (primarily forward) backed up by a second strategic echelon and a strategic reserve comprising *fronts* (and in some cases individual armies) mobilized within the Soviet Union on the basis of the strength and status of each military district. Stronger peacetime military districts will provide second strategic echelon forces and weaker districts will provide reserves. The strategic offensive will probably rely for success on the use of first strategic echelon forces to preserve strategic surprise by avoiding more than essential pre-hostility mobilization and reinforcement.[25]

This says a great deal about the likely Soviet style of war. One of the things it says is that turning this kind of offensive off, after having turned it on in the confined spaces of Western Europe, will be no small challenge for NATO. However, we have presented the Soviet operational design from the standpoint of their most optimistic expectations. What about their own vulnerabilities, especially their ability to command and control an operation of unprecedented ferocity, complexity, and potential destructiveness?

Soviet planners contemplating a conventional war in Europe would not be as sanguine as Western analysts who attribute to the Soviet Union the capability for rapid and decisive victory against NATO. This is more than professional pessimism. Apart from the Soviet policymakers' skepticism that the class struggle in Europe has taken a turn in their favor, there is the military professionals' awareness of shortcomings in the training and competency of Soviet ground forces. These shortcomings exist primarily in the ranks of enlisted personnel rather than officers, who can be expected to have undergone at least a rigorous professional education, if not the Soviets' best academic one. However, Soviet conscripts who must bear the brunt of the fighting are not of the same quality as their officers, and no one can be more aware of this deficiency than those very officers, especially the Soviet division and brigade commanders, who will have to succeed or fail on the basis of these soldiers' performances. It would be a mistake to describe either Soviet officers or rank and file as automatons, but it does concern Soviet planners that many of their rank and file do not feel that their officers are competent or that they care about the welfare of their men as opposed to their own career advancement.[26] In the ground forces of any modern army, this expectation by the "grunts" that their officers are "careerist" to the extent that they are negligent about the troops' welfare is the kiss of death for combat effectiveness. In Vietnam, U.S. army officers learned this only too well. If research shows that cohesion is the *sine qua non* for the effectiveness of armed forces in combat, and especially for the successful performance of their missions by small units, then the Soviet commanders who must motivate their troops under fire certainly have a long way to go before they are satisfied. Nor can Kremlin planners have forgotten those who departed from the front in World War I and became a reserve army of the revolutionary unemployed, eventually the coercive arm of a rising that ousted the czar. Would Soviet soldiers take the opportunity of their arrival in Western Europe to defect? Probably not, if the war were short and favorable to Moscow. But in an extended war the temptation of defection might be harder to resist, especially if maltreatment in the peacetime Soviet armed forces were as widespread as some defectors have suggested that it has been in the recent past.

A more serious issue for Soviet war planners than that of dissatisfied "grunts" and defectors is the question of whether the Soviet propensity for "top down" command systems is compatible with the kinds of fluid meeting engagements and encounter battles their armed forces may have to fight in Europe. The short answer is no and the potential incompatibility is recognized in Soviet writings and exercises.[27] A centralized command system is not necessarily inferior to one that is decentralized and relies on a great deal of tactical initiative. Much depends on the national culture and training of the soldiers in question. Thus *Wehrmacht* officers in World War II were able to draw upon a tradition of excellence and training going as far back as the origins of the German General Staff. The expectation of fighting according to *auftragstaktik*, or order that assign a general mission while allowing a great deal of flexibility and initiative in the way in which it is accomplished, was thus part of the German military psyche.[28] The Israelis have apparently got infected with this virus as well. A virus is a good analogy, because the indeterminacy of such a system plays havoc with the desire of topmost political and military leaders to manage the details of operations, on which larger outcomes sometimes depend. So, for example, in the Cuban missile crisis, former secretary of defense Robert McNamara visited the U.S. Navy command center in the Pentagon and wanted to know about the detailed procedures for intercepting Soviet ships if they ran the blockade. An argument ensued between McNamara and Admiral Anderson, chief of naval operations, with the latter quite properly reflecting military service skepticism about the interference of civilians in the details of operational planning.[29] In this instance McNamara was asserting the important point that the president sought to control the situation, even if this meant tolerating some extraordinary operational procedures. However, top-level micro-management can lead to military disaster. During the ill-fated "Desert One" rescue mission in Iran in 1980, the command system was so top-heavy that it encumbered the proper formulation and execution of the operation. After events went awry, the unfortunate commander on the scene was forced to decide whether to continue the operation or abort it, while higher military and civilian commanders (including the president) copped a plea.[30] The U.S. war effort in Vietnam was similarly blessed with a cornucopia of irrelevant command levels, in Washington and in Saigon; and experts have testified to the operational malfeasance that resulted from this self-sustaining bureaucratic excess.[31] Military bureaucracies, given their druthers, are as bureautropic as any other large formal organization. However, the armed forces have a different mission, which depends on limiting the bureau-tropic syndrome to manageable proportions. In this regard the Soviets seem to be well on the way to imitating their Western counterparts, if not exceeding them, and show an all too dangerous tendency to compensate for bureaucratic inefficiency with numbers, mass, and artificial exercises.

The related issue, suggested by the topic of administrative overdrive, is accountability. Now this might seem on the surface to be a Soviet strong point and a Western, especially American, weak one. Witness the U.S. investigation of the bombing of the Marine barracks in Beirut in October 1983, for which no high-ranking military officer was seriously disciplined or demoted. President Reagan took the blame for this unfortunate episode, which was appropriate in the larger political sense for his having decided to commit U.S. combat forces to the ambiguous "peacekeeping" mission there. It was also appropriate in a second sense, in that his minions in the White House and Pentagon enshackled U.S. Marine forces in rules of engagement that made them vulnerable to terrorism and surprise. That said, the U.S. military chain of command was a Frankenstein of incompetence for what ought to have been a small-time operation (after all, these are the armed forces which are supposed to be ready to face the Soviet union if need be).[32] In the case in Lebanon and elsewhere, it certainly appears that the phrase "*chain* of command" is apropos, extending all the way up to the level of the Joint Chiefs of Staff. There is the additional tidbit that at one time then defense secretary Caspar Weinberger had some 40 persons reporting to him directly, which is quite a span of control even for a cabinet officer of Weinberger's budgetary reach and responsibility. One might argue that this is a strictly managerial issue not pertinent to operations as such. However, the U.S. experience in Lebanon and elsewhere argues against the separation of management-control methodology from operational results. Earlier I compared the U.S. chain of irresponsibility for the situation in Lebanon with the Soviet response to the penetration of their air space in 1987 by an intrepid West German youth who landed in Red Square. Mikhail Gorbachev did not offer to take the blame for this incident; instead, he sacked leading members of the armed forces high command, including the defense minister himself.

The U.S., Soviet, and German (World War II and earlier) examples suggest, then, that there is no one right or wrong way to organize a command system, for war in Europe or anywhere else. And so, there is no one right or wrong way to prepare that system for the conduct of war termination, either. There are two problems here: one is negotiating war termination at some senior level; the other is enforcing it through *both* national chains of command. One commonality that does seem to cross cultures is that both sides must still have some capacity to fight (else why negotiate?) and some means of communicating a preference to stop fighting now, as opposed to later. Neither the Soviet command system with its apparent rigidity nor the U.S. with its pluralist confusion appears to have maximized the opportunity for wartime interaction directed toward war termination. Instead, each might be taxed to maintain effective "troop control," as the Soviets call it, without being able to task commanders with any more subtle or ambitious objectives until the fighting has almost stalemated around some clear demarcation line. So if Soviet forces invading Germany were to be bottled up at the Weser and fighting were to stabilize there, the Soviet Union might be responsive to tacit and explicit overtures for war termination instead of preferring nuclear escalation. This would seem even more appealing to them if NATO had not yet struck into Soviet territory but maintained residual capabilities to do so. As discussed in Chapter 4, this makes the coordination of naval and land warfare a difficult matter. Nuclear weapons could be introduced into one of those environments before it seemed sensible to do so in the other, and in so doing one side might throw cold water on a process of conflict termination that was just getting under way.

NUCLEAR ESCALATION AND CONTROL

Suppose now that the line between conventional and nuclear war has been crossed, either in regional theaters of action adjacent to the Soviet Union or on Soviet and U.S. soil directly, or both. U.S. officials and nuclear pundits have sometimes suggested with wry humor that Europeans would prefer to see the United States and the Soviet Union fight a nuclear war "over their heads" while they were exempted from collateral damage. This scenario is unlikely, but it does reflect the possibility of war beginning as a direct superpower nuclear conflict and then spilling backward into

Europe. This has in fact been one of Western Europe's major fears for many years—the fear of being dragged inadvertently into a U.S.–Soviet crisis and ensuing war. The opposite fear—of being abandoned in time of need—plagues other Europeans, although this fear has more to do with their expectations about U.S. help during conventional war in Europe. In the first instance—fear of involvement in nuclear war—West Europeans fear too much immersion in U.S.–Soviet disputes that are essentially bilateral. In the second instance, they fear too little immersion of America in their defense planning and deterrence signals.

Are there salient thresholds at which nuclear war between superpowers, even war that has escalated to U.S. and Soviet homelands, can be stopped, even temporarily? Let us take the harder case of nuclear strikes against U.S. or Soviet homelands, since we have discussed previously the problem of limiting war in Europe. And let us set a hypothetical experiment, in which the Soviet Union has carried out a canonical attack against some portion of the U.S. strategic retaliatory force but mostly has spared U.S. cities, economic infrastructure, and war-supporting industry. The Soviets indicate that if the United States will avoid retaliation against the Soviet homeland, and not resist Soviet occupation of Europe with conventional forces, they will not make additional attacks against U.S. forces or society. This is what Herman Kahn would have called a "constrained force reduction salvo," in which one side attempts to destroy a small but significant portion of the opponent's retaliatory force in a single strike, as a basis for further bargaining on advantageous terms.[33] (Kahn's "ladder of escalation" has this one rung *above* "slow motion counterforce war," although he admits that the two thresholds might be reversed.)[34] This scenario has become part of the standard lexicon of surrogate warfare among policy analysts, as a result of Paul Nitze's application of it to the problem of U.S. deterrent, and especially ICBM, vulnerability.[35] U.S. rationales for limited strategic options in the 1970s called for counterforce weapons that would allow these tables to be turned on the Soviets, as in selective U.S. strategic strikes against Soviet military or economic assets in response to Soviet conventional war in Europe or Southwest Asia.[36]

The first thing to be said about this scenario is how improbable it is. The second is that, however improbable it is, it is more probable than an unrestrained exhaustion of U.S. and Soviet arsenals against each other's territories. Whether the United States could or would respond to a limited nuclear attack in a limited fashion is another matter. The requirements for doing so would be severe. The president would somehow have to know the size of the Soviet attack, the targets struck, the approximate collateral damage, and the forces and options remaining for retaliation. Most important, the president would have to have some sense of what the United States wanted to accomplish in the trans-attack period, and in the postwar world. There are two kinds of non-answers to these questions. The first is to deny that the line between limited war and total war is meaningful at all. The second is to assert that the effort to distinguish between limited and total wars implies tolerance for, even interest in, the costs of nuclear war, without sufficient concern for the ethical consequences. This discussion has nothing to commend it to either school, although their frame of reference is deserving of some understanding. The impulse to prevent nuclear war *along with defending equally important political and moral values* is not disputed. The moral high ground on this issue of war prevention and limitation, properly understood, is one that requires sensitivity to value *trade-offs* as well as value absolutes.[37]

We will assume for purposes of discussion that the point of the last sentence is at least provisionally accepted by readers. The president wants to respond in some fashion, and obviously it is not in U.S. interest to respond with everything remaining in the U.S. strategic nuclear arsenal. One can question, however, whether the United States would be able to deliver constrained counterforce attacks against a precisely defined Soviet target set, in the aftermath of even limited Soviet attacks on the U.S. homeland. One issue is whether the U.S. command system can so organize and reconstitute itself that it can deliver limited, but still significantly damaging, retaliatory strikes. Perhaps it cannot, but failure to take such a scenario seriously in the planning stage makes the command system incompetent by default. Another issue is whether it wants to accomplish such attacks immediately after the Soviets have struck, or wait for a clearer assessment of surviving U.S., and Soviet, assets. A third issue is whether the Soviets will be interested in observing thresholds below total war once the United States has retaliated against their homeland.

The first issue is whether U.S. strategic command, control, and communications (C^3) can pull its act together to deliver a constrained but effective retaliation against a plausible Soviet military target set. This set would probably emphasize, although not exclusively, Soviet prompt counterforce systems capable of further attacks against surviving U.S. forces. The United States would have to have a very reliable attack assessment of its own surviving forces, communicate this assessment to national command authorities, and ensure the reception of the proper launch orders by the retaliatory forces. These forces would then have to respond according to largely preprogrammed strike plans, for there would be little or no time to improvise.[38] None of these command system prerequisites for launching discriminate and controlled attacks can be guaranteed. Attack assessments might be muddled or inaccurate. National command authorities might not receive a timely assessment even if it were accurate, or if they did, it might be misinterpreted. And the reprogramming of forces after the survivors have been polled, in order to optimize strikes against surviving Soviet targets, would be done under conditions that would fall short of the standards implicit in peacetime models.[39] A growing problem is that more of the future Soviet force than the present one may be mobile and thus difficult to target.

A complication for the command system is that it must support the various components of the U.S. strategic nuclear "Triad" (ICBMs, SLBMs, and bombers equipped with various weapons) in their operational settings, which are not identical. ICBMs deployed in fixed silos must be launched "on warning" or "under attack" in order to perform their missions, or run the risk of being rendered impotent by early Soviet attacks against their silos and command centers. Bomber operations are extremely complicated from the standpoint of demands made upon the command system. Bombers must take off to holding positions from where they will receive further, confirmatory orders that authorize them to proceed to target. Only about 30 percent of the U.S. strategic bomber force is maintained on strip alert; the rest is at least theoretically at risk from Soviet SLBMs launched form normal submarine patrol areas off the U.S. Atlantic and Pacific coasts.[40] Missiles on board submarines are less vulnerable to preemptive attack, but submarine communications are doubtfully dependable for any tasking other than serving to attack preplanned fixed targets, most of which are in urban areas.[41] Thus the most survivable weapons platforms under condition of little or no warning are those with which NCA might have the most difficulty communicating in order to revise its previous plans. This does not raise too many complications as long as the ballistic missile submarines' mission is to survive the initial exchanges and initiate World War IV. But if policymakers expect more of them, as they might following the introduction of Trident II to the fleet in 1989, then the fidelity of SSBN communications under a greater diversity of combat conditions will become an important agenda item.

The second issue is whether the United States wants to retaliate promptly and, if it does, what it wants to accomplish. The canonical scenarios posit an immediate and large U.S. retaliation against a comprehensive Soviet military target set, including C^3 assets related to Soviet countermilitary potential. This is made quite clear in authoritative U.S. government policy documents, such as the report of the Scowcroft Commission during the first term of the Reagan administration. The commission recommended that the United States deploy MX/Peacekeeper ICBMs immediately and Midgetman small, mobile, and single warhead ICBMs in the 1990s. The rationale for the MX/Peacekeeper was that it would threaten the Soviets with the destruction of their missile silos and support-ing command and control, and so pose to them the same threat that Soviet capabilities now pose to U.S. ICBMs.[42] The implied theory of war termi-nation seems to be that squeezing the Soviet countermilitary potential, by rapidly evening up our losses with theirs, would quickly disabuse the Kremlin of any interest in continuing a war. In fairness, the Scowcroft Commission (officially the President's Commission on U.S. Strategic Forces) was tasked to focus mainly on deterrence and placed less emphasis on how a war might actually be fought.

This assessment can be disputed. It would be equally logical to argue that the Soviet Union will have used the most effective proportion of its land-based strategic missile force in its opening attack. What would remain in silos would be a large number of warheads of lesser lethality, although still a substantial force. A U.S. prompt retaliatory launch against remaining Soviet ICBMs might simply cause the Soviets to launch their remaining land-based missiles on tactical warning, causing more immediate damage to the United States and no additional net damage to Soviet missile silos. It is also suggested in some analyses that the Soviet military and political command centers, regional and national, would be targets for prompt counterforce. Such destruction could either kill party, government, and military leaders in their bunkers or disconnect those bunkers from the military forces and other command nodes with which they need to com-municate. In some models these countercommand attacks spare national command centers but destroy regional political and military ones. In other models the national command centers themselves are attacked.[43]

Such attacks, even if they could wreak havoc on Soviet postattack command and control, might not be advisable. U.S. war plans apparently provide for withholding of attacks against national command centers while striking at regional ones. If top Soviet officials felt that they faced near-certain personal destruction, they would have few incentives to withhold the most comprehensive retaliatory strikes possible. Presumably, U.S. plans provide that national command centers could be attacked only as last resorts, in order to influence the behavior of Soviet leaders instead of destroying them.[44] If the initial Soviet attack greatly degraded U.S. counterforce potential, the temptation to retaliate immediately against Soviet political and military command centers of all kinds would undoubt-edly occur. Retaliatory attacks against an opponent's command system might seem to provide a more economical way of striking back with comparatively fewer forces than a counterforce duel in which the second striker would be disadvantaged. This "economy of force" could be a policy disaster if it left the opponent with no motivation except that of a dying sting.

Even if U.S. policymakers determine that large retaliatory strikes against Soviet forces and command nodes are advisable, there is no overwhelming case for doing them as rapidly as possible. Soviet ICBMs will be launched on warning or under attack before U.S. ICBMs can destroy them in their silos. The command centers are not going to move, so there is no hurry about attacking them unless they are mobile. And if they are mobile, they are going to be hard to find and to hit. U.S. sources report that the Soviet Union has dug itself in around Moscow with hundreds of command bunkers, and that other survivable command posts for the political and military leadership have been dispersed throughout the country.[45] An attack against the Soviet "command system" is a much larger and more complicated enterprise than an attack against a target list of fixed command centers. The Soviet command system in the largest sense includes the organizations, technologies, and war plans that integrate the various parts into a composite whole. The Soviet "nuclear command system" is a complex and multifaceted entity which presents to U.S. planners a formidable set of targets. As the results of the U.S. Strategic Bombing Survey after World War II showed quite clearly, the destruction of targets is not the same thing as the immobilization of an organization or an entire national defense system. Both Great Britain and Germany in World War II overestimated the effects of strategic air bombardment on the morale of the opponent's civilian population.[46]

If the United States is going to aspire to a war of attrition against Soviet forces and the Soviet military command system, it would be preferable to spread the attrition out in time, in order to draw from the use of force a measure of coercive influence. Doing the destruction as rapidly as possible simply encourages lack of restraint. Slowing it down and allowing the opponent additional time to consider whether the continuing costs of war are worth the potential gains, if any, makes more sense if one wants to conduct a war subordinated to policy.[47] Slowing down the pace of strategic nuclear war, or any war, probably makes sense if one objective of campaign planning is to allow time and opportunity for war termination. Such a planning initiative would run against the grain of military common sense, which has always believed in "getting there fustest with the mostest." The other side of the argument, which should be acknowledged, is that a response that is too drawn out may leave you with nothing left to respond with, while the other side retains competent forces.

This suggestion that war plans might attempt to slow the pace of nuclear war also has implications for the kind of force structure that U.S. planners favor. Survivable weapons with high counterforce accuracies could be delivered by slow as well as prompt launchers. Air-, ground-, and sea-launched cruise missiles can be given accuracies that make their conventional, as well as nuclear, warheads lethal to military targets in the Soviet Union or its East European allies. Submarine-launched ballistic missiles, beginning with Trident II, will have accuracies comparable to the most lethal U.S. strategic land-based missiles. Future generations of cruise and ballistic missiles with conventional warheads could destroy over great distances targets that now require a nuclear warhead within several hundred meters to assure a high probability of kill.[48] The prospects for "strategic non-nuclear war" may be far off as long as both sides fear the use of nuclear strategic missiles on the heels of conventionally armed ones, and they will as long as both sides retain large inventories of the nuclear armed missiles. No conventional weapons could completely capture the "terror effect" of nuclear warheads for the purpose of intimidation or to establish national prestige. A superpower shift toward retaliatory forces that are mainly conventionally armed, with only token numbers of nuclear weapons, is an arms controller's hope more that it is a realistic near-term possibility.

But it is *not* unrealistic to suppose that the combination of improved accuracies, increasingly sophisticated communication and control systems, and at least partly effective non-nuclear defenses against strategic nuclear weapons can make some difference in future U.S. and Soviet war plans.[49] Albert Wohlstetter has noted that these trends, separately and in combination, raise the possibility that limited and controlled war fighting might become more realistic to contemplate, and so find its way into actual war plans.[50] One should not give the impression that this would be altogether new, and even advocates of assured destruction declaratory doctrines sought to include in operational plans the possibility of selective and limited nuclear strikes.[51] Until the "Schlesinger doctrine" of 1974 these "selective" options were still very large. And the Carter administration sought to refine the Schlesinger doctrine still further. The Nixon-Ford emphasis on the destruction of a certain proportion of the Soviet economy-for-recovery was deemed less important and less feasible than the ability to damage Soviet war-supporting industry. Soviet nuclear and conventional forces were subject to large strikes, but national command authorities and population centers under the Carter policy PD-59 were presumably spared from initial retaliatory strikes.[52] The Reagan administration nuclear war plans have apparently continued the trends begun under Nixon, Ford, and Carter, toward increasing the number of targeting options in the Single Integrated Operational Plan (SIOP) and providing to policy-makers options to attack or withhold from attack political, military, and economic target sets (or "building blocks").

Carter and Reagan war plans may have anticipated the possibility of slowing down the pace of nuclear war in another way. The Carter plans purportedly called for an increased emphasis upon capabilities to fight an extended or protracted nuclear war over many weeks or months. The Reagan administration national guidance for military force planning apparently took this notion one step further in attempting to turn the Carter emphasis into actual programs for force structure and command system improvement.[53] There is reason to be skeptical about how far this process of continuing control into the extended phases of a nuclear war can go. Brookings Institution analyst Bruce G. Blair has offered a summary of the reasons for skepticism about the capabilities of the U.S. nuclear command system to support a policy of extended nuclear war fighting.[54] The policy expectations imposed by a doctrine of extended nuclear war, according to Blair, exceed the capabilities of the current U.S. command system, and this situation is likely to continue into the foreseeable future. Moreover, the U.S. nuclear command system of the present may, under some conditions, not be able to fulfill the requirements of assured destruction. More ambitious objectives imposed upon the system could simply confuse it precisely when it was most needed. As Colin S. Gray has noted, with regard to the introduction of additional subtlety in U.S. strategic nuclear war plans:

If the Soviet Union should choose to counterescalate to, and within, central war in only a very measured way (which is far from certain)—responding to U.S. countermilitary attack options and, eventually, to selective countereconomic recovery options, in kind and with roughly the same weight of attack—the United States soon would find its employment options paralyzed through the functioning of self-deterrence.[55]

It may seem that the desire to introduce selectivity into nuclear options below the full SIOP response is an objective different in kind from the goal of fighting extended nuclear war. To the contrary, selective options are more related than not to the idea of extended nuclear war fighting. If the superpowers respond to any nuclear provocation by unleashing a full SIOP or its Soviet equivalent in the first hour of war, what will have happened is something other than a war—that is, something that occurs outside the province of conflict subordinated to policy. The inhumanity of such an undertaking will be as obvious as its absurdity. The idea of extended nuclear (and conventional) war implies that less than total or nearly total responses can be expected when conflict really begins. Otherwise, national command systems will be destroyed rapidly, and war turned into a mindless series of exchanges without political point.

Future U.S. and Soviet nuclear command modernization programs will attempt to compensate for this problem by proliferating and hardening command posts for national leaders and military force commanders; by improving the survivability and redundancy of communications; by providing active and passive defenses for parts of the retaliatory force or command system, if technologies prove to be feasible and affordable; and by elaborating theories of controlled conflict that draw upon important contributions of the past. We have already noted the future conjunction of increasingly accurate offenses, partial defenses, and enhanced control and communications technologies, relative to the possibility that conventional or nuclear wars even between superpowers might be limited. Of course an equally plausible, and to my mind more convincing, argument can be made that the political parameters of conflict will determine whether it is limited, not the available technology. One needs to ask what the war is about.

This last question leads to the third issue, which is the Soviet interest in, or capability for, limiting nuclear war. The question of Soviet doctrine has been touched on earlier, although some additional and summary comments are appropriate here. The first issue with regard to the Soviet Union and war limitation is whether there is any apparent interest in the basic concept of escalation control on their part. The second aspect of this third issue is whether, interest notwithstanding, there is any apparent Soviet capability for limited nuclear war. A third aspect is whether the reciprocal interaction between U.S. and Soviet command systems can be structured so that the capabilities for, and interest in, war termination can be exploited in a timely way.

The first question—of Soviet interest—has no definitive answer. The specific circumstances would determine much. One can quote Soviet writers on all sides of the issue, up to a point. This is the point at which nuclear weapons strike Soviet territory or at which the Soviet Union decides that such an attack is inevitable. At this point, war limitation is, not impossible, but extremely difficult by all accounts in Soviet doctrine. Any war that extends onto Soviet soil, even conventional war, is an implied threat to the survival of the regime and its domination of the peripheral Eurasian heartland. On the other hand, future technologies may make possible limitations if the Soviets wish to impose them. President Reagan raised European hackles when he told an interviewer that he could "conceive" of a nuclear war limited to relatively few weapons fired in Europe. However, U.S. strategists have been conceiving of the same thing for many years. And it is official NATO doctrine that the West, if it embarks on first use of nuclear weapons, will not fire them indiscriminately. They will be fired at very specific targets in packages tailored to the requirements of the situation. There are two reasons for this requirement of specific targets and packages for NATO nuclear first use, or any early use. The first is that larger uses will require a longer period to obtain political authorization. The second is that larger uses are less controllable, in that they are less distinguishable by the victim from attacks with specific and limited objectives.

Clearly, the Soviets have not precluded limited nuclear war in Europe, or elsewhere, if it is judged advantageous to them. The recently concluded U.S.–Soviet treaty on the destruction of intermediate nuclear forces will make each nuclear weapon deployed in Eastern or Western Europe that much more important. Thus these weapons may be used sparingly, if at all, and their restricted ranges (less than 500 kilometers for the remaining ground-based missiles) will encourage attacks that are more discriminating and appropriate to the evolution of developments near the Forward Line of Troops. Some have raised the issue whether these so-called battlefield nuclear weapons should not be withdrawn from Europe as well as their longer-range cousins. NATO would then depend on conventional forces deployed in Europe, plus the U.S., British, and French "strategic" nuclear deterrents.[56] Authoritative studies have contended that affordable changes in NATO doctrine and technology would allow it to provide a credible conventional defense without resort to early nuclear first use.[57] Former U.S. secretary of defense Robert S. McNamara has been an outspoken advocate of limiting NATO nuclear weapons to the role of retaliatory deterrents, in response to nuclear aggression only.[58]

A smaller number of nuclear weapons deployed in Europe could have various effects on the problem of escalation control, depending on the remaining balance of conventional and strategic nuclear forces in the two blocs. Scenarios in which the Soviet Union overwhelms NATO conventional forces with its conventional forces and then counts on its nuclear forces to deter NATO escalation attribute to Soviet leaders great willingness to run risks, in the face of a NATO declaratory strategy that promises early nuclear use. In the equations of model builders, NATO would not take those risks, because the use of its theater and strategic deterrents would only result in the destruction of European and U.S. cities. However, in the real world of high politics and high crisis-time temperatures on the part of national leaders, NATO may value credibility more than rationality, or revenge more than prudence. On the other hand, if a drastic imbalance in superpower strategic nuclear capabilities were to evolve in the Soviets' favor, the situation might be less stable. The Soviet Union could use its strategic deterrent as a "compellent" to support a process of escalation, much to the disadvantage of the West. In this situation, it would matter more whether the battlefield nuclear weapons on the two sides were of approximately equal capability, or unbalanced in favor of either side. They would be potential detonators of the larger deterrents that were themselves unstable as a result of imbalance. Of course, from the Soviet perspective the same instability would result from a strategic nuclear imbalance drastically favoring the United States and NATO. It is sometimes argued that the United States held this favorable position during the 1940s and 1950s and did not exploit it. Therefore the consequences would not be the same as they would for an imbalance favoring the Soviet Union. However, the argument transposes the U.S.–Soviet relations of the past and the future, with uncertain parallelism. The Soviet perspective is unlikely to be so accommodating of anachronism, in order to derive a benevolent model of U.S. intentions.

A second aspect of the Soviet motivation for war limitation was whether they would have the capabilities to limit a nuclear war even if their leaders were interested. Here the answer is more straightforward, for there is no question that the Soviet Union, if it chose to do so, could limit its own use of nuclear weapons in Europe. It could even impose some restraints on its own targeting requirements for other continental and oceanic TVDs, depending on the objectives of these strikes and the reactions of opponents.[59] However, it is problematic whether the Soviet leadership would be very interested in limiting any war that had escalated to selected strikes against Soviet homeland-based forces, economic resources, or cities. There is a substantial question whether the Soviet command and control system could, for example, distinguish reliably between a limited U.S. counter-silo attack and a larger anti-city or anti-recovery strike.[60] Nor is it obvious that the Soviets could, with partially destroyed strategic forces and command systems, conduct a selective and calibrated tit-for-tat exchange with the Americans while feeling confident that their relations with other possibly hostile powers, including China, were buttoned down. So the issue of Soviet capability or willingness to fight a "limited" nuclear war in Europe must be brought down to scale. Prior to large numbers of detonations of NATO nuclear weapons on Soviet territory or near it, Soviet auto-limitation of nuclear responses is at least conceivable. Once things have gone beyond that boundary, smart wagers would be against continued restraint on escalation.

It is more realistic to believe that the Soviet Union could limit a conventional war from going nuclear, and its declaratory policy against nuclear first use, which does not preclude preemption under some conditions, should be considered in this light. U.S. maritime strategy straddles this difficult juncture, involving strategic attacks other than those with nuclear weapons, meaning that conventional weapons are used to attack targets of strategic importance. These include Soviet SSBNs in their protected "bastions," ports, naval air bases, and other war-related targets, some of which will be located on Soviet soil. How would the Soviet Union react? The assumption made by the U.S. Navy in its declaratory strategy is that the Soviet Union will feel threatened, but that nuclear escalation is not a necessary response to that threat unless the Soviet Union is desperate for other reasons, too. Critics feel that this assumption, of Soviet acquiescence to U.S. conventional attacks that threaten the survival of their strategic assets,is overly optimistic. But it is no more optimistic than the belief that, even if the U.S. Navy stayed home from war in Europe, NATO ground and tactical air forces could defeat their opponents without resorting to nuclear escalation. The U.S. maritime strategy runs the risk of not being sufficiently credible if the Soviets win too quickly in Central Europe; that is not a deficiency on the part of naval strategy, but of NATO strategy more generally.

The U.S. Navy's assumption that the Soviet Union might observe a threshold of conventional theater-strategic, although non-nuclear, war remains controversial. So does another potential Soviet threshold, in which nuclear weapons are exploded in Eastern and Western Europe but not on the superpower homelands. Although a potential threshold, it is an indistinct one. Eastern Europe is much more a part of the Soviet conventional defense perimeter than Western Europe is for the United States; geographical propinquity as well as recent historical memory of Hitler's invasion make it so. NATO nuclear weapons launched into Eastern Europe may not provoke Soviet attacks on America, and if the NATO strikes are sufficiently irrelevant to the final war outcome, they may not be met by nuclear retaliation at all. NATO's dilemma here is acute: If small demonstrative packages of tactical nuclear weapons are used, they may not be taken seriously (although not all small attacks would necessarily be demonstrative). If more comprehensive attacks are made, they may be taken too seriously. There is some evidence in Soviet writing and exercises that their leaders might recognize a threshold between regional and global nuclear use. Apparently, Soviet representatives on at least one occasion approached their U.S. counterparts about the likely U.S. reaction to a preventive nuclear attack on China.[61]

A third aspect of the Soviet motivation for limited strategic war or limited nuclear war is the interaction between the superpowers' respective command systems during nuclear crises and wars. Fortunately we have had no nuclear wars from which to generalize, but nuclear crises have also provided little in the way of solid information about the interaction of U.S. and Soviet warning and intelligence systems. We have not a single instance of which Western analysts are aware in which both sides have mobilized their strategic nuclear forces or other nuclear forces simultaneously. The fear of President Kennedy and his advisors during the Cuban missile crisis was more the anticipation of Soviet conventional pressure on Berlin, although this might have led ultimately to nuclear confrontation in Europe. A more interesting illustration of the possible effects on the two sides' intelligence and response systems was the confrontation in the Middle East in 1973. In that crisis, the United States made at least oblique nuclear threats against the potential intervention of the Soviet Union with its conventional forces in the immediate theater of war.[62] However, the extent to which the United States was willing to use its nuclear, as opposed to general-purpose, forces in the Mediterranean if the Soviets had actually intervened is indistinct. The fear in Washington was of Soviet airborne landings in Egypt to rescue the beleaguered Egyptian Third Army from destruction by Israel. This scenario lacked plausibility as a self-sufficient rationale for an alert of U.S. strategic nuclear forces. Soviet airborne landings in Egypt would have confronted Israeli forces with superior firepower at the time and place of contact. The Soviet Union, to make this intervention meaningful, would have to follow it up with support from other forces, which would surely draw in additional U.S. forces. This episode does remind us, however, of the potential for modern-day "Balkan" crises to involve the superpowers. The danger would be that one of these crises would be compounded by another, simultaneous crisis at some other trouble spot where superpower allies called for assistance. Of course, in the case of the 1973 war, some U.S. accounts have papered over the dilatory U.S. diplomacy that allowed the regional conflict to expand into more direct Soviet–U.S. exchanges. The United States initially sought to restrain the Israelis, and some U.S. government officials felt that a stalemated military outcome would lead to a postwar political settlement. For this and other reasons, including overconfidence in Israel's military competence compared to that of the Arabs, U.S. officials delayed in responding to Israeli needs for replenishment of equipment losses. This ultimately dragged out the war and led to the denouement of Soviet remonstrances about unilateral intervention, and U.S. worldwide DefCon 3 alert. The United States would have been well advised to make clear its willingness to resupply Israel earlier and to do so in a more timely manner. There is the justification that a stalemated outcome restored Arab pride better than an Israeli victory would have, and that this contributed to a postwar peace settlement. Perhaps so, although if this were the design of U.S. policy, one could argue equally well that preventing war was better than allowing it to start and hoping for a military stalemate.

To a remarkable extent, the superpowers have kept their forces from direct confrontation, and they have avoided tweaking their respective command systems with provocative measures during crises. However, the danger always exists that, in a future crisis, the U.S. and Soviet warning and intelligence systems will reinforce "worst-case" interpretations of each other's behavior, and so contribute to war. In similar fashion, the interactions between superpower command systems would be critical to terminating a war if both sides desired to do so. The problem is that peacetime procedures must be instituted within military and political organizations in order to provide any hope that, in the midst of nuclear war, authorities will feel confident about limiting it and ending it. When we say "procedures" we speak not only of the rules and regulations that are written down, but also of the expectations that persons who work in organizations have. Do they really expect that nuclear war will ever come? If it does, what will they do if they think that they are losing but are ordered by superior authorities to stop firing? Will U.S. submarine commanders, who may have contingent authority to fire their weapons under certain very specific conditions, be told that a cease-fire has been implemented? Can Soviet ASW forces that are tracking them be interrupted in midstream?

The two problems embedded here are political and provincial control.[63] Political control has to do with the larger issues of grand strategy and high politics; provincial control refers to the efficient application of military forces in their strategic and tactical missions. In the U.S. case, the provincial control of the military has generally been left to military professionals, while grand strategy has been the domain of political leadership. Most Western countries follow a similar suit, although there is variation among them in the extent to which truly *independent* military voices are heard in the highest grand strategic councils. In the Soviet Union, the picture is somewhat different. The Western references to grand strategy and high politics, as distinct from military operations, imply a cleavage or separation that is not so neat in Soviet theory or practice. In Soviet military doctrine, as we have seen, what we are now calling provincial control is the domain of military professionals up to a point, beyond which there are no party-political controversies that remain unresolved. For example, during the 1950s Khrushchev attempted to shift the balance of Soviet military investment from conventional to nuclear forces, causing great turbulence within the Soviet military establishment. This establishment focused on the problem of provincial control that it would have in executing less than nuclear missions, and so became discontented with Khrushchev's emphasis on the decisiveness of nuclear weapons per se. The military's perceived problem of provincial control led to a problem of political control for Khrushchev and his allies in the Politburo, and ultimately contributed to their demise.[64] Of course, the Soviet Union has, since its inception, been concerned with the relationship of provincial and political control, and its military doctrine has emphasized the predominant role of the party in deciding which wars to fight and to what ends. Moreover, the pervasive system of internal controls reassures Soviet leaders, at least in peacetime, that no one will rise to the top of the military professional ladder who has not been purged of "Bonapartist" tendencies or is lacking in sufficient *partiinost'*.

But peacetime conditions and wartime conditions are very different. Even an intense crisis could bring about changes in the relationship between provincial and political control for both superpowers, with results that would make war termination more difficult. Once a serious crisis or war had begun, both sides' command systems and forces would be poised to retaliate, and the strict peacetime controls against accidental or unauthorized launch would be somewhat relaxed. Both systems would shift gradually from "negative" to "positive" control; protections against accidental or inadvertent war would be less important than avoiding the loss of key forces or command systems.[65] As the Soviet and U.S. command systems shift from "safety on" to "safety off" positions, expectations of those on the receiving end of nuclear strikes will change also. Warning indicators that might be interpreted in peacetime as innocuous will have a sinister meaning during crisis or after some weapons have actually been fired.

Expectations for the efficient management of force application (provincial control) will predominate at the sharp end of the military organizations in contact worldwide: armies, fleets, and air forces. These expectations will include assumption about rules of engagement that, if authorities understand their implications, they may want to revoke. Commanders will assume under crisis or wartime conditions that they have authority not to take what appear to be unseemly risks from a purely tactical standpoint. But policymakers may want to accept these risks in order to avoid escalation if war has started, or to prevent war as the time for crisis management runs short. As the run-in between the U.S. Navy and Secretary of Defense Robert McNamara during the Cuban missile crisis suggested, the provincial control of military operations (efficient blockade) can conflict with the political control required to prevent escalation (avoiding nuclear war). When both sides have alerted forces over which they are trying to reconcile political and provincial control, the problem is compounded. In addition, the implications of political and provincial control are different for nuclear and conventional forces.[66] NATO nuclear weapons deployed with alliance general-purpose forces will be in forward and potentially vulnerable positions. Battlefield or naval commanders may want contingent authorization to fire them before they are lost in the Soviet attack with conventional forces only. This presents NATO with an acute dilemma; lose on the battlefield in order to preserve political control at the expense of provincial control, or escalate and thereby risk the loss of political control in order to restore provincial control. Nor is this less of a problem for the Soviet Union, even during a crisis:

On alert, the Soviets' dispersal of nuclear weapons might proceed randomly, their electronic warfare might inadvertently jam their own military frequencies, civil defense evacuations might be spontaneous and uncontrolled, weapons depots might explode as munitions are outloaded, and go-code disseminations might begin accidentally as radio operators were overwhelmed and confused by events.[67]

UNEXPECTED ENDINGS

If there is any universal dictum to which military historians will subscribe, it is that no war or campaign unfolds exactly as prewar theories had expected it to. Paul Bracken has outlined the theory of war termination that is widely held among U.S. strategists with regard to superpower conflict or major coalition war involving Europe. First, political objectives would be important even in nuclear war. Second, despite cultural differences, Americans and Soviets would share a common-value calculus about the prudence of avoiding gratuitous destruction of cities, control centers, and so forth. Third, problems of time scarcity and planning rigidity would not preclude innovative approaches to war termination in the event.[68] This last assumption relates to the first, about maintaining control over events in accordance with the desires of political leadership. During nuclear crisis or war the top leadership of the opposing sides will insist upon directive control: "Even if a country had never considered the doctrines of controlled escalation, once it was faced with the realities of nuclear escalation, these doctrines would soon become obvious."[69]

That organizational learning and innovation can take place under the stress of war is apparent in the German adaptation to conditions of fighting on the defensive in their campaigns against the Soviet Union during World War II. The case is interesting because it is an illustration of learning, unlearning, and relearning. The Germans quit World War I having developed innovative approaches to elastic defense. During the inter-war years these assumptions about elastic defenses remained accepted German army doctrine. Yet the operational and tactical defensive was not emphasized in the planning by the German High Command for the Russian campaign, which began with their attempted *blitzkrieg* on three main axes in December 1941. By December the German offensives in Army Group Center had ground to a halt in front of Moscow, and the Russians began a series of counterattacks that battered the German positions for several months.

As Major Timothy A. Wray has noted, once the Soviet counteroffensives began during the winter of 1941–42, the German army "was largely unable to execute the defensive techniques prescribed by German doctrine."[70] Several conditions accounted for this, including the severity of the Russian winter; the difficulties in supplying food, fuel, and ammunition to the German field forces over unprecedented distances; shortages of manpower necessary to organize an elastic defense in depth; and Hitler's "stand-fast" orders not to yield any forward territory in order to conduct defense in depth.[71] This last was especially significant at the level of operations as well as tactics. Hitler's refusal to allow local commanders flexibility in making decisions about operational defenses forced tactical commanders to improvise. The result was a series of strongpoint defenses based in Soviet towns and villages. As Wray explains, "This strongpoint defense had no basis in prewar German doctrine and was, in fact, wholly improvised to fit the particular circumstances existing at the time."[72] Hitler approved it after the fact as an acceptable alternative, preferable to the yielding of ground voluntarily. Of course, German losses in equipment, personnel, and weapons precluded a continuous linear defense. And the German Armed Forces High Command (OKW) and the Führer were justifiably concerned about a chaotic series of partial withdrawals, which if uncontrolled would disorganize the front. There was also precedent for strongpoint defensive tactics on the model of those used by advancing German panzer forces as they swept across the Soviet Union from June to November 1941. Panzers learned to adopt expedient "hedgehog" self-defense perimeters in order to protect themselves from counterattacks following an encirclement operation, until the slower infantry could catch up to complete the destruction of the trapped Soviet forces.

Thus the Germans relearned on the Eastern Front in World War II, by virtue of improvisation, what had been accepted tactical defensive doctrine at the conclusion of World War I. This change occurred informally and from the front lines to the high command, or from the bottom to the top. However successful it proved to be at the tactical level, it created some difficulties at the operational: "Already in 1943, units were creating their own vocabularies, control measures, and fighting techniques that were incompatible with those in use by other units on the other sectors of the front."[73] This created problems of interoperability among divisions from different army groups, with regard to their disparate understandings of tactical doctrine and procedures.

The Soviets might regard this as an example of "negation of the negation," in that a price must be paid for decentralization, which is one reason why the Soviet Headquarters, Supreme High Command (STAVKA), has been loath to pay it. Their approach was very directive from the outset of the war, and the disasters of the early months of 1941 were followed by a remarkable learning curve of operational art. As their forces improved in training and experience and as they were better equipped with the most modern weapons, the Soviets were able to reach back into their historical memory bank and draw from their understanding of deep operations.[74] Success did not come easily, and command and control problems for the conduct of deep operational maneuvers were not mastered until well into 1943.[75] Stalin insisted, as did Hitler, on running the war personally, requiring his approval for decisions at the operational and, less frequently, the tactical level.[76] The Soviet dictator shuttled members of the General Staff among battlefield theaters of operation much as Paul Brown used to shuttle guards in and out of his offense with each play. Stalin's methodology, however, was well suited to the Soviet tradition and temperament, whereas Hitler's was in contrast to the German historical experience with *auftragstaktik* (very loosely, mission-oriented command protocols and expectations in which great discretion is allotted to subordinate commanders).

The Soviet propensity was illustrated in the plan developed by Stalin for a multifront counteroffensive against the Germans in January 1942. The plan was briefed to the General Staff by Marshal Shaposhnikov at STAVKA headquarters on January 5, 1942, but it was actually Stalin's plan and Stalin was not about to be talked out of it. Marshal Zhukov, who had organized and commanded the successful defense of Moscow on behalf of the High Command, demurred from Stalin's recommendation. Zhukov recommended that the Soviets continue the offensive against German Army Group Center (the Soviets' Western Front), but even that would have required additional troops and equipment. Simultaneous offensives in the southwest and northwest were beyond Soviet capabilities. The chairman of the State Planning Commission also recommended against a general offensive at this time. Nevertheless, Stalin was unyielding, and the offensive went forward. "I had the impression," Zhukov later wrote, "that Stalin had called his generals to Supreme Headquarters not for a discussion of the expediency of the general offensive but to 'nudge the military,' as he sometimes loved to put it."[77] The offensive did not fulfill Stalin's expectations but Zhukov's, and stalemate opposite German Army Groups North and Center resulted. Stalin, like Hitler in the face of the necessity for retreat before Moscow, wanted to recover some of the prestige and face he had lost in the early months of Barbarossa. Hitler, successful in the earliest stages, undoubtedly felt the same need for personal satisfaction when he issued his stand-fast orders.

This is another way in which wars turn out unexpectedly. Policymakers and commanders have personal stakes in the outcomes, and in the embellishment of historical memories of those outcomes. It is not for nothing that Robert Kennedy cautioned fellow principals during the Cuban missile crisis of October 1962 that his brother, the U.S. president, did not want to go down in history as another Tojo. The analogy was perhaps stretched, but memories are based on misleadingly attractive analogies. MacArthur at Inchon pulled off a brilliant operational maneuver, a classical use of Liddell Hart's oft-recommended "indirect approach," to hit the North Koreans where they least expected it.[78] This success led to his insistence that a new strategy be adopted, one which President Truman and the U.S. Joint Chiefs of Staff were not willing to endorse. The president was unwilling to endorse a revision of strategic aims explicitly. However, he did so implicitly by not preventing MacArthur from pushing northward toward the Chinese border. The tactical logic of pursuit became the operational logic of pushing the defense perimeter northward, and then the strategic logic of unifying all of Korea under UN auspices.

The Korean War was a crucible of the unexpected. Truman's willingness to commit U.S. ground forces to a land war in Asia, and specifically to Korea, was a surprise, to Americans as well as to Koreans and Soviets. Although Stalin had undoubtedly given at least backhanded encouragement to the North Korean regime as it planned its attack, the exact timing may have caught him by surprise. The rapid push southward by Pyongyang until U.S. and allied forces were pinned in the Pusan Perimeter was surprising, as was the landing at Inchon, already noted. The Chinese entry into the war in force in December surprised MacArthur, despite previous diplomatic warnings by Beijing through third parties and despite the observation of numerous Chinese infiltrators in November 1950 by U.S. intelligence. The extension of the fighting for so long after the beginning of peace talks was unexpected, as was the number of casualties during these protracted negotiations. Finally, and most surprising in this catalogue of the unexpected, the war remained limited.[79]

The limitations observed in Korea, with regard to the number of officially declared belligerents, the targets attacked and avoided, and the restrictions of political aim eventually observed by both sides seem obvious now, with the advantage of hindsight. But these limitations were not so perceived then. The U.S. twentieth-century tradition had been one of total war, and the strategy for dealing with indirect challenges mounted by Soviet clients or surrogates had not been worked out. The need for such a strategy was barely acknowledged. U.S. principals thought that the Korean attack might be a feint to cover a preemptive lunge by the Red Army against Western Europe. Once this was determined not to be the case, the strategy of limitation had its political logic shoved down the throats of U.S. policymakers by the course of events. The choice eventually lay between even more prolonged conventional fighting, with its attendant costs, and nuclear escalation. The risk was considerable that nuclear escalation, even if restricted to Korea, would involve a direct conflict with the People's Republic of China, for which U.S. planners felt unprepared and which U.S. leaders wished to avoid.

In a modern war in Europe, a strategy of limitation might similarly be imposed by the pace of unexpected events and the starkness of alternatives. The nuclear arsenals of the superpowers are much more plentiful now, so the case for limitation could not be based on economy of force, since that consideration might have caused U.S. leaders to withhold nuclear weapons from use in Korea in 1950 or 1951. Other powers now have nuclear arsenals too, and two of these are members of NATO, although the French have withdrawn officially from the NATO military command structure. The other is the Chinese, with whom the Soviet Union has been feuding since the latter 1950s, although Gorbachev is attempting to mend fences between the Communist giants even now. Leaving aside the Chinese, which Soviet prewar calculations could not do but we will do for the purposes of exposition only, an outbreak of war in Central Europe would be most improbable. Even more improbable would be the auto-limitation by the superpowers of their war aims, if those aims were felt to include the subjugation of Western Europe on the Soviet side or the liberation of Eastern Europe on the NATO side.

However, the war aims might evolve from a contretemps that developed over crisis mismanagement, say in Poland or Czechoslovakia, extending by fits and starts into fighting between NATO and Pact forces. The superpowers would then want to attain some plausible policy objectives while de-escalating the conflict short of unlimited nuclear war. The problem for Europeans is that a "limited" nuclear war from the U.S. and Soviet standpoint is likely to be a regionally confined one, thus much more limited in its consequences for Europeans east and west. The Soviet incentive to control escalation, even after the nuclear threshold has been crossed, is to prevent dissolution of its imperium in Eastern Europe. The U.S. and Nato incentives are to do likewise, preventing defections from the alliance under the duress of war fighting, especially nuclear war fighting. These are independent but complementary interests in limitation. The common interest is in preventing escalation from jumping to super-power homeland exchanges.

Here there is a dilemma for deterrence and for war termination in Europe. A shorter fuse from the failure of conventional deterrence to the use of U.S. or Soviet strategic nuclear forces is a more intimidating factor weighing against the outbreak of *any* war in Europe. Should deterrence actually fail, neither the Americans nor the Soviets would want to have a short fuse in place. Presidents and general secretaries would demand options, and the available options would have been preplanned. Should the available options be irrelevant, new options would need to be impro-vised in circumstances for which nobody had quite prepared. This would be an improbable scenario if it had not in fact happened many times in the past. We can no more foresee how a war in Europe would end than could those who embarked on it. The only certainty is that, at the end of the line, the political objectives for which such a war might be justified, in a proper Clausewitzian sense, ought to be proportionate to the means expended. As Clausewitz would have been the first to note, this is an easier requirement to meet on paper than in reality.

NOTES

1. See George H. Quester, "War Termination and Nuclear Targeting Strategy," Ch. 14 in Desmond Ball and Jeffrey Richelson, eds., *Strategic Nuclear Targeting* (Ithaca, N.Y.: Cornell University Press, 1986), pp. 285–306.

2. Gregory F. Treverton, "Ending Major Coalition Wars," Ch. 6 in Stephen J. Cimbala and Keith A. Dunn, eds., *Conflict Termination and Military Strategy: Coercion, Persuasion and War* (Boulder, Colo.: Westview Press, 1987), p. 93. See also Thomas C. Schelling, *Arms and Influence* (New Haven: Yale University Press, 1966).

3. McGeorge Bundy, transcriber, and James G. Blight, editor, "October 27, 1962: Transcripts of the Meetings of the ExComm," *International Security* 12, no. 3 (Winter 1987-88), pp. 30–92.

4. Graham T. Allison, *Essence of Decision: Explaining the Cuban Missile Crisis* (Boston: Little, Brown, 1971), pp. 140–41; Elie Abel, *The Missile Crisis* (New York: Bantam Books/J. B. Lippincott, 1966), pp. 167–72.

5. On ExComm deliberations, see McGeorge Bundy, *Danger and Survival* (New York: Random House, 1988), pp. 391–462; Raymond L. Garthoff, *Reflections on the Cuban Missile Crisis*, 2nd ed. (Washington: Brookings Institution, 1989), Ch. 2; and James G. Blight and David A. Welch, eds., *On the Brink: Americans and Soviets Reexamine the Cuban Missile Crisis* (New York: Hill and Wang, 1989), Part One.

6. For discussion of the conflict spiral model, see Robert Jervis, *Perception and*

Misperception in International Politics (Princeton: Princeton University Press, 1976), Ch. 3. See also Jervis, *The Meaning of the Nuclear Revolution* (Ithaca, N.Y.: Cornell University Press, 1989), Ch. 5.

7. Roberta Wohlstetter, *Pearl Harbor: Warning and Decision* (Stanford, Calif.: Stanford University Press, 1962), p. 352.

8. For an analysis of the Manchurian campaign, see Lilita I. Dzirkals, "Lightning War in Manchuria: Soviet Military Analysis of the 1945 Far East Campaign" (Santa Monica, Cal.: Rand Corporation, January 1976).

9. Dzirkals, "'Lightning War' in Manchuria," p. 9.

10. Ibid., p. 11.

11. Lt. Col. David M. Glantz, *August Storm: The Soviet 1945 Strategic Offensive in Manchuria* (Ft. Leavenworth, Kans.: Combat Studies Institute, U.S. Army Command and General Staff College, February 1983), p. 39.

12. On this point see Treverton, "Ending Major Coalition Wars," *passim.*

13. See Francis Fukuyama, "Escalation in the Middle East and the Persian Gulf," Ch. 5 in Graham T. Allison, Albert Carnesale, and Joseph S. Nye, Jr., eds., *Hawks, Doves and Owls* (New York: W. W. Norton, 1985), pp. 115–47.

14. Albert Wohlstetter and Richard Brody, "Continuing Control as a Requirement for Deterring," Ch. 5 in Ashton B. Carter, John D. Steinbruner, and Charles A. Zraket, eds., *Managing Nuclear Operations* (Washington: Brookings Institution, 1987), pp. 142–96.

15. John G. Hines and Phillip A. Petersen, "The Warsaw Pact Strategic Offensive: The OMG in Context," *International Defense Review* (October 1983), pp. 1391–95; C. N. Donnelly, "The Soviet Operational Maneuver Group: A New Challenge for NATO," *International Defense Review* (1982), pp. 1177–86.

16. See V. Ye. Savkin, *Osnovnyye printsipy operativnogo iskusstvai taktiki* (The basic principles of operational art and tactics) (Moscow: Voyenizdat, 1972). U.S. Air Force Soviet Military Thought Series.

17. A recent authoritative study is Soviet Army Studies Office, U.S. Army Combined Arms Center, *The Soviet Conduct of War* (Ft. Leavenworth, Kans.: March 1987).

18. See Earl F. Ziemke, "Stalingrad and Belorussia: Soviet Deception in World War II," Ch. 11 in Donald C. Daniel and Katherine L. Herbig, eds., *Strategic Military Deception* (New York: Pergamon Press, 1981), pp. 243–76.

19. Jeffrey Richelson, *American Intelligence and the Soviet Espionage Target* (New York: William Morrow and Company, 1987), p. 243.

20. For a discussion of satellite missions during peacetime and wartime, see Paul B. Stares, *Space and National Security* (Washington: Brookings Institution, 1987), Ch. 3.

21. In addition to previously cited sources on this campaign, see P. H. Vigor, *Soviet Blitzkrieg Theory* (New York: St. Martin's Press, 1983), Ch. 9.

22. See John J. Dziak, "Soviet Deception: The Organizational and Operational Tradition," Ch. 1 in Brian D. Dailey and Patrick J. Parker, eds., *Soviet Strategic Deception* (Lexington, Mass.: D. C. Heath/Lexington Books, 1987), pp.3–20.

23. John G. Hines and Phillip A. Petersen, "NATO and the Changing Soviet Concept of Control for Theater War," Ch. 3 in Stephen J. Cimbala, ed., *The Soviet Challenge in the 1990s* (New York: Praeger Publishers, 1989), pp. 65–122, and Hines and Petersen, "The Changing Soviet System of Control for Theater War," in Cimbala, ed., *Soviet C³* (Washington: AFCEA International Press, 1987), pp. 191–219.

24. Comparison of U.S. and Soviet approaches is provided by John M. Collins, *U.S. and Soviet Special Operations* (Washington: Congressional Research Service, Library of Congress, December 23, 1986).

25. Soviet Army Studies Office, *The Soviet Conduct of War*, pp.26–27.

26. See Andrew Cockburn, *The Threat: Inside the Soviet Military Machine* (New York: Random House, 1983).

27. John Hemsley, *Soviet Troops Control: The Role of Command Technology in the Soviet Military System* (New York: Brassey's Publishers Ltd., 1982), p. 159ff.

28. Martin Van Creveld, *Command in War* (Cambridge, Mass.: Harvard University Press, 1985), p. 270.

29. Allison, *Essence of Decision*, p. 131.

30. On problems attendant to the Iran rescue operation (Desert One), see Richard A. Gabriel, *Military Incompetence: Why the American Military Doesn't Win* (New York: Hill and Wang, 1985), Ch. 4, pp. 85–116.

31. An account of this is provided in Van Creveld, *Command in War*, pp. 232–60.

32. Edward N. Luttwak, *The Pentagon and the Art of War* (New York: Simon and Schuster, 1984), p. 52.

33. Herman Kahn, *On Escalation: Metaphors and Scenarios* (New York: Praeger, 1965), p. 173.

34. Ibid.

35. Paul Nitze, "Assuring Strategic Stability in an Era of Detente," *Foreign Affairs* 54 (1976), pp. 207–33.

36. Joshua M. Epstein, *Strategy and Force Planning: The Case of the Persian Gulf* (Washington: Brookings Institution, 1987), Ch. 2, pp. 11–29, discusses U.S. plans for nuclear escalation in case of war with the Soviet Union over Iran.

37. Moral judgments involving the use of nuclear weapons are at least three dimensional: they concern motives, means, and consequences. See Joseph S. Nye, Jr., *Nuclear Ethics* (New York: Free Press, 1986), pp. 20–26.

38. A good discussion of this appears in Blair, *Strategic Command and Control*, Ch. 3, pp. 50–78.

39. See Theodore A. Postol, "Targeting," Ch. 11 in Carter, Steinbruner, and Zraket, eds., *Managing Nuclear Operations*, pp. 373–406.

40. According to Blair, *Strategic Command and Control*, p. 189, half of the 400 primary and secondary U.S. strategic C^3I targets "could be attacked by Soviet missile submarines on routine patrol." Many of these include the U.S. strategic bomber force and components of the airborne command network for postattack control.

41. U.S. ballistic missile submarine communications are evaluated in terms of SSBN missions in Ashton B. Carter, "Assessing Command System Vulnerability," Ch. 17 in Carter, Steinbruner, and Zraket, eds., *Managing Nuclear Operations*, pp. 574–78.

42. President's Commission on U.S. Strategic Forces (Scowcroft Commission), *Report* (Washington: GPO, April 1983).

43. See Jeffrey Richelson, "The Dilemmas of Counterpower Targeting," Ch. 7 in Desmond Ball and Richelson, eds., *Strategic Nuclear Targeting* (Ithaca, N.Y.: Cornell University Press, 1986), pp. 159–70; Stephen J. Cimbala, "Countercommand Attacks and War Termination," Ch. 7 in Cimbala, ed., *Strategic War Termination* (New York: Praeger Publishers, 1986), pp. 134–56.

44. Desmond Ball, "The Development of the SIOP, 1960–1983," Ch. 3 in Ball and Richelson, eds., *Strategic Nuclear Targeting*, p. 82.

45. U.S. Department of Defense, *Soviet Military Power: 1987* (Washington: GPO, March 1987), p. 15; Desmond Ball, *The Soviet Strategic Command, Control Communications and Intelligence (C^3I) System*, Strategic and Defence Studies Centre, Australian National University, Canberra, May 1985.

46. This is not to say that airpower was unimportant in the combined ground-air-maritime war against Germany, for it certainly was. See Thomas A. Fabyanic, "Air Power and Conflict Termination," in Stephen J. Cimbala and Keith A. Dunn, eds., *Conflict Termination and Military Strategy: Coercion, Persuasion and War* (Boulder, Colo.: Westview Press, 1987), pp. 145–48.

47. Stephen J. Cimbala, "How Shall We Retaliate? Slow Down and Live," in Cimbala, ed., *Challenges to Deterrence: Resources, Technology and Policy* (New York: Praeger Publishers, 1987), pp. 268–88. See also Scott D. Sagan, *Moving Targets: Nuclear Strategy and National Security* (Princeton: Princeton University Press, 1989), Ch. 2.

48. See Carl H. Builder, "The Impact of New Weapons Technologies," Ch. 8 in Cimbala, ed., *Strategic War Termination*, pp. 157–73.

49. Albert Wohlstetter, "Swords without Shields," *National Interest*, Summer 1987, pp. 31–57.

50. Wohlstetter, "Between an Unfree World and None," *Foreign Affairs* 63, no. 5 (Summer 1985), pp. 962–94.

51. See Desmond Ball, "Counterforce Targeting: How New? How Viable?" *Arms Control Today* 11, no. 2 (February 1981), reprinted with revisions in John F. Reichart and Steven R. Sturm, eds., *American Defense Policy* (Baltimore: Johns Hopkins University Press, 1982), pp. 227–34.

52. Ball, "The Development of the SIOP, 1960–1983"; Ball, "Counterforce Targeting"; and Leon Sloss and Marc Dean Millot, "U.S. Nuclear Strategy in Evolution," *Strategic Review*, Winter 1984, pp. 19–28.

53. Richard Halloran, *To Arm a Nation: Rebuilding America's Endangered Defenses* (New York: Macmillan Publishing Co., 1986), Ch. 9, pp. 268–98.

54. Blair, *Strategic Command and Control*, pp. 287–88.

55. Colin S. Gray, "Targeting Problems for Central War," Ch. 8 in Ball and Richelson, *Strategic Nuclear Targeting*, pp. 175–76. See also Ch. 14 of the same volume by George H. Quester, "War Termination and Nuclear Targeting Strategy."

56. See Dennis M. Gormley, "'Triple Zero' and Soviet Strategy," in *Arms Control Today*, January-February 1988, pp. 17–20.

57. European Security Study, *Strengthening Conventional Deterrence in Europe: Proposals for the 1980s* (New York: St. Martin's Press, 1983).

58. Robert S. McNamara, *Blundering Into Disaster: Surviving the First Century of the Nuclear Age* (New York: Simon and Schuster, 1986).

59. According to William T. Lee and Richard F. Staar, Soviet nuclear targeting strategy "appears to be insensitive to the three basic Soviet scenarios for nuclear war. Whether the USSR succeeds in preempting, launches on tactical warning under attack, or is forced into a second strike situation after absorbing an enemy attack, its targeting priorities remain the same." See Lee and Staar, *Soviet Military Policy Since World War II* (Stanford, Cal.: Hoover Institution Press, 1986), p. 139.

60. Lieutenant Commander Michael N. Pocalyko, USN, "25 Years After the Blink," *Proceedings of the U.S. Naval Institute*, September 1987, pp. 41–47.

61. Stephen M. Meyer, "Soviet Perspectives on the Paths to Nuclear War," Ch. 7 in Graham T. Allison, Albert Carnesale, and Joseph S. Nye, Jr., *Hawks, Doves and Owls: An Agenda for Avoiding Nuclear War* (New York: W. W. Norton and Co., 1985), p. 193 notes possible Soviet probing of U.S. reactions to a preemptive strike on Chinese nuclear facilities in 1969.

62. Barry M. Blechman and Douglas H. Hart, "The Political Utility of Nuclear

Weapons: The 1973 Middle East Crisis," in Steven E. Miller, ed., *Strategy and Nuclear Deterrence* (Princeton: Princeton University Press, 1984), pp. 273–97.

63. Paul Bracken, "Delegation of Nuclear Command Authority," Ch. 10 in Carter, Steinbruner, and Zraket, eds., *Managing Nuclear Operations*, p. 355.

64. Oleg Penkovskiy, *The Penkovskiy Papers*, introduction and commentary by Frank Gibney (Garden City, N.Y.: Doubleday and Co., 1965), pp. 223–60.

65. This usage is consistent with that of Blair, *Strategic Command and Control*, and John D. Steinbruner, "Choices and Trade-offs," Ch. 16 in Carter, Steinbruner, and Zraket, eds., *Managing Nuclear Operations*, pp. 535–54.

66. Paul Bracken, "Delegation of Nuclear Command Authority," Ch. 10 in Carter, Steinbruner, and Zraket, eds., *Managing Nuclear Operations*, pp. 352–72.

67. Paul Bracken, "War Termination," Ch. 6 in Carter, Steinbruner, and Zraket, eds., *Managing Nuclear Operations*, pp. 197–216, this citation pp. 210–11.

68. Ibid., p. 200.

69. Ibid., p. 201.

70. Major Timothy A. Wray, *Standing Fast: German Defensive Doctrine on the Russian Front During World War II: Prewar to March 1943* (Fort Leavenworth, Kans.: U.S. Army Command and General Staff College, Combat Studies Institute, September 1986), p. 23.

71. Ibid., p. 68.

72. Ibid., p. 71. On one commander's assessment of Hitler's orders, see Heinz Guderian, *Panzer Leader* (New York: Ballantine Books, 1957), pp. 204–5.

73. Wray, *Standing Fast*, p. 175.

74. See David M. Glantz, *Deep Attack: The Soviet Conduct of Operational Maneuver* (Fort Leavenworth, Kans.: Soviet Army Studies Office, April 1987).

75. Ibid.

76. Georgi K. Zhukov, *Marshal Zhukov's Greatest Battles* (New York: Harper and Row, 1969).

77. Ibid., p. 91.

78. B. H. Liddell Hart, *Strategy*, Second Revised Edition (New York: Praeger, 1967), pp. 339–40. According to Liddell Hart, "dislocation is the aim of strategy; its sequel may be either the enemy's dissolution or his easier disruption in battle." Ibid., p. 339.

79. Michael Doyle, "Endemic Surprise? Strategic Surprises in First World–Third World Relations," Ch. 4 in Klaus Knorr and Patrick Morgan, eds., *Strategic Military Surprises: Incentives and Opportunities* (New Brunswick, N.J.: Transaction Books, 1983), pp. 77–110.

Selected Bibliography

This bibliography emphasizes sources repeatedly cited or of special value for reference. Other important sources are cited in chapter endnotes.

Akhromeyev, Sergei (Marshal of the Soviet Union). "Doktrina predotvrashcheniya voyny zashchity mira i sotsializma." *Problemy Mira i Sotsializma*, No. 12 (December 1987), pp. 26–27.

Allison, Graham T., Albert Carnesale, and Joseph S. Nye, Jr., eds. *Hawks, Doves and Owls: An Agenda for Avoiding Nuclear War.* New York: W. W. Norton, 1985.

Ball, Desmond, and Jeffrey Richelson, eds. *Strategic Nuclear Targeting.* Ithaca, N.Y.: Cornell University Press, 1986.

Bellamy, Chris. *The Future of Land Warfare.* New York: St. Martin's Press, 1987.

Betts, Richard K. *Nuclear Blackmail and Nuclear Balance.* Washington: Brookings Institution, 1987.

Blair, Bruce G. *Strategic Command and Control: Redefining the Nuclear Threat.* Washington: Brookings Institution, 1985.

Boutwell, Jeffrey D., Paul Doty, and Gregory F. Treverton, eds. *The Nuclear Confrontation in Europe.* London: Croom Helm, 1985.

Bracken, Paul. *The Command and Control of Nuclear Forces.* New Haven: Yale University Press, 1983.

Byely, Col. B., et al. *Marxism-Leninism on War and Army.* Moscow: Progress Publishers, 1972. U.S. Air Force Soviet Military Thought Series.

Cimbala, Stephen J., ed. *Soviet C3.* Washington: AFCEA International Press, 1987.

——. *Extended Deterrence.* Lexington, Mass.: Lexington Books, 1987.

——. *Nuclear Strategizing.* New York: Praeger Publishers, 1988.

Clausewitz, Carl von. *Vom Kriege* (On war). Edited and translated by Michael Howard and Peter Paret. Princeton: Princeton University Press, 1976.

Davis, Paul K. and Peter J. E. Stan. *Concepts and Models of Escalation.* Santa Monica, Cal.: RAND Corporation, May 1984.

Donnelly, Christopher N. "Soviet Operational Concepts in the 1980s," in *Strengthening*

Conventional Deterrence in Europe: Proposals for the 1980s, pp. 105–136. Report of the European Security Study. New York: St. Martin's Press, 1983.

Douglass, Joseph D., Jr. *The Soviet Theater Nuclear Offensive*, Vol. I. Prepared for Office of Director of Defense Research and Engineering and Defense Nuclear Agency and published under the auspices of the U.S. Air Force. Washington: U.S. Government Printing Office, undated.

Druzhinin, V. V. and D. S. Kontorov. *Ideya, algoritm, resheniye*. Moscow: Voyenizdat, 1972. Published in U.S. Air Force Soviet Military Thought Series as *Concept, Algorithm, Decision*. Washington: U.S. Government Printing Office, undated.

Erickson, John, Lynn Hansen, and William Schneider. *Soviet Ground Forces: An Operational Assessment*. Boulder, Colo.: Westview Press, 1986.

Freedman, Lawrence. *The Evolution of Nuclear Strategy*. New York: St. Martin's Press, 1981.

Gareyev, General M. A. *M. V. Frunze—voennyy teoretik*. Moscow: Voyenizdat, 1985.

Garthoff, Raymond L. *Detente and Confrontation*. Washington: Brookings Institution, 1985.

Glantz, David M. *August Storm: The Soviet 1945 Strategic Offensive in Manchuria*. Fort Leavenworth, Kans.: U.S. Army Command and General Staff College, February 1983.

Gottfried, Kurt and Bruce G. Blair. *Crisis Stability and Nuclear War*. New York: Oxford University Press, 1988.

Gray, Colin S. *Nuclear Strategy and National Style*. Lanham, Md.: Hamilton Press, 1986.

Grechko, Marshal A. *Vooruzhennyye sily sovetskogo gosudarstva*. Moscow: Voyenizdat, 1974.

Hemsley, John. *Soviet Troop Control*. New York: Brassey's Publishers Ltd., 1982.

Hines, John G., Phillip A. Petersen, and Notra Trulock III. "Soviet Military Theory: 1945–2000: Implications for NATO." *Washington Quarterly*, Fall 1986, pp. 117–137.

Huntington, Samuel P., ed. *The Strategic Imperative*. Cambridge: Ballinger Publishing Co., 1982.

Ikle, Fred Charles. *Every War Must End*. New York: Columbia University Press, 1971.

Jervis, Robert. *The Illogic of American Nuclear Strategy*. Ithaca, N.Y.: Cornell University Press, 1984.

Kir'yan, General M. M. *Voyenno-tekhnicheskiy progress i vooruzhennyye sily SSSR*. Moscow: Voyenizdat, 1982.

Knorr, Klaus and Patrick M. Morgan, eds. *Strategic Military Surprise*. New Brunswick, N.J.: Transaction Books, 1983.

Kozlov, General-Major S. N., *Spravochnik Ofitsera* (The officer's handbook). Moscow: Voyenizdat, 1971. U.S. Air Force Soviet Military Thought Series.

Lebow, Richard Ned. *Between Peace and War: The Nature of International Crisis*. Baltimore: Johns Hopkins University Press, 1981.

———. *Nuclear Crisis Management: A Dangerous Illusion*. Ithaca, N.Y.: Cornell University Press, 1987.

Lee, William T. and Richard F. Staar. *Soviet Military Policy Since World War II*. Stanford, Cal.: Hoover Institution, 1986.

Luttwak, Edward N. *The Pentagon and the Art of War*. New York: Simon and Schuster, 1984.

MccGwire, Michael. *Military Objectives in Soviet Foreign Policy*. Washington: Brookings Institution, 1987.

Mearsheimer, John J. *Conventional Deterrence*. Ithaca, N.Y.: Cornell University Press, 1983.

Meyer, Stephen M. *Soviet Theater Nuclear Forces, Part II: Capabilities and Implications*. London: International Institute for Strategic Studies, Alelphi Papers No. 188, Winter 1983–84.

———. "Soviet Nuclear Operations," Ch. 15 in Ashton B. Carter, John D. Steinbruner, and Charles A. Zraket, eds., *Managing Nuclear Operations*. Washington: Brookings Institution, 1987, pp. 470–534.

Miller, Steven E., ed. *Strategy and Nuclear Deterrence*. Princeton: Princeton University Press, 1984.

Morgan, Patrick M. *Deterrence: A Conceptual Analysis*. Beverly Hills, Cal.: Sage Publications, 1983.

Ogarkov, Marshal N. V. *Istoriya uchit bditel' nosti*. Moscow: Voyenizdat, 1985.

———. *Vsegda v gotovnosti k zashchite Otechestva*. Moscow: Voyenizdat, 1982.

Panov, B. V., et al. *Istoriya voyennogo iskusstva*. Moscow: Voyenizdat, 1984.

Papp, Daniel S. *Soviet Policies toward the Developing World During the 1980s: The Dilemmas of Power and Presence*. Maxwell Air Force base, Ala.: Air University Press, December 1986.

Sarkesian, Sam C. *The New Battlefield: The United States and Unconventional Conflicts*. New York: Greenwood Press, 1986.

Schelling, Thomas C. *The Strategy of Conflict*. Cambridge, Mass.: Harvard University Press, 1960.

———. *Arms and Influence*. New Haven, Conn.: Yale University Press, 1966.

Schwartz, David N. *NATO's Nuclear Dilemmas*. Washington: Brookings Institution, 1983.

Skirdo, Colonel M. P. *Narod, armiya, polkovodets*. Moscow: Voyenizdat, 1970.

Smoke, Richard. *War: Controlling Escalation*. Cambridge, Mass.: Harvard University Press, 1977.

Sokolovskiy, V. D. *Voyennaya strategiya*. Moscow: Voyenizdat, 1962, 1963, 1968.

U.S. Department of Defense. *Soviet Military Power: 1988*. Washington: U.S. Government Printing Office, 1988.

Vigor, P. H. *Soviet Blitzkrieg Theory*. New York: St. Martin's Press, 1983.

Wardak, Ghulam and Graham H. Turbiville, Jr. *Voroshilov Lectures*, vol. I. Washington: National Defense University Press, 1989.

Yazov, General D. T. "Voyennaya doktrina Varshavskogo Dogovora—doktrina zashchity mira i sotsializma." *Krasnaya zvezda*, July 28, 1987, p. 2.

Yurechko, John J. "Command and Control for Coalitional Warfare: The Soviet Approach." *Signal*, December 1985, pp. 34–39. Reprinted in Stephen J. Cimbala, ed., *Soviet C3* (Washington: AFCEA International Press, 1987), pp. 17–34.

Zhurkin, V., S. Karaganov, and A. Kortunov. "Vyzovy bezopastnosti—staryye i novyye." *Kommunist*, No. 1 (1988), pp. 42–50.

Index

ABOUT THE AUTHOR

STEPHEN J. CIMBALA is Professor of Political Science at Pennsylvania State University and has contributed to the field of national security studies for many years. His recent titles include *Nuclear Endings* (Praeger, 1989); *Strategic Impasse* (Greenwood, 1989); and *Strategic Air Defense*. Cimbala is a member of the International Studies Association, the Inter-University Seminar on Armed Forces and Society, the Armed Forces Communications and Electronics Association, and various other professional bodies.